TX
353
.F79   Fresh food
1978

REF TX 353.F79 1978

FORM 125 M

Cop. 1   BUSINESS/SCIENCE/TECHNOLOGY

The Chicago Public Library

Received_____MAR 1 1979_____

© THE BAKER & TAYLOR CO.

FRESH FOOD

for Betsy and David

FRESH FOOD

Edited by Sylvia Rosenthal

Illustrated by Barry Ross

Tree Communications

E.P. Dutton

Acknowledgments. Our sincerest thanks to the following for their major contributions to *Fresh Food*:

Dorothy Ivens
Vicki Lindner
Lael Scott
Janet Stone
John Von Glahn
Genevieve Young

A special word of appreciation to the many friends and colleagues who shared their skill and knowledge in the making of this book, particularly to Linda Hetzer and Pace Barnes for their help and editorial guidance and to Sonja Douglas for her creativity and talent in designing this volume.

For information contact: E.P. Dutton, 2 Park Avenue, New York, N.Y. 10016

Library of Congress Catalog Card Number: 78-50682

ISBN: 0-87690-276-X

Published simultaneously in Canada by Clarke, Irwin & Company Limited, Toronto and Vancouver

The text faces for this book are Century Expanded and Spartan Book, set at David E. Seham Inc. The display face is Avant Garde X-Light set by Filmtext, Inc. Mezzotints were made by Tree Communications, Inc. The paper used is Troy Book made by the Miami Paper Corporation and supplied by the Baldwin Paper Company. The book was printed and bound by R.R. Donnelley & Sons Company.

10 9 8 7 6 5 4 3 2 1

First Edition

CONTENTS

SPEAKING OF FRESH FOOD

The family kitchen has again become a pivotal point in American life. It may not enjoy quite the same social position as it did during pioneer days when it served as the family living room and dining room as well, but it is nonetheless an area of ever-growing importance in millions of homes. With this trend has come a renewed interest in the old-fashioned goodness of fresh food, free of chemical additives and artificial flavors and colors. And whether from necessity or choice, there have never been as many good amateur cooks as there are now, with more women and men every year discovering the rewards and satisfactions of time and effort spent in the kitchen.

It belabors the obvious to note that food has been a major concern of all living things since the beginning of time. In the beginning, however, the obsession with food grew out of the need for survival. The earliest people, dressed in animal skins and armed with clubs, were not fussy about what they ate or how it tasted. Anything from fruits and berries to worms and insects was acceptable. They feasted when they found something to eat and hungered when the cold froze the fruits and grains. But as centuries passed and the refinements of civilization took over, food became something to be lovingly prepared, to be savored and enjoyed. It was no longer regarded merely as a means of survival but as a source of pleasure; its preparation became an art and an outlet for creativity.

But no amount of cooking skill can produce a fine meal unless it is preceded by an equal amount of expertise in the market. Fresh, top-quality ingredients are of primary importance to the success of a dish, and not everything offered for sale can claim the same degree of excellence. The buyer must know how to choose the best and reject the second-rate, to select the right product for the right purpose, and to have sufficient knowledge of food to change a menu at the last minute, if necessary, to take advantage of market specials or to accommodate to market shortages. Understanding ingredients and what to do with them is the key to the approach to all good cooking.

Fresh foods come into your kitchen very close to what they were in their natural state. In contrast to most of the prepared and processed foods found on supermarket shelves and in frozen-food departments, they do not require that the buyer has a degree in chemistry in order to understand what he or she is consuming beyond whatever is pictured on the box, can, or package. In this volume you will explore and perhaps renew acquaintance with a vast variety of fresh foods—delicious, flavorful products that have never seen the inside of a food factory. You will find guidelines that will help you to distinguish between the good and the not-so-good, and to determine which are the best foods in season at various times of the year. You will discover as well that efficient shopping does not always mean buying the top grade. As an example, a beef stew that needs long, slow cooking could be a disaster if an expensive, tender cut of beef such as a sirloin were used, since the meat could disintegrate before the full flavor was reached. In this case a tougher, cheaper cut is desirable.

Today's food buyers face many challenges and distractions, and they need to exercise expert judgment if their food dollars are to provide their families with the most in nutrition and eating pleasure. With constantly spiraling food costs, there is little room in most family budgets for mistakes in food buying. Price bears less and less relationship to quality, and shoppers will either resist or succumb to the blandishments and beguiling displays of a food industry that spends less money on basic food research than it does on research into finding out which food package design is likely to attract the most favorable response. The industry generally ends up making the imitation look better than the genuine article, a situation that does not necessarily extend to its taste and nutritive value. Certainly advertising does little to guide the consumer through the supermarket. But on the other hand, guidance is not the function of advertising. Its purpose is selling. It is regrettable that fresh foods, the best possible source of natural vitamins and minerals, cannot come to the market labeled according to their nutrients, as are the millions of bottles of synthetic vitamins snapped up by an eager public.

Cooking with fresh food does not mean long hours of preparation. The flavors of fine food—fresh seafood, splendid vegetables and fruits harvested at their peak—need little enhancement. The simplest cooking techniques, carefully observed, will suffice to bring out the natural goodness in their taste. Snowy cauliflower, fresh young snap beans, or brightly colored broccoli cooked to just the right degree of crisp tenderness, lightly seasoned and dressed with a bit of melted butter or margarine, cannot fail to please the most fastidious and demanding palate. Be flexible and imaginative in your use of nature's raw materials; the results will be gratifying.

It is hoped that the information in the pages that follow will help you to judge foods and encourage you to be creative in your use of them. The marketing and preparation for a meal can be a distillation of the satisfaction of challenge and the joy of creation.

VEGETABLES

For many years, vegetables were the stepchildren of the American cuisine—appendages to the pleasures of the table that some people regarded almost as a penance. ("Eat your string beans or no dessert," parents told their young.) But this is changing. Along with a new awareness throughout the world of the need for good nutrition has come a heightened appreciation of the joys of glowingly fresh vegetables cooked to crisp-tender brightness.

The fact that supermarkets across the country are reporting a decline in the sale of frozen vegetables, and an increase in the demand for those that are fresh, would indicate that a benign, peaceful revolution is taking place in the kitchens of America. And small wonder. For what processed foods, however, good, can compete against those that are free of chemical additives, artificial colors, sweeteners, or preservatives; that provide fiber and contain a full measure of vitamins and minerals; and that are appetite-provoking and taste-satisfying?

However, not all fresh vegetables grow to the same degree of perfection. Like people, some are better formed than others. Their quality can also be affected by growing conditions and the kind of care they received during harvesting, packing, and shipping. The pages that follow contain the information on what to look for when you shop for fresh produce; which vegetables are ready to eat and how to ripen those that are not; which vegetables can be stored and which must be used at once; and how to get the most in nutrition and economy from the vegetables you buy.

When you market, let your choice be influenced by what is freshest and best. Change your menu if you find the vegetables you had planned are not top quality. A tired, limp green bean or a faded, overgrown bunch of broccoli will not improve after cooking. Concentrate on the vegetables that are at their peak season, when they will be the freshest, the most tender, and the least expensive. Buy only what you need or what will store well until you need it.

The key to good nutrition is variety at every meal, and nature has been most thoughtful in providing us with a color index for our nutritional needs. By mixing a rich palette of colors and contrasts in the vegetables we serve—green, yellow, orange, red, and white, among them—we provide not only visual pleasures at our meals, but we fulfill our varied mineral and vitamin requirements at the same time. Practically all vegetables, when they are fresh, contain some vitamin C, particularly when eaten raw.

Waxing. Many consumers are distressed by the wax coating applied to some fruits and vegetables by commercial packers. Among the vegetables that are frequently waxed are cucumbers, tomatoes, rutabagas, and sweet and white potatoes. No attempt is made to disguise the wax coating; it is easily apparent to any observer. Waxing is done mainly to retard shriveling and dehydration, and not, as some people think, to improve the appearance of the vegetable. The waxes are of vegetable origin and have been approved by the United States Food and Drug Administration as safe and edible materials, completely harmless when eaten. But people who find the wax displeasing can remove it by soaking and scrubbing the vegetable with a detergent, followed by a thorough rinsing in hot water, or by peeling the skin or rind.

Vegetable cookery. You do not need a large repertoire of elaborate recipes to be a first-rate vegetable cook. Tender, fresh young vegetables require only the simplest cooking methods and the simplest seasonings. The chief contribution vegetables make to our diet, in addition to

Peak season for vegetables

Unlike many fruits that are seasonal and disappear from view during certain seasons of the year, the majority of vegetables can be bought throughout the year. There are a few exceptions, asparagus among them. The quality and cost may be up or down, depending on the season and locality, but the vegetables are available.

Most vegetables, however, have a peak season when they are freshest and at their best. But there are some that are in steady supply and of consistent quality at all times. Among them are cabbages, cucumbers, Chinese or celery cabbage, carrots, bean sprouts, various lettuces (iceberg, romaine, Bibb, Boston, etc.), chicory, escarole, mustard greens, all of the onion family, ginger root, horseradish, parsley, and potatoes. Some of these, such as cucumbers, are cheapest during the summer.

Following is a listing of the vegetables at their peak during the winter, spring, summer, and fall seasons:

January and February
Belgian endive
Broccoli
Cabbage: Savoy
Celeriac
Celery
Collards
Jerusalem artichokes
Kale
Leeks
Mushrooms
Parsnips
Rhubarb
Rutabagas
Spinach
Squash, winter: Acorn, buttercup, butternut, large banana, hubbard
Truffles, black
Turnips

March, April, May, and June
Artichokes
Arugula
Asparagus
Beans: Fava, snap
Broccoli
Celeriac
Collards (through April)
Corn (May to September)
Dandelion greens
Belgian endive
Kohlrabi (June and July)

(continued)

(Peak season for vegetables, continued)

Leeks
Mushrooms (through April)
Parsnips (through April)
Peas
Peppers (May through October)
New potatoes
Radishes
Rhubarb
Snow peas
Sorrel
Spinach
Watercress

July, August, and September
Arugula
Beans: Lima, snap, soybeans
Beets
Corn
Eggplant
Kohlrabi
Okra
Peppers
Snow peas
Radishes
Sorrel
Squash: spaghetti
Squash, summer: Cocozelle, patty pan,
yellow crookneck, yellow straightneck,
zucchini
Tomatoes
Watercress

October, November, and December
Beets
Broccoli
Cabbage: Savoy
Cauliflower
Belgian endive
Fennel, sweet
Jerusalem artichokes
Leeks
Mushrooms
Pumpkin
Rutabagas
Salsify
Turnips
Winter squash
Sweet potatoes
Truffles, white

providing fiber, is supplying an assortment of vitamins and minerals. These can be depleted easily through the wrong cooking methods.

Vitamin depletion begins in vegetables with exposure to light and air, so chop or slice your vegetables when you are ready to use them, and not hours ahead of time. Cut vegetables into the same sized pieces so they will cook evenly. Since a good deal of the vitamin content in vegetables is water soluble, and heat also increases nutrient loss, cook the vegetables in a little liquid and for as short a time as possible. Vegetables are at their best when they are crisp and undercooked.

Vegetables may be steamed, sautéed, or stir-fried. No costly equipment is needed for any of these cooking methods; a large skillet with a tightly fitting cover can be used for any of them. Also popular for steaming foods is an inexpensive metal basket on legs that is widely available; the size is adjustable and fits comfortably into almost any pot. Baking and broiling are also satisfactory methods of preparation. Vegetables in their skins (potatoes, winter squash, onions, beets) or peeled vegetables in broths or sauces in a covered casserole are put into a preheated oven and baked until tender. When vegetables are sautéed, the coating of oil seals in flavor and natural juices. The stir-fry method, an outgrowth of interest in Chinese cooking, is a welcome addition to vegetable cookery. The method evolved originally out of the shortage of fuel in China and the necessity of cooking all foods as quickly as possible. The foods are cut into small pieces and tossed quickly in a small amount of hot oil in a wok or skillet over medium-high heat.

The important nutrients in many vegetables are concentrated in the skins or just below it, so it is advantageous to leave them unpeeled when possible. Peels also provide a source of fiber. We often peel vegetables more out of habit than necessity. Vegetables such as carrots, tomatoes, potatoes, summer squash, eggplant, and cucumbers, if young and tender, can be cooked and eaten with skins left on. The liquids in which the vegetables were cooked should be saved for soups and sauces.

Plan your cooking so that the vegetables are ready at the time you serve them. Do not cook them ahead and reheat. Leftover vegetables, too, should not be reheated. Toss them in a vinaigrette and serve as a salad, or use them in your next vegetable soup.

Be adventuresome on your next marketing trip. Try some new products that you have never served before—a different leafy green or a root vegetable that has been a stranger in your kitchen. You may discover a whole new family of vegetables that your family will enjoy knowing.

ARTICHOKES

The globe, or French, artichoke, with its special nutty, meaty flavor, is a most interesting vegetable. It may be boiled, baked, or steamed, eaten hot or cold. It can serve as an appetizer, as a vegetable course by itself, or as the main attraction of a hot-weather luncheon or light supper. Eaten leaf by leaf, the artichoke offers the additional attraction of keeping the diners busy (with a minimum of calories) as they scrape off the delicious light-green bit at the base of each leaf with their teeth. It is a popular vegetable among many children, since it is one of the few foods that makes good manners out of eating with your fingers.

Artichokes may be cooked and served whole or trimmed and pared, leaving only the tender, delicious bottom to be filled with a vegetable purée; or they may be hollowed out, the choke removed and replaced with any one of a number of vegetable, meat, or seafood stuffings.

Peak season. Artichokes are available the year round, but their peak season is in March, April, and May, when they are at top quality and their price is the most reasonable.

Amount to buy. One whole artichoke makes an individual serving, one to two filled artichoke bottoms will serve one person.

Selection. Size has little to do with the quality or flavor of artichokes, since some are ready to pick when they are small and others do not mature until they grow larger. Select only those that feel compact and heavy and yield slightly to pressure. Leaf scales should be large, fleshy, tightly closed, and of good green color; a few darkish spots have no significance

A flowering vegetable

Artichokes are actually the unopened flower buds of a plant in the thistle family. They must be picked while the heads are tightly closed and bright green. If they were allowed to open fully, they would turn into large purple thistles and a splendid vegetable would be lost.

Artichokes, one of the oldest foods known to man, originated in the Mediterranean regions in Italy and have been highly prized in European kitchens since the time of the ancient Romans. The name is derived from the Italian *articiocco* and *archiciocco*. In French, artichoke is *artichaut*; in Spanish, *alcachofa*; in German, *Artischocke*.

Artichokes—like asparagus— have always had a certain elegance about them, although there are those who complain that they are the only vegetable of which there is more after it is eaten than before. Detractors aside, artichokes have had a distinguished history enhanced by royal approval. Hearts of artichoke are said to have been a favorite food of sixteenth-century Catherine de Medici, the wife of Henry II of France.

Artichokes began to be commercially cultivated in the United States around the beginning of the twentieth century, in the midcoastal regions of California, where the climate—cool, foggy, and comparatively free of frost—is the friendliest possible for artichoke growing. In the United States today the town of Castroville, south of San Francisco in Monterey County, California, is known as the "artichoke center of the world."

How to eat an artichoke

Pull off a leaf with your fingers and dip the bottom into the accompanying sauce, then scrape off the morsel of flesh on the leaf between your teeth. The rest of the leaf is discarded. If the choke—the fuzzy center growth—has not been removed, you will eventually reach it. Lift the choke out, scrape the artichoke bottom clean, and cut it into pieces with a knife and fork, dipping each piece into the sauce.

For hors d'oeuvres

Individual leaves from a cooked artichoke provide a splendid starting point for an hors d'oeuvre. Detach the leaves after the artichoke has been cooked and place a small portion of a cold salad—tuna, minced mushroom, shrimp, crabmeat, chicken— over the edible portion of each leaf. Your guests will eat the juicy morsel of the artichoke along with whatever you have seen fit to place on it. Calorie counters will thank you.

Artichoke hearts vs. artichoke bottoms

The canned, bottled, or frozen artichoke hearts are not exactly the same as artichoke bottoms, although many people use the two terms synonymously. The commercially packaged artichoke hearts come from tiny artichokes widely available in California but scarce on the East Coast; they have almost no choke at all. The artichoke hearts consist of a portion of the bottom with a few small tender leaves, while the artichoke bottom refers specifically to the meaty, round base of the vegetable without the leaves.

as long as the leaves feel fresh and full. Winter is a critical period for artichokes, and freezing temperatures can cause spots of discoloration (the artichokes are then known in the industry as "Winter Kist"). This does not necessarily impair quality, although it may tend to discourage the buyer.

Storage. Artichokes may be kept up to four or five days. If you are not going to use them at once, wrap them, unwashed, in a damp towel and store them in a plastic bag in the refrigerator to prevent their wilting and drying.

Preparation and serving. Wash artichokes by holding each head under cold running water, spreading the leaves a bit to give them a thorough washing. Place each artichoke on its side on a cutting board. Slice off the bottom stem and trim the base so the artichoke will rest firmly on its bottom and not topple over. Pull off any small or coarse leaves at the base. Next, slice an inch (2.54 cm) off the top of the cone and trim half an inch (1.27 cm) off each of the remaining leaves with kitchen shears. To prevent discoloration, rub all the cut places with lemon. As each artichoke is prepared, place it in a bowl of cold water to which a few tablespoons of lemon juice or vinegar have been added (acidulated water).

To remove the choke before cooking—a chore that may also be done after or even by the diner himself—open the center of each artichoke with your fingers, pushing the leaves apart and exposing the fuzzy choke at the center. Dig out the choke with a teaspoon to expose the flesh of the artichoke bottom and scrape off the fuzz adhering to it. Rub with lemon juice, then press the cone of leaves closed.

To cook, place the artichokes, base down, in a deep kettle so they fit snugly together. (Use an enamel or stainless-steel pot; aluminum turns artichokes grayish.) Cover completely with boiling salted water. Bring to a rolling boil and boil gently, uncovered, for 30 to 45 minutes. Start testing for doneness after 30 minutes by piercing the bottom of an artichoke with a small, sharp-pointed knife; if the knife encounters no resistance, the artichoke is done. If the water level gets low during the cooking, add more boiling water so the cooking process is never interrupted.

When done, remove the artichokes from the water with kitchen tongs or two long-handled spoons. Place upside down and allow to drain. Serve hot or warm with melted butter or hollandaise sauce; serve cold with vinaigrette dressing.

The part of the artichoke that remains after the leaves and choke have been removed is called the "artichoke bottom" (*fond d'artichaut* on French menu). It is slightly concave, a convenient shape to hold stuffings or sauces. To prepare artichoke bottoms, cook artichokes until tender, then pull off the leaves, remove the chokes, and trim the bottoms to make them smooth and neat. (Some cooks prefer to trim the artichoke bottoms before the artichokes are cooked. The bottoms are then simmered until tender [20 to 30 minutes] in boiling salted water to which about 2 tablespoons [30 ml] of lemon juice have been added.) The bottoms may be filled with finely chopped mushrooms or puréed broccoli or green peas or almost anything your fancy dictates.

Dietary information. The calories in 3½ ounces (100 g) of cooked artichokes range from 6 to 44, depending on whether they are fresh or stored. Among other elements and minerals, they contain appreciable amounts of calcium, phosphorus, sodium, and potassium.

ARTICHOKES, JERUSALEM *See* Jerusalem Artichokes.

ARUGULA

A plant with many names
Arugula is known by many names—roquette, rocket, rocket salad, rocket cress, rugula, rucola, ruchetta, ruca, and perhaps others. The Greeks call it *roka*.

How to account for this torrent of names? The scientific name of the plant, *Eruca,* means "rocket." It is logical to assume that "arugula" is a corruption of that name, which then went through other changes in other languages.

Seasoned butter
Arugula adds special flavor interest when it is minced and blended with butter for sandwiches and canapés.

Arugula is a salad green that has been better known in the European Mediterranean countries than on these shores, but that is now gaining in popularity in the United States. It has a distinctive peppery flavor, and a few leaves added to a salad can impart a zingy taste and perhaps a touch of mystery. When young, the green leaves are narrow and pointed. As the plant matures, the leaves grow larger and the peppery flavor intensifies, so arugula is not everyone's favorite thing; people who like the tangy taste of watercress will probably like it. It is available generally at fine greengrocers and in good Italian restaurants, where a salad made of it commands a high price.

Peak season. May to October.

Amount to buy. Arugula is usually sold in small bunches. One bunch will be adequate for two servings of salad when used alone, but if combined with other salad greens it can serve six to eight.

Selection. As with all salad greens, the leaves should be clean and look fresh. The small leaves are the youngest and will be the tenderest and taste the best. Avoid greens with wilted and/or discolored leaves.

Storage. Place washed and dried arugula in a container with a tight-fitting cover and store in the coldest part of the refrigerator; it is, however, advisable to use it within a day or two of buying.

Preparation and serving. Arugula is likely to be sandy and, like spinach, must be thoroughly washed in cold water and drained well. Remove root stems and dry the leaves on a towel or absorbent paper before storing or using. Leaves may be broken or, if desired, used whole in the salad. Toss with French dressing just before serving.

Dietary information. Arugula contains vitamin C, calcium, phosphorus, and potassium, as well as other vitamins and minerals; calories are negligible.

Green vs. white asparagus

Asparagus is a member of the lily family, which also includes such flavorful and decorative plants as onions, garlic, leeks, lilies, tulips, and gladioli.

The two leading varieties are the dark green, which is the most important, and the light green or whitish spears. The dark green type is an early spring crop and is cut as soon as the tips of the stalk grow about 8 inches above the ground. The light asparagus is the same variety, but it is cut while most of the stalk is still below ground. The light-colored varieties are different from the white or blanched asparagus that is grown for canning.

California, New Jersey, Michigan, and Washington are the chief sources of supply.

A long and honorable history

The origin of asparagus is uncertain, shrouded in the mists of time. We do know that it was cultivated in the eastern Mediterranean area for more than two thousand years. It has been a herald of spring since ancient times, when the Persians called it *asparag*, meaning "sprout."

Long before it was used as a food, it was prized for its medicinal qualities. The Greeks and Romans believed it was useful in relieving toothache and preventing bee stings.

But even the ancients were aware of the evils of overcooking asparagus. It is said that the Emperor Augustus, fond of the tender green spears, originated the saying, "Quicker than you can cook asparagus."

ASPARAGUS

There is no more pleasant harbinger of spring than the appearance in our markets of the first asparagus. Asparagus enjoys a relatively short season; consequently, among asparagus enthusiasts it is almost a daily "must" at meals, the frozen or canned varieties being a poor substitute for the fresh.

Peak season. April to June.

Amount to buy. One pound generally serves two persons as a vegetable. If you are serving it as a separate course—either appetizer or salad—you will need from four to six fat asparagus (or an appropriate number of thin ones) per person.

Selection. Look for straight, fresh-looking stalks that are bright green, unstreaked by white markings, and have compact, pointed tips; avoid those with tips that are opened and spread out. Nicely rounded stalks are superior to the flat ones, which can be tough and stringy. Asparagus presents one of the rare situations where fat is better than thin, for the thicker the spear the more tender it is likely to be.

Asparagus frequently comes in bundles of about a pound (454 g) but do buy it loose where possible so you can select stalks of uniform thickness that will cook evenly.

Storage. When you get the asparagus home, cut off an inch (2.54 cm) or so of the stem, wrap the bases in a damp paper towel, and store in the coldest part of the refrigerator in a plastic bag. The asparagus will keep for a few days, but use as soon as possible; it loses flavor if kept too long.

Preparation and serving. A great deal has been said and written about cooking asparagus in an upright position so the tough stems can be boiled and the delicate tips just steamed; there are special asparagus cookers for this purpose. However, if the stems are peeled—a highly recommended procedure—they will be as tender as the tips and the whole spear will cook at the same time. A pot like a large skillet or chicken fryer, in which the asparagus can lie flat in the boiling water, will do nicely.

Wash the spears thoroughly with cold water and peel the stems to within 2 inches (5.1 cm) of the tip, using a swivel-bladed vegetable peeler. If you are dealing with a few dozen spears, you might want to tie them with kitchen string in bundles of ten for easy removal. Three inches (7.6 cm) of boiling water are adequate to cook asparagus; use about a teaspoon (5 ml) of salt per quart of water. As soon as the water reaches a fast boil, add the asparagus. Cover the pot until the water returns to a boil, then remove the cover immediately. The spears should cook in between 5 to 8 minutes, or until a sharp, pointed paring knife pierces the end easily. You can sample the tip of one, but make sure you do not overcook; asparagus is too fine a product to come to the table with a limp, bowed head. The moment it is tender, remove from the water with two kitchen spatulas—one a broad one— and drain on a folded kitchen towel. If the asparagus are to be served cold, refrigerate them; if hot, transfer them to a warmed serving platter.

Asparagus makes a splendid first course, cold, resting on a bed of greens and dressed with a vinaigrette and perhaps a strip of pimento for color. Hollandaise sauce, melted butter or margarine, or browned bread crumbs are appropriate for hot asparagus.

Dietary information. Asparagus is rich in vitamins A and C; it is low in sodium and high in calcium, phosphorus, potassium, and iron. One pound (454 g) of asparagus, uncooked and untrimmed, contains 66 calories.

AUBERGINE *See* Eggplant.

BEANS

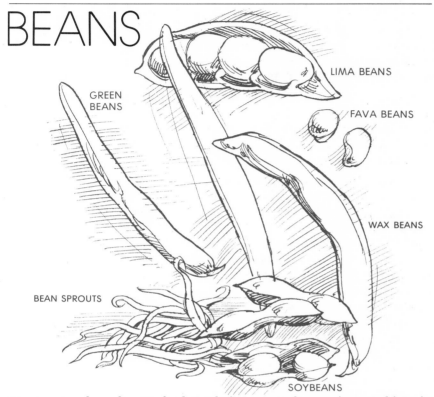

GREEN BEANS

LIMA BEANS

FAVA BEANS

WAX BEANS

BEAN SPROUTS

SOYBEANS

Beans have been a food staple in many cultures since prehistoric times, providing nourishment for royalty and peasants alike, as well as for their livestock. Today beans are among the most popular and important foods produced, and hundreds of varieties are grown throughout the world. It would be difficult if not impossible to categorize every bean; there are so many, and their names and even characteristics change from country to country. Some varieties, such as green beans, are eaten whole with their pods when they are young and fresh; others are shelled, pods discarded, and the beans often dried.

GREEN BEANS

Green beans, also known as "snap beans," "string beans," and "French beans" or "haricots" are one of the most familiar bean varieties for cooks as well as for home gardeners. They are in reality the immature pods of kidney beans picked while the seeds are tiny. Plant breeders have virtually eliminated the stringy filament that used to run along the length of the bean, although occasionally beans with strings do show up (to the dismay of the cook). Some beans are flat, some are round, some are yellow (wax beans), but all are equally good. Wax beans do not seem to enjoy the same popularity as the green ones, although they have a distinctiveness of their own and can be most attractive when mixed with their green relatives in a cold salad.

Bean lore

The ancient Greeks and Romans used beans for balloting, both in the courts and for elections. The black bean signified opposition or guilt; the white stood for agreement or innocence. The beanstalk was a common Roman funeral plant, and Scottish witches were said to take their moonlight rides on beanstalks instead of broomsticks. Roasted beans were buried to ward off toothache and smallpox.

Armenian green bean salad

  1 pound green beans
  1 large onion
  1 tablespoon salt
  2 tomatoes, peeled, seeded, and diced
  ½ cup finely minced fresh parsley
  ¼ cup snipped fresh dill
  ¼ cup salad oil
  2 tablespoons vinegar
  ½ teaspoon salt

Break the beans into ½-inch lengths. Cook in boiling, salted water until only crisp-tender; do not overcook. Drain, rinse in cold water, and set aside.

Slice the onion into thin rings and place in a shallow bowl. Add 1 tablespoon salt. With the heel of your hand crush the onion with the salt until it becomes limp and the juices run out. Rinse the onion rings in cold water to wash out the salt and drain thoroughly.

Return the onions to the bowl and add the tomatoes, beans, parsley, and dill. Toss lightly with the oil, then add the vinegar and ½ teaspoon salt and toss again. Chill until ready to serve. Serves 4 to 6.

At the beginning

While dried beans were a staple of colonial life, and Boston's baked beans were a part of American tradition, green or snap beans were of little importance in early American kitchens. And no wonder! According to the recipes of that time, they were to be boiled until they could be mashed or else they were cooked for hours with a piece of fatback into a gray, greasy glob. The green bean, like the potato, had to travel from the New World to the Old Country and await the cooking skills of the French before it could come into its own. The French picked the beans while they were young—a lesson unknown in this country at that time—and then cooked them quickly, thereby giving this fine vegetable the treatment they deserve.

History

It is thought that the lima bean originated in Central America and was then taken to South America, where it was cultivated and improved. The beans are reputed to have been named after the city in Peru where they were found by Spanish explorers. Travelers carried the bean up through Mexico, and it was grown by Indians living in the southwestern and eastern sections of this country.

Since early times lima beans and corn have been closely associated. We are told that in the early seventeenth century the explorer Champlain reported that the Indians in Maine planted a number of beans with their corn because the beanstalks served as a natural pole to support the corn as it grew. History goes on to say that, soon after the Pilgrims arrived in 1620, an old Indian pit was opened up, and in it were found some corn and a bag of beans—undoubtedly the first succotash!

Succotash

1 cup cooked lima beans
1 cup corn kernels (about 2 ears), cooked
2 tablespoons butter or margarine
1 teaspoon salt
⅛ teaspoon of paprika
 Freshly ground pepper
1 tablespoon chopped parsley
Combine all the ingredients in a saucepan and heat gently over a low flame until hot. Serve at once. Serves 3 or 4.

Peak season. Available all year. Peak season June through August .

Amount to buy. One pound (454 g) of snap beans should be adequate for three servings.

Selection. Choose brightly colored beans, green or yellow, according to variety. They should be unblemished, young, tender, and crisp enough to snap easily between your fingers when bent. When the pods look ridged and bulgy, the beans are usually old, tough, and leathery. A tired green bean that was picked too old and kept too long in the supermarket can be a disaster, and is guaranteed not to improve with cooking. If this is the best your market offers, pass it up.

Storage. Wash beans and store in an airtight plastic bag in the vegetable crisper in the refrigerator and use as soon as possible. Washing them before placing them in the refrigerator will prevent their drying out. The beans will keep for a few days, but an extended delay will not improve their quality.

Preparation and serving. Wash the beans and snap off the ends. Beans may be left whole, if small and young; they may also be broken into 1-inch (2.54 cm) lengths or French-cut into thin diagonal strips.

Beans may be steamed or cooked by being plunged into a generous amount of fast-boiling, salted water and boiled uncovered. (The greater the amount of water, the more quickly it will return to a boil after the beans are added, thus cutting down on the time the beans will need to be in the water.) Add the beans a few at a time so the boiling does not stop. After they have all been added and the water returns to a full boil, reduce the heat. Boiling will take about 12 to 15 minutes; steaming, 15 to 20 minutes. Start tasting after 7 or 8 minutes; beans must never be overcooked. Drain the beans well and return to the saucepan. Shake well to dry, then season.

Properly cooked fresh snap beans are so delicious they need little embellishment. Toss them with a little oil or butter, salt, pepper, a few drops of lemon juice, and a sprinkling of fresh minced parsley, chopped fresh mint, or dill. Water chestnuts, almonds, or mushrooms (thinly sliced and browned in a bit of oil or butter) may be mixed with the beans for added texture and color. Served raw, they make an interesting addition to a platter of *crudités*, and they are also delicious pickled.

Don't reheat cooked beans; the heat further destroys vitamin content. Instead, add them to the greens in your salad bowl.

Dietary information. Snap beans contain calcium, phosphorus, potassium, and vitamins A and C. One pound (454 g) of untrimmed green beans contains 128 calories.

LIMA BEANS

The flattish, kidney-shaped lima beans have a vast array of names— Madagascar, wax, or butter beans. The smaller sizes are called "baby" or "butter limas" and the larger beans "potato limas." The best fresh ones are the baby limas that are just mature enough to be shelled from their pods but are not quite fully ripe. If limas are allowed to grow too big, they become tough.

Peak season. Spring and summer months.

Amount to buy. One pound (454 g) of lima beans in the pod will yield about 1 cup (240 ml) of beans, so you will need about 3 pounds (1.3 kg) for four people.

Selection. Look for clean, well-filled pods of a good green color. The pods should be crisp, unblemished, and not too bulging; pods that are flabby, too, generally indicate inferior quality. The bean itself should be plump, with a tender skin that is green or greenish white .

Storage. Store uncovered, in the pods, in the refrigerator and use within three to five days. Do not shell the beans until you are ready to use them.

Preparation and serving. Pop the shells open along their seams and remove the beans. Or you can split the pods at the rounded end and the beans will come out fairly easily. Pick them over carefully and discard any that appear discolored or wormy.

To cook lima beans, pour about ½ inch (1.27 cm) of water into a heavy saucepan with a tight-fitting lid. Add salt, cover, bring to the boiling point, and add the beans. Cover, lower the heat, and steam gently 15 to 20 minutes, or until the beans are tender. Time will vary according to their freshness, but don't allow them to overcook or they will get mushy, a sorry state for a lima bean—or any other vegetable, for that matter. The beans should be tender but offer the slightest suggestion of resistance when tasted. Drain thoroughly and return to the saucepan. Shake well over heat to get rid of all moisture, then season.

Lima beans may be served hot, dressed with melted butter or margarine and chopped chives or dill, with onions and sliced mushrooms that have been sautéed in oil or butter, or with cooked, crumbled bacon. They may also be served cold, in a tangy vinaigrette as an appetizer or salad.

Dietary information. Limas contain protein and iron and other minerals, and vitamins A and B. Three ounces (90 g) of boiled, drained young lima beans contain 94 calories. The same amount of boiled mature lima beans contain almost half again as many calories.

FAVA BEANS

Fava beans, or broad beans, are long and round, with velvety pods, not unlike lima beans except that they are rounder, and their pods are thick and somewhat larger.

In the opinion of some food experts, fava beans are superior to lima beans in taste and texture. They are certainly easier to shell, and they do have better flavor. They may be substituted for lima beans in any recipe, and they will work well. They are generally available in specialty markets and fine greengrocers.

Peak season. Spring and summer months.

Amount to buy. The pods and skins of the fava beans are heavy; 5 pounds (5.5 kg) of unshelled favas will serve about four.

Selection. Young beans are quite tender, but as the beans mature, the skin covering the bean becomes coarser and tougher. Then the outer skin has to be removed, or "slipped," before they are eaten. With this word of warning, always try to find the smallest, youngest broad beans.

Storage. Store in the refrigerator and use within a day or two. Shell just before using.

A new bean is introduced

Fava or broad beans are comparative newcomers to America. Most other beans were natives of the Americas, but these were brought to our shores either by the Italians or by the English, who call them "broad beans." To the rest of Europe they are known as *fave* or *fèves*. . However, they are now in general use in this country.

As an hors d'oeuvre

Very young, very fresh fava beans may be added to your platter of *crudités* along with the raw string beans, carrots, and cauliflower. Either remove the beans from the pods or allow the guests to extract them themselves. Serve with a bowl of coarse salt for dipping.

Uses of soybeans

There are over a thousand varieties of soybeans—white, yellow, brown, black, and multicolored. Missionaries brought the soybean to Europe from the Orient during the eighteenth century, but it did not come to the United States until the nineteenth.

Although as a food it has much merit and many ardent champions, it has never achieved widespread popularity as a vegetable in this country. Its by-products, however, have many industrial uses. It is useful in renewing soil, for example, and entire farms are given over to it for the production of plastics and glue. Foam materials for fire fighting are also made from soybeans.

Preparation and serving. Shell the beans and wash thoroughly. Place in boiling, salted water and cook quite rapidly, uncovered. The small ones will cook in 10 to 12 minutes; the larger ones may need up to 25 minutes. Drain well.

Taste the beans after cooking, and if you find the outer skins tough you will have to remove them. After the beans cool—you can hurry this by pouring cold water over them—slip off the outer skin of each one. Reheat the beans and add seasonings.

The beans may be served coated with melted butter or margarine, seasoned with salt and freshly ground pepper, and sprinkled with chopped parsley or basil.

Dietary information. Fava beans are similar to lima beans in nutritional value and calories.

SOYBEANS

Soybeans, or soya beans, are the ancient beans of the Orient. For thousands of years, they were the leading source of protein for the people in that part of the world. When fresh, soybeans may be eaten like fresh limas. When dried, they may be sprouted or ground into flour, made into soy milk, soybean oil, or the soybean curd *tofu*, fermented soy cheese often used in Oriental dishes. They are the source for soy sauce, a fermented brown liquid known to anyone who has ever dined in an Oriental restaurant.

Peak season. Available in some areas in the late summer or early fall.

Varieties. There are two types—vegetable type and field type. The vegetable type is used for cooking. The beans are larger and milder than the field-type soybeans, which are used for oil and commercial flour production.

Amount to buy. One pound (454 g) yields about 1⅔ cups (400 ml) and will serve two to three. Each soybean pod generally contains about two beans.

Selection. For cooking, use only the young vegetable type. They are ready to eat when the pods—which have a fuzzy surface and are not edible—are bright green and plump.

Storage. Fresh soybeans may be kept, in the pod, in a covered container in the refrigerator for a few days, but it is better to use them as soon as possible.

Preparation and serving. Shell the beans only when you are ready to use them. Some people shell them dry, but it is easier if you first immerse them in boiling water to cover. Cover the pot, and after 5 minutes drain the beans and cool them. Break the pods crosswise and squeeze out the beans.

To cook, add 2 cups (480 ml) of shelled soybeans to 1 cup (240 ml) boiling water with ½ teaspoon (2.5 ml) salt. Return to a boil, cover, and cook gently for 10 to 20 minutes, or until tender. Cooked soybeans are similar to green peas or lima beans in color, but they have a firmer texture and a nutty flavor. They may be served with a simple butter or cream sauce, or as a substitute in any of your lima bean recipes. They combine well with garlic, green onions, mushrooms, and rice.

Salted, roasted soybeans can be as habit forming as peanuts. To prepare, spread the cooked beans over a greased cookie sheet, dot with butter or margarine, and heat in a 350°F (177°C) oven until brown.

Dietary information. Soybeans, valued chiefly for their high protein content, are also rich in iron, calcium, and phosphorus and contain substantial amounts of vitamins A, B, D, and E. Four ounces (113.5 g) of boiled soybeans contain 134 calories. The fat in soybeans is highly polyunsaturated.

BEAN SPROUTS

These crunchy morsels have been a mainstay of Oriental cookery for centuries. Cooked or raw, they have a fresh, delicate flavor that adds interest and texture to all manner of foods. Plastic-wrapped packages of fresh sprouts are now widely available in many supermarkets and at many greengrocers.

Peak season. Available all year.

Varieties. Alfalfa, soy, and mung bean sprouts, among others, are commonly available. They are interchangeable in use.

Selection. Make sure the sprouts look fresh and crisp, with tips that are not dry. The shorter the bean sprout, the younger and the more tender it will be.

Amount to buy. One pound (454 g) of fresh sprouts yields 4 cups (1.1 l) ready-to-use sprouts. When cooked, 2 cups (480 ml) of raw sprouts diminishes to 1 cup (240 ml). The amount of sprouts needed depends upon how you are planning to use them.

Storage. Store in a tightly sealed plastic bag in the vegetable crisper of the refrigerator. They will keep for 3 to 5 days.

Preparation and serving. Wash sprouts well in cold water and float off the loose particles. Chill in ice water for half an hour before serving to make them crisp, then drain well. The sprouts can be added to fresh salads or sandwich fillings; they may be added to soups or other vegetables shortly before serving. They may also be served, independently, as a vegetable, sautéed in oil or butter until crisp-tender and seasoned with salt and pepper or a bit of soy sauce. Bean sprouts are most versatile, and you can be as creative as you wish in finding uses for them.

Dietary information. Sprouts are low in calories. One-half cup (120 ml) of mung bean sprouts contains 15 calories; the same amount of soybean sprouts contains 25 calories. Soybean sprouts have more nutritional value than the same amount of mung bean sprouts; they both have a high content of water in addition to some protein, vitamins, and minerals.

Grow your own bean sprouts

The pleasant prospect of a product that can be grown throughout the year, requires neither light, soil, nor special equipment, and is ready to eat in three or four days brings us to bean sprouts. The most popular beans for sprouting are mung beans and soybeans, although any dried bean will do. Mung beans sprout in about three days; soybeans take about six. Dried mung beans may be bought from a Chinese food store. They are inexpensive and will keep for months in a covered jar.

Soak ¼ cup of beans overnight in a cup of lukewarm water. The next day drain and rinse the beans a few times with warm tap water until the water is clear. Transfer the beans to a quart jar. Cover the top with cheesecloth secured with a rubber band and place the jar on its side in a warm, dark place, such as under the sink near the hot-water pipe or in your oven. It does not have to be pitch black, but bean sprouts must never be in direct sunlight if you want them munchy, tender, and white. Rinse the beans with cool water four or five times a day and drain well. It is essential that all water be drained to prevent growth of mold; if any beans do become moldy, discard them. The sprouts should be an inch or two long within two or three days and ready to eat. Give them a final rinse and refrigerate them in a tightly covered jar. Beans produce six or seven times their volume: about ⅓ cup of beans will yield about 2 cups of sprouts.

Chinese saying

The technique of raising bean sprouts at home in a dark, secluded place has given rise to a colloquial expression used by the Chinese when someone disappears from public view. He is said to be "sprouting at home."

Sugar beets

The sugar beet, cultivated commercially throughout the temperate zone, today provides about one third of the world's sugar. Technological advances in harvesting have reduced production costs so that beet sugar can compete with cane sugar in cost. About 100 pounds of beets are needed to produce 5 pounds of sugar. Garden beets and sugar beets must never be planted near each other, because the pollen of sugar beets is windborne and cross-pollination takes place readily. It can ruin the seeds of both.

Beet greens

Beet tops are often removed from young plants, bunched, and sold as salad greens. How good they taste depends upon how young and tender they are, and their color and appearance give us a clue. They should be thin-ribbed, fresh green, and not wilted or slimy. The greens are prepared exactly the same way as spinach (see page 70). Their use as a food was recognized long before the beetroot became popular. Until the later centuries of the Roman Empire, only the greens were eaten; the roots were used medicinally as a cure for toothaches or headaches.

BEETS

Beets are a versatile and attractive vegetable with good flavor. They can be served hot as a vegetable, cold, pickled, sweet and sour as a salad or relish, or as the leading ingredient of a soup (borscht). In the South and Midwest, the beet tops, cooked like spinach, are preferred by many over the tuber, or bulb, part.

Peak season. Beets are produced commercially in 31 states from New Jersey to California the year round, with the peak season running from June through October.

Amount to buy. Bunches usually carry from five to seven beets, which should serve three to four people. You will need about a dozen of the tiny ones for the same number of servings.

Selection. Fresh, first-quality beets should have a good globular shape, with smooth, firm flesh and a deep red color. Soft, wet spots on beets indicate decay, and a rough, shriveled feel flashes a warning that the beet will be tough. Choose small- or medium-sized beets over large ones, which can be woody and coarse. Poor-looking beet tops are not necessarily a sign of inferior quality, because beet tops deteriorate rapidly without affecting the quality of the root.

Storage. Beet tops are extremely perishable, but the beets themselves, because of their thick skins, store well. They should be refrigerated in a plastic bag or in the vegetable compartment, where they will hold for up to two weeks. When storing beets, remove all but 2 inches (5.1 cm) of the tops.

Preparation and serving. Trim the beets, leaving 2 inches (5.1 cm) of the tops and the root ends. Do not scrub beets before cooking, since this might puncture the skin and allow the juice to escape—a process known as "bleeding," which drains the beets of their rosy color. Wash the beets gently, then put them in boiling, salted water to cover, cover the pot, and simmer slowly. Young beets take from 30 to 45 minutes; older beets 1 to 2 hours. Testing with a fork for doneness will also cause bleeding, so do not pierce the beets unnecessarily. Rather, remove one from the pot with a spoon and feel it. If it gives a bit and is tender to the touch, it is done.

When tender, plunge the cooked beets into cold water, drain, and slip off the skins. (If you've cooked the beets ahead, leave them in the cooking liquid until you are ready to use them.) Beets may be sliced and heated in a saucepan with a few tablespoons (30-45 ml) of butter or margarine, a generous splash of lemon juice, salt, and freshly ground pepper. They are delicious pickled and served cold. They may also be baked in their skins, 1 to 1½ hours in a covered casserole in a 425°F (220°C) oven. Let cool, peel, and slice. Serve at room temperature, dressed with vinegar and oil, salt and pepper, or bathed in sour cream or plain yogurt, seasoned to taste.

Dietary information. Beets contain calcium, phosphorus, sodium, potassium, vitamin C, and a small amount of vitamin A. One-half cup (120 ml) of boiled, sliced beets contains 32 calories.

BELIGIAN ENDIVE (WITLOOF) *See* Endive.

BOK CHOY

Bok choy, or Chinese chard, resembles both chard and celery and is also called "white mustard cabbage." A leafy vegetable with white stems and green leaves, it is a popular ingredient in many Chinese dishes. It has a stronger flavor than that of Chinese cabbage, but adds an interesting piquancy to soups or combinations of other vegetables. It can usually be bought at Chinese greengrocers.

Amount to buy. Bok choy is generally sold by the pound. One pound is adequate for most purposes since it is rarely used alone.

Selection. Good quality leaves are dark green and shiny. Avoid those that look wilted or limp.

Storage. Store in a plastic bag in the refrigerator and use within a day of purchase.

Preparation and serving. Wash leaves and cut into 1-inch (2.54 cm) squares. Cook for 7 to 9 minutes, following the instructions for steaming spinach (page 70). Season with salt, pepper, and a bit of butter or margarine. If used in soup, add to the soup during the last 10 minutes of cooking. It may also be stir-fried in oil.

Dietary information. Fresh bok choy contains 69 calories per pound (454 g), untrimmed. It is high in protein, vitamins A and C, calcium, and other minerals.

A New England tradition

Harvard beets have been part of the culinary lore of New England for decades.

⅓ cup granulated sugar
2 teaspoons cornstarch
¼ cup vinegar
¼ cup liquid in which beets were cooked
2½ cups sliced, cooked beets
1 tablespoon butter

In a saucepan, combine the sugar, cornstarch, vinegar, and beet liquid. Cook, stirring, until the mixture becomes thickened and smooth; then add the sliced beets and butter and cook until heated through. Serve at once. Serves 4.

Note: In James Beard's Yale version of Harvard beets, ½ cup of orange juice and 1 tablespoon of lemon juice are substituted for the vinegar and beet liquid, and the sugar is increased to ½ cup.

What's in a name?
Broccoli is sometimes called "Italian asparagus"—an odd situation, for, while broccoli and cabbage have a common ancestry, asparagus is in no way related. The name "broccoli" comes from the Latin word *brachium,* which means "arm" or "branch"—understandable in view of its general construction. In France broccoli is known as *chou broccoli* ("cabbage broccoli") and, in Central Europe, *broccoli-rabe.* It appears that it was known to the early settlers of this country, as "brockala." James Beard tells us that old manuscript cookbooks contain occasional recipes for it under that name.

Not for eating only
The flower buds of the broccoli plant are so attractive they are sometimes used in floral decorations.

BROCCOLI

Although broccoli, a first cousin to cauliflower, is an ancient vegetable, its popularity in American kitchens is comparatively recent. Modern plant growers have improved the varieties of broccoli enormously, and it is far better today than it was some fifty years ago. There are two general types: heading, or cauliflower, type, which has dense white buds like a cauliflower; and sprouting, which has branching clusters of compact flower buds, dark green or purplish green, that crown a thick, lighter green stalk. Green sprouting broccoli is sometimes called "Calabrese." It is believed to have originated in Calabria, Italy, and is the most usual type found in the United States markets. We can use it in many different ways—raw as an hors d'oeuvre with a dip, cooked and served cold in a salad, boiled, baked, steamed, stir-fried, sautéed, puréed…its possibilities are endless.

Peak season. Available fresh all year, with peak season from October to May.

Amount to buy. Broccoli is usually sold in 2-pound (908 g) bunches, which will serve four.

Selection. Look for fresh green color in the heads, leaves, and stems. Stalks should be tender and firm, with compact buds in the head. Overly mature broccoli will give itself away by yellow "flowers" showing inside the buds—and as the yellow flowers increase, its desirability decreases.

Storage. Wash broccoli well, wrap it in plastic, and store it in the vegetable compartment of your refrigerator. It will keep for two or three days, but it is better to use it as soon as possible.

Preparation and serving. Rapid cooking and very little water help to preserve nutrients, and broccoli lends itself nicely to this procedure. Cut it into florets and peel the thin, green skin off the stalks with a swivel-bladed vegetable peeler. The peeling will make all the difference between a tough vegetable and a tender, fast-cooking one. Broccoli requires 8 to 10 minutes of cooking in boiling salted water, or until a knife pierces the stems easily. It is also delicious sautéed. Slice the stems in ¼-inch (.635 cm) rounds and, using a large skillet, cook gently for about 5 minutes in a few tablespoons (30-45 ml) of oil seasoned with a clove of minced garlic (optional). Add the broccoli florets, season with salt and pepper, cover the skillet, and simmer for another 5 minutes, or until the florets are crisp-tender. Shake the pan from time to time. The broccoli will be beautifully green, and there will be absolutely no odor.

Dietary information. As with other leafy greens, broccoli is a good source of vitamins A and C. It also contains vitamin B, calcium, and iron. One cup (240 ml) of cooked broccoli contains 40 calories and it is also high in fiber.

BRUSSELS SPROUTS

Brussels sprouts look like miniature cabbages and have a similar, but slightly more delicate, taste. We are told that they were first grown in the Belgian city of Brussels in the thirteenth century, whence comes their name. Properly cooked, they can be as crisp, well flavored, and inviting as any vegetable, in spite of their somewhat tarnished reputation, brought about by decades of poor preparation and overcooking.

Most Brussels sprouts are grown in California, Oregon, and New York. Although this vegetable needs a long, cool growing season and can withstand freezing temperatures quite well, "sunny California" is the leading state in sprout production.

Peak season. Sprouts are available about ten months of the year, but peak season is from October through December.

Amount to buy. One pound (454 g) will serve four.

Selection. Good sprouts are firm, compact, fresh looking, and of good green color. Puffy, soft sprouts are usually inferior in quality and flavor, and leaves that are wilted or yellow indicate aging. Brussels sprouts are usually sold in one-pound (454 g) baskets containing varying sizes. There was a time when they were graded according to size and you could buy small, medium, or large, but, like other minor luxuries, that custom has passed. The only uniformly small-sized ones generally available are the frozen baby Brussels sprouts.

Storage. Brussels sprouts should be stored in an airtight plastic bag in the refrigerator crisper to keep freshness and good color. They will hold for a few days, but for best results they should be used as soon as possible.

Preparation and serving. Cut off the stem (being careful not to cut too closely or the leaves will fall off during cooking) and remove any loose or discolored leaves. Brussels sprouts may be steamed or boiled. To boil, place the prepared sprouts in an ample quantity of boiling, salted water. Boil uncovered, briskly, until they are just tender. This will take from 5 to 15 minutes, depending on how big they are and the degree of crispness you desire. Be careful not to overcook; as with all vegetables, a sodden, mushy product defeats its purpose. Drain the sprouts well and return to the saucepan for a minute to dry out. Add a lump of butter or margarine and toss until thoroughly covered, then sprinkle with freshly ground pepper and salt, if needed. Sautéed sliced mushrooms, or sesame seeds or sliced almonds browned in butter mixed with the sprouts provide tasty variations.

Brussels sprouts are a hearty vegetable and go well with hearty dishes that can stand up to them—beef, lamb, roast chicken, roast pork, and so forth, but they should not accompany foods in subtle wine or herb sauces, since they will overpower the delicate flavors.

Dietary information. Raw Brussels sprouts are high in vitamins A, C, and B_1 and iron; prolonged cooking can destroy vitamin C. One-half cup (120 ml) of boiled Brussels sprouts contains 32 calories.

History

Brussels sprouts, one of the few vegetables to have originated in northern Europe, are descended from the wild cabbage. They are about four hundred years old, which makes them relatively new. They came to the United States in about 1800, but they have been grown commercially only since the early 1900s. Unlike broccoli and other members of the cabbage family, there is no mention of Brussels sprouts in the early cookbooks. It may be that, because they were so badly prepared, no one thought they were worth writing about. They are a popular vegetable among the English, who were probably responsible for introducing them to the American scene.

The United States now raises close to sixty-nine million pounds of Brussels sprouts annually, of which less than one third are consumed fresh. The rest are canned or frozen.

As a decoration

In nature, Brussels sprouts grow close together on a single tall stem. This "baby cabbage" is so decorative that it is sometimes used as a centerpiece in the form of a tree. The little sprouts are wired into a pyramid shape attached to a tall stem. This is then sprayed with gold. Quite lovely and completely inedible.

The origin of coleslaw

In case you've wondered how raw-cabbage salad came to be known as "coleslaw," the name derives from *colewort,* an archaic English word that was originally a general name for any plant of the cabbage family.

In the beginning

There is evidence that cabbage was introduced into Rome a few centuries before the birth of Christ, and for hundreds of years after that the Romans revered it as a medicine. Although unrecognized at the time, its high vitamin C content undoubtedly was making its contribution to the general well-being of the population. Particularly recommended were poultices made from red cabbage for the treatment of warts, tumors, and sores and to prevent rheumatism.

Cabbage comes to the New World

It is possible that it was the Dutch who brought cabbage to the New World, for it is first mentioned in connection with New Netherlands. It was grown by the Swedish colonies in Delaware, and it must also have reached New England shortly after the first settlers arrived. It then earned a permanent place in culinary history by becoming a tradition in the New England boiled dinner.

Sauerkraut

Huge amounts of cabbage were salted and made into sauerkraut during the early years of our country. With no refrigeration, this process offered an effective way to preserve cabbage for the winter and added a welcome fillip of acidity to meals—which could account for the traditional custom of serving sauerkraut with turkey in Maryland. Sauerkraut is a popular dish when served hot as an accompaniment for game, such as duck and pheasant, and cold as a salad as well. Originally made by the Dutch and Germans, the name in German literally means "sour plant."

CABBAGE

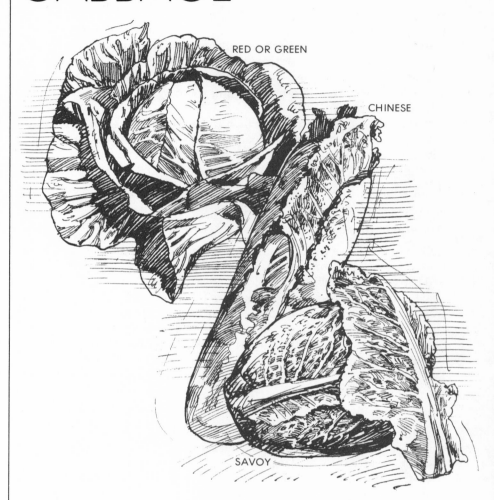

RED OR GREEN

CHINESE

SAVOY

Cabbage, one of the oldest known vegetables, has a history of cultivation that goes back four thousand years. The development of the huge cabbage family, which includes cauliflower, Brussels sprouts, broccoli, and kale, can be traced in the Mediterranean area, in Asia Minor, and in northern and western Europe. A splendid, hardy vegetable that can be served in many ways, it can be eaten raw, shredded for salad, or it can be pickled, braised, boiled, stuffed, or steamed; it also gives a good account of itself as an ingredient in soup. Actually, cabbage would have needed great merit to have withstood the centuries of poor preparation that earned it the undeserved reputation of mushy consistency and offensive cooking odor. It is the cooking method and not the cabbage that must take the blame for this.

Peak season. Available the year round. Peak season for Savoy cabbage is September through March.

Amount to buy. A 2- to 3-pound (1 to 1½ kg) cabbage will serve four persons.

Selection. Choose well-trimmed, reasonably solid heads that are heavy for their size and show no discolored veins. The outer leaves should have a fresh appearance, with no sign of puffiness or wormholes.

Varieties. The varieties most often seen in our markets are the smooth-leaved green or white cabbage, the red cabbage, and the curly-leaved Savoy. Their use is interchangeable. Summer cabbage is small and the leaves are a rich, dark green. Their heads usually weigh about 2 or 3 pounds (1 to 1½ kg). The winter cabbage, called "old cabbage," has whiter leaves inside with gray-green outer leaves, and the heads range from 4 to 6 pounds (2 to 3 kg). The red, or purple, cabbage, streaked with white inside, is used for special recipes and pickling, as well as raw in salads. The Savoy, or curly-headed, cabbage is more delicate and flavorful than the winter cabbage, which has come out of storage, and it has the additional attraction of being pleasing to the eye. Its yellowish, crimped leaves form a head that is about as hard as iceberg lettuce.

Storage. Undamaged, unwashed heads can be stored in a plastic bag in the refrigerator for up to a week or ten days. If there is evidence of worm or insect damage, soak the head in cold, salted water for ten minutes to drive out the culprits. Savoy cabbage should be used as soon as possible, because it does not keep as well as the green and white varieties.

Preparation and serving. Remove all the outer leaves that are coarse or torn. Cut the cabbage in half and cut each half in two or three sections; or shred finely or coarsely, according to how you want it. Unless you like the core cooked with the cabbage, you can cut it out and perhaps munch it yourself as you prepare the cabbage—a bonus for the cook. Use a stainless steel knife to cut or shred the cabbage; its juices discolor ordinary steel, which then discolors the cabbage.

The cabbage can be steamed in about ½ inch (1.27 cm) of boiling, salted water or a shallow filming of oil on the pan. Cook, covered, until crisp-tender, 5 to 10 minutes, depending on whether it is shredded or cut in larger sections. Add salt and freshly ground pepper to taste. Cooked in this manner, cabbage is delicious, has pleasant texture, and does not give off any cooking odor. It combines well with creamed white onions.

Red cabbage should always be cooked with wine or vinegar or lemon juice (or apples) to prevent the color from fading or changing. The acid counteracts the alkalinity of the water and of the salt that dilutes the red color.

Dietary information. Raw cabbage is rich in vitamin C and has a fair amount of vitamin B_1. The early varieties of green-leaved cabbage have the largest amount. The more quickly cabbage is cooked, and the least immersion in water, the more vitamins will be retained. Cabbage also has significant amounts of calcium, phosphorus, and potassium. One cup (240 ml) of finely shredded raw cabbage contains 24 calories.

Cabbage with caraway seeds

1 medium-sized cabbage
3 tablespoons cooking oil
1 large onion, sliced
½ teaspoon salt
   Freshly ground pepper
   Water or dry white wine, if necessary
2 tablespoons caraway seeds

Wash the cabbage and drain, then cut into quarters and remove the core. Cut the cabbage into thick slices and set aside.

In a large, heavy skillet with a cover, heat the oil and cook the onion until limp and transparent, then add the cabbage, salt, and pepper. Cover the skillet and cook over a low flame until the cabbage is crisp-tender, about 8 to 10 minutes. Shake the pan from time to time. If the cabbage seems in danger of scorching, add a splash of water or dry white wine to the pan. Sprinkle with the caraway seeds and mix through; then transfer to a warmed bowl and serve. Serves 4.

An educated cabbage

During their growing period, cauliflowers are sensitive to changes in temperature and require a cool, moist climate. At a certain time the large inner leaves have to be drawn together and tied loosely to shield the head from the sun, or the quality will be affected. Cauliflowers don't just grow—they require care and watching.

Cauliflower is certainly queen of the cabbage clan, which is probably what evoked Mark Twain's famous remark, "Cauliflower is nothing but cabbage with a college education."

Which came first?

Some food historians claim that the artichoke enjoyed by the ancient Greeks and Romans was not the globe, or French, artichoke but the cardoon. Others claim that the cardoon came later, developed from the artichoke by a long process of cultivation and selection. However, the course of history would not have been affected in either case.

The cardoon has been introduced into South Amercia, where it has grown wild extensively on the Pampas.

The mysterious cardoon

Cardoons are a mystery to most Americans, but the Italians, who know them as *cardi* or *cardoni,* and the French, who call them *carde,* hold them in highest esteem. They are distinctive, with a subtly sweet and interesting flavor, slightly reminiscent of artichokes.

They require special treatment in their preparation, because, like artichokes, they darken quickly when cut. It is best to handle them in 2- or 3-inch slices, instantly dropping the scraped portions into cold water seasoned with either lemon juice or vinegar. In their preparation, their larger ribs must be scraped and stripped of their strings, and portions of the outer ribs that seem hollow or woody must be discarded. The tenderest part is the center core, which is cut into crosswise slices. The French like the tender inner ribs slivered raw and added to a salad as an extra bit of crunch.

Cardoons are most versatile. They may be served hot with butter, cream sauce, or tomato sauce; cold with a lemon and mustard vinaigrette; coated with a batter and deep fried; baked with tomato sauce and cheese; or served *au gratin* with Parmesan cheese and bread crumbs. They may also be puréed as a vegetable or as the basis of a cream soup.

CELERY CABBAGE

This is a pale green and white cabbage that forms compact, cylindrical heads. This sweetly flavored, leafy member of the mustard family has some of the characteristics of both romaine and cabbage. It is frequently found in Chinese dishes and is delicious either raw or cooked.

Peak season. All year.

Amount to buy. About 1 pound (454 g) of celery cabbage will serve four.

Selection. Stalks should be firm, fresh, and white.

Storage. Celery cabbage may be stored, unwashed, for a few days in a plastic bag in the refrigerator after any damaged outer leaves have been removed.

Preparation and serving. Remove any tough outer leaves. Wash well and crisp the cabbage in ice water if it is to be served raw. It may be mixed with other greens in a salad, cooked as greens, or sliced in ½-inch (1.27 cm) slices and stir-fried in oil. It can provide a crunchy contrast to other vegetables in vegetable soups if added shortly before serving.

Dietary information. Celery cabbage contains appreciable amounts of vitamin A and potassium. Three and one-half ounces (100 g), uncooked, contain 14 calories.

CARDOON

The cardoon is a long, celery-like vegetable, measuring nearly 2 feet (61 cm), with a long, narrow, coarse top leaf. It is related to the globe artichoke. The edible portions are its young leaves and undeveloped stalks, which are grown in the dark to keep them white and tender.

Selection. Select a cardoon with a small shank, which indicates a young, tender plant. Leaves should be very dark green.

Storage. Trim, rinse, and shake off excess moisture before storing the cardoon in a plastic bag in the refrigerator. It will keep for a week.

Preparation and serving. Remove and discard the outer stems, since they become tougher when cooked. The inner leaves and stalks have a pleasant flavor and can substitute for celery. To keep the cardoon white when cooked, add a teaspoon (5 ml) of vinegar to each cup (240 ml) of water used. Boil the cardoon, uncovered, until crisply tender. The roots and leaf stalks are usually cooked and used in soups.

Dietary information. Cardoon is low in calories and contains vitamin A, potassium, and other minerals.

CARROTS

Carrots grow in all shapes, sizes, and colors in various parts of the world, but the most popular in the United States is the Mediterranean type, which is fairly long and deep yellow or orange in color. Carrots belong to the same family as celery, parsnips, parsley, caraway, and fennel, among many others—about twenty-five hundred in all.

Carrots are rich in carotene, the substance that gives them their yellow-orange color and that is converted into vitamin A by the liver. Doctors tell us that vitamin A is useful in improving night vision. Three-quarters of a cup (180 ml) of raw carrots supplies about double the amount of vitamin A needed daily by the average person.

Carrots are a most versatile vegetable. They can play a part in every course of a meal—raw, to accompany the predinner drink; as a soup, a vegetable, and a salad; as a marmalade, flavored with orange and lemon; and they can provide a splendid crescendo to a dinner as an important ingredient in a delicious cake.

Peak season. Fresh carrots are available all year, with no distinct peak and large supplies at all times.

Amount to buy. Bunches generally weigh 1 to 1½ pounds (454 to 681 g); this will serve two to three. It's a good idea to buy extra, for carrots are always useful as seasonings, for salads, and as a nibble.

Selection. Choose firm, well-formed, smooth, deeply colored carrots. The carrots with a bright orange color contain more carotene than the paler varieties. Avoid wilted, flabby, shriveled, soft carrots, or carrots with large green areas (sunburn) at the top. Reject topped carrots that have green shoots and bunched carrots that have yellow tops; these are signs that they have not been stored properly or that they are too old.

Most markets carry carrots either packaged in plastic bags or by the bunch with the tops attached. The latter are generally fresher and more desirable, although not always available. The feathery green tops may be combined with other greens for cooking.

Storage. Carrots may be stored in a plastic bag or vegetable crisper in the refrigerator for several weeks. If the carrots have tops attached, be sure to remove them before storage, since they drain moisture from the carrots and the carrots will become limp and dry within a day or two. Carrots do not lose any nutrients when properly stored. A test indicated that the carotene actually increased after twenty weeks in commercial storage, and then remained the same for the next ten weeks.

Preparation and serving. Carrots are simple to prepare. Wash and trim as necessary. Some young, smooth carrots need only a good scrubbing with a firm-bristled vegetable brush, but if they are older scrape them with a swivel-bladed vegetable peeler, which will remove a minimal amount of the peel. Carrots may be diced, sliced across or diagonally, shredded, cut into julienne sticks, or left whole. They should be cooked or steamed in a small amount of boiling, salted water in a heavy saucepan with a tightly fitting cover. Shredded carrots will cook in 4 to 5 minutes, cut slices in 10 to 12 minutes, and whole carrots in less than 20 minutes. Do not overcook; they should be tender but still crisp. Cooked carrots may be served with melted butter or margarine, sprinkled with chopped

History

Carrots were cultivated in the Mediterranean regions before the Christian era, but they did not become popular as a food until about the thirteenth century in Europe. The ancient Greeks looked on them as an aphrodisiac, and the ladies in the Middle Ages used their delicate foliage to ornament their hair and hats.

There is no specific account of the introduction of the first carrot into America, but it seems safe to assume that it came with the first settlers. It became a favorite crop with the Indians, who liked carrots so much that they took them from the early settlers' gardens when they would take nothing else.

Carrot juice

Many health-conscious people take their carrots liquefied to assure themselves of an adequate supply of vitamin A. Carrot juice is featured in many health-food bars and is also available canned. But a word of warning must be sounded. There is possible harm in taking too much vitamin A, and an excess of carrot juice in the body can give the skin a decided orange hue. Moderation in all things—even carrot juice!

Honeyed carrots

    3 tablespoons butter or margarine
    3 tablespoons orange juice
    1 tablespoon lemon juice
    ½ teaspoon salt
    ¼ teaspoon powdered ginger
    ¼ cup honey
    4 cups carrots (about 8 carrots),
        scraped and cut into julienne strips

In a large, heavy skillet with a cover, melt the butter or margarine. Add the orange and lemon juices, salt, ginger, and honey, and mix well. Add the carrot strips and cook, covered, over low heat for 15 to 20 minutes, or until crisp-tender. Keep your eye on them while they are cooking and stir frequently so they won't scorch and will take on an even glaze. Serves 4 to 6.

Crécy

The next time you see the term *Crécy* on a French menu, know that it means either made of or garnished with carrots. And *purée Crécy*? Carrot soup, of course.

Cauliflower Mornay

1 medium cauliflower, separated
into florets
3 tablespoons cooking oil
3 tablespoons all-purpose flower
1½ cups hot milk
½ teaspoon salt
Freshly ground pepper
1 cup grated Cheddar cheese
½ cup buttered bread crumbs

Steam the cauliflower florets until barely tender, about 8 minutes. Drain well and return to the saucepan for a minute or two to dry out over very low heat. Arrange in a shallow 8-by-10-inch baking dish.

In a saucepan, blend the oil and flour. Add the milk, stirring constantly with a wire whisk, and cook over low heat until thickened and smooth. Season with salt and pepper.

Cover the cauliflower with half the grated cheese, pour over the cream sauce, then sprinkle on the remaining cheese. Top with the buttered bread crumbs. Heat in a 350° oven for 15 minutes, or until the topping is brown and bubbly. Serves 4.

parsley, marjoram, or chopped dill. Carrots need not be boring. Properly cooked and imaginatively seasoned, they can be delicious. If you are braising a beef pot roast or a veal roast, throw in a few whole carrots to cook along with the meat; they will take on a lovely flavor.

Dietary information. Carrots are high in vitamin A and contain minerals. One whole raw carrot, 5½ inches (13.9 cm) by 1 inch (2.54 cm), contains 20 calories.

CAULIFLOWER

Cauliflower is a cultivated descendant of the common cabbage and has much in common with its green relative, broccoli. It came from Asia to the Italian coast and then through Europe. In French it is *chou-fleur*, "cabbage flower," but the English name is derived from the Latin *caulis*, "stalk." Cauliflower grows on a single stem. The head, known as the "curd," is a crown of undeveloped white flower buds. Broad green leaves surround the curd and protect it while it is growing. Cauliflower has become an important crop in the United States only since the 1920s. It is eaten cooked or raw in salad, and is popular both as an ingredient in mixed pickles and as an hors d'oeuvre, served raw with a dip.

There was a time when basic instructions for choosing a good cauliflower included the phrase "should wear a jacket of bright green, denoting freshness," but today most cauliflower is shipped stripped of its perishable leaves, the head encased in clear plastic wrap. The plastic wrap helps to preserve freshness, and eliminating the heavily ribbed leaves saves a large portion of the cost of shipping.

Peak season. Cauliflower is generally available all year, but supply is greatest from September through November.

Amount to buy. One medium-sized head will serve four.

Varieties. In addition to the usual white or creamy white cauliflower, a new green variety has been developed commercially. It is a cross between conventional cauliflower and broccoli, and it stays green when cooked. The head resembles cauliflower, but the color is chartreuse, rather than the dark green of broccoli. It is a pleasant, tasty vegetable that cooks more quickly than cauliflower and is less apt to give off an odor while cooking.

Selection. The head should be white or only slightly creamy white, firm, and compact. A yellowed or speckled surface means it is not fresh. Avoid loose, open flower clusters or a head that is described as having a "ricey" appearance. If there are surrounding leaves, they should be fresh looking and green. The size of the head does not affect quality, nor do the tiny leaves you occasionally see growing through the curd.

Storage. Store cauliflower, wrapped in plastic, in the vegetable crisper of the refrigerator and use as soon as possible, although it will keep for up to five days before it begins to deteriorate in quality. If for any reason you need to freshen the head, soak it, head down, in cold water containing a teaspoon (5 ml) each of vinegar and salt for 30 minutes. This will also drive out any insects or other infestation.

Preparation and serving. Wash the cauliflower well, remove outer leaves and heavy stem, and cut out any bruised sections. Leave the cauliflower whole or break it into florets. The first makes a handsome presentation on a vegetable platter surrounded by other vegetables, but the florets will cook more quickly and evenly. Cauliflower can be steamed in about an inch (2.54 cm) of boiling, salted water in a heavy, covered saucepan. Add a teaspoonful (5 ml) of fresh lemon juice to the water to keep the cauliflower white. The whole cauliflower will take from 20 to 30 minutes and the florets from 9 to 15 minutes. Do not overcook. Mushy cauliflower is uninteresting and unpalatable; it should be just crisply tender. When the stem end yields to the touch of a fork, it is done. Drain well and serve with buttered bread crumbs or a butter sauce, a sprinkling of Parmesan, chopped chives, or parsley, or a hollandaise.

Dietary information. In addition to calcium and potassium, in its raw state cauliflower has a large amount of vitamins A and C. One-half cup (120 ml) of cooked florets contains 14 calories.

CELERIAC

Celeriac (pronounced se-LER-i-ak), also known as "celery root," "turnip-rooted celery," "knob celery," and "celery knob," is not the root of the stalk celery, as some people think. It is a round, brownish root with rough skin and green tops that is grown for the root alone. More popular in Europe than it is in the United States, it is still worth knowing. It is useful in salads, both raw and cooked, and does well in combination with other vegetables, potatoes among them. While it is not a pretty vegetable—the bulbs are large and usually covered with a collection of little brown roots—it does afford a pleasant change from other vegetables. It is most familiar to American food sophisticates as a French hors d'oeuvre, served as a salad called *céleri-rave rémoulade.*

Peak season. Primarily a winter vegetable.

Amount to buy. About 1½ to 2 pounds (681 to 908 g) of celery root for four persons. It is often sold in bunches of three knobs, but it can sometimes be bought by the piece.

Selection. Choose firm knobs that are small, since the smaller roots will be more tender and less woody.

Storage. Trim roots and tops and store in the refrigerator.

Preparation and serving. Peel the celeriac and cut it into slices. Drop it into a saucepan with boiling, salted water to cover and boil slowly, covered; it should be tender in 6 to 10 minutes. A little vinegar or lemon juice added to the water will keep the celeriac white. The boiled slices may be served tossed in melted butter, then sprinkled with chopped chives or parsley, or mashed with an equal amount of cooked potatoes and seasoned with salt and pepper.

Dietary information. Celery root contains phosphorus and potassium. Three and one-half ounces (100 g) contain 40 calories.

Céleri-rave rémoulade
(Celery root in mustard sauce)

This is a popular appetizer in France and Switzerland. It also serves as a pleasant accompaniment for cold poached fish.

    1 pound celery root
    ¾ cup mayonnaise
    3 tablespoons Dijon-type mustard
    2 teaspoons wine vinegar
      Crisp lettuce leaves
    2 to 3 tablespoons chopped parsley

Peel the celery root and cut into thin strips the size of matchsticks. Plunge into a pot of boiling, salted water and boil for exactly 5 minutes. Rinse the pieces in cold water, then drain well and dry in a towel to remove excess moisture.

Combine the mayonnaise, mustard, and wine vinegar in a small bowl and add to the celery root. Allow it to marinate a few hours or overnight. Serve on crisp lettuce leaves, sprinkled with chopped parsley. Serves 4 to 6.

Special dishes for a special dish

Still to be found in antique shops are the "celery glasses," vaselike containers, often footed, that were specially designed to hold the stalks of celery that were consumed in American homes a few generations ago. They are still used in France and England, but gradually in the United States oblong celery dishes in china and cut glass replaced the upright holders, and the celery was served from a horizontal position, often topped with some crushed ice to keep it crisp and some olives and radishes to keep it company.

A bland, gentle vegetable

Celery is a bland vegetable that does not overwhelm the taste of other foods. It has a distinctive, delicate flavor that, unlike artichokes and asparagus, never overpowers anything it accompanies. A wine fancier about to embark on a great wine may nibble a piece of celery to "clear the palate," so the full impact of the wine can be savored without any previous taste distractions. It also serves as an important detergent vegetable, cleansing the teeth.

CELERY

Like potatoes, onions, and carrots, celery is a year-round staple in many kitchens. From salads to soup to stews, the crispy, crunchy, flavorful celery stalk is a virtual necessity. Rarely does nature provide a product with so little waste, since every part is suitable for use: the leaves are perfect for soup, stews, or salads; the outer ribs of the stalk can be boiled, braised, or creamed, even parboiled, dredged in flour, and fried; the hearts, or inner ribs, give a good account of themselves on the relish tray. Celery seeds are flavorful seasonings for other dishes, a sprinkling of them being a common addition to coleslaw.

Amount to buy. Cooked as a vegetable, a bunch of celery will serve four. For braising, one heart can be split to make two servings.

Varieties. There are two kinds of celery: Golden Heart, which is bleached white, and Pascal, which ranges from light green to a deep, robust green. At the beginning of the nineteenth century, some well-intentioned plant scientists came up with the notion that celery could be bleached of its green color to make it milder tasting, but better judgment has since prevailed. Bleaching diminishes some of the nutritional value, and the green celery is superior to its pale counterpart in flavor, lack of stringiness, and nutrients.

Selection. Characteristics of quality in both varieties are the same. Leaf stems or stalks should be brittle enough to snap easily and should be of medium length and thickness; they should look fresh and crisp and be free of bruises. Light green, glossy-surfaced stalks will taste best. Celery hearts that are sold in units of two per package are most convenient for braising.

Storage. Trim, rinse, and shake off excess moisture before storing in a plastic bag in the refrigerator. Use as required. Celery will keep well for at least two weeks.

Preparation and serving. When preparing celery for eating or cooking, wash it thoroughly under cold running water to remove all sand. For serving raw, cut in any lengths you wish. Crisp in cold water with ice cubes for an hour before serving; drain well.

To steam-cook, strip the leaves from the stalks and remove any strings you find. Slice or dice the celery or cut in julienne strips 2 to 3 inches (5.1 to 7.6 cm) long and ½ inch (1.27 cm) wide. Pour a scant inch (2.54 cm) of water into a heavy saucepan with a cover. Add salt, bring to a rolling boil, and drop in the celery. Cover, reduce the heat, and steam until the celery is crisp-tender, about 10 minutes. (You may use chicken or beef broth instead of water.) Drain thoroughly and combine with melted butter, salt (if needed), freshly ground pepper, and a few squirts of lemon juice. Whole braised heart of celery is also a delicious dish too often overlooked in our meal planning.

Dietary information. Celery has a fair content of vitamins—A and C—as well as many essential minerals. It is high in sodium. The Pascal or green celery contains a greater amount of vitamins than the bleached. One-half cup (120 ml) of boiled, cut-up celery contains 11 calories; one large, raw, outer stalk, 7 calories.

CHARD

Chard—often called "Swiss chard"—is actually a beet whose root is hard, woody and inedible, unlike other beets. It is cultivated for its large leaves, which can be about 7 inches (17.8 cm) long, and the stalks to which the leaves are attached. Chard leaves resemble spinach, and the vegetable is, in effect, two vegetables in one, for the leaves may be cooked as greens and the white stems may be cooked as celery or asparagus. Chard is not a large commercial crop, but it can be found in markets, in season.

Peak season. From July until the frost.

Amount to buy. One pound (454 g) serves two.

Varieties. Light and dark green are the most common colors, but red chard, which resembles rhubarb, is being grown in larger quantities in the United States.

Selection. Like all salad greens, the leaves should be fresh, crisp, firm, and well colored.

Storage. Store in the vegetable compartment of the refrigerator in a plastic bag and use within a few days. After that the leaves will start to wilt and become limp.

Preparation and serving. Slice off the thick stems and wash the leaves carefully under cold running water to remove any dirt. The leaves should be cooked like spinach, using only the water that clings to them after washing. (The stems should be saved and cooked separately.) The leaves are delicate and should be steamed, never boiled. They are done when tender. Cream of chard soup, made like cream of spinach soup, is a lovely prelude to a luncheon or supper.

Dietary information. Chard is a source of vitamins A and C, with potassium, phosphorus, and calcium, and is high in magnesium. One-half cup (120 ml), boiled, contains 17 calories.

CHAYOTE *See* Squash.

CHICORY *See* Endive.

CHIVES *See* Onions.

CILANTRO *See* Parsley.

History

Wild chard, like other wild beets, may have originated in the Mediterranean region in prehistoric times. It is still to be found there, as well as in the Near East and in Asia Minor. Interestingly, the cultivated varieties of chard are not greatly different from their ancient ancestors.

Chard seems to have been one of the earliest cultivated vegetables. Aristotle mentions it as far back as the fourth century B.C., but it was classed with cabbage and therefore thought of as indigestible and fit only for peasants. It was part of the fare of the Romans, too, and by the seventh century it had found its way to China. Gradually it rose in the social scale, and by the Middle Ages soup made with chard was acceptable to all classes of society.

History

The name "collards" is a distortion of coleworts, an archaic English word for any plant in the cabbage family. Collards, also known as "collard greens," are still very much what they were in their primitive states about four thousand years ago. They grew wild in areas of England and continental Europe, and, although now cultivated they have not changed greatly.

Soul food

Fads and trends sweep through the world of food just as they do in hairstyles and skirt lengths. A few years back there was a great vogue for "soul food," and small family-run restaurants featuring the specialty proliferated. "Soul food" was the term for a variety of dishes that were favorites of generations of black Americans and southern whites. Featured were such foods as fried chicken, corn bread, fatback (the fat of salt pork with no lean meat on it), collard greens (also known as "collie greens"), turnip greens (frequently served with fatback), and "pot likker," which is the vitamin- and mineral-laden liquid from the pot in which the greens were cooked. This trend brought collard greens to the attention of many who were formerly unfamiliar with the vegetable.

As with coleslaw, the name "collard" comes from the Anglo-Saxon "coleworts," meaning cabbage plants. Collards are not too unlike kale, both of which are in the cabbage family and are older than recorded history.

COLLARDS

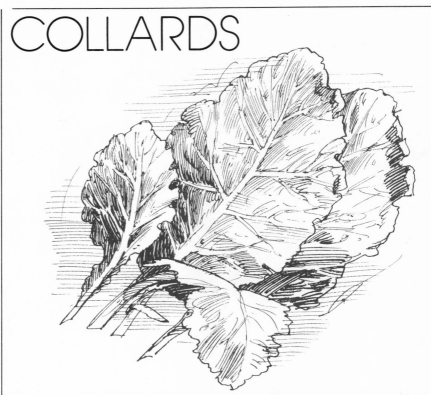

Closely related to kale and sharing the same history, collards, an open, cabbage-like plant with green leaves, are low man on the totem pole of cabbages and are considered one of the most primitive and oldest members of that family. Georgia and Virginia have the largest acreages, but a good many other southern states also grow a large supply. Collards have had a unique association with the South for many generations, where they are traditionally cooked with some pork product.

Peak season. Supply is fairly constant throughout the year, but most plentiful from January through April.

Selection. Good-quality collards are freshly crisp, clean, and free from insect injury. They should have a healthy, unblemished green color.

Storage. Do not store for any length of time. Keep in the refrigerator in a plastic bag and use as soon as possible. Some crushed ice in the bag will help keep collards fresh.

Preparation and serving. Collard greens should be washed well under cold running water. Fry pieces of bacon or salt pork and add the washed collard greens, shredded. Cover and simmer until tender—10 to 15 minutes—with very little water. A splash of vinegar will zip up the taste.

Dietary information. A pound (454 g) of raw collard leaves contains 140 calories, with heavy amounts of calcium, phosphorus, ascorbic acid, and vitamin A, as well as other elements and minerals.

CORN

A seasonal prospect that gladdens the heart of many Americans is the arrival in markets of the supply of local sweet corn, which can come to the table from the growing field within hours. A native of America, corn is a vegetable not really understood or appreciated by some European cultures, which consider it suitable only for fodder. It makes superb eating when it is freshly picked, quickly cooked, and simply served.

There are over two hundred varieties of sweet corn being grown in the United States. These are generally hybrids, which are grouped by the color of the kernel—yellow, bi-color, and white— with the most important commercial varieties being yellow hybrids. New varieties are constantly being developed. But whether white or yellow, the most properly developed corn will have an even-numbered row of kernels—generally twelve to fourteen. There is also an eight-row corn, a native of Pennsylvania, which is considered very fine. But basically corn falls into two categories: indentata, which is high in starch and provides us with our cornstarch; and saccharata, which is table corn, or our common sweet corn.

Peak season. Sweet corn is available in fresh form practically throughout the year, but heaviest supplies are from May to September. Winter supplies are grown in California and Florida.

Amount to buy. Who can say how many ears of fresh corn an individual is capable of ingesting? The calorie-conscious may limit themselves to one; the more adventuresome may go much, much further. You have to know and recognize the capacities of your corn eaters.

Varieties. White and yellow are the most common; choice is based on personal preference.

Selection. In top-quality corn, the husk is a fresh green color and free from decay where the silk ends. If possible, pull back the husk and puncture a kernel with your fingernail. If the corn is fresh, the kernel will exude a milky liquid; if not ripe, it will exude water; and, if past its prime, the kernels will be tough and the milk will be doughy.

Storage. Try to cook and serve your corn as soon as possible after picking. If it must wait, place the unhusked ears, uncovered, in the coldest part of your refrigerator and use within a day or two.

Preparation and serving. Remove husks and silk, cut off the stems, and, if you wish, remove the tips. Corn can be roasted in the husks, wrapped or unwrapped, or buried in hot embers. Kernels can be cut off before cooking and used for casseroles, fritters, puddings, soup, chowders, and pancakes. The most popular method for lovely fresh corn is boiling. Craig Claiborne, the knowledgeable food editor of *The New York Times* suggests a foolproof and perfect method for cooking corn. Place the shucked corn in a kettle containing enough boiling water to cover it. Do not add salt; it toughens the corn. Cover the corn, and, when the water returns to the boil, remove the kettle from the heat. Let the corn stand in the water 5 to 10 minutes and serve without further cooking. The corn may stand in the water for as long as 20 minutes without damage to flavor or quality. It should, however, be served immediately after being taken

Corn or maize

A more accurate designation for corn is "maize," which is what everyone outside the United States calls it. If you were British, "corn" would mean "wheat" to you; or, if you were Scottish, it would stand for "oats." During Biblical times all grains were called "corn," which perhaps takes us back where we started.

The corn grown by the American Indians before the arrival of the Europeans was not the sweet variety we know, and Columbus' men apparently did not care for it. In the days of the early settlers, the Indian corn was a colorful sight, with a mixture of red, white, yellow, and black kernels in each ear. We still see it about, particularly at Thanksgiving time, when it is used ornamentally.

About popcorn

Contrary to some opinion, popcorn is not regular sweet corn that has been treated in a way that will make it pop. There are three main varieties of corn: the sweet corn that you eat; the field corn grown for fodder; and popcorn, the popular snack that sustains life for thousands of people while they're watching movies. Popcorn is the only variety of the three that will pop when exposed to high heat. It is thought by scientists that the popping occurs as a result of a combination of the hard shell and the internal moisture of the popcorn kernel.

Most of the world's popcorn is grown in the midwestern part of the United States—particularly in Indiana, Iowa, and Nebraska, where the summers can get very hot. Legend has it that one summer the heat became so intense that the corn in the fields began to pop right off the stalks. The cows and pigs became so confused they thought it was a blizzard and lay down and froze to death.

A versatile vegetable

Although corn is one of the most important food crops in the United States and a staple in most of South America, parts of eastern Europe, and eastern and southern Africa, considerably less than 10 percent is used as a vegetable. Corn is processed for cornstarch, oil, and other by-products; it is ground into meal and cereal (processed beyond recognition into cornflakes); and mashed and distilled for bourbon. Nor must we overlook the contribution of the dried cobs in pipe making. In earlier times, the South American Incas accepted corn as currency, and even in the latter part of the seventeenth century the inhabitants of Martha's Vineyard used corn for balloting. The corn signified an aye vote, and beans the nay.

Cool as a cucumber

"Cool as a cucumber" is an expression that is based in fact. Actual tests conducted on a hot day proved that the interior temperature of the vegetable can be as much as 20 degrees cooler than the outside air.

A popular cosmetic

For centuries cucumber juice has been used throughout the world in cosmetics for whitening and softening the skin. Indeed, in France a special kind of white cucumber was cultivated for this particular purpose.

But the beneficial effect of cucumbers was not limited to its surface application; it was considered equally effective for the skin when eaten. Might this account for the popularity of cucumber sandwiches at English tea tables? If this is so, it would be a pleasant way to have a facial.

out of the water; the kernels shrivel and lose their plumpness if they are made to wait.

Dietary information. Sweet corn contains carbohydrates and a variety of vitamins and minerals. Yellow corn provides a fair amount of vitamin A, along with vitamin C and other vitamins. It is low in sodium. One pound (454 g) of corn on the cob with the husks removed contains 240 calories; one cup (240 ml) of boiled kernels cut from the cob has 114 calories.

CUCUMBERS

The cucumber is notable for its crisp, crunchy texture. Like its relatives, summer squash and watermelon, it has a high water content, which is what gives it its cooling, thirst-quenching properties and makes it such a refreshing addition to summer salad meals. It originated in India over three thousand years ago and was brought to America on one of Columbus' expeditions. It can be served raw or pickled, as a soup, or as a cooked vegetable, in which form it is a fresh-tasting and pleasant change from the usual selection of vegetables.

There are three classes of cucumbers, based on their use: the field-grown, for slicing or table use; the pickling varieties, also field-grown and smaller than the slicing varieties; and the greenhouse varieties adapted to development under artificial heat. Actually, there is little difference between the pickling and slicing cucumber except for size. A not-fully-grown slicing cucumber can be pickled; a large pickling cucumber can be sliced.

Peak season. Cucumbers are a year-round vegetable, but they are at their best and least costly in the summer.

Amount to buy. Two medium-sized cucumbers will serve four.

Varieties. There are about twenty species of cucumbers and innumerable subspecies—green, white, and yellow; long, short, and thin; smooth-skinned and rough-skinned; early and late maturing. The most familiar is the dark green cucumber with smooth skin. A comparative newcomer—and a welcome one—is the cultivated cucumber, medium green in color, that is about 2 to 2¼ inches (5.1 to 5.7 cm) in diameter and 12 to 20 inches (30.5 to 50.8 cm) in length. Known by a number of names—among them, European or English cucumber—it is of the seedless type (known technically as parthenocarpic), bred especially for greenhouse culture. Its delicious seedless crispness makes it superior to many other types.

Selection. Choose cucumbers that are slender, firm to the touch, and of good green color. The shade of color is important, because older ones can become dull green or sometimes yellow. Avoid overgrown cucumbers with shriveled ends, which indicate toughness and bitter flavor.

Cucumbers are one of the vegetables that are frequently waxed when they are to be shipped. The wax is used to enhance appearance, but, more than that, to prevent and retard shriveling and drying; its presence should be self-evident to any buyer. The wax is harmless, and there are no bad effects from eating it, but if you prefer you may scrub the wax off with a stiff vegetable brush or remove the peel with a vegetable peeler. Fresh farm produce is not waxed.

Storage. Wrapped in plastic, cucumbers will remain fresh in the refrigerator crisper drawer for about a week.

Preparation and serving. Tender, fresh young cucumbers need not be peeled if eaten raw. Those with unusually tough skins or the heavily waxed ones may be scored with fork tines or peeled; they can then be sliced or diced. To remove excess water, sprinkle cucumber pieces with salt, let stand for 10 or 15 minutes, then drain. The pieces can then be added to a tossed salad. Some people do not care for the cucumber seeds. To remove them, slice the cucumber lengthwise and scoop out the seeds with a teaspoon; the slices will then have an attractive crescent shape. Cucumbers cut lengthwise into strips with the skin left on add color to a relish tray. Sliced thin and dressed with plain yogurt, snipped dill, salt, and pepper, they make a pleasant side dish. Sliced cucumber and tomato garnished with watercress and moistened with mayonnaise on toasted bread makes a refreshing sandwich. Cucumbers can also be steamed or fried as a hot vegetable, which goes well with fish.

Dietary information. Cucumbers are more than 95 percent water, but they do provide some vitamin A and vitamin C. Half a pound (227 g) of cucumber eaten with the skin contains 33 calories; the same amount eaten without the skin contains 23 calories.

DAIKON *See* Radishes.

DANDELIONS

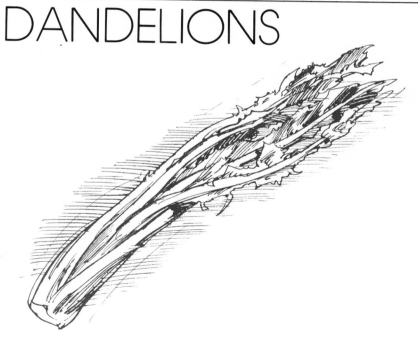

The dandelion, the yellow flower you see growing wild along the road, is really a vegetable; its leaves, known as "dandelion greens," have been used for food for centuries. Highly nutritious, they were probably the first spring tonic for the colonial settlers, who looked forward to them after a winter of only root vegetables. The dandelion is a common, stemless plant of the sunflower family.

For the convenience of those who prefer not to forage in the fields for their dandelion greens, they are now grown commercially throughout the

Crisp cucumber salad
    2 large cucumbers
  ½ cup white vinegar
    2 tablespoons water
  ¼ cup granulated sugar
  ½ teaspoon salt
    Few grinds of black pepper
    2 tablespoons chopped parsley

Peel the cucumbers, leaving bands of the green skin here and there for color and eye appeal. Slice thin.

In a deep bowl, combine the remaining ingredients and mix well. Add the cucumber slices, cover them with a plate, and a weight. Refrigerate about 3 hours; drain the cucumbers to serve. The marinade can be saved and used again. Serves 4.

The ubiquitous pickle
Pickles have probably been around as long as cucumbers. In the first century A.D. the Greek essayist and biographer Plutarch wrote that the Romans often used salad and pickles. Pickling was one of the most effective ways the ancient peoples had of preserving foods long past their growing season, and pickled cucumbers enjoyed the reputation of promoting health. Before the early part of the nineteenth century housewives made their own pickles—barrels of them—but since then commercial pickling has become a major industry, and certain pickles are cultivated just for that purpose.

The lion's tooth
The name "dandelion" may be a corruption of the French *dent de lion*, "lion's tooth," because of the saw-toothed edge on the dandelion leaf.

The plant has many other names, which have come from children who blow the fuzzy seeds—ever so gently—to tell fortunes, time, or the weather. It has been called "weather-glass," "what's o'clock," or "fairy clock," as well as "rabbit meat," "dog's grass," and "stink faire." One can only guess at what the children were describing.

A feast of dandelions

A type of beer is made from the leaves of the dandelion and a wine from crushing the flowers. The roots can also be roasted, dried, and ground to make a beverage resembling coffee. Thus a feast could be produced from the wild dandelion, beginning with an *apéritif* of dandelion wine, a main course of steamed and buttered dandelion roots accompanied by a salad of dandelion greens, finished off with a cup of dandelion coffee.

History

It is believed that the Arabs were among the first people to think of eating eggplant. They took it to Spain in the twelfth century, and over the next hundred years it found its way to Italy—where it was not entirely respectable. The Italians used it for decoration, but they did not eat it, possibly because eggplant belongs to the deadly nightshade family—a distinction shared by potatoes and tomatoes.

However, by the sixteenth century some of its sinister aspects had dissipated. The Spaniards favored it greatly, considering it an aphrodisiac, but northern Europeans of the time labeled eggplants "mad apples" and believed that they could cause insanity. In time the legends melted away, and the eggplant found its place in the culinary structure of the world.

southern and southeastern seaboard states during the spring and early summer months. Winter supplies originate primarily in Florida, Texas, and California.

Peak season. Dandelion greens are available in some markets practically all year. The wild dandelion greens should be gathered and eaten when they are young and tender, in early spring, before the plant blooms.

Amount to buy. One pound (454 g) will serve three to four.

Varieties. The cultivated leaves are larger, lighter green, and less bitter than those which grow wild.

Selection. Good quality is evidenced by a fresh green appearance and comparatively large tender leaves. Those with a portion of the root attached will be juicier. Avoid leaves that are excessively dirty, show insect damage, or are wilted, flaccid, yellow, or tough.

Storage. Store in the refrigerator in a plastic bag and use as soon as possible. Some crushed ice in the container or bag with the leaves will help keep them fresh.

Preparation and serving. Dandelion leaves may be used as salad greens in a tossed salad. They may also be steamed or wilted in a hot oil dressing, as with spinach.

The root itself is also eaten. Peeled and sliced, it, too, can go into a salad, or it can be used to flavor soups and stews. It may also be sliced and fried like parsnips. For this purpose, the roots must be young and juicy, best gathered in winter, at which time the sap they contain becomes thick and sweet, losing much of its bitterness.

Dietary information. Dandelion greens are extraordinarily high in vitamin A, iron, and calcium. One pound (454 g), uncooked, provides 204 calories.

EGGPLANT

ggplant, or aubergine as it is known in Europe, is a handsome, purple, pear-shaped vegetable that originated in India and China. Widely used in Oriental and near-Eastern cookery, it is a basic ingredient in many notable Greek, Italian, French, and Spanish dishes as well. In recent years, it has become increasingly popular in the United States, and many of our recipes are American adaptations of foreign recipes. There are many interesting ways of serving eggplant. It combines well with oil, tomatoes, olives, onions, green pepper, garlic, anchovies, zucchini, capers, ground meat, or cheeses. It is an enormously versatile foodstuff that can serve as a cold appetizer; stuffed, as a main course; and as a vegetable accompaniment to almost every meat. The Italian *caponata* and the French *ratatouille* are both based on eggplant.

Peak season. Available all year, with peak season in August and September, lightest in February.

Amount to buy. One large eggplant—1½ to 2 pounds (681 to 908 g)— will serve four.

Varieties. Among the varieties of eggplant are white, purple, purple-black, yellowish white, red, or striped, but most of the world's production is the dark purple, pear-shaped variety. The sizes also vary, ranging from the miniature ones just adequate for an individual serving to the large economy-size product.

Selection. Purple eggplant should have a clear, dark, satiny color that covers the entire surface evenly. It should feel firm and not bounce back if you press on it with your thumb. Do not buy an eggplant by size or weight. A large, heavy eggplant will usually have more seeds than the smaller ones, and the flesh will not be as firm. Eggplants that have not been allowed to grow too large will have small seeds that are hardly noticeable and a tender skin that need not be pared.

Storage. Eggplant can be stored for about a week in a cool room (about 60°F [16°C]) or in a plastic bag in the refrigerator. The plastic bag helps to retain moisture.

Preparation and serving. It is unnecessary to peel tender, young eggplant. Just wash well and cut off the stem and top before cooking. Unless the skin seems very tough, it can remain. Eggplant can be sliced, cubed, or diced; baked, steamed, or fried or split, scooped out, and stuffed; served alone or in combination with other vegetables; eaten hot, at room temperature, or cold. Leftover cooked eggplant whirred in the blender into a paste and seasoned with lemon juice, salt, and pepper makes a delicious dip served with crisp crackers or celery sticks.

Dietary information. Nutritionally, eggplant is not distinguished for any one vitamin or mineral. Its substantial quality makes some people look on it as a main-dish item, but its protein content is low. However, if it is combined with cheeses, mozzarella and grated Parmesan, as in eggplant *parmigiana*, it becomes acceptable as a meat substitute. It is low in calories: one cup (240 ml) of boiled eggplant contains 38 calories.

To salt or not to salt

There has been a discussion for years between two schools of thought vis-à-vis salting/not salting eggplant slices. It boils down—with apologies for the cooking term— to individual taste. There are some people who find the slightly bitter flavor of eggplant unpleasant. Salting the slices definitely ameliorates that flavor and has made eggplant admirers of people who formerly could not abide it. If you don't mind the taste, don't salt. If the bitterish, puckery flavor bothers you, try salting and see how you feel about eggplant then.

Since salting makes eggplant slices a bit limp, cut them at least ½ inch thick so they won't fall apart. Salt both sides and let stand for about 30 minutes. Drain well, then rinse the slices and dry.

Broiled eggplant

Eggplant absorbs an enormous amount of fat, so instead of frying them we'll save calories by broiling. Add a chopped garlic clove or two to some oil. Paint eggplant slices lightly with the seasoned oil, then sprinkle with salt, pepper, and sweet paprika. Broil 5 minutes, or until lightly browned on each side. Serve at once.

In the beginning

The endive has been a salad vegetable since antiquity. It probably originated in the Mediterranean region, and it was eaten long before the birth of Christ by the Greeks, who obviously recognized a good thing when they ate it. In the first century A.D. the Romans used it in salads and as a cooked vegetable. Pliny, the great Roman naturalist, who lived at that time, recognized its medicinal properties and advocated endive juice mixed with vinegar and rose oil as a remedy for headache.

A coffee extender

There is still another form of chicory that is grown for its large roots. Chicory—or "succory," as it is sometimes called—produces a lovely blue flower that looks something like a blue dandelion, with petals that project like the rays of the sun.

The roots of the plant are dried and ground and used as a supplement for coffee. Some people prefer the flavor of the coffee when it has been combined with chicory. It has been long used in France.

ENDIVE

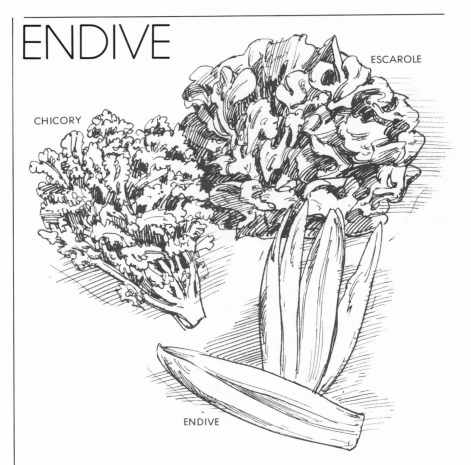

ESCAROLE

CHICORY

ENDIVE

There are three greens in the endive family that, because of local customs—or personal misunderstandings—are frequently misnamed. Shoppers ask for one type when they have another in mind. For example, in some localities endive is called "escarole" or "chicory," chicory is known as "endive," and escarole is called "chicory." A thoroughly confusing situation. Let us try to identify each leafy green correctly.

Chicory or **curly endive** or **chicory endive** grows in a bunchy head whose narrow, raggedy-edged leaves are frizzled at the ends like an overdone permanent wave. The leaves at the center of the bunch are yellowish white and are milder in flavor than the darker green outer leaves, which may be slightly bitter. If you'd like the center leaves to be lighter in color, you can bleach them further by covering them overnight with a damp cloth.

Escarole is a variety of endive with a bushy head made up of broad leaves that do *not* curl at the tips. It is also known as "Batavian endive," but it is marketed almost universally as "escarole."

Belgian endive or **French endive** is botanically known as "witloof chicory," although few people would recognize it under that name. It is a small, cigar-shaped, rather tightly folded plant that grows upright in a thin, elongated stalk, quite different from the bunchy chicory (curly endive) or escarole. This vegetable is usually bleached while growing. Its color is creamy, and the leaves have pale yellow tips. Originally it was imported from Europe, but now a limited amount is grown in the United

States. More expensive than most other greens, it has a crisp texture and a delicately bitter flavor. It is one of the cleanest of all lettuces, requiring very little washing. It is often braised and served hot as a vegetable.

Peak season. Chicory and escarole are available the year round. Peak season for Belgian endive is October through May.

Amount to buy. Plan on about 2 cups (480 ml) of loosely packed greens per person. If served alone, one Belgian endive will serve two.

Selection. Look for fresh, crisp, tender leaves and a good green color in the outer leaves of the bunchy types. Avoid heads with brownish or yellowish discolorations. Belgian endive should have firm, well-bleached stalks about 4 to 6 inches (10.1 to 15.2 cm) long.

Storage. Remove two or three of the outer leaves of the Belgian endive and wipe with damp paper towels. Wrap in plastic and store in the crisper of the refrigerator. Wash chicory and escarole, leaving the heads intact. Shake off excess water, roll in several thicknesses of paper toweling or a dish towel, and place in a plastic bag in the refrigerator. The greens should stay fresh for a few days, but use as soon as possible.

Preparation and serving. Because of the slightly bitter taste of the chicory and escarole, it is best to combine them with other greens if you are using them in a tossed salad. They should be broken into bite-sized pieces. They may also be steamed in a heavy saucepan with a tight-fitting cover. Let them wilt over medium heat for about 15 minutes, then dress with melted butter and a splash of lemon juice or vinegar. Belgian endive can be quartered, broken into leaves, or sliced for salad. It combines well with other lettuces, raw mushrooms, or sliced, cooked beets. Split in half lengthwise, it may be braised in consommé or chicken broth and sprinkled with chopped walnuts. It will need about 5 to 10 minutes of cooking.

Dietary information. As with most leafy green vegetables, endive, escarole, and chicory are all good sources of vitamin A, with a fair amount of vitamin C and some of the B vitamins. Used raw, they are one of the detergent vegetables helpful for dental health. Eight ounces (227 g) of Belgian endive, raw and untrimmed, contain 31 calories; 8 ounces (227 g) of chicory or escarole contain 46 calories.

ESCAROLE *See* Endive.

FENNEL

According to the neighborhood you are in, sweet fennel may be known as *finocchio* or *fenucchi* or "anise." A stalk vegetable that is somewhat like celery with a bulb at the bottom, fennel has delicate green leaves or fronds and a licorice or anise flavor. It has always been popular in French and Italian country cooking and is becoming more widely known and used in the United States. Fronds or bulbs, with their faintly licorice flavor, can add a bit of taste magic to whatever foods they are combined with.

Peak season. Fennel is a winter vegetable, available from October through March.

Amount to buy. If you are planning to use it as a cooked vegetable, figure on three large or four to five small fennel bulbs for four persons.

A distinctive flavor

The taste quality that most distinguishes the endive family from other lettuces is the marked bitter taste not present in other lettuces. Some people find this marked bitter taste most agreeable. For those who do not, blanching (cooking for a few minutes in boiling water) reduces the bitterness. Unfortunately, blanching also lessens food value and is thus not a recommended practice. Actually, the bitter quality can be an advantage in pepping up a bland soup or some mild greens that could do with additional flavor.

Flaming fennel

Some varieties of fennel are cultivated for their bulbs, some for their seeds, and some for their stalks. One of the great eating experiences is a grilled sea bass served on a bed of flaming fennel stalks, a French specialty called *loup grillé, flambé au fenouil.* The fennel used for *loup grillé* in the south of France is the long, stalky variety that grows wild along the coast. After the stalks are harvested, they are made into smallish bundles 6 to 8 inches long and weathered until they are dry enough to flame. The flame and smoke from the fennel twigs lend drama to the presentation and some flavor to the fish, making it a most appetite-provoking performance. As a compromise for this elaborate procedure, which is not without hazard in a confined kitchen, a few fennel seeds sprinkled inside the fish will impart the subtle flavor of wild anise to the fish as it cooks. If you would like the excitement of a controlled blaze, you can flame some fennel seeds in warmed brandy and pour it over the fish just before serving.

Garlic for health?

The poor garlic bud has been a subject of controversy since earliest times. The priests of ancient Egypt declared that garlic was unclean and an abomination and forbade anyone with garlic on his (or her) breath from entering the temple. But this did not prevent its use. It was fed daily to the thousands of slaves engaged in building the great pyramid in Cheops to give them the strength and endurance they needed to carry the weighty stones.

Beginning with Aristotle, who praised the medicinal qualities of garlic, and Pliny, the Roman naturalist, who listed over sixty-one different ailments that could be cured by garlic, a succession of authorities of varying degrees of competence over the centuries have claimed medical triumphs for the pungent root. These triumphs have ranged from giving immunity from the plague to lowering blood pressure, beautifying the complexion, and improving the intellect. None has stood the test of time or scientific corroboration. The continued use of garlic has been solely as an indispensable cooking ingredient in many kitchens.

Varieties. There are two basic types, one squat and bulbous, the other flat and elongated. The squat one is crisper and sweeter and should be the only kind used for salads. Either variety may be cooked, but, again, the bulbous one gives better results.

Preparation and serving. Cut away any wilted or bruised parts, then trim the green fronds from the heads and save them to use, minced, in place of parsley to garnish and flavor dishes. Fennel may be prepared as celery and eaten raw or minced and used in a salad. It is also delicious cooked—sweeter than in its raw state. To prepare for cooking, trim off the tops of the stalks, down to the knobs. (The stalks are excellent for soups and stews.) Cut the bulbous lower parts into vertical slices no more than ½ inch (1.27 cm) thick and cook until tender, 25 to 40 minutes. The slices may also be braised in broth or sherry.

Dietary information. Fennel leaves are extremely high in vitamin A and potassium, in addition to containing other minerals. One pound (454 g) contains 118 calories.

GARLIC

Garlic is a member of the same family as the onion—the lily family. Native to western Asia, it has been cultivated for over six thousand years, during which time it has been both vilified and revered. The root, which is what we use, is a compound bulb made up of a number of smaller sections, or cloves, enveloped in a papery skin.

Garlic has been described as "the atomic bomb of the vegetable world." With its undeniable, characteristic odor and flavor, evoking strong likes or dislikes from the eating public, it is a most important cooking ingredient in the countries around the Mediterranean, the Mideast, and Asia, although it is largely ignored in northern Europe. It can be used to flavor almost any dish—meats, shellfish, vegetables, stews, poultry, soups, salads, sauces—and in the preparation of pickles and sausages.

Garlic bulbs grow from individual cloves, not seed, and develop entirely underground. They are ready to be harvested when the leaves and flowers that grow aboveground wither. California supplies a good deal of the United States needs, which are augmented with imports from Mexico, Italy, Spain, and Peru.

Peak season. It is available the year round, with the heaviest supply from July through September.

Amount to buy. One or two garlic bulbs will generally take care of kitchen needs for a while. (A bulb usually contains about eight cloves, although there are some varieties that have as many as twenty to forty).

Varieties. The most popular types of garlic are the Creole and the Italian. The Creole generally has larger cloves than the Italian, which does, however, provide the strongest flavor. They are both pinkish in color. There is another type called "Tahiti," which has large, individual cloves that are generally darker in color than the first two. However, most experts claim that this is not a true garlic and have named it "elephant garlic."

Selection. Select large, firm white heads.

Storage. Store in a screw-top jar in the refrigerator. Garlic will keep for weeks this way.

Preparation and serving. One or two cloves are generally sufficient for seasoning a dish. The secret of the success of the use of garlic is prudence: some of the world's finest dishes owe their success to a delicate undertone of garlic, with "delicate undertone" the key words. When you are ready to use it, peel a garlic clove and either smash it with the side of a heavy cleaver (Chinese style) or mince it or slice it. A garlic press is not recommended; it releases oils that give the garlic a stronger and even unpleasant taste. If you wish, instead of adding the chopped garlic to the food, you can season the cooking oil with a whole, peeled garlic clove, which should be discarded when it becomes slightly brown. Burnt garlic will give any dish a bitter taste, so care must be taken. However, there is no substitute for the flavor of fresh garlic; garlic powders are a poor imitation.

Dietary information. A medium-sized bulb contains 74 percent water, 20 percent carbohydrate, and small amounts of protein, fat, ash, and fiber. A pound (454 g) contains 450 calories.

Twenty-four cloves of garlic

A classic chicken recipe from Provence calls for twenty-four cloves of garlic in its preparation, which on first glance seems a terrifying prospect.

However, the garlic cloves are left whole, with their inner skin completely intact, and are distributed among the chicken pieces for the last 20 minutes of cooking. This gives the dish a delicate flavor, and even people who hate garlic admit that the dish has a pleasing and rather mysterious charm.

Erasing the memory

Many different methods have been proposed to eliminate the pungent aftertaste and breath odor left by garlic. Among them are chewing a coffee bean, raw parsley, or other fresh green herbs. Commercial breath fresheners are also a possibility. To remove the odor from hands, it has been suggested that they be sprinkled with salt and rinsed in cold water or, alternatively, rubbed with fresh-cut lemon.

While on the subject of the pervasiveness of garlic odor, the story is told of the great French chef Francatelli. He was asked how he managed to achieve the extraordinary degree of mouthwatering taste in his salads. His answer, in his inimitable French accent, was that at the very last moment he chewed a "leetle clove of garlic" and then breathed gently over the salad!

Dry ginger for ginger root?

Dry ginger or ground ginger powder are really not adequate substitutes for the fresh ginger root. The taste is not quite the same.

However, you can substitute fresh ginger root for powdered ginger and you'll end up with a superior taste. If your recipe calls for ⅛ teaspoon (a pinch) of powdered ginger, try using one tablespoon of grated or shredded fresh ginger root in its place.

GINGER ROOT

G inger root, a brown-skinned, irregularly shaped tuber, is probably one of the least prepossessing items in the entire produce department, but it can bring a sparkle to the taste of a wide variety of fish, shellfish, meat, poultry, and dessert dishes. Only a few slices of fresh ginger root are needed to create a fine taste effect. Native to India and China, it is available at many greengrocers, Oriental food stores, and American food specialty shops.

Peak season. Available all year.

Amount to buy. One ginger root will suffice for many uses.

Selection. Choose tubers that are fresh looking and firm. The little sprouts that appear on the sides of the ginger root are more delicate in flavor than the main part of the root.

Storage. To store fresh ginger root, scrape the skin off each piece and wash and dry the pieces. Place the ginger in a jar, add enough dry sherry to cover, and cap tightly. Store in the refrigerator and it will keep indefinitely.

Preparation and serving. Ginger root may be sliced, shredded, or grated, depending on how you want to use it. It will enhance the character of meat dishes, vegetable combinations, or fresh fruit salads.

Dietary information. Ginger root is low in calories, with three and one-half ounces (100 g) containing 49 calories. It contains vitamin A, calcium, phosphorus, iron, and potassium.

GREENS FOR SALAD

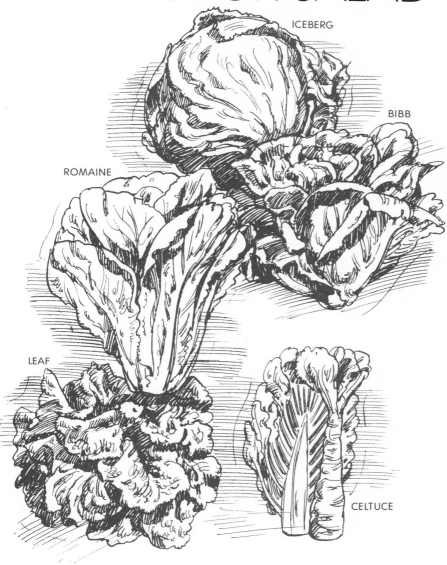

ICEBERG

BIBB

ROMAINE

LEAF

CELTUCE

Salads through the ages

Lettuce has been cultivated for thousands of years, and is believed to have originated in the Mediterranean or the Near East. It is possible that lettuce was used as one of the bitter herbs in the Jewish feast of Passover. The Persian kings were served lettuce, and the Romans had many varieties of it. Our romaine lettuce, so popular today, got its name from "Roman."

At the beginning of the sixteenth century, lettuce was introduced into England. Down through the centuries, it was often boiled rather than eaten raw. The sixteenth-century English botanist and barber-surgeon, John Gerard, made the original observation that lettuce should be "boyled in order that it be sooner digested and nourish more."

During the eighteenth and nineteenth centuries, all raw vegetables fell out of favor and the salad along with them. In America, for example, the pioneer fathers considered salad effete and more or less "women's food." But, in the twentieth century, with improved knowledge of nutrition the salad again assumed a position of importance in the eating habits of the world, and it is today one of the most important items on the menu. Salad items are served as appetizers, as main courses, as vegetable courses, hot or cold—providing splendid fare for all seasons.

Tired lettuce

Lettuce that has lost its pristine brightness and crispness can be turned into a most agreeable cream soup. You will need about a pound of lettuce; cook it for 5 minutes and purée it in a blender. Sauté a couple of tablespoons of grated onion in 2 tablespoons of butter, blend in 2 tablespoons of flour, and stir in slowly 1 quart of milk or beef or chicken stock. Season with salt and a pinch of sweet paprika. Add the puréed lettuce and mix well. Heat the soup and serve with a sprinkle of grated Parmesan cheese. Serves three or four.

A n essential part of a good meal is the salad. It does not have to be exotic; indeed, crisp, fresh greens, tossed with a simple oil and vinegar dressing, can add interest and variety to any meal. Don't confine yourself to just one kind of green, however; a variety of tastes and textures are desirable.

There are five general types of lettuce: *crisphead*, such as iceberg; *butterhead*, such as Boston and Bibb; *Cos*, such as romaine; *leaf*; and *stem*. These represent the major types of lettuce that are the most popular in today's salads. They can be supplemented with other greens and vegetables that double as salad greens (arugula, cabbage, chicory, dandelion greens, spinach, watercress, etc.).

The same general rules governing selection, storage, and preparation apply to all. With improved methods of transportation and refrigeration, most lettuces are available all year. When buying them, make sure they

Preparing green salads

Start with fresh, crisp, washed greens. It is of prime importance that the salad greens be completely dry, so if any moisture remains on the leaves, pat them dry with paper toweling. Moisture on the leaves will dilute the dressing and make the finished result tasteless and soggy.

It is difficult to be specific about quantity, but on an average you can figure about 2 cups of loosely packed greens per portion—less if other ingredients or vegetables are to be added.

Break the greens into bite-sized pieces by hand; cutting them can bruise the tender leaves. You can do this well in advance of serving time and refrigerate in a covered container. Each piece should be a size that is comfortable to spear with your fork and eat.

When you are ready to serve the salad, add the dressing and toss lightly. This last step is an important one in salad preparation. Too vigorous tossing will bruise the greens and result in a limp salad. Gently does it.

Dressings: Choice of dressing rests with the cook. The basic French dressing consists of about three or four parts oil to one part vinegar, sparked with salt, pepper, a pinch of dry mustard, and perhaps a clove of garlic that is removed before serving.

Some salad buffs perform the ritual of tossing with great ceremony, first coating the greens with oil, then adding the vinegar, salt, pepper, and dry mustard, in that order. Others maintain that the coating of oil prevents the leaves from being properly flavored with the vinegar and they start with the vinegar. There is enough documented opinion to make a case for either technique; the final choice is yours.

The only point on which everyone agrees is that there should be just enough dressing to coat the greens and make them shiny— not to drown them. A puddle of dressing at the bottom of the salad will not enhance either the presentation or the texture.

are fresh, crisp, and not wilted. When you get them home, wash them well under cold running water. The loose, dark green outer leaves are called "wrapper leaves," and, if these are undamaged, don't discard them; they contain a good deal of the nutrients. Loose leaves may also be saved for soup. Drain the greens well in a colander, wrap in a kitchen towel, and store in the refrigerator in a plastic bag. They will keep well for a number of days.

For a crisper salad, place your prepared salad greens (covered with plastic wrap) in the freezer for a few—*and not more than a few*—minutes before serving. Then add the dressing and toss. Your super-chilled salad will crackle with crispness.

Dietary information. Lettuce contributes a fair amount of vitamins A and C, iron, and calcium, as well as other vitamins and minerals. The Boston and Bibb lettuces are high in iron. The addition of lettuce to sandwiches not only adds taste and texture but nutrients as well. Raw lettuce is high in fiber and is an important detergent food, promoting good mouth hygiene. It is low in calories—an entire head of iceberg contains 65 to 70 calories.

ICEBERG. When buying iceberg (*crisphead*) lettuce, look for heads that are firm but not hard. Lighter, springier heads have a sweeter taste and are easier to separate for salads and sandwiches. Iceberg may not have quite as much flavor as some of the other lettuces, but the hearts, well crisped and broken into small chunks instead of unmanageable wedges, have a pleasant taste and interesting texture. Iceberg should be cored before washing so that the water can flow between the lower leaves to rinse out any sand that is clinging to them. To core iceberg, hold the head, core down, and whack it briskly on the kitchen counter. Then twist and lift out the core with your fingers. Wash the lettuce and shake it vigorously to remove all water possible, then drain thoroughly, core side down. Dry off any moisture remaining with a paper towel and store in the refrigerator in a plastic bowl with an airtight lid or in a plastic bag. Iceberg will keep for two weeks or more if it was in good condition to begin with.

BOSTON OR BUTTER LETTUCE. This is softer and lighter than iceberg, and not so crisp. Pale green with light yellow leaves inside, and loosely packed, this tender, round lettuce takes dressing well. Remove the core as in iceberg lettuce. Boston lettuce is fragile and must be washed and dried gently.

BIBB. Grown principally in greenhouses, Bibb is considered the choicest member of the lettuce family; it is also the most expensive. This small, cup-shaped lettuce, which is exceptionally green and crisp, received its name from Major John Bibb, who developed it. He never really gave it a name; his neighbors called it "Mr. Bibb's lettuce," and eventually it came to be known as "Bibb lettuce." Sweet and tender, with a delicate, buttery taste, it requires thorough washing, for dirt gets caught in the little indentations of the leaves. Wash it by sloshing the heads up and down in warm—not hot—water. This wilts the leaves and releases the dirt that has crept into the indentations. Then crisp the heads in a basin of very cold water. To dry, shake off as much water as possible, wrap the heads, root side up, in a fresh dish towel and chill in the vegetable crisper of the refrigerator.

ROMAINE OR COS. A popular lettuce, romaine has crisp, long, bright leaves. The leaves seem to be coarse, but they are actually tender and have good flavor, with less bitterness than other greens. The outer leaves are deep green and the inner ones golden yellow. The core of the lettuce is slightly bitter but pleasant, and can be trimmed and sliced into the salad.

LEAF LETTUCE. This category includes a number of varieties with leaves loosely branching from their stalks that do not form heads. Leaf lettuce has a crisp texture that many people prefer. The curly green and the curly red-tipped are the most common, the red-tipped adding interesting color contrast to a green salad. There are also a number of lettuces with flat leaves. Leaf lettuces have delicate, tender leaves that do not store well. They should be used as quickly as possible. They wilt easily, also, and they must not be overtossed.

CELTUCE. Celtuce (SEL-tuss) is the only variety of stem lettuce that is available for sale in the United States, where it is a comparatively new vegetable, although it has been grown in China for many years. It is a crossbreed, developed from seeds a missionary from western China sent to an American seed company in the late 1930s. Like all stem lettuce, it has an enlarged stem and no head. The leaves are not palatable. The stems, however, may be peeled and eaten raw or they may be boiled, stewed, or creamed. Celtuce, which is often used in Chinese dishes, has a flavor that is a combination of celery and lettuce, hence its name. Select and store as you would lettuce.

LAMB'S LETTUCE OR FETTICUS. Also known as "corn salad," this is a lovely green that comes in small bunches. It does not travel well and is therefore not widely available. Its leaves are generally used raw, in combination with other greens, or may be cooked like spinach.

FIDDLEHEADS. These are the young shoots of the ostrich fern, which grow wild, chiefly in eastern Canada. Their name comes from their coiled shape, which resembles the scrolled head of a violin. The stems have the flavor of asparagus and artichoke. They can be served as a vegetable, salad green, or an ingredient in soup. Fiddleheads may be gathered wild, but they are more likely to be found frozen in food specialty stores.

HEARTS OF PALM

Hearts of palm, a tropical vegetable, is the young terminal bud, or heart, of a tropical palm tree, usually the cabbage palmetto. It is a popular vegetable in Brazil but in the United States is available, fresh, only in Florida. The heart, a creamy white cylinder, is from 1 to 2 inches (2.54 to 5.1 cm) in diameter and about 12 inches (30.5 cm) or more in length. It is encased in wrappings that must be slit open to expose it. It cannot be stored for any length of time or it loses its soft whiteness. It is cut into pieces and cooked, without salt, for about 10 minutes, or until tender. It may also be eaten raw, like cabbage.

Generally it is only the canned hearts of palm that are known to North American kitchens.

Limitless horizons

Prosper Montagné, in his monumental food, wine, and cookery encyclopedia, *Larousse Gastronomique,* describes salads as "dishes made up of herbs, plants, vegetables, eggs, meat and fish, seasoned with oil, vinegar, salt and pepper, with or without other ingredients." This surely establishes a broad base for the operations of any creative and ambitious salad maker. However, the one thing that Monsieur Montagné was insistent about was the use of a good wine vinegar in the dressing. He considered that no useful purpose could be served by replacing the vinegar with lemon juice—unless, he conceded reluctantly, the wine vinegar was of doubtful quality.

In any event, the ingredients that can come together successfully in a salad bowl are endless. In addition to basic tossed salads, there are main-course salads made of fish, meat, or poultry; salads of cold pastas, rice, bulgur, or beans, moistened with a creamy mayonnaise or a dressing of oil and vinegar, and combined with bits and pieces of leftover vegetables or slivers of meat or poultry. And then there are hot salads, such as combinations of potatoes and string beans sparked with a tangy dressing, and eye-filling molded salads in aspics, shimmering with color and design.

The most popular salad in the United States is the classic Caesar salad, often presented with great flourish in top-flight restaurants. It provides the opportunity for a four-star performance by the maître d', as he crushes the garlic, tosses the bite-sized pieces of romaine with the oil and vinegar, gently adds the garlic-flavored croutons, salt and pepper, anchovies, and finally the lightly coddled or raw (no one seems able to agree) egg, finishing with freshly grated Parmesan cheese. A most titillating performance, even before you take your first bite of the delicious mélange.

Serving hearts of palm

Hearts of palm can be chilled and used as a cold hors d'oeuvre, served with a suitable dip, or as a salad bathed in a vinaigrette or mayonnaise dressing. It is frequently sliced or cut into chunks and baked in a cream sauce topped with grated cheese.

A bitter herb

Horseradish was one of the five bitter herbs of the Passover Seder dinner, along with coriander, nettle, horehound, and lettuce. Over the years, substitutions have been made for many of these in the Passover observance, but horseradish has remained.

Horseradish sauce

An interesting sauce to accompany cold smoked brook trout or any other cold smoked fish:

1½ to 2 cups sour cream or 1 cup of
    whipping cream
    Freshly grated horseradish
1 teaspoon Dijon mustard

Combine the cream with horseradish to taste; then fold in the mustard. Serve cold.

HORSERADISH

Horseradish, or German mustard, is grown mainly for its root, which is grated fine and mixed with vinegar as a condiment. It contains a pungent oil, which gives it its familiar "hot" taste. A member of the mustard family, it is believed to have originated in an eastern European country, although it comes to us from Great Britain.

Horseradish is often found growing in moist locations, such as on the banks of streams and in damp meadows. In some places, particularly New York State, it can grow as a troublesome weed.

Peak season. Available all year.

Selection. Select firm roots with no soft spots; shriveled roots indicate lack of freshness. Horseradish that has been harvested after the cold weather has set in will keep better.

Storage. Store, wrapped in plastic, in the refrigerator. Horseradish will keep for about three months, but after that it develops an unpleasantly bitter taste.

Preparation and serving. Horseradish is used raw and grated. It is added to cocktail sauces or dressings and is also popularly served with cold meats and fish. Grating it will inevitably cause the eyes to tear. Some horseradish is "hotter" than others, and, since tastes differ, you will have to use your own judgment, adding a small amount at a time and tasting as you go. Commercially prepared horseradish is simply a combination of grated raw horseradish root, vinegar, and salt (sometimes beet juice is added to make it red), but in your home-prepared product you may substitute lemon juice for the vinegar if you wish.

Dietary information. Three and one-half ounces (100 g) of raw horseradish contain 87 calories and phosphorus, potassium, and calcium. The same amount of prepared horseradish contains 38 calories.

JERUSALEM ARTICHOKES

Never was a product so misnamed as the Jerusalem artichoke: it has nothing whatever to do with Jerusalem and is not even distantly related to the globe artichoke. One of the true native North American products, it is actually a tuber, the root of a variety of sunflower plant, and it is sometimes marketed under the name "sunchokes."

The Jerusalem artichoke, which looks like a cross between a knobby potato and a ginger root, is a crunchy, sweet-tasting vegetable with a delicate, nutty flavor. In spite of the fact that it is a distinctly American product, it is unknown to many people in the United States. Versatile, with many uses, it can be a dunk for a dip, a hot vegetable, or a meat extender. It contains inulin, a natural sugar that is well tolerated by people on low-carbohydrate diets. A variety known as the "American artichoke" is ground into a flour from which commerical breadsticks and noodles are made.

Peak season. The season is uncertain, and fresh Jerusalem artichokes may appear at any time throughout the year.

Amount to buy. One pound (454 g) will serve four.

Selection. Choose firm, fresh-looking tubers that don't seem shriveled.

Storage. Jerusalem artichokes are perishable when stored indoors, so they must be kept in a tightly closed plastic bag in the refrigerator. Properly stored, they will keep for a few weeks.

Preparation and serving. Scrub Jerusalem artichokes with a vegetable brush. They have tender skin and don't really need to be peeled, but, if you insist on peeling, scrape them as you do potatoes and plunge them immediately into cold water to which salt and small amounts of lemon juice or vinegar have been added to keep them from turning dark. They may also be peeled after cooking. Jerusalem artichokes cook quickly— usually in about 15 minutes—and should not be overcooked or they will fall apart. Raw, they may be sliced and used in salads, or as a garnish for soups. They can be boiled, broiled, sautéed, creamed, or mashed— any cooking method you use for a potato. Mashed, they can be added to a meat loaf or a vegetable loaf; whole, they may be baked with a roast. The French make a soup from them that they call *potage Palestine*.

Dietary information. When freshly harvested, Jerusalem artichokes contain 7 calories per 3½ ounces (100 g). During storage, however, some of the inulin is converted to sugar, and after a long period of storage the same amount of Jerusalem artichokes will contain 75 calories. They also contain various vitamins, particularly B_1, and potassium.

A new vegetable is found

It is believed that the Jerusalem artichoke was first encountered by Sir Walter Raleigh's expedition in Virginia in the late sixteenth century. These sunflower roots were grown and eaten by the American Indians of that time. After the colonists in the New World established trade with Europe, sunflower seeds were carried to Italy and then on to England. Early French explorers learned to grow and eat them from the Huron Indians and took the tubers back to France in the seventeenth century. In Europe, and particularly in France, the vegetable was cultivated and improved, and now there are over two hundred varieties.

The Jerusalem artichoke gets its name

In the growing fields of Italy, where the sunflower seeds were first cultivated many hundreds of years ago, the flowers turned or "gyrated" toward the sun, so they were appropriately called *girasole*, "turning toward the sun." Thus the Italian word *girasole* standing for "sunflower" was born. When the plant later reached England, *girasole*, a strange sound to English ears, was corrupted into "Jerusalem."

In ancient times

Kale and its first cousin, collards, closely resemble the original cabbage, which was leafy and did not form a head. The ancient Greeks and Romans cultivated kale thousands of years ago. It still grows wild in England and northern Europe.

Kale is not an important agricultural crop in the United States, and elsewhere throughout the world it is grown as a feed for sheep, but there was a time when it was a mainstay in Scotland. Kale soup was an essential part of Scottish meals; even the pot in which the soup was cooked was called a "kail."

Sea kale

A broad-leaved, green plant called "sea kale" is sometimes confused with kale. Sea kale is very different from kale; indeed, it is not even a member of the cabbage family. It is a wild vegetable, probably related to the cresses, and grows along seashores in the British Isles and in western Europe. It is used as a potherb in Europe, and sometimes during the winter the fishermen's wives use it as a substitute for cabbage.

JICAMA

Jicama (HEE-ka-ma) is a root tuber grown in tropical America. It has the same importance for Mexican families as the potato does in the United States. It has the reputation of being a great favorite with travelers, for it quenches thirst and is highly nutritious. It is eaten raw. The jicama looks like a turnip, but it has a bland flavor, similar to a water chestnut, and is an excellent substitute for this more costly vegetable.

Selection. Choose firm, relatively smooth, clean, well-shaped tubers; they should not be cut or bruised. The smaller ones are better than the larger, which tend to be woody.

Storage. Store in a plastic bag in the refrigerator. Use within a week.

Varieties. There are two known forms, one called *agua*, with a watery juice; the other *leche*, with a milky juice. They are distinguishable only by taste.

Preparation and serving. Wash well and cut into thin slices. Sprinkle with lemon juice and salt.

KALE

Kale is a hearty, hardy, curly-leafed green, which is also known as "borecole," or "curly greens." This cabbage-like plant, native to the eastern Mediterranean or to Asia Minor, has been cultivated for so long its origin has been lost. It can be eaten raw, but its coarse texture makes it less desirable for salads than for cooking. It is grown extensively in New York, Maryland, and Virginia and is a popular home-garden vegetable because it is easy to grow.

Peak season. It is available all year and is abundant throughout the winter.

Amount to buy. A pound (454 g) will serve two.

Varieties. Curly kale, which looks like large parsley, is the most popular, although there are others that are yellow-green, red, or purple, with either plain or deeply frilled leaves. A silver kale is cultivated mostly for floral arrangements.

Selection. Dark green kale is best, but, should a few leaves have slightly brown edges, they can be easily trimmed. Look for leaves that are crisp, clean, and free from bruising or crushing.

Storage. Wash, drain well, and store in the refrigerator in a plastic bag or crisper. Use within one to two days.

Preparation and serving. To prepare kale, wash it well and remove the leaves from the tough stems, which should then be discarded. Shake the leaves to remove some of the moisture and cook them in the water that remains on them. Cook until wilted—about 10 minutes—and season with salt, pepper, and a dollop of margarine or butter.

Dietary information. Kale is quite rich in vitamin A, calcium, and iron; it also contains vitamins B and C and other minerals. A pound (454 g) of trimmed, raw kale contains 154 calories.

KNOB CELERY *See* Celeriac.

KOHLRABI

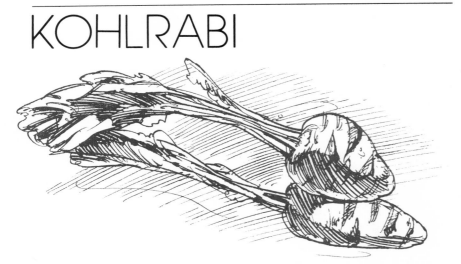

Kohlrabi (coal-RAH-bi) is a member of the cabbage family and native to northern Europe. It has an unusual appearance that sets it apart from other members of the cabbage family. Instead of a head of closely packed leaves, there is a bulbous swelling of the stem, a few inches (5.1 to 7.6 cm) in diameter, just above the ground. From this bulb, leaves similar to those of a turnip arise. It is grown for the bulb, but if the leaves are crisp and green they may be cooked like spinach. The green tops are usually attached when purchased. Young, small bulbs have a pleasant, sweet, mild, turnip-like flavor and crisp, tender texture.

Peak season. Peak season is June and July, although kohlrabi is available fresh from May through November.

Amount to buy. One medium kohlrabi bulb per serving.

Varieties. Light green and purple kohlrabi are grown, but the light green is the most popular.

A newcomer to the vegetable world
Kohlrabi is among the world's newest vegetables, for the plant has become a food only within the last five hundred years. It is better known to Chinese and European cuisines than to that in the United States.

Kohlrabi has been unflatteringly called "the mongrel of the vegetable kingdom" because it appears to be "a turnip growing on a cabbage root." Actually, it is a member of the cabbage family. The name is German and accurately describes it: *kohl* means "cabbage" and *rabi* means "turnip." It is, of course, closely related also to the Brussels sprout. This is not as unlikely as first appears, for if you take a close look at the leaves of both plants, you will see a marked family resemblance.

Creamed kohlrabi
Kohlrabi would have difficulty in a popularity contest, less because it is disliked than because it is unfamiliar. For a different vegetable-eating experience, you might try it creamed.

You will need about eight kohlrabi for four servings. Cut off the tops and pare the roots. Drop them in rapidly boiling water and cook them, uncovered, until they are barely tender. Drain well. Cook the tops separately in the same way. Drain, chop them very fine, or purée them in a blender and combine them with the sliced roots. Make a cream sauce with 2 tablespoons butter, 1½ tablespoons flour, and 1 cup of milk. (To cream any food, always figure on 1 cup of cream sauce to every 2 cups of solids.) Mix together the cream sauce and vegetable and serve hot, sprinkled with nutmeg.

Selection. Look for small- to medium-sized kohlrabi bulbs (about 2 or 3 inches [5.1 to 7.6 cm] in diameter) with fresh green leaves. The skin should be tender. Avoid the large bulbs; they can be tough, woody, and bitter.

Storage. Store in the refrigerator and use within a few days.

Preparation and serving. Raw kohlrabi—washed, peeled, and sliced, served with a dip—gives a good account of itself on a relish tray. The globes may be cooked before or after peeling. To peel, insert a knife under the tough fiber at the base of the globe and strip off the skin. Steam-cook kohlrabi, covered, in about an inch (2.54 cm) of boiling, salted water. Raw julienne strips will cook in about 15 minutes; larger slices take about 25 minutes. Serve with melted butter or margarine, salt, pepper, and a sprinkling of thyme or with a rich cream sauce. The julienne strips can be marinated in French dressing for an hour while still warm. Then drain and chill and serve as an accompaniment to cold meats.

Dietary information. In 3½ ounces (100 g) of trimmed, cooked kohlrabi there are 24 calories. Kohlrabi is a fair source of calcium, phosphorus, potassium, and vitamin C, in addition to some vitamin A and other nutritional elements.

LEEKS

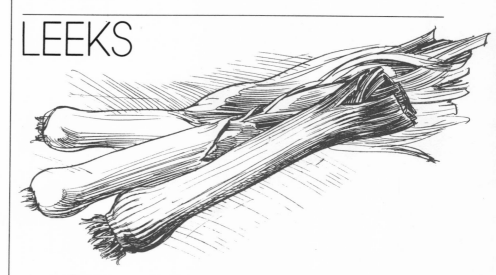

Leeks are the sweetest and mildest members of the onion family. Time was when they were considered the "asparagus of the poor" in France, and they enjoyed a similar status in this country. However, in the early part of the twentieth century they came into their own. Louis Diat, the French chef at the Ritz Carlton in New York, created there his cold vichyssoise soup, the classic potato and leek soup of his native country. Immediately, leeks grew in demand and became expensive.

Peak season. Peak season is October to June, although leeks are available throughout the year.

Amount to buy. Two leeks per person make a suitable portion.

Selection. Leeks come by the bunch or are sometimes sold separately. Look for bunches with leeks of uniform, medium-sized necks. Tops should be fresh and green. The leeks should "give" a bit to the touch, to assure their not being woody inside.

Storage. Store in the refrigerator and use within a week.

Preparation and serving. Leeks hold dirt between the layers of leaves, and great care must be taken to wash out all of it. Slit the stems lengthwise to within an inch (2.54 cm) of the white section and wash under cold running water, spreading the leaves apart. Soak for 30 minutes in a bowl of cold water to which a tablespoon (15 ml) of lemon juice or vinegar has been added. Both the white and green parts may be used, or the white parts alone. Steam the leeks in a small amount of boiling, salted water until just tender, about 20 to 30 minutes. Cooked, drained leeks may be served cold with a vinaigrette sauce, and hot with hollandaise or melted butter or margarine. They can be cut into slices for stews and soups. They may also be braised in the oven in chicken broth for 40 minutes. They can substitute for onions in any recipe that calls for mild onion flavor. They are also a must for two famous soups—the cold French vichyssoise or the Scottish cock-a-leekie.

Dietary information. In 3½ ounces (100 g) of the uncooked bulb and lower leaf portion of leeks, there are 52 calories. Leeks also contain calcium, phosphorus, and vitamin A.

LETTUCE *See* Greens for salad.

MUSHROOMS

O riginally a delicacy reserved for the very wealthy, mushrooms are now grown on a commercial scale in enormous supply and are a standard supermarket product. Mushrooms are not a vegetable, but an edible fungus. There are hundreds of edible species, but all the mushrooms that are available fresh in the stores are of one variety, cultivated from the wild field mushroom. In some European countries wild mushrooms are sold in the markets, but this practice is illegal in the United States. Mushrooms have countless uses in meal planning; entire cookbooks have been devoted exclusively to the mushroom and ways to serve it.

It was formerly believed that darkness was essential for growing good mushrooms, but scientists say this is not so. Most important is a constant correct temperature and protection against drafts. In some parts of the world, Thailand and Japan among them, mushrooms are grown outdoors, but the United States does not have a suitable climate for outdoor production. In parts of the eastern United States, and also in France, they are grown in natural caves or in specially designed windowless buildings in which ventilation, humidity, and temperature are carefully controlled.

Peak season. Available fresh all year, with peak production from November through April. August is the low point for production.

Amount to buy. One pound (454 g) of mushrooms will serve three to four persons, but for avid mushroom eaters you might increase the amount to 1½ pounds (681 g). One pound of raw mushrooms will make about 5 cups sliced, which cook down to about 2 cups. There are about thirty-six to forty-six small button mushrooms in a pound; twenty-five to thirty medium (1½ to 2 inches [3.8 to 5.08 cm]); and twelve to fifteen large ones.

To grow mushrooms

The way has been cleared for people who wish to grow their own mushrooms. There are commercially prepared kits, complete with container and growing medium, that are available from mail-order seed houses and garden stores.

Essential are even moisture and a steady temperature of 50 to 70°F. Darkness is not necessary, but dark places such as a cool basement are usually best because it is easier to maintain even temperatures and dampness in such a setting.

The first crop, which is usually the best, comes in less than a month, and the mushrooms quickly reach harvestable size. They are followed by successive growth spurts of mushrooms about ten days apart over the next six weeks.

Dried mushrooms

Dried mushrooms are a popular ingredient in Chinese dishes and for soup making. They have a much more intense flavor than the fresh ones. They must be soaked in several changes of water before being used in cooking.

You can dry your own mushrooms by threading firm, fresh, washed and dried mushrooms on a string (or place them on a wire screen) and putting them in the sun for 6 to 8 hours. When thoroughly dry, store them in sterile, tightly sealed glass jars. Before using, wash mushrooms briefly in three waters and soak in hot water for a few hours. They can be used as ingredients for soups, casseroles, stuffings, and so on—but not as a cooked side dish.

Stalking the wild mushroom

Much has been written about the ubiquitous and fascinating field or wild mushrooms that nature has designed in a broad range of glorious colors, sizes, and shapes, with the added bonus of flavor that is often superior to that of the cultivated variety we buy in our markets. And what a comfort to have this natural bounty of delicious morsels waiting only to be gathered!

But nature can be perverse and deceptive, and a loud note of caution must be sounded for the inexperienced mushroom hunter.

There is no foolproof way for anyone but an expert to distinguish the edible wild mushrooms from the look-alike poisonous varieties. The deadliest poison is contained in the loveliest of all—the pure white, deadly *Amanita verna*— "Destroying Angel"—with its tall, stately stem and wide, graceful cap. Hunting wild mushrooms is not a sport for the uninformed.

However, there are many books and reliable field guides that can be helpful to the amateur interested in mycology—the study of fungi. There are actually some fifty mushrooms that may be eaten with safety and delight, but one must know which they are. Poisonous mushrooms are sometimes called "toadstools," and anyone who goes off on a "mushroom walk" is strongly advised to learn to recognize a toadstool at sight. There is no margin for experimentation in this area.

Varieties. The only variety in cultivated mushrooms is in size and stem length. Size does not affect quality, nor is it a reliable indication of whether the mushrooms are tender. Some brown mushrooms are sold in California and other areas, but they are not too common.

Selection. Freshness, color, and shape are the most important considerations. The white portion on top, the cap, should be closed around the stem or just slightly open to reveal the rows of tissue (gills) under the cap. The caps should be cream colored or white, although a darkened or spotted mushroom is not necessarily spoiled. Avoid those with wide-open caps and dark gills, those that are markedly pitted or discolored, and those with a spongy texture. Choose small mushrooms for buttons; medium for slicing, chopping, or caps; and large for stuffing or broiling.

Storage. Bright, attractive mushrooms can be kept in a tight container or a plastic bag in the refrigerator for a few days, although it is better to use them as soon as possible. Do not wash them until you are ready to use them. However, all mushrooms will oxidize and darken, particularly if exposed to room temperatures. This occurs more slowly when the mushrooms are refrigerated.

Preparation and serving. Number one rule in preparing mushrooms is *Do not peel*. Much of the flavor and nutritive value is in the skin, so peel only if the caps are very discolored. Wipe the mushroom clean with a damp paper towel; do not soak them in water. Cut off and discard a thin slice from the bottom of each stem. Mushrooms can be used whole, sliced, chopped, or minced, stems removed or left; sliced raw in salads or left whole as an appetizer with a dip; marinated or pickled or stuffed. They can be sautéed broiled, baked or deep-fried.

Dietary information. Although mushrooms contain some protein and minerals, they are largely composed of water and have limited nutritive value. They are low in calories—a pound of raw mushrooms (454 g) contains 103—which has value for dieters, since it gives them a feeling of having eaten well with a minimum of calories.

MUSTARD GREENS

Mustard greens are one the minor leafy vegetables, but they are popular in the South, which is the leading producer. They have a pungent yet delicate flavor that has won them a place in other cuisines as well and we find them used in a number of Italian and Chinese dishes.

Peak season. Available all year.

Amount to buy. Two pounds (908 g) will serve four.

Varieties. The type most often grown for commercial marketing is called "leaf mustard." Mustard spinach and tender green mustard are frequently grown in home gardens.

Selection. Select the smaller leaves, 6 to 12 inches (15.2 to 30.5 cm) long, as they will be more tender. Mustard greens should be of good color, fresh, tender, and crisp. Poor quality is evidenced in leaves that are dirty, discolored, wilted, or spotted. Seed stems indicate age and toughness.

Storage. As soon as you get them home, wash the greens in several waters to keep them from wilting and assure their crispness. Shake off as much water as possible and spread the loose leaves out on paper towels to dry. Refrigerate them in a plastic bag. The leafy greens should keep fresh in the refrigerator for a week or more.

Preparation and serving. Discard any brown or faded leaves. The young, tender leaves of mustard greens can be used as salad leaves either alone or in combination with other greens. The older leaves are used for cooking. Cook them only in the water that clings to the leaves after washing. Use a heavy saucepan with a tight-fitting cover. Place the washed greens in the pan, add a teaspoon (5 ml) of salt, and cover. Let them wilt over medium heat for 15 to 18 minutes. When cooked, drain well and chop if you desire. Dress with melted butter or margarine and a few squirts of lemon juice or vinegar.

Dietary information. Cooked mustard greens are exceedingly high in vitamins A and C as well as iron, and useful amounts of other vitamins and minerals, including folic acid. A cup (240 ml) of cooked greens contains 35 calories.

A useful plant

Some species of the mustard family are cultivated for their seeds. They are ground up and mixed to a paste with vinegar or oil, spices, and other ingredients to create the golden topping without which a hot dog would be a pallid thing instead of the great American pastime that it is. Strangely enough, mustard does not have any pungency until it is mixed with liquid. Only then does it become hot. Prepared mustards range from very mild to very hot, depending upon the preparation and balance of the other ingredients.

Whole mustard seed is used primarily in pickling and in marinades for meat or shrimp. Powdered mustard, which is the seeds reduced to a powder, is used to flavor mayonnaise, French dressings, and a variety of sauces, besides many other uses in cooking.

History of okra

Okra is believed to have originated in Africa in the region of present-day Ethiopia, where it still grows wild, and it was also cultivated in ancient Egypt.

Okra first came to this country with its African name, *kingumbo*, or *quingumbo*, which was shortened to the more familiar "gumbo." In some parts of the world it is still called "lady's fingers."

It was probably taken from North Africa to the European continent by the Moors. It is known that the Spanish Moors and the Egyptians of the twelfth century were familiar with the Arab word for "okra." Since okra is so popular in the French cookery of Louisiana, it is assumed that it was introduced into the New World by the French colonists of Louisiana in the early 1700s, where it has flourished ever since.

Appetizer

- 1 pound young, small, uniformly sized okra with stems
- ½ cup mayonnaise
- ½ cup plain yogurt
- ½ teaspoon prepared Dijon-style mustard
- 2 teaspoons chopped onion

Wash the okra but do not trim or disturb the skin. Plunge the okra all at once into boiling, salted water. Time from the moment the water returns to a boil and boil for exactly 7 minutes. Drain immediately and chill.

Arrange the okra on individual plates, placed like spokes of a wheel. Combine the remaining ingredients and spoon into a lettuce cup in the center of each plate so that the pods can be dipped into the sauce and eaten by hand. For variety, the pods may be kept warm and served with hollandaise in the same manner. Serves 4 to 6.

OKRA

Okra, a pod vegetable used in soups and stews, is also called "gumbo," the name by which it is known in most countries outside the United States. It is a member of the mallow family, which makes it directly related to the inedible but economically important cotton plant. Okra is popular in the South, where it is prepared in a number of different ways—boiled, baked, or fried. It occupies an outstanding place in the Creole cookery of Louisiana: what would a southern gumbo be without it? Young okra pods have a pleasant flavor and combine successfully with tomatoes and other vegetables such as corn and green pepper. Okra is distinctive for the thick, gluey sap that oozes out of the sliced pods as they are cooked, giving body and substance to stews and soups.

Peak season. Available fresh June through November, with July the peak month.

Amount to buy. One pound (454 g) will serve four.

Varieties. There are ridged and smooth varieties. They are interchangeable in use.

Selection. Okra of good quality may be green or white; pods may be long and thin or short and chunky. In any case, freshness can be determined by the tenderness of the pods—they should bend easily or puncture on slight pressure. Young, tender, fresh, clean pods of small to medium size—2 to 4 inches (5.1 to 10.2 cm) —are generally of good quality. Overgrown pods are tough and fibrous. Avoid dull or discolored, dried, or shriveled pods.

Storage. Okra should be refrigerated in a plastic bag and used within three to five days.

Preparation and serving. To prepare for cooking, remove the stem ends and wash the pods. If the pods are used whole and cooked quickly, the juice will not run out and the pods will have a crisp, crunchy texture instead of the slippery quality that some people find objectionable. Okra must not be subjected to long cooking unless in a gumbo or stew. Steam-cook in a small amount of boiling, salted water about 10 minutes, or until just tender. They can be served with melted butter, salt, and pepper or with a vinaigrette sauce.

Dietary information. Fresh okra provides calcium, phosphorus, potassium, iron, and vitamins A and C. One pound (454 g) of raw okra contains 140 calories.

ONIONS

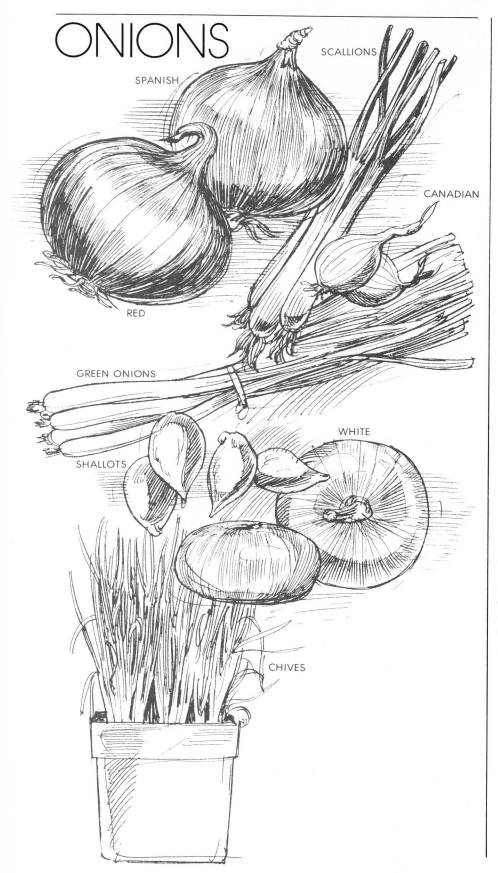

SPANISH

SCALLIONS

CANADIAN

RED

GREEN ONIONS

WHITE

SHALLOTS

CHIVES

An object of reverence

The onion was worshiped in Egypt long before the Christian era, and huge amounts of gold were spent to buy onions and garlic for the workmen building the great pyramids. Onions were believed to have the power to avert evil, and people wore them on their bodies and hung them in their houses for good luck and to prevent disease.

An old proverb states that if you eat onions in May, the following year the doctors can play, the inference being that doctors without sick people to care for will have more leisure. For some reason, onions have had a long history as a home remedy. The onion has been recommended for everything from a treatment for burns to bee stings. It has been rubbed on the head to cure baldness and its juice combined with honey to cure a chest cold. A roasted onion was a common remedy for earache and neuralgia, but it is not made clear whether it was to be eaten or applied to the affected part.

Weep no more

No one who has ever cut an onion is unaware of the eye tearing this activity induces. A great number of techniques have been recommended, each of which has its champions and its detractors. Among the suggestions are to run cold water over the onions before peeling; to run scalding water over the onions before peeling; to peel them under water of any temperature; to cut the onion without removing the stem end; to breathe only through the nose, keeping the mouth shut tightly while peeling the onion; to hold a crust of bread between your teeth with one end projecting outward.

Onion odors

"Eat no onions nor garlic, for we are to utter sweet breath," says William Shakespeare in *A Midsummer Night's Dream.* Eating half a dozen sprigs of parsley lightly dipped in salt will achieve Shakespeare's objective of "sweet breath." The onion odor can be removed from a knife by running it through a raw potato, and for hands tainted with onion odor try rubbing them with celery salt or lemon before washing.

Baked onions

This is a hearty, delicious onion dish that can cook along with the poultry or beef that is roasting in the oven.

  8 medium-sized yellow onions
  ½ cup consommé or chicken broth, more if necessary
     Salt and freshly ground pepper
  4 to 6 tablespoons grated Parmesan cheese

Oil a 10-inch casserole with a cover. Peel the onions and arrange them in it. Add the broth and sprinkle the onions lightly with salt and a few grinds of pepper. Cover the casserole and place in a 350°F oven for an hour, or until the onions are tender. Take a look from time to time and add more liquid if they are drying out. When the onions are tender, sprinkle grated cheese over them and return to the oven, uncovered, until the cheese is melted. (You can run the onions under the broiler for a few minutes to bubble the cheese.) Serve at once. Serves 4.

A food writer once observed that onions would be prized above truffles and caviar if they were not quite so abundant. Not many cooks would argue that point, and in most kitchens throughout the world onions are the quintessential cooking ingredient. There are few dishes, other than desserts, that do not include at least a hint of one form or another of onion. They were one of the first crops of our early settlers, but they have been known for over four thousand years—so long, in fact, that no one is sure where they originated, although it is suspected that it was Asia Minor. Botanically, onions are "kitchen lilies," belonging to a family that is a cross between the lily and the amaryllis.

Peak season. Available fresh all year.

Amount to buy. Figure one large, two medium, or three or four small onions per serving. Most households stock onions as a staple and buy them a few pounds at a time.

Varieties. The *chive* is the baby of the onion family, picked before the bulb has had a chance to form. It is snipped and sprinkled over food just before serving. The *scallion* is a shoot that has been pulled before the bulb has formed. It is also snipped or sliced and used raw. The *green onion* is an adolescent chive. An onion that is harvested green, it has a definite bulb formation. The *Canada onion*, which has a very small bulb, is cultivated especially for pickling and for use as a cocktail onion. These white baby pearl onions are processed and are available only in jars.

The *sweet red Italian,* or *creole,* onion, is believed to have been originally developed in Italy but is now grown in large quantities in the United States. It is without peer for eating, sliced paper thin for sandwiches or to top a hamburger, or sliced or chopped in a salad. However, its flavor is too subtle to make much impact in a stew or soup. Onions grown in warmer climates are generally sweeter and milder than those grown in colder areas.

The *sweet Bermuda,* or *Spanish,* onion, may have originated in either one of those places, but now Texas produces enough to take care of the needs of the United States. It is generally larger and a little stronger than the red Italian, and, although still gentle enough to be eaten raw, it has enough flavor to make a contribution when boiled in soups and stews.

The *leek,* another important member of the onion family, is discussed on page 50.

The *small white boiling onion* is ideal for use as a vegetable—creamed, glazed, or sautéed—or added to chicken or meat stews and casseroles. It is a firmly constructed little globe and holds its shape and texture even in a stewpot.

The *shallot* is a cross between the onion and garlic. Like garlic, it is divided into cloves, but, unlike garlic, it is subtle and sweet in flavor and its odor does not remain on the breath. It is becoming more available in markets everywhere. A few cloves, minced and added to the other onions, impart a pleasant flavor. Shallots may be stored in the refrigerator in a plastic bag for a number of weeks. One-half pound (227 g) perform yeoman's service in many dishes.

Yellow globe onions, the workhorses of the onion family, are the most common and are considered primarily a cooking onion. They have a strong flavor. "Yellow globe" is a commercial term applied to several varieties and strains that come to the markets at various times of the year and represent about 75 percent of the world's onion supply.

Selection. Onions should be firm and well shaped, with dry, paperlike skins. Avoid onions that are sprouting or those with a wet, soggy feeling at the neck. This can be a sign that decay is starting. Size of onions has nothing to do with quality.

Look for green, fresh tops for green onions, scallions, and chives.

Storage. Store scallions and green onions in the vegetable compartment of the refrigerator and use as soon as possible, within a day or two.

All other onions may be stored in a cool, dry place, in a loosely woven mesh container, for many weeks, or in the refrigerator. Use before they soften and sprout. Onions should never be stored with potatoes because they will take on moisture from the potatoes and decay quickly.

Preparation and serving. Onions can be used as a main vegetable dish; in soups, stews, and sauces; boiled, baked, creamed, steamed, French-fried in rings, or roasted; sliced or diced raw in salads. Chives are snipped with a kitchen scissors and added to foods raw. Green onions and scallions are trimmed of their roots, tops skins peeled off, and minced or sliced. Scallions may be left whole and eaten raw. Shallots are broken apart and the cloves peeled and chopped or minced. Small white onions can be peeled more easily if they are plunged into boiling water for 15 or 20 seconds and peeled at once. Cut a cross at the root end to keep the center core from falling out while cooking.

Dietary information. Mature onions are not notably high in nutrients, but they do have some iron and vitamins A and C. One pound (454 g) of raw onions, untrimmed, contains 157 calories.

PARSLEY

Parsley is actually an herb, but it is so rich in nutrients—containing more vitamin A than carrots per ounce, three times as much vitamin C as oranges, and twice as much iron as spinach—that it deserves more attention than being used to garnish a platter, only to be ignored and set aside. In addition to its other virtues, it is a natural breath freshener, neutralizing any side effects caused by garlic and onions. It is grown in the United States as well as several European countries.

An ancient crop

The subject of what crops were grown at which time in world history has fascinated many historians. According to one study, published in the late nineteenth century, there were some twenty-seven plant crops cultivated in the Old World more than four thousand years ago. Among them were almonds, cabbage, tea, watermelon, turnips, and onions.

But wild onions also grow abundantly throughout most of the world. They grow in every state of the United States, and none is poisonous. We know that the early settlers found wild onions growing in the New World. An Indian tribe named the place near the southern end of Lake Michigan where these wild onions grew in profusion *She-khe-ony*. When white men built a town in that area, the Indian name was turned into one that we all know: Chicago.

Parsley lore

Parsley is native to the Mediterranean shores and has been used as a garnish for thousands of years. The ancient Greeks crowned their brows with parsley leaves, less for the cosmetic effect than the belief that the leaves would stimulate and excite their brain, thereby heightening their appetite and spirits.

Peter Rabbit, Beatrix Potter's greatly loved little animal, obviously knew something that has eluded many mortals. We read that Peter ate some lettuce and some French beans and then some radishes—after which he felt rather ill and went to look for some parsley.

Storing parsnips

Parsnips require a long, cool growing season and have the highest yield when they are planted in early spring, grow during the summer, and are harvested in the late fall after the first frost. Some growers leave the parsnips in the ground for the entire winter where they are safe and snug, in spite of the freezing ground that surrounds them. Actually, this is when they improve in flavor, since freezing converts the carbohydrates to sugar.

Peak season. Parsley is available fresh all year, with heaviest supplies from October through December.

Varieties. The curly-leaf variety is the most commonly seen, but the flat leaf, sometimes called "Italian parsley," is also available. Italian parsley has a highly distinctive and pleasant flavor, and some people prefer it.

Selection. Select parsley that is crisp and firm, with a healthy, all-over dark green color. There should be no yellowing, which indicates age. Black, watery areas indicate bruising.

Storage. Wash in cold water and shake dry. Refrigerate in a covered, airtight plastic container in the vegetable crisper, where it will keep fresh for a week or more. It may also be stored in the refrigerator with the stems in a container of water, covered with a plastic bag.

Preparation and serving. In addition to its use as a garnish, parsley can be chopped and added to salads, vegetable dishes, soups, marinades, and spreads for bread. Add it chopped or shredded to the butter or margarine you use for sandwiches, garlic bread, or sweet corn.

Dietary information. One tablespoon (15 ml) of chopped parsley contains 1 calorie; 8 ounces (227 g) contain 100 calories.

CILANTRO (coriander). Sometimes called "Chinese parsley" or "Mexican parsley," *cilantro* is actually the parsley-like leaf of the coriander plant, which supplies the seeds that have served as a spice and seasoning from ancient times. The Spanish name for coriander is *cilantro*. The leaves are tenderer than parsley, and may be used in exactly the same way as parsley. However, cilantro has a much zestier taste, one that lingers in the mouth. For that reason it must be used in smaller quantities when substituted for parsley in any recipe.

Cilantro should have good, green color and unwilted leaves. It is handled and stored like parsley.

PARSNIPS

Parsnips, a root vegetable, are available all year, but are at their best during the winter months when many vegetables are in poorest supply. Growers try to wait until after the first heavy frost to harvest parsnips, at which time they have a sweeter and more delicate taste. They are one of the hardiest vegetables on the market and hold up well in all temperatures.

Parsnips are a member of the family that includes carrots and celery. They look rather like dingy white carrots, with stems and leaves that resemble celery. A most delicious and satisfying vegetable, parsnips deserve more usage than they get.

Peak season. January through April.

Amount to buy. One and a half to two pounds (681 to 908 g) will serve four people.

Selection. Small- to medium-sized parsnips are usually the most desirable (the very large sizes are likely to have a woody core), and they should be firm, clean, well shaped, and smooth. Softness may indicate decay and discoloration may indicate freezing. Parsnips that have been stored are preferable to the freshly harvested ones.

Storage. Store in the refrigerator and use as desired. Parsnips keep well for a couple of weeks.

Preparation and serving. It is quicker and easier to peel parsnips after cooking, which also keeps them from discoloring. Scrub them well with a vegetable brush and steam them in boiling, salted water. This will take from 20 to 40 minutes, depending on the size of the parsnips and the time of year they were grown. Do not overcook; when properly steamed, they have a sweet, nutty flavor. Drain and let them cool before skinning. (Plunging them into cold water will hasten the cooling process.) Since parsnips may have a woody core, slice them lengthwise so there is less waste. They can be mashed and combined with potatoes, or creamed, sautéed, or deep-fried in thin slices in a batter. Cold, they make an interesting addition to salads.

Dietary information. One pound (454 g) of raw parsnips contains 293 calories. Parsnips are high in vitamin A, phosphorus, iron, sodium, and potassium besides other vitamins and minerals.

PEAS

It seems a pity that there are children today who have never experienced the succulent sweetness of a fresh green pea as it is popped out of the pod. Peas out of cans, boxes, and plastic bags are all very well—some are better than others—but they are a far cry from what nature provides in the fresh state. Only a small proportion of the peas grown are shipped fresh, for most of them go into those cans, boxes, and plastic bags.

Peas have been used as food for humans as far back as prehistoric times. Originally they were cultivated only for their dry seeds, and it was not until the late eleventh century that "green peas" began to be mentioned in England. Many fine varieties were developed, and they soon became known throughout the world as "English peas." Their popularity among the English undoubtedly assured their inclusion among the first vegetables to travel across the Atlantic, and in their dried form they provided a good source of winter food for the early settlers.

Peak season. March through June.

Amount to buy. You will need 3 to 5 pounds (1.3 to 2.3 kg) of peas in pod, depending on their size, to adequately serve four. One pound (454 g) of peas in pod yields a cup (240 ml) of shelled peas.

Varieties. The two main varieties are the English, or garden, peas, and the sugar peas, or "snow peas" (see below). *Petits pois* are not a separate type but simply peas gathered before they are mature. They are considered top quality.

Selection. Look for young pods, uniformly green and well filled. A yellowish pod indicates overmaturity. To remove all doubt about quality, split one and taste a pea to make sure that it is fresh and sweet.

Storage. The ideal situation would be to pick your peas out of the garden, shell, cook, and eat them immediately. Failing that, store them uncovered in their pods in the refrigerator and use them as soon as possible. Garden peas, like sweet corn, tend to lose part of their sugar content when stored.

Favored by royalty

History tells us that Catherine de Medici introduced tiny green peas to France when she married the Duke of Orleans (later to become Henry II, king of France) in 1533. The French were most enthusiastic about them and called them *petit pois,* a name that has survived over the years. During the late sixteenth and early seventeenth centuries, these peas became very fashionable, and very expensive. They were equally prized by the English, who imported them from Holland.

Varieties of peas

Marrowfats are a variety of garden peas that are used mostly for canning and freezing. They are large and wrinkled.

Field peas originated in Africa and were cultivated in Egypt thousands of years before the Christian era. The flowers of field peas are purple and the seeds are gray, yellow, or spotted, in contrast to garden peas, which have white flowers and yellowish white or bluish green seeds. The seeds are dried for use as split peas. The pigeon pea is one type of field pea.

Asparagus peas flourish mostly in southern Europe. In spite of their name, they have no resemblance to asparagus, nor do they look like other peas. They have hairy pods marked with vertical ribs and brown seeds. The entire pod is ready to be eaten when it reaches an inch in length.

Cowpeas are believed to have come to America from Africa with the first slaves. They thrive in warm climates and are now indigenous to the South. When southerners speak of peas, they generally are referring to cowpeas; garden peas are identified as "English peas." Botanically, cowpeas are closer to beans than they are to peas. They are often dried. The most popular kind of cowpea, especially in the South, is the black-eyed pea. It grows on a vine and, true to its name, has a black "eye" on a white seed.

Roasted peppers

Roasted red or green bell peppers, cut into strips and marinated in some garlicked oil, make a fine accompaniment to a main course, or as an appetizer in combination with rolled or flat anchovies.

Wash the peppers well and place a whole uncut pepper directly over each of your gas burners, turned medium high. Use long kitchen tongs to turn the peppers until they are completely black and charred. During the process, the pepper will cook and soften. This goes quite quickly, perhaps 10 minutes or so are all that are needed. As soon as the peppers have cooled sufficiently so you can handle them, scrape off all the blackened skin. Cut a crosswise slice from the stem end and discard. Remove the seeds and membranes and cut the peppers into thin strips.

Marinate the strips in oil to which you have added some minced garlic and a pinch of salt. Keep in a covered jar in the refrigerator, where they will hold for weeks. Serve at room temperature.

Preparation and serving. Rinse the pea pods if necessary and shell peas immediately before serving. Do not wash the peas before cooking and do not salt them until *after* they are cooked. Half a teaspoon (2.5 ml) or so of sugar may be added when cooking to increase sweetness. Cook peas in as little water as possible. The French method of cooking is to line a saucepan with wet lettuce leaves, pour in the peas, and cover with more wet lettuce. Cook, covered, over medium heat until tender, 8 to 10 minutes, depending upon the youth of the peas. Test for doneness by tasting them, and butter, salt, and pepper the peas before serving. Young fresh peas may also be eaten raw. For purées and soups, boil peas until very soft.

Nutritional information. Peas are rich in vitamins A and B. One pound (454 g) of shelled raw peas contains 381 calories.

SNOW PEAS

Snow peas are also known as "Chinese peas," *mangetout*, "sugar peas," and "Chinese pea pods." The flat peas used extensively in Chinese cooking, they are picked before the seeds form, and the entire pod can be eaten.

Peak season. May through September.

Amount to buy. One pound (454 g) will serve four.

Selection. Pods should be bright green and crisp.

Storage. Store in a plastic bag in the refrigerator and use the snow peas as soon as possible.

Preparation and serving. Rinse and remove any withered blossoms. Pea pods can be cooked whole or shredded. Steam as you would regular peas or stir-fry in a small amount of oil. They should be crisp and crunchy and a vivid emerald green when cooked. They must not be overcooked or they will lose their fine, crisp texture. Serve with melted butter or margarine alone, or with sautéed mushrooms or toasted almonds.

Nutritional information. Snow peas have the same nutritional values as regular peas, but about half the calories; one pound (454 g) contains 196 calories.

PEPPERS

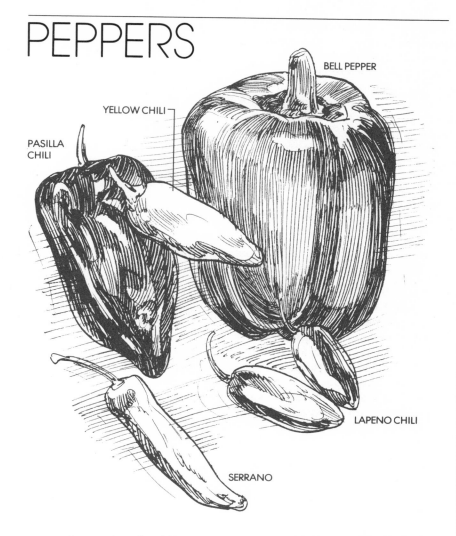

BELL PEPPER

YELLOW CHILI

PASILLA CHILI

LAPENO CHILI

SERRANO

The green and red bell-shaped peppers we use as vegetables are in no way related to the Asiatic vines whose berries are used for the ground black and white pepper. The green and red peppers are members of the *Capsicum* family, specimens of which Columbus carried back to Spain from his voyages of discovery to the New World. The Europeans found them useful, mainly as a seasoning. Curiously, although peppers were originally American, they had to be reintroduced to the United States from Europe, where they had been used since the middle of the sixteenth century. Peppers of one kind or another of varying degrees of pungency are now eaten all over the world and come in a dazzling display of colors—brilliant green, yellow, and red. However, in the United States, the sweet, mild bell pepper is the most popular. It may be green or red, depending upon its state of maturity, for as the green pepper matures it turns bright red.

Peak season. Green peppers are available all year, their peak May through October. The red ones are more seasonal, generally in good supply in the fall.

Amount to buy. Two large or four small sweet peppers will generally serve four people as a side dish. For stuffed peppers, you need one large pepper per serving.

Some like it hot

When the Spanish explorers came to Central America in the fifteenth century, they found hot peppers being cultivated by the native Indians. It was the desire for the precious spice, pepper, that made Queen Isabella of Spain willing to pick up the tab for Columbus's voyage across unknown oceans and made the trip possible in the first place. The Spaniards mistook the plants growing in the New World for the spice, and called the plant "pepper," although it has no relationship to peppercorns. Correct or not, the name stuck and later became "chili peppers" (from the Mexican Nahuatl Indian *Chilli*).

Hot peppers are gaining popularity because of increasing interest in hot ethnic foods now in vogue—Thai, Vietnamese, Szechuan, Indian, Arab, Spanish, and Mexican. When used with restraint and care, hot peppers can add a new dimension to the pleasure of eating for those who like their food lusty and with bite.

The leading fresh, canned, or dried hot peppers on the market are known by a variety of names, and they are frequently identified differently by different experts:

Cayenne is a smooth-skinned red pepper with a pungent flavor. It is found both fresh and dried on strings.

Chili and *chilitepines* are red, whole, and dried and are often sold on strings. They are popularly used in the Southwest in Mexican food.

Jalapeño and *serrano* are small green chilies. Serrano is milder than the jalapeño, and both are used extensively in Mexican cooking.

Poblano is a dark green chili pepper shaped like a bell pepper but with a tapered end. It is mildly hot and is found fresh and canned.

Tabasco is a bright red, tapered pepper, 1 to 1½ inches long. This fiery pepper is found both fresh and bottled whole and is used for sauces.

The potato gets its name

Potatoes were unknown in Europe until the Spanish conquistadors found the Inca eating them in the Andean region of South America in the sixteenth century. The Inca word for them was *papa*. The Spaniards brought the potatoes to Spain, where they were grown and sold in public markets. The Spaniards were fond of the other South American tuber, the sweet potato, which they called *batata*. The white potato got its Spanish name *patata* from *batata*. Actually, the white potato and the sweet potato are not at all related; the former is a plant of the nightshade family and the sweet potato is a member of the morning-glory family.

In France the potato was regarded at first as an ornamental plant. They called it *pomme de terre*, "apple of the earth." In Holland it is *aardappel*, "earth apple," not because of its texture, which somewhat resembles the crispness of a fresh apple, but because many different fruits were called apples in the Middle Ages.

The potato was introduced to Great Britain in the 1580s and a few years later to Ireland. It grew so well there it became the staple food of the country. It was easy to plant; all that was needed was a spade to dig trenches. The word "spade" became convoluted in a mix of Gaelic and cockney English and turned into "spud," which is what the Irish called potatoes and is an expression used even now. The term "Irish potatoes" is so entrenched in our language that many people mistakenly think Ireland is the country where potatoes originated.

Why potatoes darken

Many cooks are distressed by the potato's tendency to turn dark after cooking. This graying or darkening does not affect flavor, texture, or nutrient content of the cooked potato; it is purely cosmetic. It is also unavoidable, and not caused by your inept handling. It may be inherent in the variety used, or the potatoes may have been stored in a too-cold location along the way to your home. Potatoes grown in an acid soil may tend to gray when they are cooked. There is no way of knowing in advance which potato will darken after cooking; they will all look the same before being cooked.

Varieties. The numerous varieties of garden peppers can be classified in two categories, sweet and hot or pungent. The most common type in the American diet is the sweet bell pepper, large and bell-shaped, which is often eaten while green or else as fully ripe.

Chili, cayenne, and pimiento are varieties of hot peppers. Tabasco sauce is made from pickling chilies. Another long, bright-red pepper, cultivated in Hungary, is called "paprika." It is ground into a powder and can be pungent or mild.

Other types of peppers are the small, thin, light green Italian pepper, whose mild taste makes it excellent for flavoring, and the small, round, and very hot cherry pepper, which can be red, yellow, or purplish.

Selection. Look for peppers that are firm and well shaped. They should be thick fleshed and either bright red or green. Avoid those that have punctured skins or look wilted or tired.

Storage. Refrigerate peppers at once in an airtight container or plastic bag in the vegetable crisper. They will keep for a week or so.

Preparation and serving. To prepare peppers for cooking, wash them thoroughly and remove the cores, seeds, and membranes, leaving only the shells. The seeds of bell peppers are bitter, and the seeds of chili peppers exceedingly hot, so they should always be discarded.

Peppers can be used whole, cut in quarters, sliced, or chopped. For most recipes they are cut in julienne strips or in rounds. They can be stuffed with a combination of rice and meat and baked, or they can be added to casseroles, stews, soups, and sauces. They can also be served raw in salads or cut into strips accompanied by a dip as an appetizer. Italian or bell peppers are delicious cut into strips and lightly sautéed in oil seasoned with garlic.

Dietary information. Peppers are high in vitamin C, and contain some vitamin A and a variety of other vitamins and minerals, plus fiber, which is desirable for body functioning. One medium pepper contains 15 calories.

POTATOES

The potato is the world's most important vegetable. Grown in at least eighty countries, it has kept entire nations alive during periods of stress and, imaginatively prepared, has brought glamour (as well as substance) to Lucullan feasts. Like the tomato, it is one of the vegetables that originated in the Western Hemisphere, traveled through Europe, and was later reintroduced to the New World by European settlers. Experimentation over the years has developed new strains and improved growth, which have brought the potato to its present high level of excellence.

Idaho and Maine are the leading potato-producing states in the United States; Germany, the Soviet Union, and Poland lead potato production in Europe.

There are a great many varieties of potatoes, and potatoes differ in every region of the country. The seed used, climate under which the tubers were grown, the amount of fertilizer and water, the temperature and humidity of the storage before shipping—all of these conspire to create variations in the product that finally reaches your table. The

Idaho potato, used for baking and for preparations requiring a mealy potato, is known throughout the country, but many other types are regional. Food shoppers need to be familiar with the potatoes available in their own area and know which potato is best suited to the purpose for which they are using it.

Many countries have contributed fine potato dishes to the world's cuisine: puffy soufflé potatoes and potato soup from France; fried potatoes from Germany; boiled potatoes from England; and, from the United States, hash browns, home fries, potato chips, and the splendid baked potato. But at the top of the list in popularity are French fries. It is mind boggling to think of the mountains of these consumed each day.

Peak season. Available all year. New potatoes are available in late winter or early spring, although they may appear in some areas at other times of the year.

Amount to buy. For most preparations, one medium-large potato per person generally suffices. Figure one baking potato per portion. Small potatoes are more difficult to gauge, but 2 pounds (908 g) will generally serve four.

Varieties. The potato industry generally classifies potatoes in five basic types, among which the Russet Burbank is the most widely grown. But, for the purposes of the consumer, potatoes may be divided into three categories: baking, general-purpose, and new.

BAKING POTATOES. The best-known baking potatoes are the long, oval-shaped Idaho bakers (the Russet Burbank). The flesh is dry, mealy, and fluffy. They are also good for French fries.

GENERAL-PURPOSE POTATOES. Mature potatoes are the general-purpose potatoes of many varieties. Either round or oval in shape, they can be boiled, mashed, fried, and in some cases even baked successfully.

NEW POTATOES

Unlike the majority of the United States potato crop that must be stored, the early or "new" potatoes are shipped directly from the field after harvesting. New potatoes are characterized by relatively thin, or "feathering," skin. They are either red or brown and range in size from a tiny ball to the size of an average all-purpose potato. Their best use is boiling or creaming. The little ones should be boiled and served in their jackets, perhaps with a strip peeled from their circumference before boiling to enhance their appearance. Red-skinned potatoes have a waxy quality that makes them a good choice for use in dishes like potato salad because the potato will not soak up the dressing or crumble when cut into cubes or slices.

Selection. Choose potatoes that are well shaped, firm, and unsprouted; contain few eyes; and are free from blemishes and "greening." The green discoloration is caused by the development of a toxic substance called "solanine." This occurs in potatoes that have been exposed to sunlight or artificial light. Considerable greening gives the potato a bitter taste, and a large amount can cause the eater to become ill. It is best to peel away the green area of the potato completely, and, if you find several potatoes green, return them to the seller for replacement.

The maligned potato
Few foods are as maligned by dieters as the potato, which has been made the patsy for all the additional calories heaped on it in the form of butter, cream, and cheese. A medium-sized baked potato contains only about 90 calories, the same as an apple, an orange, or one slice of buttered toast. Its mealy softness can be delicious by itself, or when sprinkled with freshly ground pepper, a favorite herb, or a spot of plain yogurt.

The number of calories with which the potato ends up depends not only on its embellishment, but also on how it is prepared. Three ounces of French-fried potatoes contains about 345 calories; the same amount pan fried, 240 calories; the same amount plain boiled, 71 calories.

When the salt shaker slips
If by mistake you have put too much salt in a soup or sauce, cut a raw potato in half and add it to the pot. Boil for a short time until the oversaltiness disappears, then discard the potato.

Nutritionally speaking. . .
Any cooking process destroys some of a food's vitamin C and the potato is no exception. More is lost as cooked potatoes are kept for later use, particularly if they are at room temperature. Serve potatoes as soon as possible after they are cooked, and always refrigerate whatever is left. It should be noted that dehydrated instant potatoes contain almost no vitamin C.

A bit of camouflage
Some red potato varieties are artificially colored with a nontoxic red dye or wax to enhance appearance and preserve freshness. FDA regulations require that such treated potatoes be identified and make it illegal to color white-skinned potatoes red. Boiling a color-waxed potato with the skin on leaves an objectionable residue in the pan, and many states have laws prohibiting their sale completely. Some areas also clear-wax their russet and white varieties to enhance their appearance and preserve freshness.

To make perfect mashed potatoes

Use all-purpose potatoes—not new ones. Peel potatoes and cut them into quarters. Add enough boiling water to almost cover and throw in a pinch of salt. Bring to a boil, cover, and cook until tender, 20 to 40 minutes. Drain off the water and return the pan to the heat to dry out, shaking the pan gently. For a perfect, lump-free result, put the potatoes through a food mill, ricer, strainer, or a food processor (using the steel blade and running for about 12 seconds, or until mashed). Season with salt and pepper and a lump of butter or margarine, if desired.

Pumpkin seeds

Pumpkin seeds, also known as *pepitas*, are a popular snack, rich in all manner of minerals and B vitamins and contain protein and polyunsaturated fat. One pound contains 553 calories. You can buy them raw or roasted, or you can create your own supply by saving the seeds, allowing them to dry naturally, and toasting them in the oven. The outer husk should be peeled off and just the kernel eaten.

Roasted pumpkin seeds

  2 cups washed, hulled, and dried
     pumpkin seeds
1½ tablespoons oil
  1 teaspoon salt

Heat the oven to 250° F. Combine the pumpkin seeds with oil and salt, then spread the coated seeds on a shallow baking pan and bake for 30 to 40 minutes, until the seeds are browned and crisp. Shake the pan frequently so the seeds will brown evenly. Makes 2 cups.

Storage. Store potatoes in a cool, dry, dark area, as greening takes place more rapidly at room temperature than in cool. If stored properly, general-purpose and baking potatoes will keep for several months and new potatoes for several weeks. Look them over before you store them and set aside any that are bruised or cracked to be used first.

Preparation and serving. Whenever possible, serve the potatoes in their skin, since most of the nutrients of the potato are concentrated in the layer beneath. To bake potatoes, scrub them well with a stiff vegetable brush, dry them, rub with oil, and prick the skin with a fork to prevent their "exploding" while in the oven. An aluminum or stainless-steel baking nail in the potato helps promote uniform baking. Bake between 45 and 60 minutes in a 400°F (205°C) oven. If you have other foods in the oven that need a lower temperature, allow additional time for the potatoes. Serve at once or they become soggy.

Boil potatoes with the skins on, in a covered pot, in the least amount of boiling, salted water until just done. Depending on the size, this may take from 25 to 40 minutes. They may also be thinly pared before cooking, but leaving the skins on is preferable.

French-frying potatoes is a two-step operation. Use a deep, heavy-bottomed kettle or large saucepan with a wire basket for easy removal of food. Fill kettle no more than half full of cooking oil or melted vegetable shortening. Heat fat to 375°F (190°C). Test temperature with a 1-inch (2.54 cm) cube of bread. If it browns in 60 seconds, you've achieved the proper temperature. Drop in potato strips. Cook 2 minutes. Skim out potatoes and drain on absorbent paper. Cool about 5 minutes, reheat oil to 375° and drop potatoes in again. Finish frying them for about 3 minutes. They should be golden brown and will be crisp when drained on absorbent paper.

Test a baked potato for doneness by squeezing to determine softness; use a clean kitchen towel to protect your fingers. Test boiled potatoes with a fork for tenderness; taste a cubed or sliced potato; judge a fried or French-fried potato by its rich golden color.

Dietary information. Potatoes contain a fair to large amount of vitamin C, in addition to some of the B vitamins, iron, phosphorus, and other minerals. One medium potato (three to a pound) contains 92 calories.

See also Sweet Potato.

PUMPKIN

A vegetable of autumn, the pumpkin is a member of a large family that includes squash, watermelons, cucumbers, and gourds. But custom has made it more than a mere vegetable. It has become a symbol of Halloween for American children and of Thanksgiving-dinner dessert for meal planners.

Pumpkins grow on long vines and come in assorted sizes—from several inches (7.6 to 10.1 cm) to 2 feet (60.9 cm) in diameter. They grew in South and Central America and Mexico long before the arrival of the first Europeans. Pumpkin is one of the few main-course vegetables that can practically claim being a fruit, since it does so well as a pie filling or in custards.

Peak season. Late October.

Amount to buy. A 5-pound (2.3 kg) pumpkin yields about 4½ cups (1.1 ml) of mashed, cooked pumpkin.

Selection. The shape is unimportant, unless you are planning on making a jack-o'-lantern. Look for bright-colored, firm, unblemished pumpkins. For cooking, the smaller ones have less waste and usually more tender flesh.

Storage. Keep cool until ready to use.

Preparation and serving. Halve or quarter the pumpkin and remove the seeds and stringy portions. Cut into small pieces and peel off the rind. Cook, covered, in a small amount of lightly salted water for 25 to 40 minutes. A large amount of water is not recommended, since the pumpkin is a watery vegetable. Drain after cooking and mash thoroughly, then place in a strainer and allow to drain for 30 minutes to get rid of excess liquid. (Pumpkin may also be baked; *see* Squash, page 71.) Cooked, mashed pumpkin is used for many preparations such as pie, bread, muffins, custards, and puddings as well as for stuffing with various combinations of meats and vegetables or seafood.

Dietary information. Pumpkin is high in vitamin A and has other minerals. One pound (454 g) of raw pumpkin with rind and seeds contains 83 calories.

RADISHES

The radish, a member of the mustard family, is a fine vegetable with interesting taste and texture. Its use should not be confined to being an object that is carved into a rose as a garniture for other foods. Crisp radishes served with cheeses and crusty French bread make a lovely snack or summertime lunch.

Peak season. Available fresh all year, with peak season May through July.

Amount to buy. Two bunches or bags will serve four to six.

Varieties. The main varieties are the globular red radish and the long, white, mild-flavored radish called "icicle." The globular ones range in size from 1 to 4 inches (2.54 to 10.2 cm) in diameter; the long ones, from 3 to 10 inches (7.6 to 25 cm) in length. There are also globular white, long red, and long black radishes. The black radish has a sharp flavor and is often grated into a salad.

Selection. Radishes should be smooth, crisp, and firm; those that are soft, spongy, or wilted should not be used. Since radishes keep better without their tops, they are often sold in plastic bags containing from 4 to 8 ounces (113.5 to 227 g) of topped radishes.

Storage. Radishes will keep in the refrigerator for at least two weeks if their tops have been removed.

Preparation and serving. Radishes, well scrubbed, may be served whole, or they may be sliced, chopped, and grated and added to salads. They may also be cooked and eaten with a cream sauce or sliced and sautéed with other vegetables. In some countries, radish tops are cooked and eaten as greens.

Radish lore

Radishes, believed to have originated in China, were highly regarded in ancient Egypt. As a measure of the esteem in which they were held in ancient Greece, they were served in gold dishes, while beets and turnips rated only silver or lead. Many centuries later in Europe, they were accredited with all manner of magical healing properties, from detecting the presence of witches to curing insanity and warts. It was said that radish juice was even effective in curing corns.

Raise your own

Radishes are the easiest and fastest vegetable to grow. Even if you don't have a plot of ground, you can make do with a 6-inch container and a window sill that gets five or six hours of sun or the equivalent under fluorescent lights. The container should have drainage holes in the bottom and be about 12 inches deep. Radishes mature in about three weeks, and you can keep sowing for a continuous crop.

A good potting mix is equal parts of packaged soil, peat moss, and vermiculite mixed in with a bit of bonemeal. Follow the plant directions on the seed package and keep the seedlings moist but not soggy. Once the radishes come up, thin the seedlings to about 1 inch apart and water generously.

Rhubarb as medicine

"Rhubarb and soda" has been part of the pharmacopoeia for centuries. The rhubarb used medicinally is entirely different from the garden variety that ends up as a pie filling. The first comes from the root of a plant and has been used as a combined cathartic and astringent for thousands of years.

The plant is thought to have originated in the cold regions of central Asia and was grown in China and Tibet. For a long time it was imported into Europe through Russia. The root was called "Turkish" or "Russian rhubarb" and is now known commercially as "East Indian" or "Chinese rhubarb."

Dietary information. There are 17 calories in 3½ ounces (100 g) of radishes. They supply some vitamin C and have a fair amount of potassium and magnesium, besides other minerals and vitamins, but their leading value is as an appetite stimulant. They are also a valuable detergent food for the teeth.

DAIKON

Daikon (DIE-kon) is a Japanese radish, huge quantities of which are grown in both Hawaii and Japan. It is long and tapered, from 8 to 10 inches (20.3 to 25.4 cm) long and about 1¼ to 1½ inches (3.2 to 3.8 cm) in diameter at the top. Similar in taste to the regular radish but slightly hotter, it keeps very well in the refrigerator, as do other radishes.

Daikons are often pickled whole and served shredded as a relish; thinly sliced they are added to soups or cut into thin strips and combined with other vegetables.

Daikon is high in vitamin C, calcium, phosphorus, and potassium. One pound (454 g) contains 67 calories.

RHUBARB

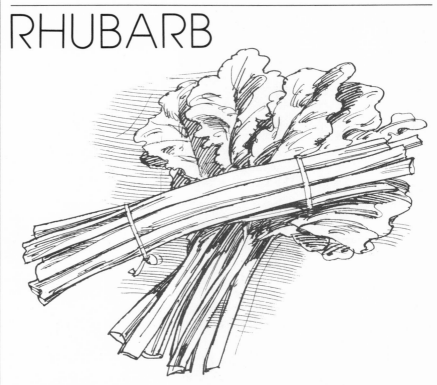

In contrast to the plants that are botanically fruits but are eaten as vegetables—tomatoes and eggplant, to name just two—we have the reverse situation in rhubarb, which is botanically a vegetable but is eaten as a fruit. It is frequently referred to as "pie plant," for reasons that anyone who has ever eaten a tart, mouth-watering rhubarb pie can figure out. Rhubarb is a member of the same family as sorrel.

Peak season. February through June.

Amount to buy. One and one-half pounds (681 g) of rhubarb will serve four people.

Selection. Look for crisp, long stalks that may vary in color from light pink (hothouse variety) to cherry red. The stalk, flat on one side and round on the other, should be fairly thick. Stale rhubarb gives itself away by its wilted, flabby look; it will not be flavorful. The condition of the leaves (which, however, are not always present) is a reliable guide in judging freshness. The younger stems with immature leaves are usually the most tender and have the most delicate flavor.

Storage. Fresh rhubarb stalks in good condition can be stored in the refrigerator for two to four weeks. They wilt quickly at room temperature.

Preparation and serving. Wash rhubarb and peel, if necessary, but discard the leaves. Not only are the leaves bitter, but they also contain oxalic acid, which, if ingested in large quantities, can cause death. Only the rhubarb stalk is suitable for eating. Besides being made into pies, tarts, or puddings, rhubarb may be cut up and stewed (for about 10 minutes after it has come to a boil) or baked (about 20 minutes), and served as a breakfast dish, a side dish with other meals, or dessert. Rhubarb needs a considerable amount of sugar to counteract its acidity. It combines well with strawberries or apples.

Dietary information. Rhubarb provides a fair amount of vitamins A and C, in addition to potassium and magnesium. One pound (454 g) of fresh, partly trimmed rhubarb contains 54 calories; ½ cup (120 ml) of cooked, sweetened rhubarb, 169 calories.

ROMAINE *See* Lettuce.

RUTABAGAS

Rutabagas are often called "yellow turnips," although they are a different species from turnips. Rutabagas (*rotobagge*, in Swedish) are called "Swedish turnips" or "Swedes" in Europe. They are nutritionally superior to the turnip, but they are not as widely used. In appearance they are elongated globes, more yellowish and firmer fleshed than turnips. The flesh is usually deep yellow or orange, like that of the sweet potato. They have a strong flavor that many find most pleasant.

Rutabagas are introduced

Rutabagas were used for family food and livestock fodder in France and southern Europe during the seventeenth century. There is no record of the vegetable before that, so it is comparatively new—far more recent than the turnip, which is an ancient vegetable. The rutabaga's ancestry indicates that it may be a hybrid—a cross between a type of cabbage and a turnip. It has cabbage-like leaves and a swollen neck with ridges—different from the turnip.

The English have always been very fond of this vegetable and were the first to bring the "Swedes," the name by which they were known in Europe, to this country. In some parts of the United States Swedes are a traditional part of Thanksgiving dinner, either mashed or buttered.

The "John-go-to-bed-at-noon" vegetable

The salsify has a flower like a huge dandelion that closes in the middle of the day. Consequently, in England it is known as the "John-go-to-bed-at-noon" vegetable.

Salsify has been known in southern Europe and North Africa for about two thousand years. It was in the United States before the nineteenth century and was one of the vegetables that Thomas Jefferson experimented with on his farm in Virginia. It was a popular root vegetable in the United States a few generations back, until for some unknown reason it fell into disfavor, but it now seems to be winning new friends.

The young leaves of the salsify plant can be used in salads. Home gardeners find salsify a satisfactory crop because the roots do not freeze in cold weather. They can remain underground and be picked throughout the winter as needed. Indeed, the flavor is improved after exposure to cold temperatures.

Peak season. October through February.

Amount to buy. One large rutabaga should serve four or more. One pound (454 g) of cooked rutabagas will make 2 cups (480 ml), or about two portions.

Varieties. There are white-fleshed and yellow-fleshed rutabagas, but the commercially grown ones are mostly yellow fleshed.

Selection. Rutabagas should be smooth-skinned, firm, and heavy for their size, although size does not affect quality.

Storage. Store at cool room temperature (about 60°F [16° C]). Storing below 50°F (10°C) can chill and injure the vegetable. Properly stored, a rutabaga will keep for several months.

Preparation and serving. Peel the rutabaga, cut into chunks or slices, and cook in a large quantity of boiling, salted water until tender. Rutabagas are generally dipped in edible wax to preserve them and improve their appearance before being sent to market, but, since they *must* be peeled before cooking, this will present no problem. Drain well, and mash and season with butter or margarine, salt, pepper, and herbs of your choice. Rutabagas can also be served as fritters or pancakes or fried. They combine well with mashed potatoes, carrots, apples, and other fruits and vegetables. They can be cut in strips and eaten raw.

Dietary information. A 3½-ounce (100 g) portion of raw rutabaga contains about 46 calories; cooked, 35 calories. They have more vitamins A and C than turnips, and more of other vitamins and minerals, but less iron. They are low in sodium.

SALSIFY

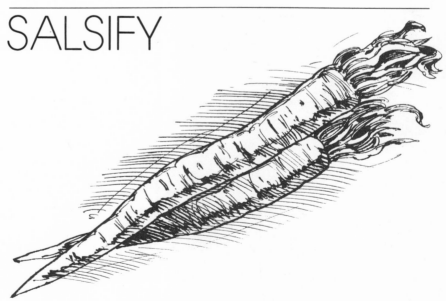

Salsify is an early-fall root vegetable that is sometimes called "oyster plant," "vegetable oyster," and, incorrectly, "vegetable marrow." It was given the name of oyster plant because it was said to have the flavor of oysters, a claim some people would dispute. However, it has a bland, pleasant quality, and, when carefully prepared, is most satisfactory.

Salsify looks somewhat like parsnips, except that the tops look like heavy grass. Like the parsnip, its flavor improves after exposure to cold temperatures. Salsify is long, rather black on the outside (although there is also a white-skinned variety), and about 1 inch (2.54 cm) in diameter at the heart.

Peak season. October and November.

Amount to buy. Plan on two roots for each average serving.

Selection. Select plump, firm, small- to medium-sized roots without blemishes or soft spots.

Storage. Salsify may be stored for several weeks in the vegetable crisper of the refrigerator.

Preparation and serving. The root discolors on exposure to the air, so scrape well and toss immediately into water to which some lemon juice has been added. (Salsify may also be cooked unpeeled.) The scraped roots may be cut into 2- or 3-inch (5.1 to 7.6 cm) pieces or cooked whole. Cook in boiling, salted water until just tender, 10 to 15 minutes. Remove and drain thoroughly. Salsify may be dressed with melted butter or margarine, salt, and pepper and sprinkled with chopped chives or parsley; it may also be served in a rich cream sauce or sliced and sautéed.

Dietary information. Raw salsify ranges in calories from 13 per 3½ ounces (100 g) for the freshly picked vegetable to 82 calories after storage. The corresponding range for cooked salsify is from 12 to 70 calories. It contains potassium, phosphorus, calcium, and iron. It is low in sodium and in vitamins.

SCALLIONS *See* Onions.

SHALLOTS *See* Onions.

SORREL

The slightly lemon-flavored sorrel, or sourgrass, has always enjoyed more popularity in Europe than in this country. The French call it *oseille* and make many fine dishes with it. Sorrel is handled like spinach, which it resembles in texture but not in taste. Its leaves, light green and rather dull in color, are narrow and often pointed in shape, like an arrowhead. Its acid taste adds a refreshing sharpness to soups, sauces, salads, omelettes, and cooked greens like spinach and chard. It is perhaps best known as the principal ingredient in a soup called schav. Schav is traditionally made with sorrel and chicken or veal broth and eggs, and is served either hot or cold.

Peak season. Spring and summer.

Amount to buy. Sorrel is usually sold in bunches. One bunch (about 2 cups [480 ml] of leaves) is sufficient for most purposes, but if you are planning to serve it as a creamed vegetable, figure on 2 pounds (908 g) for four persons.

Selection. Leaves should be fresh-looking and unblemished. Young, small leaves are best for salad.

Storage. Wash and dry leaves well and store in refrigerator crisper in a plastic bag. Use as soon as possible.

Preparation and serving. Strip the leaves from the stalks and discard the stalks. When the leaves are fresh, they may be finely shredded and

Sorrel omelet

The tang of sorrel leaves lends a special brightness and flavor to an egg omelet.

1 small bunch sorrel
6 eggs
½ teaspoon salt
Freshly ground pepper
2 tablespoons butter or margarine

Wash the sorrel leaves, dry, and coarsely chop enough to give you about ½ cup. Break the eggs into a deep bowl, add salt and pepper, and beat with a wire whisk only enough to break up the yolks and mix smoothly with the whites. Do not overbeat.

Stir the sorrel leaves into the egg mixture and let stand at room temperature for at least 45 minutes. When ready to serve, heat a 10½-inch omelet pan, add the butter or margarine, and, when melted, tilt the pan to grease the bottom and sides. Lightly beat the eggs once more and pour them quickly into the pan. Make the omelet, lifting it with a spatula as it cooks to let the top liquid run underneath the cooked portion, so the omelet will cook in layers. When there is no more liquid on the top, the omelet is done; it will finish cooking on its way to the table. Fold the omelet into a half-moon shape and flip it onto a heated platter. Serves four.

Wanderings of the spinach plant

History tells us that spinach originated in Persia, where it was cultivated in the fourth century, but Europeans did not learn of it until seven hundred years later. The Moors developed such a liking for it that they called it the "prince of vegetables" and brought it to Spain, along with their architecture and other influences. The Crusaders returning home to England from Asia Minor also took spinach back with them. In many parts of Europe spinach became known as the "Spanish vegetable," and during the Middle Ages the monks ate it on their fast days—not, we hope, as a penance.

Spinach reached the New World in colonial times and by the nineteenth century was a well-established part of the American cuisine, even though at that time it was considered necessary to cook it until it became a sodden, limp mass.

Spinach and mushroom casserole

This preparation is puffy and light enough to have people mistake it for a soufflé.

    2 pounds spinach
    3 tablespoons cooking oil
    1 clove garlic, minced
    1 pound mushrooms, finely chopped
    3 tablespoons lemon juice
    ½ teaspoon salt
       Freshly ground pepper
    ½ cup dried bread crumbs, plus addi-
       tional for topping
    ⅔ cup mayonnaise
    1 tablespoon Parmesan cheese

Cook the spinach according to the directions in "Preparation and serving." Drain well and chop, then set aside.

Heat the oil in a large skillet; add the garlic and heat until it turns golden. Add the mushrooms, then sprinkle with the lemon juice, salt, and pepper and cook over medium heat for 3 to 4 minutes, before the mushrooms begin to give off liquid. Remove from the heat and add the chopped spinach, ½ cup bread crumbs, and mayonnaise and mix well. Taste for seasoning. Place the mixture in a shallow, oiled casserole or glass pie dish, sprinkle with the Parmesan cheese and additional bread crumbs and place in a 350°F oven for about 15 minutes, or until heated through. Serves 4.

added to a salad or sliced tomatoes dressed with oil and vinegar. The leaves should be cooked like spinach in the moisture that adheres to them after washing. Cook, uncovered, about 10 minutes, stirring a few times, until wilted. Drain well, chop leaves finely, and season with salt, pepper, butter or margarine, and a few tablespoons of cream.

Dietary information. One pound (454 g) of sorrel contains 89 calories. It is extraordinarily high in vitamins A and C, in addition to other vitamins and minerals.

SPINACH

Spinach is one of our most commonly used vegetables and the most important crop grown for greens in the United States—this in spite of its having been badly treated by generations of people who overcooked it and by the likes of the cartoon character Popeye, who relentlessly reminded the children of a few decades ago that they had better eat their spinach if they wanted to grow up strong. This was scarcely a public image that would enhance the taste possibilities of a food or titillate an appetite. Actually, spinach is a beautiful, versatile vegetable with fine flavor. Besides serving as an accompaniment to the main course, it can be used in salads, soufflés, sauces, tarts; as an appetizer or for cream soups; as a bed for poultry, fish, meat, or eggs; and in combination with a wide range of other ingredients, such as chopped mushrooms or clams. It is used to give a green color to noodles and mayonnaise (*sauce verte*).

Peak season. Available fresh all year, with peak in January through May.

Amount to buy. Usually 2 pounds (908 g) of spinach will serve four persons. One pound (454 g) of raw spinach will yield 4 cups (960 ml) of leaves and 1½ cups (360 ml) cooked.

Varieties. Either curly or flat-leaf types are good for cooking. Other varieties include the beet grown throughout the summer and fall only for its spinach-like leaves.

Selection. Leaves should be a good green color, clean and fresh looking. Avoid bunches with yellow leaves that are wilted, bruised, or crushed. Spinach often comes prewashed and packed in bags. The bags should feel full and spring back easily when pressed.

Storage. After spinach is washed and drained, it can be stored in a plastic bag in the refrigerator crisper drawer from three to five days, although it is better to use it as soon as possible.

Preparation and serving. Spinach now comes to the market cleaner than in the past, but it must still be washed carefully to remove all grit. Trim off the roots and heavier stems, and wash the leaves in a sinkful of lukewarm water to which a little salt has been added; this will remove dirt more effectively than cold water. Spinach that is especially sandy should be washed in two or more waters. Repeat until there is no grit remaining at the bottom of the sink. Lift the leaves out of the final water, rinse in cold water, and drain well in a colander or salad spinner.

Before cooking spinach, rinse the leaves again. Chop the large or coarse ones. Steam the spinach in a covered pot, with only the water that clings to the leaves, only until it is wilted—5 to 8 minutes. Turn once or twice with wooden spoons. It may be served *en branche*, as cooked, or chopped. Season with melted butter, salt, pepper, and a pinch of nutmeg, or a splash of lemon juice or vinegar. It is delicious creamed or stir-fried, Chinese style, in hot oil seasoned with a garlic clove. The stir-frying takes under five minutes.

The fresh taste and pleasing texture of very young, tender spinach leaves are a splendid addition to salads, either alone or mixed with other greens. Raw spinach with raw sliced mushrooms tossed with a hearty French dressing makes a fine salad, worthy of a main luncheon course.

Dietary information. Raw spinach provides vitamin A, some vitamin C, and calcium, iron, potassium, magnesium, and other minerals. One pound (454 g) of untrimmed raw spinach contains 86 calories. Raw spinach is considered a helpful detergent food, one that cleans the teeth.

SQUASH

The squash family offers a wide diversity of flavors, colors, and textures. The many varieties of squash are divided into "summer" and "winter" categories. These terms are not quite accurate and can be confusing, because, actually, "summer" types are available all winter and "winter" squash is in the markets in the late summer and fall as well as in winter.

However, there is a difference between the two types. The summer squash are quick growing and are picked and eaten while still immature, before the seeds and rinds harden. Outside of the United States they are generally referred to as "vegetable marrows." The winter types are all hard shelled and are adapted for long storage. The seeds are expected to be hard and inedible and are scooped out before or after cooking.

SUMMER SQUASH

The popular varieties in the soft-shelled, immature category include the *yellow crookneck* and *yellow straightneck*, shaped as their names describe. They are moderately warted, with light yellow skin that becomes deeper in color in the mature stage; the flesh is creamy yellow. *Zucchini* and *cocozelle* are cylindrical and dark green with smooth skin. Zucchini is also called "Italian marrow" and is known as *courgette* in some European countries. *Scallop*, also known as *pattypan* or *cymling*, is a scalloped white or whitish-green disk that looks somewhat like a small cushion with a scalloped edge.

Peak season. Generally available all year, but most plentiful in the summer.

Amount to buy. Two pounds (908 g) will serve four people.

Selection. The squash should be obviously fresh, with good, characteristic color and heavy for its size. The rind should be tender enough to puncture with your fingernail.

Storage. Store in a plastic bag in the refrigerator and use within a week.

Preparation and serving. Summer squash does not need to be peeled if tender. The crooknecks or straightnecks can be sliced or cut into strips.

An American vegetable

Squash was another gift from the New World to the Old. Distinctly American, it originated in Central America and Mexico. It was grown by the American Indians throughout the country, and it was not until the sixteenth century that the Europeans learned about it. Squash is a member of a very large botanical family that includes gourds, melons, pumpkins, and cucumbers.

Smaller can be better

It was not so many years ago that the pattypan and yellow crookneck and straightneck squash were allowed to mature until they reached an obscenely large size. The pattypan was grown to 8 to 10 inches across, and the yellow squash reached similarly monstrous proportions. The results were a coarse-meated, large-seeded, thoroughly forgettable foodstuff. An enterprising West Coast farmer decided to sell them small and underdeveloped, and an enthusiastic public welcomed them. And instead of boiling them for hours into a flavorless sodden pulp, as was done years back, cooks discovered that young, tender squash, lightly sautéed or steamed, provided a delicious dish.

The very small zucchini or *courgette*, when available, has a lovely delicate flavor and texture and is worth looking for. It needs only to be boiled or steamed and requires no embellishment, except perhaps some melted butter or margarine, salt, and pepper.

Names and more names

As we have seen, the summer squash, particularly zucchini, parade under a wide assortment of names—vegetable marrow, Italian squash, Italian marrow, and *courgette*. Pattypan is known as "cymling," "scalloped squash," "scallops," and "custard squash." Chayote is known to Creole cooks as "mirliton," and in South America it is called "mango squash." Floridians call it the "vegetable pear," and Mexicans call it *chayote*.

Potage vert

This is a delicious cold soup whose origin will elude most people. The rather bland vegetables that create it take on a most delightful and hard-to-identify flavor.

  3 medium-sized yellow squash
  3 medium-sized zucchini
  1 scant cup water
  1-1½ cups chicken broth
   1 small clove garlic, crushed (optional)
   Salt and freshly ground pepper
  ¾ cup diced, cooked chicken
  ¼ cup plain yogurt

Wash the squashes well, unpeeled, and remove the stem ends. Slice about 12 paper-thin slices from the ends of the zucchini, chop coarsely, and set aside for garnish. Slice the remaining squashes and cook, covered, in a saucepan in the water seasoned with the chicken-broth cube and crushed garlic. When soft—about 10 minutes—pour the vegetables and liquid into the blender and blend until liquefied.

Transfer to a bowl and add enough chicken broth to give you the consistency you want; the soup should be on the thick side, like heavy cream. Add salt and pepper; how much seasoning you need will depend upon the saltiness of the chicken broth. To serve, add a heaping tablespoon of the diced chicken, a spot of yogurt and a sprinkle of coarsely chopped zucchini slices to each portion. This may also be served hot. Serves 6.

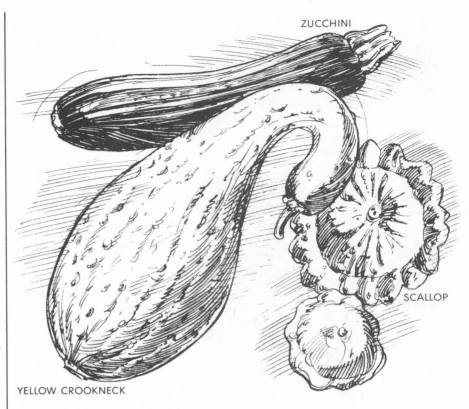

ZUCCHINI

SCALLOP

YELLOW CROOKNECK

Zucchini, one of the most delicious of all the squash family, can be cooked whole if small, or sliced or cut into strips. It can be scooped out and stuffed with meat or vegetables and baked. Both the yellow squash and zucchini are splendid raw served with a dip, or added to a salad. They also make a wonderful soup. The pattypan can be left whole or cut into quarters. Squash is a watery vegetable, so it should be cooked in very little water. It can be steamed, fried, or sautéed in oil or butter.

Dietary information. Soft-shell squash contain vitamins A and C, potassium, and magnesium; they are low in sodium. One-half cup (120 ml) cooked zucchini or cocozelle contains 9 calories; the same amount of scallop, 19 calories; the same amount of yellow, 14.

WINTER SQUASH

Popular varieties of the hard-shelled mature squash, with their hearty orange-yellow flesh, include the dark green, deeply ridged *acorn*, shaped as its name implies. It is exactly the right size for two servings and the right shape to hold a variety of stuffings. The massive *Hubbard* can weigh as much as 15 pounds and is sometimes used instead of pumpkin in pie or pudding recipes. The dark green *buttercup* is named for the turban-like cap at the blossom end. Others are the smooth, hard *butternut*, shaped like an elongated pear and dull tan in color, and the nearly cylindrical *large banana*, which changes from a pale olive gray to a creamy pink in storage. There is also the lesser-known *chayote* (chay-o-tee), a tropical product, better known in Mexico. It is dark green, round to pear shaped, and has light green flesh.

Peak season. Available fresh all year but most abundant in fall and winter.

Amount to buy. Two to three pounds (908 g to 1.3 kg) should serve four people. With the larger winter squash, the number of portions you need will determine how much you should buy.

Selection. Rinds should be hard, smooth, and unblemished. A soft rind indicates immaturity and thin flesh.

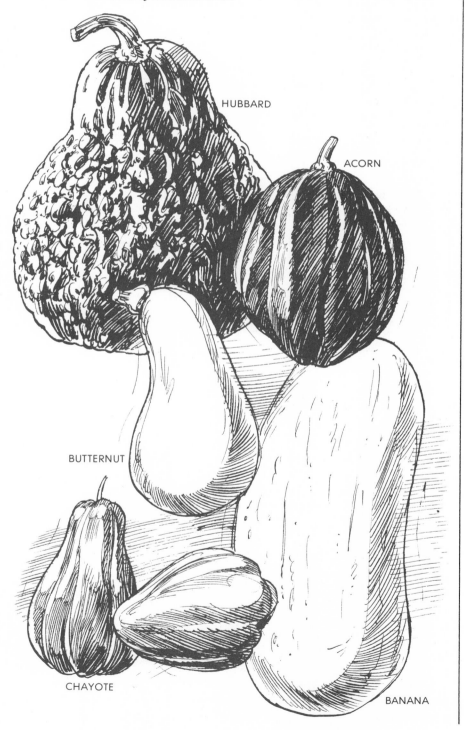

HUBBARD

ACORN

BUTTERNUT

CHAYOTE

BANANA

Baked acorn squash

2 acorn squashes
1 tablespoon oil
½ teaspoon salt
Paprika
4 teaspoons butter or margarine
4 teaspoons light brown sugar

Cut the squashes in half crosswise, parallel to the stem end. Trim a thin slice from the top and bottom so they will sit firmly on their bases and not topple. Remove the seeds and stringy pulp from the cavities, brush the cavities with the oil, and sprinkle lightly with salt and paprika. salt and paprika.

Cover the bottom of a flat baking dish with about ½ inch of hot water and place the squashes, cut side down, in the pan. Bake in a 375° oven for 35 minutes. Take a look once in a while to make sure the water has not evaporated, and add a bit more boiling water if necessary. Remove from the oven, pour out any water remaining in the pan, and turn squashes cut side up. Brush the cavities and tops with the butter and sprinkle with the brown sugar. Return to the oven for another 10 or 15 minutes, or until soft and tender. Serves four.

Variations: Sprinkle the cavities and tops with browned sesame seeds.

Fill the cavities with cooked green peas or a combination of green peas and sliced mushrooms.

Brothers and sisters under the skin

Pumpkins, squashes, watermelons, cucumbers, muskmelons, and gourds all belong to one family—the cucurbit family. It is a big family and also a clannish one, as evidenced by the ease with which vegetables of the same type can be substituted for each other. For example, summer squashes such as zucchini and cocozelle can be used interchangeably; and either one can take the place of cucumbers or eggplant in almost any recipe.

Pumpkins and winter squashes, too, are interchangeable. There is basically no difference between the two, except for the names. These have been traced back to the early settlers who chose to differentiate between them. Had it not been for these hardy souls, we might carve a Halloween squash instead of a Halloween pumpkin at the end of October.

A pleasant casserole can be made from either winter squash, such as hubbard, or the inside of your Halloween pumpkin. You will need about five pounds of squash or pumpkin. Bake in a 375°F. oven for about an hour or boil the vegetable until tender. Mash well and mix with one stick of melted butter or margarine, a teaspoon of salt and an equal amount of freshly ground pepper, a pinch of nutmeg and ¼ cup of dry sherry. Transfer to a well-greased baking dish and garnish the top with toasted pecan halves. Bake in a 375°F. oven for 15 minutes, or until heated through. Serves 4 to 6.

Storage. Hard-skinned squash can be stored for months in a cool, dry temperature. At higher temperatures they will dry out and not remain edible for as long.

Preparation and serving. The simplest way to prepare winter squash is to cut it into halves (as with acorn squash) or portion-sized wedges, scrape out the seeds and center fibers, and bake in the rind until the pulp is tender. It can be served with butter or margarine, honey, or a sprinkling of brown sugar, cinnamon, nutmeg, or sesame seeds. It can also be peeled and cut into chunks and steamed or boiled, then mashed and served like potatoes. Butternut squash is delicious prepared in this manner.

Dietary information. Winter squash is higher in vitamin A and contains less water than the summer varieties. It does not lose any nutritional value during storage; rather, the carotene content increases. Half a cup (132 ml) of baked winter squash averages about 70 calories.

SPAGHETTI SQUASH

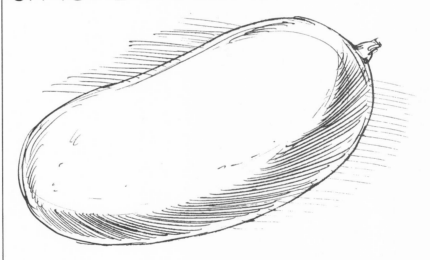

Although spaghetti squash is classed as a squash, it is actually an edible gourd and not a true squash. It is also known as "cucuzzi," "calabash," and "suzza melon." It has a smooth skin and is very light green in color, somewhat like an unripe honeydew melon. It is a most interesting vegetable, for after it is cooked the flesh falls into long strands, like spaghetti.

Peak season. Summer months.

Amount to buy. Three pounds (1.3 kg) will serve four.

Selection. Rind should be firm and hard, without blemishes.

Storage. Store in a cool, dry place. Spaghetti squash will hold for weeks.

Preparation and serving. Wash well and bake, whole, for 1 hour at 325°F (163°C). Cut in two and remove the seeds. The squash may be served in the shell, or the spaghetti-like strands scooped out and seasoned with a lump of butter or margarine, salt, pepper, and a sprinkling of Parmesan cheese or a tomato sauce.

Dietary information. Spaghetti squash is similar to other summer squashes in nutritional values. It is low in calories.

SWEET POTATOES AND YAMS

The sweet potato, one of the most complete foods known, is a staple for the populations of some tropical and subtropical regions. An elongated or roundish tuber, its skin color can range from light yellowish tan to brownish red. The flesh is white or yellow; the latter is more popular in the United States.

There are many varieties of sweet potatoes, but mainly they are of two types: those with dry, yellow flesh and those with soft, sweet, moist, deep yellow or orange-red flesh, erroneously called "yams." Actually, yams are a different species, one rarely seen in the United States. The Louisiana yam with its orange-colored moist flesh was so named to distinguish it from the dry sweet potato.

Peak season. Available all year, with peak season October through December.

Amount to buy. Allow one potato per portion. There are about three medium-sized potatoes to a pound. One pound (454 g) of cooked and mashed sweet potatoes will yield 1¾ cups (420 ml).

Varieties. Dry-meated and moist-meated types.

Selection. You can disregard skin color in buying sweet potatoes, but look for thick, chunky, medium-sized sweets that taper toward the ends. They should be bright and clean and free from blemishes. Avoid those with any sign of decay, such as shriveled, discolored ends, for such deterioration spreads quickly and affects the taste of the entire potato.

Storage. Store in a closed bag or box in a cool, dry place—not the refrigerator—and use as soon as possible. Sweet potatoes decay more rapidly than the white and are good for only short periods of storage.

Preparation and serving. The moist-meated and dry-meated sweet potatoes are interchangeable in use, although some people prefer the moist-meated for baking and glazing. They may be baked, or boiled, then fried, mashed, or glazed. To bake, scrub well and place in a 400°F (204°C) oven for 35 minutes to 1 hour, or until they feel soft. (Protect your fingers with a towel.) Boil the potatoes, unpeeled, in enough boiling, salted water to cover. Test for doneness with a fork. The skins slip off easily after cooking, so drain, peel, and season with melted butter or margarine, salt, and pepper. Sweet potato is also used in biscuits, muffins, pies, custards, cookies, and cake.

Dietary information. One medium boiled, peeled sweet potato provides more than twice the recommended daily allowance of vitamin A for an adult, besides a goodly amount of vitamin C and other vitamins and minerals. Three and a half ounces (100 g) of boiled sweet potato contain 114 calories; the same amount, baked, contains 141 calories.

SWISS CHARD *See* Chard.

Same name, different family

Except for the similarity in being tubers of about the same size, sweet potatoes and potatoes are in no way related. The sweet potato belongs to the morning-glory family, and when grown in the tropics it produces a long trailing vine and lavender blossoms like the morning glory's. The white potato, on the other hand, belongs to the same family as the nightshade. It is said that it was the sweet potato—called *batata*—that Columbus first found in the West Indies, which would tend to give the sweet more claim to the name of "potato" than the white tuber, with which it was later confused.

Sweet potato plant

Most commercially available sweet potatoes are treated to prevent bud sprouting, but, if you can find an untreated potato, you can grow an attractive houseplant.

Place the uncut sweet potato in a large vase or jar of water so that just the bottom touches the water. Place in a bright, warm place. Soon sprouts will begin to emerge and eventually leaves and vinelike growth. After the shoots appear, it can be potted in rich soil with a bit of sand, or it can continue to grow in water.

Poi

Taro root is believed to have come originally from China, and it was the staff of life for the ancient Hawaiians. They worked hard to plant the crops of taro, irrigating the fields by sending water through bamboo pipes. Poi is made by pounding or grinding the roasted peeled roots of the taro plant, and this starchy food paste is still eaten.

Poi, which has been basic to the diets of many Asian and Oceanic countries for a long time, is easily digestible; indeed, it might be noted that the Kanaka language used in many poi-eating lands has no word for indigestion.

When is a fruit not a fruit?

The answer could be when it is a tomato. Botanically, the tomato is a fruit—more specifically, a berry—but its use in soups and as an accompaniment to the main course, never as a dessert, has earned it the designation of a vegetable. This was affirmed by a decision of the U.S. Supreme Court in 1893, when an importer claimed that tomatoes were a fruit and therefore not subject to duty. The Supreme Court decided otherwise; tomatoes remained a legal vegetable.

History of the tomato

Most authorities agree the tomato originated in South America—probably in what is now Peru, Ecuador, and Bolivia. Its name is derived from the Aztec word *xtomatle.* The first tomatoes were brought to Europe from the New World in the late 1400s, but a persistent superstition about their lethal properties prevented their widespread acceptance as a food for hundreds of years.

To freeze tomatoes

It is a simple matter to freeze tomatoes when they are at their best in peak season and provide your household with a supply of ripe, frozen tomatoes for use in cooking. Select tomatoes that are fully ripe but firm. Plunge them into boiling water for 30 seconds and then into cold water. Peel off the skins and cut out the cores and stem ends. Pack in freezer containers or plastic freezer bags, or wrap in freezer-weight aluminum foil or freezer paper and seal with freezer tape. At 0°F or below, they will keep for eight to twelve months— much less if the freezer temperature is only a few degrees higher.

TARO ROOT

Taro root, also known as "dasheen," has become familiar to travelers and others largely through its extensive use in the Pacific Islands. In Hawaii taro is eaten mostly in the form of poi, a slightly fermented sticky food paste that usually accompanies meat, fish, or vegetables. Some travelers find poi palatable, while others are less complimentary.

Taro is raised and used mostly in the southern states; it is also cultivated in many warm regions of the temperate zone, such as Egypt, Syria, Japan, and New Zealand—wherever there is wet soil and a long growing season.

The flesh of cooked dasheens ranges from purple or violet to a light cream shade. The more deeply colored violet "corms," as the taro roots are called, are considered superior in flavor to the cream-colored ones.

Peak season. Available all year in its natural growing regions.

Selection. Taro roots should be firm and unblemished, leaves and stems fresh looking.

Storage. Store in the refrigerator and use as needed.

Preparation and serving. Taro root may be baked, steamed, boiled, or used in soup like potatoes; it is inedible unless cooked. Skins are removed after cooking. Taro is also baked into cakes.

Dietary information. There are 98 calories in 3½ ounces (100 g) of the tubers of raw taro and a goodly amount of minerals and vitamins, including vitamins A, G, and others. A similar amount of leaves and stems contain 40 calories, plus calcium and a small amount of protein.

TOMATOES

Less than one hundred fifty years ago tomatoes were totally unknown in this country, but today they have become a year-round vegetable, grown in every state, including Alaska. A kitchen without them is almost unthinkable, and it is regrettable that they are not possessed of the same mouth-watering goodness all through the year.

The best tomatoes are to be found during the summer months, because for the rest of the year the only ones available are those that were artificially cultivated in hothouses or those that had to endure the rigors of being shipped from warmer states. Ripe tomatoes are extremely delicate, so those that must travel long distances are usually harvested when fully grown but still green and hard. They are exposed to ethylene gas during shipping, which changes their color to a deceptively ripe red hue but does nothing to bring the fruit to full maturity. Such tomatoes are really only symbols of tomatoes. They are tasteless, have a mealy texture, and a lower vitamin content than fully grown tomatoes that have ripened on the vine. To distinguish a vine-ripened tomato from a gas-ripened one (without tasting it), smell it. Gassed tomatoes are odorless, and vine-ripened ones have a telltale tomato-y fragrance.

The solution, of course, is to try to buy vine-ripened tomatoes, and to take full advantage of them when they are in season.

Peak season. June through August.

Amount to buy. One pound (454 g) serves two to four, and equals 1½ cups (360 ml) peeled and seeded.

Varieties. The most common are the garden tomatoes, which are large, red, and round. True, old-fashioned beefsteaks are rarely seen commercially, but descendants known as beefsteak varieties are available. They can be recognized by their flat, somewhat elliptical shape from top to bottom and a round or oval-shaped circumference. The small, oval Italian tomatoes known as "egg" or "plum" are excellent for cooking and also for salads. Cherry tomatoes are the smallest of all—about 1 inch (2.54 cm) in diameter. They are either red or yellow and are frequently superior in taste to the garden tomatoes.

Selection. Choose firm, plump tomatoes with a tomato-y smell. Avoid soft, overripe tomatoes with blemishes, bruises, soft spots, or growth cracks. For most purposes, yellow or red just-ripe or slightly underripe tomatoes are best. Ask the retailer for the locally grown varieties; they are more likely to be vine ripened and less likely to be waxed. Underripe tomatoes are preferable to gas ripened. Those harvested with even a slight natural tinge of pink will have good taste when properly ripened at home.

Storage. To ripen at home, store tomatoes in a warm location away from direct sunlight, standing on the flat stem end. (Some people put them in a paper bag.) Once ripe, a tomato can be held in the refrigerator for up to a week. Keep them uncovered on an open shelf, not in a vegetable drawer, where they can be bruised.

Preparation and serving. Wash tomatoes, just before using, in tepid water, which helps to remove chemical fertilizer and pesticides. A good, ripe tomato usually does not need to be peeled, but if the skin appears to be coarse, do peel. There are two methods of peeling tomatoes. Either drop the tomatoes in scalding water for 30 seconds or so—the water should be at the boil—and remove; peel as soon as cool enough to handle. Or hold them, impaled on a long-handled fork, over the gas flame for a moment or two, turning until the skin pops. You can then strip off the skin easily. Raw tomatoes taste best at room temperature or very slightly chilled. To seed a tomato, cut in half crosswise, squeeze gently, and scoop out the seeds. Sprinkle lightly with salt and drain upside down in a colander. Firm green tomatoes can be sliced, dusted lightly with seasoned flour, and fried. They also are delicious pickled.

Dietary information. Tomatoes are high in vitamin C, low in carbohydrates and protein, and a good source of fiber. One small fresh tomato (4 ounces [113.5g]) contains 24 calories.

"Love appele" or deadly poison?

Few foods have had a more checkered past than the tomato. Spanish conquerors introduced the tomato, which was then small and yellow, to Europe via Italy. There it was known as *pomo dei moi* ("apple of the Moors") and *pome d'ore* ("apple of gold"). This soon became *pomme d'amour* ("love apple") in French. By the end of the sixteenth century, both red and yellow *pommes d'amour* were grown in Europe but were used only as garden and table decorations. It seems Europeans were not quite sure what to do with the notorious tomato, for by this time it had acquired the dual reputation of aphrodisiac/poison. The fear of its toxic qualities, which persisted until 1900, can be attributed to the fact that the tomato belongs to the botanical family *Solanaceae*, some of whose other members (such as nightshade) are poisonous. The origin of its rumored aphrodisiacal qualities is not so neatly traced. Certainly the French adulteration of its Italian name had to have played a part in giving it its amorous connotation.

In spite of this less than encouraging beginning, the tomato eventually became an integral part of nearly every cuisine in the world. People ate them and survived, and as time went on, tomatoes became universally accepted. Today we can scarcely imagine cooking without them.

Home gardening

To enjoy fresh-picked, vine-ripened tomatoes, especially those varieties not normally found in the market, grow tomatoes at home. They are easy to raise, and are the most popular vegetable for the home gardener. The smaller varieties can be grown in containers on rooftops, terraces, patios, and even indoors, provided there is enough light. Cherry tomatoes make a charming hanging plant. Tomato plants may be started from seeds or grown from established seedlings, which are sold in plant stores and garden centers.

Juicy tomato slices

When slicing tomatoes for salads or sandwiches, place the tomato stem side up and cut vertical slices as you would cut a loaf of bread. The slices will be firm and retain the juice more effectively than the horizontally cut slices.

For centuries, Europeans have used pigs and dogs to hunt truffles. Although there are some people who claim the ability to detect the odor of truffles growing underground, animals seem to have more talent in this area. Dogs are preferred over pigs because they can be taught to obey commands and not eat the find. The Russians have attempted to train bear cubs and the Sardinians have tried goats, but truffle hounds and truffle pigs are more in general use. After the animals have sniffed out the hiding places, the owner unearths the truffles.

TRUFFLES

More expensive than caviar, the bulbous and unimpressive-looking truffle is a gourmet's delight. To describe it as a wild, subterranean edible fungus—which it is—is to ignore its mystery and distinctive aroma. It has a unique, faintly garlicky scent that permeates any food to which it is added and that, for its admirers, justifies its wildly extravagant cost.

No one has ever been able to cultivate truffles. They grow from 3 inches (7.6 cm) to a foot (30.5 cm) or more underneath the roots of trees, especially scrub oak or beech trees. Their scent while underground cannot generally be detected by humans, but can be sniffed out by animals.

Peak season. All truffles in the United States are imported. Black truffles are shipped fresh in January and part of February, and the white are shipped in October and November. Canned truffles are available all year, but they are far inferior to the fresh and not worth the cost.

Varieties. The two leading varieties are the white, found in parts of northern Italy, and the black from various regions of France, particularly the Périgord region. The black are deep black, with a warty exterior, and their flesh is dark gray veined with white.

Selection. Although the best truffle variety by most people's standards is the black, some food connoisseurs prefer the white Italian. It might be mentioned that dishonest merchants have been known to dye white truffles black. Truffles cost about $20 an ounce and weigh between 1 and 3 ounces (28 to 84 g).

Storage. Fresh truffles should be mixed with dry rice and stored in a covered bowl in the refrigerator. They will stay fresh for up to a week or ten days.

Preparation and serving. The white is rarely cooked. It is generally served raw, in thinly shaved slices, over poultry or meat dishes. The black is usually cooked, although it may also be eaten raw. It is particularly known for its use in pâté.

TURNIPS

The turnip may not be everyone's favorite vegetable, but this indifference could be caused by lack of familiarity with it. The round white tuber with a purple band across the top of the skin, when young and fresh, has a flavor somewhere between a tart apple and a crisp radish. Unfortunately, too many turnips reach the markets when they are oversized and overage and have become woody and bitter.

Some varieties of turnips have been developed especially for the production of greens. Turnip tops have more vitamins and minerals than the roots and can be used raw in salads or cooked as spinach and other greens.

Peak season. Available all year.

Amount to buy. Two pounds (908 g) will serve four.

Varieties. Turnips come in a variety of shapes and colors, all with much the same flavor, but the most common are the white roots with a colorful purple band.

Selection. Some turnips are sold with the tops removed. If the tops are present, they should be young, fresh, and green. Look for small, firm, fairly smooth young tubers, about 2 or 3 inches (5.1 to 7.6 cm) in diameter. Avoid large turnips with obvious fibrous roots.

Storage. Store the tubers in the refrigerator and use as needed; cut off the greens, place them in the crisper drawer of the refrigerator, and use within a week.

Preparation and serving. Remove the turnip tops, and, if they are young and fresh, cook them as you do spinach or serve them raw in a salad. To prepare the tubers, cut a slice from the rootlet end and a slice from the stem end. Turnip skins can be bitter, so peel them first. Turnips can be cooked whole, but they will cook more quickly sliced, diced, or cut into strips. Cook in 2 inches (5.1 cm) of boiling, salted water until just tender; whole turnips will take about 30 minutes and diced or sliced from 10 to 20 minutes. They can be baked with a roast in its drippings, and a turnip or two—not too much or it will overpower the other flavors— will be effective in a stew or vegetable soup.

Dietary information. There are 14 calories in ½ cup (120 ml) of cooked, drained turnip greens; the same amount of boiled, mashed turnips contains 27 calories. Turnip greens are rich in vitamins A and C, with a good amount of magnesium and calcium.

The turnip's past

The turnips we use today are direct descendants of the European varieties that developed in the Mediterranean regions thousands of years ago. The turnip is hardy and will grow in sandy soil where little else thrives.

There was a time when turnips were a symbol of disapproval. They were thrown at any unfortunate in disfavor, much as eggs and tomatoes are used today. A girl who gave a suitor a turnip was giving him a message that in today's vernacular would translate into "Get lost." But gradually the turnip lost its unpleasant connotation, and during the Middle Ages it again became a popular and respected vegetable.

Turnips in mustard-maple sauce

This goes well with poultry or meat. It needs a green vegetable to go with it, however, because it looks very much like white potato when cooked.

    2 pounds small white turnips
    3 tablespoons butter or margarine
    2 teaspoons dry mustard
    1 tablespoon dark brown sugar
    2 tablespoons maple syrup
    Salt and freshly ground pepper

Wash and scrape the turnips. Slice ¼-inch-thick slices and drop into a pot of rapidly boiling, salted water. Cook for exactly 5 minutes after the water has returned to a boil. Drain and set aside. Preheat the oven to 350°F. In the same pot in which you cooked the turnips, melt the butter or margarine and blend in the dry mustard, brown sugar, maple syrup, and a pinch of salt and pepper. Add the turnip slices and coat well. Grease a round shallow baking dish or pie plate and arrange the slices neatly in a single layer in the bottom of the dish. Cover tightly with aluminum foil and bake for 35 minutes. Taste for doneness; the slices should be crisp-tender. Serves 4.

A proliferating plant

The growing of watercress is a reversal of the usual order, for it was cultivated before it grew wild and then not cultivated again until the early nineteenth century. An examination of the way watercress grows will explain this unusual situation. Not only does watercress sprout from seeds, but it also roots easily when just tossed into fresh running water. If the surroundings are favorable, the plant will flourish and spread. It is important that the water in which it is growing be pure and unpolluted. If pollution is present, the watercress may be eaten with safety only if cooked. Watercress is so prolific that one plant will yield a succession of crops in one year and may grow for ten years.

An ancient medicine

As with many other vegetables, watercress was used widely as medicine by the ancient peoples. The Persians believed it helped their children grow and fed it to them liberally. The ancient Greeks saw to it that soldiers ate it for their health, and the Romans believed that eating it would make their hair thick and luxuriant. The application of watercress juice was believed effective in ridding the skin of blemishes.

WATERCRESS

Watercress, a peppery-tasting green, grows best in cool, gently flowing water. It has long stems and small substantial leaves that have a pungent flavor—which is understandable, since it is a member of the mustard family.

Peak season. Watercress is available all year but is most plentiful from May through July.

Amount to buy. Watercress is usually sold in small bunches. One bunch will be adequate for most purposes.

Selection. Leaves should be fresh and bright green; stems should be crisp. Wilted, bruised, or yellowing leaves are signs of inferior quality and improper handling.

Storage. Wash leaves gently but thoroughly in cold water, drain well, and dry on absorbent paper towels or in a salad spinner. Place in a container with a tight-fitting cover and store in the coldest part of the refrigerator. Use as needed. Watercress will keep for a week or more. Keeping watercress loose in the vegetable crisper, where it can be crushed by other vegetables or fruits, is not recommended.

Preparation and serving. Both the tangy leaves and tender stems are used. Clusters of fresh watercress make a most effective garnish for hot or cold dishes. Watercress can be mixed with other greens in salads, but it wilts quickly when dressed and might be better served as a garnish for the salad. Puréed, it makes a delicious soup. The Italians use whole sprigs in their minestrone, and the Chinese include it in their won ton and other soups. It also makes a fine sandwich ingredient.

Dietary information. Watercress is high in vitamin C and also contains iron, calcium, phosphorus, potassium, and vitamin A. There are 19 calories in 3½ ounces (100 g) of watercress.

YAMS *See* Sweet Potatoes and Yams.

ZUCCHINI *See* Squash, Summer.

HERBS

Placebos or panaceas?

Just about every culture in the world has experimented with herbs as cures. The Greeks and Romans believed herbs had the power to heal a wide variety of ailments, and Claudius Galen, the most renowned physician of the ancient world, specialized in herb therapy in treating the patients who flocked to his sanatorium in Pergamum.

The Orientals, too, were early students of herbal medicine, and to this day ginseng and fo-ti-teng, contributions of China and Korea to the field of herbal panaceas, have loyal advocates who believe in the power of these herbs to increase vitality and prolong life.

To Indian medicine men, herbs were as important as are the pharmacists' drugs to the modern physician, and the Indians used plant remedies to cure everything from snakebite and general malaise to epilepsy and the common cold.

Modern medicine discovers herbs

For a long time modern pharmacology dismissed most of the ancient remedies as naive folk medicine. No reputable doctor ever prescribed foxglove as a remedy for rapid heartbeat or a brew of juniper to ensure the birth of a girl—both highly respected medical treatments in many parts of the world for hundreds of years.

But modern medicine has "rediscovered" plants, and twentieth-century pharmacologists readily acknowledge their debt to herbs as the source of some of our most effective drugs. Belladonna and atropine are extracted from deadly nightshade, digitalis is found in foxglove, and male and female sex hormones come from herbs once used by primitive people to combat impotence and increase virility. Obviously, not all ancient remedies and old wives' cures were as absurd as they seemed.

A posthumous Cordon Bleu citation should be awarded to the first courageous cook who, thousands of years ago, tossed a handful of strange, aromatic leaves into a steaming caldron, thereby creating *haute cuisine*. Thanks to that early culinary innovator, we now have countless ways of transforming the simplest fare into a gastronomic treat, simply and inexpensively.

Herbs have become indispensable ingredients in the kitchens of the world. What character would a French bouillabaisse have without a liberal sprinkling of thyme? What would Italian pasta taste like without generous amounts of oregano or basil added to its sauce? How could the Danes cook without dill, or the Indians without coriander?

Until recently, American cooks relied chiefly on the simplest seasonings to flavor their food. Although their colonial ancestors had planted herb gardens outside their kitchen doors, most modern Americans approached herbs with reservation, if not with downright suspicion, and "good American cooking" usually meant a traditional roast along with unadorned potatoes, vegetables, and salad—all hearty and satisfying, but with little personality. Now, however, the American palate, probably inspired by exotic fare sampled in distant lands, has been whetted for more imaginative diets, and there's been a revolution in the American kitchen.

The possibilities of herb cooking are infinite, depending only upon the availability of the right herb and the creativity of the cook. There are no rigid rules. If you're a novice, you'll probably want to follow a good recipe at first, or experiment with simple combinations of just a few herbs. Soon you'll get the "feel" of how much dill or mint to snip into your carrots, how much tarragon to add to a fish sauce, or how much sage and thyme to use in poultry stuffing. Before long you'll be creating your own combinations: a subtle blend for a *fines herbes* omelet for a special Sunday brunch, or a bouquet garni (sprigs of a few of your favorites tied together) to transform an ordinary beef stew into a delicious ragout.

Over three thousand different kinds of herbs have been identified throughout the world, though only some of these have culinary uses. Culinary herbs can be annuals, perennials, or biennials, and most have three generally recognized characteristics: they have pliant, woody stems; the plants die back to the ground at the end of the growing season; and it is most often the aromatic leaves that are used for seasoning. (This last, incidentally, is what distinguishes them from spices, which are made of the dried roots, bark, buds, or berries of plants that grow mainly in the tropics.)

Growing herbs. Although not all culinary herbs have exactly the same growing requirements, most of them do tend to conform to a few general rules. To grow well, most herbs need good soil, good drainage, plenty of sun, and frequent watering. The leaves, the parts you'll use for seasoning, should be harvested when they're young, green, and tender, not yellowed and aging. Nurseries now offer many varieties of herbs, and even greengrocers and supermarkets sell potted chives, tarragon, and dill. If you have a small plot of ground, you can grow herbs from seeds or young plants; if you're an apartment dweller you can raise many kinds on a sunny windowsill. Consult your nursery about the special idiosyncrasies of the herbs you buy.

Storage. Herbs perish rather rapidly after harvesting. For the best flavor they should be used at once, but some will keep reasonably well for several days if the stems are placed in a jar of water on a refrigerator shelf. If you've raised a bumper crop of different kinds of herbs and plan to use them over a long period of time, they can be preserved by freezing or drying.

Drying. To dry herbs, keep them out of the sun. Place the leaves on a drying screen with a wooden frame so that air circulates freely and the leaves dry uniformly. If you're drying your herbs out-of-doors, a few words of caution: beware of a sudden breeze that might scatter your precious harvest, and be sure to move the frames indoors at dusk so the leaves are not affected by evening and morning moisture. Another drying method is to tie whole sprigs of herbs together and hang them from a beam or an eave. Or, if you live where it's not convenient to dry your herbs out-of-doors, you can lay them on a baking sheet and place them in a slow oven (about 150°) until all moisture has been removed. The length of time for drying will depend on the method and on the herb itself. Outdoor drying might take a few days; oven drying, several hours. When all the leaves are crackly and brittle, they'll be sufficiently dry.

Freezing. Many people freeze herbs to preserve them, and you might prefer this method. Most herbs do best if they're blanched before being frozen. To blanch, drop whole sprigs into hot water for a few seconds, then dip them quickly into ice water. Remove the leaves, chop them if you like, package them, and place them in the freezer. Frozen herbs can be added to cooked foods just as they are; defrost them before adding them to salads.

ANGELICA

Angelica is so rewarding, both in the garden and in the kitchen, that it deserves greater popularity. In the garden it grows quite tall, so it makes an excellent background plant. Its rounded, umbrella-like tops bear small white flowers, and its large leaves resemble those of a begonia plant; it has a delicate licorice flavor. In the kitchen every part of the plant can be put to use. The stems can be candied or stewed, the ground seeds can be added to puddings, and the leaves add delicious flavor to fish dishes. Angelica is native to the Northern Hemisphere, and in medieval Europe people thought it capable of warding off evil spirits.

BASIL

One of the most popular of all herbs, the shiny, dark leaves of sweet basil have a pungent, spicy flavor. If you freeze basil, try sprinkling a bit of olive oil over the leaves first. The flavor of basil is a perfect addition to sauces and is, of course, the chief ingredient of Italian *pasta al pesto*. It adds zest to pot roasts and poultry, and even glorifies the humble hamburger. Basil is the perfect seasoning for tomatoes, either raw or cooked. The herb's name probably comes from the Greek word *basilikon*, meaning "royal," and the French call it *l'herbe royale*.

Do-it-yourself fragrance

Before the days of mass-produced cosmetics, perfumes, and air fresheners, these products were made at home from herbs and garden plants.

One of the simplest ways of preserving dried herbs for fragrance is to assemble them into a potpourri. Potpourris can be made of almost any blend of herbs, although those with the strongest scents are best. The following "recipe" is just an example.

Combine the dried leaves of lemon verbena, rose geranium, and rosemary with some dried orange peel, cloves, and cinnamon. Add a fixative, such as orris-root, and an aromatic oil—attar of roses or carnation. Place the mixture in a covered jar and let it stand for several weeks, lifting the cover and stirring the mixture from time to time. After six or eight weeks place the jar, with the lid removed, in your living room or bedroom, where the herb mixture will give off a pleasant fragrance.

Some culinary hints

For some reason, herb cooking has frequently been treated as a kind of mysterious and exotic culinary art not recommended for the timid novice, and as a result cooks with limited experience sometimes become unnerved by a recipe that contains a foreign-sounding ingredient or a long list of unfamiliar herbs. Actually, it's not much more difficult to season food with fresh herbs than it is to use the spices and condiments called for in more conventional recipes. Here are a few tips to eliminate the mystique of cooking with herbs:

Even the simplest dish can be improved by the addition of an herb. (Add some chopped chervil leaves to a cream soup, dill to a consommé, chives to a baked potato.)

If a recipe calls for several different herbs, don't panic if one is unavailable: substitutions or omissions are often permissible.

Dried herbs have a more concentrated flavor than fresh ones, so use them sparingly.

Common herbs that lend mild pungency are sage, rosemary, and savory. Those with a stronger, more distinctive flavor are oregano, basil, dill, thyme, and marjoram.

Fines herbes usually means chopped chervil and chives, plus any other compatible herb.

For a bouquet garni for soup or stew, tie together sprigs of bay leaf, thyme, and chervil, or wrap dried, chopped leaves in a square of cheesecloth. Basil, marjoram, and savory can also be used.

BAY

The disadvantage of this lovely evergreen is that it is difficult to grow, so most people prefer to buy bay leaves already dried and packaged. A member of the laurel family, the bay bush needs considerable care. Planted in the ground, a tall bay tree adds a welcome touch of green all year; potted shrubs brighten living rooms and kitchens. Native to the Mediterranean area, bays and their relatives long symbolized nobility and courage, and wreaths of laurel and bay were often placed on the heads of nobles and heroes. Bay leaves add subtle flavor to stews, pot roasts, and soups. They must be used with discretion; fresh or dry, one leaf is generally sufficient to season a large roast or stew.

BORAGE

A member of a large family that includes heliotrope and forget-me-not, borage is a satisfying addition to an herb garden. Its bright blue flowers bloom for many weeks atop hairy stems. Borage leaves can be cooked alone and eaten as a vegetable, or the raw leaves can be added to salads. When added raw to vegetables, borage provides a delicate, cucumber-like flavor. The flowers can be candied.

BURNET

A member of the rose family, burnet is a hardy perennial that grows well in temperate climates. The feather-shaped leaves tend to toughen quickly, so they should be picked almost as soon as they appear. Ideally, burnet should be planted every year to ensure the most delicate flavor. The ancients used poultices of burnet to stop bleeding and believed that applications of the herb hastened healing. Today burnet is used for the subtle, cucumberish flavor it adds to salads. Add a few sprigs to vinegar or salad dressing.

CHERVIL

Curly chervil leaves enhance the flavor of herbs they're combined with and are a must for a bouquet garni. Used alone, they're a refreshing alternative to parsley and a particularly pleasing addition to egg dishes. Long valued as a medicinal plant, chervil roots were prescribed to ward off plague during the Middle Ages. Chervil will grow well in partial shade, and the more its leaves are picked, the fuller the plants will become.

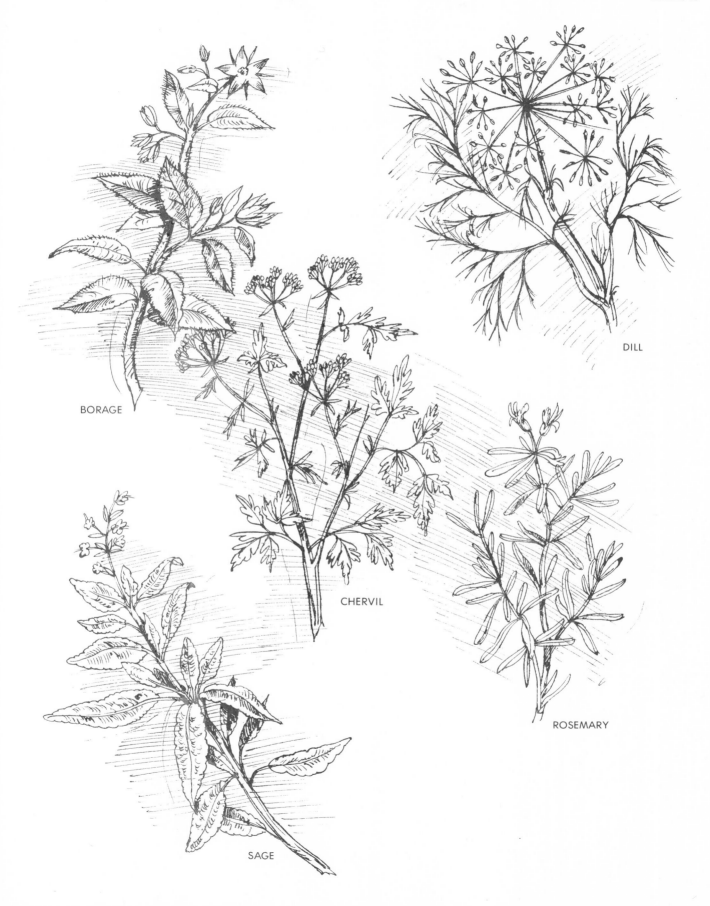

BORAGE

DILL

CHERVIL

ROSEMARY

SAGE

Herb or erb?

The word herb is derived from the Latin word herba, meaning grass. In England it was spelled erb until 1475 but even after the h was added, it was not pronounced until the nineteenth century. Today, herb is preferred in England. In New England we say erb but everywhere else one hears herb. Either pronunciation is correct.

Bouquet garni

A bouquet garni is a combination of herbs, usually tied together into a faggot. They are added to soups and stews during cooking and discarded before serving. Basic herbs for a bouquet garni are parsley, thyme, and bay leaf, to which may be added

1 chervil, tarragon, and celery;

2 rosemary, savory, and sage;

3 basil, lovage, and savory;

4 marjoram, borage, and chervil.

CHIVES

Of all the herbs, chives are the ones most often found in pots on grocers' shelves. Snip the grassy green spikes before the purple, clover-like flower appears at the tips and dice them finely over salads, into cottage and cream cheese, and on vegetables for a delightful onion-y flavor. Chives can be frozen without blanching.

CICELY

Sweet cicely, sometimes called "giant chervil," has a licorice-like taste similar to that of fennel. Given good soil in a semishady spot, cicely will thrive. The plant bears attractive, small white flowers; the leaves and stems are covered with a soft down. Chopped cicely leaves add interest to fish and salads.

DILL

This herb got its reputation by transforming the bland garden cucumber into a zesty pickle, but the feathery leaves will also pep up salads, soups, and sauces. Add a few sprigs to the liquid for poaching fish and to chicken soup, and snip generous amounts into sauces for fish and lamb. Dill, whose name comes from the Norse word *dilla*, meaning "to soothe," was always prized as a digestive aid.

HOREHOUND

Because of its somewhat bitter taste and long association with colds and sore throats, horehound has never achieved much popularity. Actually, the horehound plant is attractive enough to grace any herb garden. It bears small white flowers and oval gray leaves and is so hardy that in many places it is regarded as a troublesome weed. Both the leaves and the flowers can be used for flavoring. Besides its well-known use in candy, horehound does well in cookies, meat sauces, and tea.

HYSSOP

Hyssop, with its attractive blue flowers and shiny, dark green leaves, is familiar as a hedge in shady areas. When clipped, it makes an excellent border in an herb garden. Tea made with the leaves, stems, or flowers of hyssop is often helpful in treating congestion of the nose and throat. The leaves, which have a rather sharp, minty taste, give a spicy, pungent flavor to soups and stews.

LOVAGE

The young leaves of the lovage plant taste like strong celery. The plant grows tall and makes an excellent background in an herb garden. Native to southern Europe and now cultivated in many parts of the world, lovage is a plant of many uses. Oil extracted from its roots has medicinal properties; a liqueur is made from its fruit; and the leaves add a pungent quality to salads, vegetables, and soups. The flavor of lovage is quite sharp, so the leaves should be used sparingly in uncooked foods. The seeds may be pickled like capers.

SWEET MARJORAM

The most popular member of a large family, marjoram's grayish oval leaves add a pleasant flavor to fish, soup, and vegetables. To the ancients, marjoram symbolized contentment. The Greeks used it medicinally to cure convulsions and placed it on graves to ensure an untroubled sleep for the deceased. Wreaths of marjoram sprigs adorned the heads of bridal couples in ancient Rome.

MINT

The tangy flavor of mint is a familiar flavoring in tea, juleps, fruit punches, and jellies. Try it, too, in salads and homemade applesauce and ice cream. A word of caution if you're planting mint out of doors: Runners proliferate rapidly underground, and, if beds are not thinned regularly, mint will overtake your herb garden.

How does your garden grow?

Herb gardens, along with skirt lengths and hair styles, are subject to the whims of fashion and, like miniskirts and moustaches, are in and out of style. Ancient peoples surely must have planted herb gardens, however simple. Egyptian papyri tell of physician-priests who raised medicinal herbs. Greek and Roman manuscripts describe elaborate banquet dishes prepared with herbs, and the beautiful Helen, so the legend goes, was gathering an herb called "elecampane" when Paris spirited her away.

During the early years of Christianity and throughout the Dark Ages, herbs, long associated with mystery and magic, fell upon bad times. The Church discouraged their cultivation, and herb gardens virtually disappeared. But the Church later reversed its stand, and medicinal gardens, with the unromantic but descriptive name of "physick gardens," were planted in the cloister of almost every monastery and convent.

For many centuries herb gardens represented the height of horticultural fashion, and Europe's greatest monarchs, from Charlemagne to Louis XIV, set the tone by ordering famous landscape architects to design herb gardens for their royal estates. Charlemagne's garden was planted with seventy-five herbs, about eighteen of which we know today, and an extensive area of Louis's famous gardens at Versailles was turned over to the cultivation of herbs.

For a long time afterwards interest declined. Herb gardens became as passé as powdered wigs and were regarded as a quaint relic of a bygone era. Today, however, herbs are "in" once again, so if you're a trend setter, now's the time to plant your own herb garden.

Planning an herb garden

1. Decide where you want your garden. Outside the kitchen door guarantees that your herbs will be handy when you need them for cooking, but consider the possibility of planting along walks, around terraces, or at the base of trees and bird baths.

2. Once you've picked the spot, make sure there's good soil, sufficient drainage, and plenty of sun with enough shady areas to suit the plants that can't take full sun all day.

3. Pay a visit to your local nursery and select the herbs you'll most enjoy using.

4. Plan your design. Your garden needn't be complicated, but even simple designs make for greater interest. Naturally you'll want to use the taller herbs like lovage and borage for background, with dill, chervil, rosemary, or oregano in the front.

5. If you're a novice, plant your herbs according to the advice you get from the nursery. In the last analysis, however, trial and error will be the best test. If your dill doesn't do well the first year, switch to something else the next.

6. Once planted, your herbs will be quite self-sufficient unless, of course, you run into a dry spell when they'll have to be watered.

7. Sit back and await harvest time, then use them.

OREGANO

Another member of the marjoram family, oregano is sometimes called "wild marjoram." This staple of Italian kitchens is also popular with Mexican and Spanish cooks. Its distinctive flavor, stronger than that of sweet marjoram, does wonders for sauces as well as for squash, eggplant, and tomato dishes.

PARSLEY *See* page 57.

ROSEMARY

The green, needle-like leaves of this hardy perennial have a mild pine scent. Add them to a marinade or to a basting sauce for poultry or lamb for an interesting, pungent flavor. Ancient Greeks and Romans used rosemary as incense, European housewives placed it in clothes cupboards, and its strong aroma made it a popular room freshener long before modern deodorizers. It was long believed that rosemary prevented forgetfulness, and for that reason it was often called the "herb of memory."

SAGE

The grayish leaves of this hardy perennial can be identified by their coarse, bumpy surfaces. Their best known use is probably as a seasoning for poultry stuffing, but the dried leaves also add interesting flavor to roast pork and lamb. Be careful to use it sparingly: its pungent flavor has a way of overwhelming other seasonings. Its name probably comes from the Latin word *salvia*, meaning "sane or healthy," and the plant has always been considered rich in therapeutic properties.

SAVORY

The popular annual variety bears tiny green leaves that give a slightly peppery flavor to fish, meats, and poultry stuffings. If the Pilgrims stuffed their game birds on the first Thanksgiving, they probably seasoned the dressing with savory they had brought from England, and the attractive plant was a staple in colonial gardens along the East Coast.

TARRAGON

The pointed, dark green tarragon leaves are redolent with a strong anise-like aroma, and their faintly licorice flavor is a tantalizing complement to poultry, meats, and sauces. Salad dressings made with tarragon-flavored vinegar perk up the most ordinary greens. The French call this herb *estragon*, which, connoting as it does "little dragon," possibly refers to its sharp, spicy flavor.

THYME

An attractive ground cover as well as a versatile seasoning, thyme is one of the few herbs that does not object if its soil is allowed to go quite dry. Thyme once symbolized courage and strength. Like other highly aromatic herbs, it had a long career as a moth repellent, a deodorizer, and, when mixed with water, a fragrant cleansing agent. Whatever its other virtues, thyme lends distinctive flavor to foods. Try it in fish soups and stuffings for poultry and veal roasts.

Cook's guide to herbs

Soups
Basil, bay, chives, dill, oregano, parsley, tarragon

Eggs
Basil, coriander, cress, dill, parsley, tarragon, thyme

Breads
Caraway, chives, dill, garlic, marjoram, parsley, rosemary, tarragon

Fish
Chives, dill, fennel, parsley, tarragon

Meats
Basil, dill, marjoram, mint, oregano, rosemary, sage, summer savory, thyme

Poultry
Basil, dill, lemon balm, lovage, sage, tarragon, thyme

Salad and salad dressings
Basil, chives, cress, dill, garlic, marjoram, oregano, parsley, savory, tarragon

FRUIT

With today's methods of growing and storing fruits, improved refrigeration, and fast transport, a huge variety of fresh fruits have been made available to the consumer every month of the year. Certainly a choice of dessert or a snack for hungry times need never be a problem when the fruit markets smell and look like flower shops and are just as tempting, spilling over with melons, berries, grapes, apples, pears, and other splendid fruits, fragrant with natural sweetness and as nutritious as they are good tasting. And, as an added bonus, fruits are one of the least caloric nibbles one can eat; few fruits contain more than a hundred calories.

But still the twentieth-century methods of growing and shipping fruits are not without disadvantages. Fruits are often picked unripe, held in cold storage, and offered for sale when they are not at their best. In some instances, fruit cultivators provide us with fruits that are bred more for appearance and ability to store well than for flavor. Modern fruit production does present us with excellent fruit that we might not have tasted otherwise, but there are times when it gives us products of inferior quality that never achieve their true taste and juicy texture.

Buying fruit. To be assured of fruits that are at their best, consumers must learn to recognize prime fruits when they are at their peak without depending upon the packager or produce clerk to do it for them. The following pages describe how to select, home-ripen, and store individual varieties of fruit for maximum eating pleasure. There are a few general rules for the buyer to keep in mind:

Don't buy fruit only on the basis of its size and appearance. Large-sized fruits are not necessarily the best in quality or the most economical, and may not be suited to the purpose you have in mind. Although the outward appearance of many fruits is related to their eating quality, this is not always so. Fruit with minor skin blemishes or poor color may have a good eating quality, whereas large, beautifully colored fruit may be mealy and uninteresting in flavor.

Buy only fruit that you need. Some fruits are highly perishable, and, even though refrigerated, most fruit deteriorates in quality in a few days. Citrus fruits are an exception.

Buy fruits in season and, whenever possible, from local orchards. Fruit in season is lower in price and higher in quality than out-of-season fruit, which has usually been picked green and shipped great distances.

Grades for fruit. The Agricultural Marketing Service of the United States Department of Agriculture has established grade standards for many varieties of fresh fruit, based on color, size, maturity, and lack of defects. The grading standards are used voluntarily by fruit producers, and the packages must contain fruits that conform to these standards. Some states have similar grading standards. Top grades are either U.S. Fancy or No. 1.

Ripening and storing fruit. Many varieties of fruit can be bought when they are still hard and then ripened at room temperature. But they must be mature enough to have developed their full potential of sugar. To ripen fruit at home, place it in a warm, dry spot away from drafts and out of direct sunlight. Except for bananas and pears, most fruits ripened at home will never be as succulent as tree-ripened fruit,

Peak season for fruits

A country with as great a variety of climates as are found in the United States has correspondingly different growing seasons for fruits, and it would be difficult to pinpoint the peak season for every fruit in every region of the country. However, the following list provides a general guide to the time of year when our most popular fruits are in greatest supply and at top quality:

January and February

Apples, fall and winter: Golden Delicious, Red Delicious, Rhode Island Greening, Rome Beauty, McIntosh, Stayman, Winesap, York

Cantaloupe: Mexican varieties

Oranges: Seedless navels, pineapple oranges, Florida Temples, tangerines, and mandarins (through January), tangelos, Florida and Texas Valencias

Grapefruits: Florida and Texas

Kumquats

Kiwi

Papayas

Fall and winter pears: Anjou, Bosc, Comice, Winter Nellis

Persimmons

Pineapple

Quince

Ugli

March, April, May, and June

Apples: McIntosh, Winesap

Apricots (June)

Soft berries: Huckleberries (June), loganberries (June), raspberries (June), strawberries (April)

Cherries (June)

Grapefruit: Florida and Texas

Grapes: California and Arizona Emperor, Tokay, Cardinal, Thompson seedless, Ribier

Lemons (May, June)

Limes (June)

Loquats

Mangoes (June)

Melons (some varieties in June)

Oranges: California and Florida Valencias, California navels, Jaffa, blood, last of Florida tangerines

Papayas

Pears: Anjou, Comice, Winter Nellis

Pineapples

Plums (early spring)

Watermelon: Mexican

July, August, and September

Apples: Jonathan (latter half of September), Delicious (last part of Sep-

(continued)

(Peak season for fruits, continued)
tember), Gravenstein, Granny Smith.
(Summer apples are not the best; wait
for the fall crop.)
Apricots (July)
Berries: blackberries (July and August),
blueberries (July), cranberries (Sep-
tember), currants (July), gooseberries
(July), huckleberries (through August),
loganberries (July), raspberries (July),
strawberries
Cherries (July)
Figs
Grapefruit: Florida, Texas (September)
Grapes
Kiwi
Lemons (through August)
Limes
Litchi nuts (early July, short season)
Melons
Nectarines
Oranges: California and Arizona Valen-
cias
Papayas
Peaches (July and August)
Plums: Santa Rosa, Laroda, El Dorado,
Greengage
Fresh prunes
Pears: Bartlett (mid-July), Clapp
Favorite (August, September), Seckel
(late August)
Pineapple

October, November, and December
Apples, fall and winter:
Clementines
Coconuts
Cranberries
Dates (November)
Grapefruit: Florida and Texas
Grapes: Concord and Delaware
Kiwi
Kumquats (November, December)
Mandarins (November to February)
Melons: Casaba (October), honeydew
(October), honeyball (October)
Oranges: California navels (November to
June), Temples (December), Florida
and Texas Parson Browns and Hamlins,
tangerines (late November), Florida
tangelos
Papayas
Pears: Anjou, Bosc, Clapp Favorite, Co-
mice, Winter Nellis, Seckel
Persimmon
Pineapple
Pomegranate (October)
Prickly pears
Quince
Ugli

although they may have an acceptable flavor and texture. Among the fruits that cannot be ripened at home are grapes, pineapples, watermelons, and berries. Muskmelons may improve when held for a few days at room temperature, but, with the exception of honeydews, melons do not technically ripen. Ripe fruit should be refrigerated or stored in a cool place and eaten as soon as possible. Wash and dry all fruits (except berries and cherries) before placing in refrigerator.

About waxing. Most citrus fruits, apples, and sometimes plums are waxed before shipping. This is done to replace nature's protective coating of wax, which was washed off by the fruit grower along with the debris accumulated in the orchard before packing and shipping. The wax is added to retard spoilage and improve the appearance of the fruit. Very little wax is added; to give you an idea of how little, just one gallon (3.8 l) of wax will protect and polish five tons of apples; six drops of wax will protect one orange. All waxes used for fruit have been approved by the United States Food and Drug Administration as completely safe and edible materials, nontoxic to humans.

Vitamin content of fruits. All fruits contain some vitamin C, but in varying amounts. Those rich in vitamin C include oranges, grapefruit, cantaloupes, papayas, and strawberries. Those with smaller amounts are apricots, avocados, bananas, blackberries, blueberries, honeydew melons, pineapples, red raspberries, tangerines, and watermelon. Cantaloupes and apricots are rich in vitamin A.

Serving fruits. Wash all fruits with an edible peel thoroughly whether you serve them raw or cooked. If you choose to peel fresh fruit, keep the parings as thin as possible, and never cut a fruit until it is ready to eat. Do not serve overly chilled fruit. Extreme cold masks the taste.

Cooking fruit. Fruit can be cooked in many appetizing ways and served as an accompaniment to main courses and as dessert. Often fruit that is slightly less than ripe can be cooked successfully.

Broiling. Broiled apple rings, bananas, peaches, and nectarines are delicious eaten with meat. To broil most fruits, dot them with butter, sprinkle them with a sweetener and favorite spice, and broil for a few minutes until the fruit is brown and bubbly.

Sautéing. Sautéed bananas, apple rings, peaches and pineapple can be served with meat or as a breakfast food. Fruits are sautéed on both sides for about 8 to 12 minutes total. After cooking, sprinkle with sugar, cinnamon, or salt before serving.

Baking. Apples, pears, and peaches may all be baked. Cut the fruit in half, core it, and arrange in a shallow buttered baking dish. Dot the fruit with butter and sprinkle with sugar and spices if you like. Add liquid to the bottom of the pan and baste the fruit with it periodically while it is baking. Bake, uncovered, until the fruit is tender.

Simmering or poaching. Fresh fruit cooked in a sugar syrup makes a delicious dessert that can be stored at length in the refrigerator. In general, use only enough sugar to bring out the flavor of the fruit, and cook it until it is tender, but not soft and mushy. To simmer fresh fruit, mix sugar and water and bring to a boil. Add the fruit to the boiling syrup. Cover and return the syrup to a boil, then reduce the heat until the liquid simmers. Stir as little as possible to avoid breaking the fruit. When tender, remove from the heat and let cool in the liquid.

AKEE

The akee is a finger-shaped fruit, about 3 inches (7.6 cm) long, that grows on a tropical evergreen tree and is a favorite Jamaican food. The fruits turn yellow and red as they ripen. They are a most beautiful fruit, but a demanding one as well—for unless they have ripened to the point where they open themselves, they are poisonous. No fallen, discolored, or unripe fruit may be eaten. The mature fruit splits open in three segments, exposing three large shiny black seeds that are attached to white flesh. The seeds, too, are inedible and must be discarded. Although akee is technically a fruit, it is served hot or cold with meats or fish like a vegetable. Its flavor has been likened to that of scrambled eggs.

Amount to buy. Two akees per serving.

Selection. Use only firm, unbruised, open akees.

Preparation and serving. Hull the akees and remove the seeds. Place the white pods in boiling water to cover, reduce the heat, and simmer until soft. Strain and coarsely mash and season with salt, pepper, and Parmesan cheese or chopped nuts. Akees can also be curried, baked, or cooked with fish.

APPLES

GRANNY SMITH

McINTOSH

GOLDEN DELICIOUS

RED DELICIOUS

WINESAP

CORTLAND

Blighia sapida

Akee is also known as *seso vegetal*, but, more interestingly, its botanical name is *Blighia sapida*, named for no less a person than the notorious Captain William Bligh of *Mutiny on the Bounty* fame. Akee is as basic to the Jamaican diet as plantain (in spite of its being poisonous until ripe). It is believed that Captain Bligh may have introduced akee to the West Indies along with breadfruit from Tahiti. (This was a number of years after he recovered from his famous, cataclysmic altercation with his crew.) The breadfruit never did quite take off in the West Indies as a replacement for plantain, but akee has flourished.

Forbidden fruit?

The apple has been held responsible for contributing to the fall of man, since it was supposedly the apple that tempted Eve. Although it is easy to see how the crisp, juicy apple might have proved irresistible to the first couple, biblical scholars tend to doubt the charge. The Tree of Knowledge in the Scriptures bears little resemblance to the modern apple tree, and besides, they observe, the climate in the Garden of Eden was probably too warm for apple trees to flourish. It is more likely that the forbidden fruit was an apricot or quince; some think it might have been a banana. No amount of scholarly persuasion, however, has absolved the apple completely.

Fresh apple sauce

A blend of two or more varieties of apples will make an interestingly flavored sauce. Quarter, peel and core 6 medium-sized apples. As you cut them, place the apple quarters in a bowl of cold water to which you have added a pinch of salt to prevent discoloration. Slice the apple quarters and put them in a saucepan with as little water as possible—just enough to keep them from scorching. Cover and simmer until the apples are almost soft. Sweeten to taste; the amount of sugar you will need depends on the variety of apple. Add a little at a time, until the sauce is sweet enough. Continue simmering for a few minutes to dissolve the sugar and complete the cooking of the sauce. For more tartness, add a dash of lemon, and for a spicier taste add cinnamon, nutmeg, ground cloves, allspice, or mace. Serves 4.

Apples to eat and drink

The English colonists brought apple seedlings to Massachusetts about a decade after the Pilgrims landed. As time went on and more Europeans settled in the New World, they developed many new varieties of apples. The multitude of ways these crisp fruits could be prepared, the ease with which they grew in cold climates, and their ability to store well made them the most important fruit in colonial America. They were eaten raw and baked into pies, but their greatest importance was for cider. Milk was a hazardous drink in the early days of this country; it was produced and sold under conditions that would now be considered outrageously unhygienic, and it was a frequent cause of severe illness. Abraham Lincoln's mother died of the "milksick." Cider was the popular drink. Besides apple cider, there was pear cider ("perry") and peach cider ("peachy"). Cider was cheap and plentiful. In addition, it hardened into an alcoholic drink that answered some needs for a hardworking society.

Today's cider mills may not legally sell anything alcoholic, so apple juice is treated to keep it from fermenting beyond a specific point. It is not really cider, but simply apple juice.

Known to antiquity as the "fruit of immortality," but to contemporary society as the vital ingredient in an American dessert as highly regarded as motherhood, apples are one of the world's best-loved fruits. Their many uses and taste-pleasing qualities have made them known as the "king of fruits." The ancestor of the apple tree we know today was a wild variety that grew in the mountains of southwestern and central Asia and that bore a fruit similar to a crab apple. There are countless varieties of apples; some say as many as seven thousand. At least twenty-five different ones are cultivated in the orchards of the United States and Canada. They come in a wide range of skin colors, textures, and tastes, from deepest red to palest yellow, from crisp to mellow, from sweet to tart.

It is important for the shopper to be familiar with apple varieties, since not every apple is suited to every purpose. The Red Delicious, for example, is a superb eating apple but can be disappointing when cooked. Green apples are commonly thought of as cooking apples, but there are some species, such as the Newtown Pippin and Granny Smith, that are excellent for eating. Following is a list of some of the most popular varieties and the ways they are best used:

BALDWIN. Red skin. Tart, juicy, and crisp. Excellent for pie and sauce.

CORTLAND. Bright red, crisp, and sweet. Good for eating, in fruit cocktails and salads, and in pies.

DELICIOUS, GOLDEN. Yellow, sweet, firm. Excellent raw as a dessert apple and for apple tarts.

DELICIOUS, RED. A red, juicy apple, sweet and firm. Best eaten fresh, used in fruit cocktails, or sliced with cheese.

GRANNY SMITH. A tart green apple from Australia. All-purpose, from eating to cooking. Holds its shape when cooked.

GREENING, RHODE ISLAND. Standard green cooking apples, excellent in pies and sauces.

JONATHAN. Yellow, heavily overlaid with red. Very good for eating fresh and in pies and applesauce, but poor for baking whole.

LADY APPLES. Small white apples blushed with red. Good to eat, their diminutive size makes them decorative in a bowl of fruit.

MCINTOSH. Red-striped appearance. Crisp, juicy, slightly tart. Excellent for eating fresh or in salads or dumplings, or for poaching whole. Makes wonderful applesauce.

NEWTOWN PIPPIN. A tart, green or bright yellow all-purpose apple that can be eaten fresh, or made into pies and sauces or baked.

ROME BEAUTY. Red, mild-flavored classic baking apple.

STAYMAN. Red striped or mottled. Tart, semi-firm, all-purpose apple, for eating fresh, puddings, and sauces. Tends to get mushy when cooked.

WINESAP. A deep red, moderately tart apple, very juicy. For eating fresh, salads, pies, and general cooking.

YORK. Light red, dotted with russet. Firm, crisp, and sweet and holds shape when cooked. Used for general cooking, pies, and baking.

CRAB APPLES. The parent stock of all modern apples are used only in jellies and preserves. They are too bitter to be eaten fresh.

Peak season. Apples are on the market all year, but they are at their best and least expensive from about September through November, when they are newly harvested. After November, almost all apples on the market come from cold storage.

Amount to buy. Apples store well and are a good fruit to keep in the refrigerator for "hungry times." There are about three medium apples to a pound (454 g). One pound will yield about 2 2/3 to 3 cups (638–720 ml), peeled and sliced. You will need about 3 pounds (1.4 g) of apples for a pie.

Selection. Choose apples that have good color for their variety and are firm to the touch. Firmness is important, particularly when buying the larger sizes. Big apples tend to mature more quickly than the smaller ones, and a soft apple usually has a mealy or mushy texture and an overripe flavor. Skins should be smooth and reasonably bruise free; too many bruises end up as decay spots. The background color on red varieties should be slightly yellowish green; the darker and greener it is, the more immature the apple. Apples must be mature when picked in order to have good flavor, texture, and long life in storage. Most apples are lightly waxed with a harmless, tasteless, edible wax.

Apples are graded by federal or state inspectors according to their variety, maturity, lack of defects, color, and size. Grade U.S. Extra Fancy, U.S. Fancy, and U.S. 1 are the best grades. Generally the grade of an apple is determined more by its color than the general defects of its skin; apples with less color (as long as they are not greenish) can provide excellent flavor and will cost less.

Storage. Store apples in the refrigerator or in a very cool spot. They will keep for a week or more. Warmer temperatures cause apples to ripen rapidly and lose crispness and flavor.

Preparation and serving. Wash apples thoroughly, whether you serve them raw or cooked. When you pare apples, make the parings as thin as possible. To minimize discoloration in apples after you cut them, dip them in lemon juice (or any other citrus juice—lime, orange, or grapefruit) or pineapple juice.

Apples may be baked whole; used in pies, cobblers, and cakes; fried into fritters; and cooked into sauces. Cut into rings, they can be sautéed or broiled and served with meat dishes. Use them raw and sliced or diced in fruit cocktails and fruit salads. They can be candied, spiced, and preserved. They are made into vinegar, juice, cider, and brandy.

Dietary information. A medium-sized apple contains from 80 to 100 calories; there are 242 calories in one pound (454 g). They are rich in pectin and fruit acids as well as minerals. Eaten raw with the skin left on, they provide bulk to the body system.

Cleaning tips

Clean discolored aluminum pots and pans by boiling apple peelings in them. When juice from your apple pies stain your oven, sprinkle salt on the sticky puddles; they will be easier to remove.

The real Johnny Appleseed

"Apple pies and apple fritters, apple cores to feed the critters," sang Johnny Appleseed, one of the heroes of modern folklore. Not a legendary character, Johnny Appleseed was a real man named John Chapman, born in Massachusetts in 1774. He will be forever remembered as the person who spread the apple tree from East to West by sprinkling its seeds from a burlap bag wherever he walked. Excited by tales of pioneers trekking westward, John Chapman joined the movement, traveling about new territories, developing nurseries of fruit trees. He was a gentle man with a sincere love of nature and all mankind, including the Indians he met on his travels. He died in Indiana at the age of 71, having accumulated twelve hundred acres of orchard.

Poached apricots

Peel 12 apricots and cut them in half. Do not discard the pits. Bring 1 cup of sugar and a cup of water to a boil and cook for 5 minutes. Add apricots, pits, and a dash of lemon juice. Reduce the water to a simmer and cook until the fruit is tender (8 to 10 minutes). Baste the fruit with the liquid while it is cooking. Remove the apricots and boil the liquid until it is reduced; this is the sauce. If you wish, you may add an ounce of liqueur of any kind to the sauce, and serve the apricots with the sauce, topped with whipped cream.

Growing apricots

Sometimes called "eggs of the sun," apricots are the fruit of drought-resistant trees. An apricot tree may survive from fifty to one hundred years. Its pure white blossoms, however, are extremely sensitive to cold, and since they appear early in spring, an entire crop of apricots can be ruined by a late frost if the trees are not properly protected. Apricots do best where summers are warm and sunny, winters are cool, and where late frosts are rare.

History of the apricot

Even the inscrutable Chinese could not keep the apricot a secret. Before the time of Alexander the Great, apricots were cultivated in Southwest Asia, and from there they traveled to northern Africa. At the close of the thirteenth century, Marco Polo returned to Europe from China, bringing with him coffers full of Oriental treasures, among them the seeds of an apricot tree. The secret was out, and apricots were soon grown throughout southern Europe. Spanish missionaries brought the fruit to the New World and planted apricots in southern California.

APRICOTS

First cultivated in China by skillful gardeners, growing as early as 2000 B.C., apricots were the first fruits planted in California by the mission fathers in the eighteenth century. Today the Pacific coast states, Utah, and Idaho produce more than 90 percent of the American crop. Apricots are also raised in Iran, Spain, Italy, and Syria.

Fresh apricots are extremely delicate and ship poorly, making them a luxury in many areas. Most people are more familiar with the dried version of the fruit and have never known the delight of a fresh, tree-ripened apricot.

Peak season. June and July. Imported apricots may be available in December and January.

Amount to buy. There are three to six apricots in a pound (454 g), depending on the variety. If poached, allow three to four apricots for each serving.

Varieties. Apricots range in color from pale yellow to deep orange, and some varieties are flecked with tiny red dots. The color of the flesh, too, may also range from yellow to orange. The best known American varieties are Moorpark, Royal, and Tilton; about eleven varieties are grown in all.

Selection. Choose apricots that have a rich yellow or orange color, and are plump and firm but yield slightly to the touch. An apricot that is heavily tinged with green will not make good eating, even when allowed to ripen at room temperature. Avoid apricots that show bruise marks, are wilted or shriveled, or are very soft to the touch.

Storage. Apricots are perishable, and, while they may be refrigerated for three to five days, storing will not improve them. It is better to buy a few at a time and use them as soon as possible.

Preparation and serving. Apricots may be eaten out of hand, or mixed with other fruits in fruit salads. They may be poached or else peeled, sliced, and served with sugar and heavy cream. To remove the skin from a fresh apricot, drop it in boiling water for a minute. The fruit also makes delicious jams, pies, fritters, and puddings, and in Norway it is even used to make a soup. The puréed pulp is often used as a glaze for cakes and pastries. Both fresh and dried apricots are used in Mideastern recipes with meat and fowl; a Chinese specialty is duck with apricots. Apricot nectar is a commercially bottled drink made of apricot concentrate and sugar.

Dietary information. Fresh apricots are high in Vitamin A and are a good source of other minerals. One pound (454 g) of apricots contains 217 calories. Dried apricots are rich in iron.

AVOCADOS

Many species of avocado hide their rich, buttery flesh under a tough, leathery hide, which gives them their nickname, "alligator pear." On the inside, however, the avocado bears no resemblance to either an alligator, a pear, or any other fruit. Its taste is neither acid nor sweet, but pleasantly bland. The avocado contains more oil than any fruit, except the olive, which makes it more like a nut in chemical composition. Extremely versatile, the tender meat of the avocado can be eaten as a vegetable or sweetened and incorporated into ice creams and blender drinks.

Peak season. Available all year.

Amount to buy. One good-sized avocado is sufficient for a large salad. Half an avocado will serve one person, if used alone.

Varieties. There are more than fifty species of avocado, which differ significantly in size and appearance. There are small, dark, smooth-skinned avocados and large, smooth-skinned green ones that turn dark brown or purple when ripe. Others have rough, textured skins and turn black when ripe. Some are no bigger than a plum; others weigh as much as 4 pounds (1.8 kg). The interior of all avocados, however, looks and tastes much the same. The most common avocados on the American market are the rough-skinned, pear-shaped green avocado that turns dark as it ripens and the smooth-skinned, shiny green one that turns reddish brown. They usually weight about 8 ounces (227.2 g).

Selection. Avocados are ready for eating when they yield to light pressure. However, they may be purchased slightly underripe and ripened at ordinary room temperature. Avoid avocados with dark, sunken spots

The avocado comes north

Legend has it that the first European to taste avocados was Hernando Cortès, the Spanish conquistador, during his foray into Mexico in 1519. Perhaps Montezuma served them at a dinner party in a diplomatic gesture toward appeasement. The Spaniards liked them so much they exclaimed "Bocados," which translates into "A mouthful!" And that, some would have us believe, is how the avocado was named. It will have to do until a better story comes along.

We then lose sight of the avocado for a few centuries until it was introduced into the United States in 1833, at which time it was already growing in Africa, Polynesia, and Hawaii.

Until comparatively recently, avocados were considered a luxury food, but today with year-round production in California and Florida, this former delicacy is a common supermarket product.

Inside the avocado is a tree

An avocado seed can produce a houseplant or a six-foot tree. Wash the avocado seed in warm water. Place the bottom or broad end of the seed (the point is the top) in a container of warm water, submerged about half an inch. Prop it in place with three or four toothpicks in the sides of the seed, resting them on the top of the container. Keep water on the warm side and change it often. Place the plant in a warm, bright spot out of direct sunlight.

Roots will appear during the next two to six weeks and stems should begin to inch their way up. When the main stem reaches seven or eight inches in height, cut it back, leaving about three inches of stem coming out of the seed. This will keep the plant from growing tall and spindly, with sparse leaves. In about two weeks when the leaves are well established, transfer to a 10-inch clay pot. Place pieces of broken pottery around the drainage hole and fill most of the pot with humus-enriched potting soil.

Remove the toothpicks from the avocado seed and set the plant gently into the pot. Add soil, leaving half of the seed exposed. Water well with the water from the jar, which will settle the soil, and add more soil until the level is again halfway up the seed. Water daily with warmish water.

Guacamole

A delicious dip for cocktail snacks is the Mexican salad, guacamole. Mash the fruit of one avocado in a bowl and add lemon juice to taste, salt, pepper, 3 tablespoons chopped onions, 3 tablespoons chopped tomatoes, a teaspoon of chili powder, and a dash of cayenne. Two tablespoons of yogurt or sour cream will give it a creamier texture. Vary the recipe by adding chopped garlic or chopped peppers. Serve with corn crackers.

Avocado soup

In an electric blender combine 1 large avocado, peeled and chopped, with 1 ten-ounce can of chicken broth, heated to the boiling point. Blend until smooth. Then add 2 cups heavy cream or milk or yogurt, ½ cup dry white wine, and 2 teaspoons lemon juice. Season to taste with salt, pepper, and a pinch of cayenne. Blend. Serve the soup cold or warm (heat in the top of a double boiler), garnished with fresh dill or chopped parsley. Serves six, and extra may be frozen.

The traveling banana

The banana is known for its wanderlust and its antiquity. Botanists say that the banana plant dates back to an era a million years ago. It took an early voyage in the time of ancient man, when it was discovered that banana roots could be dried, carried great distances, and replanted. The banana traveled in this form from southern Asia to the Pacific Islands, then with the Arabs from India to the Holy Land, and it went from tribe to tribe across Africa to New Guinea with cargoes of ivory and slaves. In New Guinea the banana was discovered by the Portuguese and carried off to the Canary Islands. In 1850 the first cargo ships brought bananas to the United States, and fifty years later the United Fruit Company was founded in Central America in order to keep the banana moving to foreign ports. Today the banana is still on the road. It is the one exotic fruit we regard as a year-round staple, even though it is not grown in the United States.

or signs of bruising. Irregular light brown markings or a very dark skin are normal and do not indicate a spoiled fruit. Besides the "squeeze" test, you can test an avocado for ripeness by sticking a toothpick in the fruit at the stem end. If it goes easily in and out of the fruit without encountering any resistance, the avocado is ripe and ready to be eaten.

Storage. A ripe avocado should be stored in the refrigerator. Refrigeration slows down the ripening process, but use the avocado before it gets too soft. If unripe, place it in a dry spot at room temperature; in three to five days, it will be ready to eat. You can shorten the ripening time by storing the avocado in a partially closed paper or plastic bag kept at room temperature.

Preparation and serving. Do not cut an avocado until it is ripe. To extract the flesh of the avocado, cut the fruit in half with a sharp knife from stem end to bottom, avoiding the large pit in the center. The flesh can then be either scooped out of the shell or cut out in slices. An avocado may also be peeled like an orange. Once avocado flesh is exposed to air it will turn brown rapidly unless coated with lemon or lime juice. The avocado can be diced and used in salads, spread on bread or crackers like butter, or eaten right from the shell with a dash of salt, pepper, and lemon juice or a vinaigrette dressing. The cavity in the avocado provides a natural container for a stuffing, and half an avocado filled with poultry or seafood salad makes a fine appetizer or main luncheon course. The avocado is the basic ingredient of the popular Mexican *guacamole*, a cocktail dip served with crackers.

Dietary information. Avocado is very high in essential nutrients: vitamins A, C, and E and many of the B vitamins, in addition to potassium. It is also high in monounsaturated fat. There are about 150 calories in 3½ ounces (100 g).

BANANAS

Bananas are among the most popular of all fruits. Their daily availability, ease of eating, high nutritional value, and fine, sweet taste make them appealing to people of all ages. There are about three hundred varieties of banana cultivated today, many differing significantly in size, color, and taste. Almost all the bananas we consume in the United States are imported from South and Central America. The United States and Japan are the two leading world importers of bananas. Properly refrigerated, bananas are easy to ship and store. They are one of the very few fruits that do not have to be tree ripened to reach peak flavor. Actually, a banana that turns yellow on the plant loses its flavor, and, even when they are eaten where they are grown, they are not allowed to ripen on the plant. The finest flavor develops only when the fruit is cut while green and ripened afterward.

Peak season. Available all year.

Amount to buy. Buy according to need. Bananas will ripen at room temperature, and if you buy a large bunch they will all ripen at once, perhaps leaving you with more ripe bananas than you can use. If you are using them for dessert, figure one banana per serving.

Varieties. The most common variety of banana is the Cavendish, the familiar yellow banana 6 to 8 inches (15.2 to 20.3 cm) long. Its distinguishing feature is that the tips are blunt and generally curved. We rarely see the red banana, which is inclined to break off the stalk. The silk-fig banana is known as the "apple banana" because its pink fruit tastes like a combination of an apple and a banana. Tiny dwarf bananas, the size of a finger, are sweet and tender.

PLANTAINS are greenish long, thick bananas with rather rough skins. Never eaten raw, they are a staple food in tropical countries, where they are used primarily as a starchy vegetable. They can be baked, mashed, or fried as an accompaniment to meat, fish, or eggs. They can be deep fried to make banana chips. They should not be refrigerated until they become very soft. Plantains contain 119 calories in 3½ ounces (100 g). They are high in potassium and contain goodly amounts of vitamin C and some phosphorus.

Selection. Select bananas that have not yet become quite fully yellow so that they will be firm and free of bruises when you get them home, where they will ripen easily at room temperature. They are ready to eat when the skin is deep yellow and studded with a few brown spots. Bananas with green tips and little yellow color are not ready to eat, but if you are planning to bake or broil them, the slightly green banana will retain its shape better. Choose bananas that are bunched, rather than the single unattached ones. Avoid bananas with discolored, dull, grayish, or aged-looking skins because they have decayed or been improperly stored.

Storage. Bananas ripen best in a temperature between 60° and 70°F (15.5°–21°C); they ripen too quickly at higher temperature. Once the bananas are at the proper stage of ripeness, place them in the refrigerator. The cold will turn the skins dark brown, but it does no harm to the fruit inside the peel except to slow down further ripening. The fruit will remain unchanged for three days or so before it begins to discolor.

Preparation and serving. Bananas are a delicious and nutritious snack. Sliced, they can start the day over breakfast cereal and finish it over ice cream. Fully ripe mashed bananas can be used in cakes, muffins, and bread, cookies and milk shakes. They can be broiled and baked as a dessert or as an accompaniment for poultry or fish.

Dietary information. A medium-sized banana contains about 100 calories (there are 262 calories in 1 pound [454 g]). The banana is very high in potassium, an important mineral not present in large quantities in most foods. It also has appreciable amounts of vitamin A and phosphorus, in addition to other minerals and vitamins. Bananas are high in carbohydrates. They should be eaten only when they are fully ripe, since they are more digestible at that point.

Baked bananas

The banana is as tasty cooked as raw. One of the best ways to cook a banana is to bake it in the oven, sprinkled with sugar and spice and other things nice, such as a liqueur. Peel a banana for each serving; halve them lengthwise and lay them in a lightly buttered baking dish, flat side down, You have several options: you may sprinkle them with brown sugar or granulated sugar, glaze them with honey, or spread them with several tablespoons of a favorite preserve. Dot with butter, add cinnamon or nutmeg, and bake for 15 minutes in a 350°F oven until tender. If you like, add ⅓ cup of rum or sherry to the baking dish, or wait till the bananas are done. Then, pour some warmed brandy over them and flame them for a grand entrance. Baked bananas can also be served with the main course; dot with butter, sprinkle with lemon juice, and bake.

How bananas grow

The banana plant is often called a tree, but it is not a real tree because there is no wood in the stem rising above the ground. The stem is made up of leaves growing very close together, one inside the other. When the plant is old enough to bear fruit, the stem is from 9 to 16 inches wide and the plant from 15 to 30 feet high.

Bananas grow in bunches. Each bunch is made up of nine to sixteen clusters of fruit called "hands," and each hand has from ten to twenty separate bananas, called "fingers." A plant bears just one bunch of fruit, which can weigh well upwards to 60 pounds. The seeds of bananas do not propogate, and when one bunch is cut, the whole plant is chopped down and another one planted.

How berries got their names

There's little doubt about how blueberries and blackberries earned their names, but what about gooseberries, cranberries, and strawberries?

Some gooseberries have a downy texture, like the soft feathers of the fowl they're named for. The etymology of "strawberry" is less clear cut, since they neither look nor taste like straw, but it is thought that they were once stored under beds of it, which has a kind of logic.

The origin of the word "cranberry" is also obscure. The early colonists called the fruit *ibimi* which means bitter berry, the name given it by the local Indians. Some historians believe that they were first called "crane berries" because cranes inhabiting the salt-marsh bogs ate them. Others theorize that the name grew out of the resemblance of the shape of the cranberry's bud and stem to the head and neck of a crane. We mustn't forget that cranberries were once also known as "bounce berries," because their ripeness can be tested by their ability to bounce. (Try it.)

Naming berries surely was no easy task, because there are innumerable varieties of this fruit, many of which look and taste alike. It had to have taken a good deal of ingenuity to come up with names such as juneberries, pokeberries, whortleberries and cloudberries, among others.

BERRIES

GOOSEBERRIES

LOGANBERRIES

STRAWBERRIES

BLACKBERRIES

BLUEBERRIES

BLACK CURRANTS

Innumerable varieties of berries abound in the woods and fields of North America and other temperate zones. First discovered by the Indians, who used them as medicines, dyes, and food preservatives, berries are still prized as one of our most delicate and delicious fruits, whether eaten fresh or cooked into tangy jams and pies. Good-tasting teas with medicinal purposes are also made from the leaves of almost all berries.

Today we no longer depend upon a whim of nature to supply us with berries. Thousands of acres of berries are cultivated for commercial purposes in many parts of the country. Various hybrids of berries are being produced constantly in an unending search for berries that ship and store better and have superior flavor.

Buying and storing berries. There are a few general rules that apply to buying and storing all soft berries, such as blackberries, black raspberries, raspberries, strawberries, and boysenberries. When buying, look for bright, clean berries with good uniform color, typical of their species. Stem caps should not be attached; only the strawberry is permitted to wear its little green cap as a sign of maturity. Berries are usually sold in cardboard containers. Look at the bottom of the container to make sure it has not been stained from mushy or moldy fruit. If possible, check the fruit at the bottom of the carton.

Berries are sold by the pint (480 ml) and quart (960 ml), raspberries, in half-pint (240 ml) containers. There are 2 cups (480 ml) per pint and you should generally allow about a cup (240 ml) of fresh berries per serving. For a 9-inch (22.9 cm) pie you need about 1 quart (960 ml) of berries.

Most berries should be used the day of purchase. As soon as you get them home, spread them out on a square of waxed paper and discard any that are bruised, spoiled, or moldy. Mold spreads quickly from berry to berry. Place berries in a flat container so they won't be mashed and refrigerate until you are ready to use them. Do not wash or hull the berries until then. When ready to use, wash carefully in cold water and drain thoroughly in a colander. Make sure there are no bits of stem or bush included in the berries. If the berries become soft, mash them and cook briefly in a simple sugar syrup to use as a topping for ice cream or cake.

BLACKBERRIES

The blackberry is a large, purplish-black berry with a sweet, yet acid flavor. It is cultivated and also grows wild. It is distinguishable from the dewberry only in that dewberries grow on trailing, ground-covering vines, while blackberries grow on an erect plant. Both are especially delicate and must be used immediately after purchase. They are a splendid dessert berry eaten with cream and sugar, and for pies, puddings, jams or jellies, and wine. Avoid dull-looking fruits, stained containers, and containers with too many red, unripe berries.

Peak season. Blackberries ripen in the summer months, usually in July and August, but they are sometimes available from June through September, depending on the area.

Dietary information. There are 58 calories in 3½ ounces (100 g) and large amounts of vitamins A and C, in addition to potassium and other minerals.

BLUEBERRIES

Blueberries are among the most popular of the noncitrus fruits in the United States. Easy to handle, they involve no peeling, no puttering, no pitting, and no waste. The cultivated blueberries we find in our markets are dark blue in color with a typical silvery gloss, which is a natural, protective waxy coating. Choose berries that are plump, firm, and uniform in size. Watch out for stained or leaking containers. Blueberries are among the hardier of berries; unwashed, they may be kept in the refrigerator for three to five days. One pint (480 ml) will serve three to four. They can be frozen successfully, as is (dry pack), in freezer bags.

Before using, wash blueberries by placing them in a bowl of cold water to float off bits of stems and leaves and repeat a few times until no more particles appear. Like all berries, blueberries are delicious with sugar and cream, puréed as a sauce for ice cream, or preserved in jellies or jams or for the traditional blueberry pie. They are also very good in

Taming the wild blueberry
Blueberries were first gathered by the American Indians, who ate them, baked them, and dried them to use in winter in their soups and stews. This round, blue berry with the tart-sweet taste grows wild on low bushes in sandy areas. It has been gathered and canned for commercial use since the Civil War. Today blueberries are grown commercially, and manpower has been replaced by mechanical pickers. However, some blueberry fanciers think the wild varieties have a more distinctive flavor. The wild blueberry is a pale bluish lavender with a silvery gloss. People frequently confuse the wild blueberry with its relative, the huckleberry. Huckleberries are smaller, darker, and more tart than blueberries, with harder seeds.

Blueberry soup
This is a traditional Polish soup recipe that is best eaten for dessert. Combine one pint of blueberries (you may use blackberries, too) in a saucepan with a thinly sliced lemon, 2 cups of water, a cinnamon stick, and sugar to taste. Bring the mixture to a boil and simmer it for 10 minutes, or until the berries are tender. Stir in 2 cups of sour cream or yogurt and chill. Serves six.

Cranberries for Christmas

In this age of plastic and aluminum Christmas tree baubles, few of us brighten our branches with the favorite ornament of preindustrial days—the string of cranberries. Arm your children with a needle and thread and watch them enjoy creating the original biodegradeable ornament—just as pioneer children did.

Cranberry relish

A relish can be made of raw or cooked cranberries. For raw relish, grind 2 cups of raw cranberries and combine them with ½ cup apple cider, ¼ cup honey, and ¼ teaspoon of allspice. For variations add grated apple, diced pineapple, orange rind, raisins, or chopped nuts. If you prefer a cooked relish, simmer a pound of cranberries with a cup of cider, a cup of honey, grated lemon rind, and ¼ teaspoon ground mace for 5 minutes. You may also include apples and raisins in the cooking pot. Serve with roast meat or fowl.

Cranberry-apple pie

The next time you make apple pie, combine a cup of chopped cranberries and a tablespoon of grated orange rind with the apples for a new, tangy taste.

muffins and pancakes. To prevent their sinking to the bottom of baked goods, give them a quick dunk in flour before adding them to the batter.

Peak season. Available according to area from May through September. Peak month is July.

Dietary information. Blueberries contain 61 calories in 3½ ounces (100 g), vitamins A and C, potassium, phosphorus, and calcium.

CRANBERRIES

Unlike the wild berries known to the early settlers in the New World, today's cranberries are cultivated to be larger, brighter in color, and superior in flavor. There are a number of varieties of cranberries that differ in size and color but taste much the same. Generally they are glossy, firm, plump, and red. Avoid cranberries that look shriveled or dull, or are soft and sticky. See that the container is not stained.

Cranberrries are sold in supermarkets in 1-pound (454 g) containers or bags. Place them, unwashed, in their original container in the refrigerator; they will keep for a week or more. Just before cooking time, rinse them in cold water and remove any stems or bruised berries. It is a good idea to buy berries when they are in season and freeze them. Just place the unopened box or bag in the freezer, and they will be ready to use whenever you want them without thawing. They will keep firm and fresh for months in the freezer. There is 1 quart (960 ml) in 1 pound (454 g) of fruit, which will yield about 1 quart (960 ml) of whole berry or jellied sauce.

Cranberries are extremely tart and are usually cooked with sugar. They are served with poultry and meat, as ice-cream, cake, or custard topping, a glaze for ham, or chopped raw in a relish with fruits and spices or for bread. When cooking cranberries, cook them only until they pop. If cooked longer, they become bitter. Cranberry jellies are also made, and cranberry juice is bottled commercially.

Peak season. September through January.

Dietary information. Raw, unsweetened cranberries contain 46 calories in 3½ ounces (100 g), vitamins A and C, potassium, calcium, and phosphorus.

CURRANTS

Currants are small berries that grow in clusters like grapes. There are red, white, and black currants, both wild and cultivated. The glossy, sweet-sour red currants are eaten raw, added to fruits compotes and salads, or made into jams and jellies. They are used in the manufacture of a liqueur called cassis. Black currants may be made into pies, but their best use is in jams and jellies. White currants are eaten raw or used in fruit salads.

When selecting currants for jelly making, choose firm currants that are not overripe. Overripe fruits do not "jell" so well.

Peak season. All currants are in limited supply. When available, the season is from June to August, with peak month in July.

Dietary information. In 3½ ounces (100 g) of currants, there are about 52 calories, vitamins A and C, and calcium, phosphorus, potassium, and iron.

ELDERBERRIES

Elderberries are small black berries that grow on the elder bush. They are used primarily in preserves, pies, and wine.

GOOSEBERRIES

Gooseberries were among America's earliest products, brought from England and planted by the colonists. A close relative of currants, they resemble grapes somewhat and may be 1 to 1½ inches (2.54–3.78 cm) long. They may be green, red, yellow, or white, but the most common variety is yellowish or whitish with translucent skin revealing a series of white veins. The outside may be smooth or have a downy texture. In England, the home of gooseberry pie, they are also eaten raw with cream; in this country they are generally cooked. They are usually available only in farmers' markets or through local suppliers. Gooseberries carry a fungus that destroys the white pine tree, and consequently their cultivation and transportation is regulated by state and federal laws.

Ripe gooseberries can be recognized by their light amber color and softness. The large ones are generally of better quality. Avoid mushy berries or those with skins marred by splits or blemishes. They should be stored unwashed in the refrigerator and will hold for three to five days. One quart (960 ml) will serve four generously.

Wash gooseberries carefully before using and remove both the stem and blossom end. Ripe gooseberries may be eaten fresh with cream or made into jams, purées, and relishes. They can be substituted in any favorite berry recipe for pies. The French make a gooseberry sauce to serve with mackerel; another European favorite is gooseberry fool, or a thick purée of gooseberries and whipped cream.

Peak season. In season May through August, with June and July peak months.

Dietary information. Gooseberries contain 39 calories in 3½ ounces (100 g), vitamin A and potassium, and some vitamin C, phosphorus, and calcium.

HUCKLEBERRIES

Huckleberries grow wild and are usually sold in local markets because they do not ship well. They are smaller and more acid than blueberries and have ten large seeds that crackle as the berry is eaten. Blueberries have many more seeds, but they are so small they are unnoticeable. Huckleberries are interchangeable in use with blueberries.

Peak season. June through August in limited quantities.

Dietary information. Similar to blueberries.

Berry picking

Berries of all kinds spring up like weeds in any vacant wooded spot. Picking tiny berries one by one, especially when the bushes are spiked with thorns and loaded with mosquitos, is not everyone's favorite sport, but the rewards are unsurpassed. Minimize damage by wearing long sleeves, mosquito repellent, and a hat to shade you from the sun. Some berries must be picked by performing a series of deep knee bends. Blueberries and huckleberries grow on low shrubs; dewberries grow in creeping vines near the ground, as do wild strawberries.

Pêche Cardinal

One of the most glorious ways to combine raspberries with another fruit is in the classic French dessert, *pêche Cardinal*—or a poached peach covered with raspberry purée. Dissolve a cup of sugar and 2 tablespoons vanilla extract in enough water to cover peaches (figure one peach per serving). Bring the water and peaches to a simmer and simmer about 8 minutes, until tender but firm. Let the peaches cool in the syrup for 20 minutes, then peel. Chill. Purée the raspberries by blending them with sugar to taste in an electric blender and chill. When ready to serve, spoon the raspberry purée over the peaches and top with whipped cream.

Dessert strawberries

One can never fault the choice of strawberries to top off a fine dinner. When they are at their peak—large, perfect, juicy—serve them unadorned, hulls intact, heaped in a pretty bowl. Pass the strawberries accompanied by a bowl of confectioners' sugar, and let your guests ladle out their own servings of berries and sugar on their dessert plates and do their own dipping.

LOGANBERRIES

Loganberries are large, long, dark red, acid, and highly flavored. They are the oldest trailing blackberry variety of the Pacific coast. They are highly perishable and are most often canned. They are used in making jams, preserves, tarts, and pies.

Peak season. June and July, in limited amounts.

Dietary information. Fresh loganberries contain 62 calories in 3½ ounces (100 g), calcium, phosphorus, potassium, and vitamins A and C.

RASPBERRIES

Raspberries come in all colors—yellow, golden, apricot, amber-colored, black, red, purple, and various shades in-between. They grow wild and are also cultivated. Most commonly seen are the red and black. They are always sold with the hulls removed.

Raspberries are perishable and expensive. Look for berries that are plump and fresh looking in dry, unstained containers. These berries must be used as soon as possible after purchase. They are delicate and must be handled and washed most gently.

Raspberries are delicious eaten with cream or unadorned and dusted lightly with confectioners' sugar. They also make fine jams and preserves and are interchangeable in use with strawberries.

Peak season. Available in limited quantities from mid-April through November, with peak supplies in June and July.

Dietary information. Red raspberries contain 57 calories in 3½ ounces (100 g); black contain 73 calories in the same amount. Red are high in vitamin A, while black have only a trace. Both contain vitamin C, calcium, potassium, and phosphorus.

STRAWBERRIES

The strawberry is one of our most popular fruits and is certainly the star of the berry family. Tiny, sweet wild strawberries, once nicknamed the "oyster of summer," still abound in woods and shaded areas, but enormous quantities of strawberries are cultivated in both America and in Europe.

Many varieties of strawberries have been developed; some are huge, bright red, and well shaped. Unfortunately, the flavor of oversized berries does not always measure up to their appearance, and smaller berries are frequently sweeter and more distinctive in taste. When choosing berries, look for full, red color and firm flesh, with the green stem cap attached. Avoid berries with uncolored areas, patches of mold, or that look overripe. Examine the container to make sure it is not stained. Strawberries are usually sold by the pint (240 ml). One pint (240 ml) will serve two, and 2 pints (480 ml) will provide enough fruits for a 9-inch (22.9 cm) strawberry shortcake.

Discard soft or moldy berries at once and store the rest, unwashed, in the refrigerator. As with all berries, they should be used as soon as possible, but they will keep for a day or two. Wash them just before using in a bowl of tepid water. They must be washed thoroughly because they are often sandy. After washing, lift them from the bowl with your hands and spread them on paper towels to dry. Hull them *after* they are washed; never before, or they will absorb some of the water.

Strawberries are perfection, lightly sugared, with or without cream, and served as dessert. They combine well with other fruits in a fruit cup, make excellent jams and purées and fillings in pies and tarts.

Peak season. Available all year, with peak production and lowest prices generally between mid-April and mid-July. Lowest supplies in October and November.

Dietary information. Strawberries contain 37 calories in 3½ ounces (100 g). They are high in vitamin C and contain minerals and some vitamin A.

BREADFRUIT

Staple food in Polynesia, breadfruit is a watermelon-sized fruit. It is also grown in South and Central America, and in the South Sea Islands it is regarded as the staff of life. Breadfruits, which may weigh as much as 15 pounds (6.8 kg), are oval or round with a yellowish green rind. The pulp is fibrous in texture and white to yellowish when mature. The starchy pulp, when roasted in its skin, tastes like baked potatoes with sweet milk.

Varieties. There is a cultivated breadfruit that is seedless and a wild breadfruit with seeds called "breadnut." Breadnut is grown for its seeds, which are roasted or boiled. They closely resemble chestnuts in flavor and texture and may be used in place of chestnuts in any recipe. Seeds are available packaged in American markets.

Preparation. Breadfruit is cooked like potatoes.

Dietary information. Raw breadfruit has 103 calories in 3½ ounces (100 g) (compared to 76 in potatoes for the same amount) and some minerals and vitamin A.

CARAMBOLA

The carambola is an unusual egg-shaped fruit with four or six prominent ribs that run longitudinally. It ranges in size from a small plum to a large orange. The skin is a bright golden yellow; the flesh is juicy and has a crisp texture. The carambola grows in the West Indies and Hawaii and in small quantities in southern California and Florida.

Varieties. There are sweet and sour types; the sweet is superior.

Preparation and serving. Carambolas are peeled and can be used raw in fruit or vegetable salads, as a flavoring for beverages, or cooked into jellies and jams.

Dietary information. There are 35 calories in 3½ ounces (100 g) of carambolas. They contain appreciable amounts of carbohydrates, vitamins A and C, and potassium.

Mutiny on the Bounty

In case you've ever wondered about the nature of Captain William Bligh's mission in 1787 when the famous mutiny on his sailing ship, the *Bounty,* occurred, it was to reach Tahiti in order to bring back specimens of the breadfruit tree to the West Indies as a source of food for England's colonies in the Caribbean. The good captain had been called "Breadfruit" Bligh since 1772, when he first discovered the virtues of the melon-shaped fruit. As you may remember, he didn't quite make it on his first trip, but four years later he set out again, and this time he completed his mission. (The ship was the *Providence*.) He loaded his decks with breadfruit plants in Tahiti and planted hundreds of them on the islands of St. Vincent and Jamaica. The young trees had to be watered daily on the long sea voyage, and the trees got their water even if the crew did not.

But the breadfruit was not a success in West Indies. The trees thrived, but the West Indians preferred their familiar staple starch of plantains, which has remained their favorite starch in spite of Captain Bligh's efforts.

Beauty that is skin deep

The carambola's chief claim to fame is its unusual appearance, which makes it a dramatic addition to gift packages of fruits. The fully ripe fruits have an agreeable flavor that ranges from mildly acid to sweet, but its main distinction is its looks, rather than its flavor.

The carambola is popular in southern Florida as a dooryard tree, but its supersensitivity to cold weather and water has deterred growers from attempting large commercial production.

Cherimoya relatives

There are several other fruits in the cherimoya family that resemble it in taste and texture. One is the sweetsop, also called "sugar apple" and its more acid relative, the soursop, also known as "guanabana," which has spines on its green rind. The llama, grown in Latin America, is another variety of cherimoya and has a similarly flavored, mildly acid pulp. Both the soursop and sweetsop are high in vitamin C, carbohydrates, and contain minerals. There are 94 calories in 3½ ounces of sweetsop; 65 in the same amount of soursop.

The Japanese cherry

The cherry had its origin in China more than four thousand years ago and is cultivated in many countries. Nowhere, however, is the cherry more popular as a subject of verse and legends than in Japan. The Japanese cherry tree bears a small, acid fruit, but it is the cherry blossom that stirs the imagination in the land of the rising sun. According to legend, a fifth-century Japanese emperor was boating on a lake surrounded by cherry trees. A few pink blossoms drifted into his sake cup. He was struck with the poetic magnitude of the moment and resolved to drink wine beneath the cherry trees every spring. Today, cherry orchards are still the scene of festive spring celebrations in Japan. The cherry is so highly regarded in Japan that the city of Tokyo sent the Japanese variety of the tree as an official gift to adorn the streets of Washington, D.C., in 1912.

CHERIMOYA

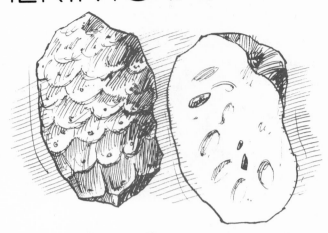

The cherimoya is an almost heart-shaped green fruit, with skin faintly etched in medallions. The pulp is white and has a sherbetlike consistency when chilled—which explains why it is called "sherbet fruit" and also "custard apple." The ripe cherimoya has a sweetly acid flavor that is said to resemble a combination of strawberry, pineapple, and banana. It is grown primarily in California, Australia, the West Indies, and southern Florida.

Selection. Choose fruits with a fairly uniform green color. The larger sizes are superior to the small ones. Avoid cherimoya with mold or cracks at the stem end, or those with dark brown skins, as they are overripe. Surface brown scars do not indicate poor quality.

Storage. Ripen at room temperature until the cherimoya yields to gentle pressure between the palms of the hands. Refrigerate and use promptly.

Preparation and serving. Cut into halves or quarters and eat with a spoon, removing the seeds as you eat it. If you have the patience and fortitude to remove all the seeds, you can cut it into cubes and use in fruit cups and salads.

Dietary information. There are 94 calories in 3½ ounces (100 g) of cherimoya. It is high in vitamin C and contains carbohydrates, minerals, and small amounts of vitamin A and some B vitamins.

CHERRIES

The cherry has been glorified in legend and literature, not only for the succulent taste of its fruit but for the loveliness of its pink blossoms, which herald the end of winter in many countries throughout the world. Just as the cherry blossom symbolizes the spring, its ripe fruit marks the beginning of the summer season. There are no less than six hundred varieties of sweet cherries grown in temperate climates. Sour cherries, too, abound (more than three hundred varieties); these usually go straight from the tree to processing plants, where they are canned and frozen and made into other commercial products.

Peak season. May through July. June cherries have the best flavor. Cherries are available through August in some areas.

Amount to buy. One to 1½ pounds (454–681 g) will serve four people. You need about a pound (454 g) of cherries, canned or fresh, for a pie.

Varieties. There are many excellent varieties of both sweet and sour cherries. The favorite sweet eating cherries are Bing, Lambert, and Royal Ann. The Bing matures before the Lambert and is large, round, and plump with a deep mahagony color. It ships well from the western states, where it is grown. The Lambert matures a week to ten days after the Bing and is grown in the same areas; it is longer and heart shaped, with much the same flavor. The Royal Ann is distinguished by its light color. Royal Ann has a good flavor but ships poorly, because slight bruises show on its pale skin. Sour cherries are lighter in color and tart in taste. They are more easily found canned than fresh. They are grown primarily in the Midwest and eastern states.

Selection. Good-quality sweet cherries are dark in color with bright, glossy, plump surfaces; inside they are firm and juicy. The stems should appear fresh, not shriveled or dried. Avoid cherries that are soft, leaking, or too dark in color; the natural dark color of cherries often conceals signs of decay. Most cherries, including Bing, are deep maroon to almost black in color; Lambert cherries are lighter red. The best way to test cherries before buying is to sample one.

Storage. Cherries are delicate, bruise easily, and must be handled with care. They will keep a day or two in the refrigerator. Do not wash until just before eating.

Preparation and serving. Cherries should be washed thoroughly because they are sprayed with insecticide; do not allow them to soak in water, however, or they will become waterlogged. If you find pitting cherries a tiresome chore, try using a fresh, strong penpoint inserted in a clean holder. The now-scarce hairpin also works very well. Sweet cherries are delicious eaten out of hand. They may be poached, soaked in liqueurs, and flamed for cherries Jubilee, spooned over ice cream, or made into jellies and jams.

Dietary information. There are 70 calories in 3½ ounces (100 g) of sweet cherries; sour cherries have 58 calories in the same amount. Cherries contain calcium, vitamin A, and phosphorous, as well as a small amount of protein and iron.

CITRON *See* Lemon.

Cherries are for the birds

Birds love cherries as much as people do, and their greedy little appetites are a problem for cherry cultivators. Cherry growers often scare birds away from the crop by setting off timed explosives of firecrackers. The birds never become used to the loud noise and fly away, leaving a few more cherries for human consumers.

Cold, warm, or flaming

A big bowl heaped with ripe, juicy cherries is a lovely dessert. So are poached cherries. So are flaming cherries.

To poach cherries, make a syrup of 1 cup of sugar and 2 cups of water in a saucepan. When it comes to a boil, add 1½ pounds of pitted, stemmed cherries—Bing, for instance. Cook just until they are heated through. Don't overcook; if you must make a mistake, let it be on the underdone side. Remove from the heat and add a dollop of kirsch or cherry brandy, if you like. Serve them warm or chilled, or, for a really festive dessert, you can serve them flaming over ice cream.

Cherries Jubilee

⅓ cup cherry juice
2 tablespoons sugar
½ cup finely shredded orange peel
2 cups poached cherries
¼ cup orange liqueur
½ cup brandy, warmed
1 quart vanilla ice cream

Combine the cherry juice, sugar, and shredded orange peel in a small saucepan and simmer over low heat for 3 or 4 minutes. Add the cherries and liqueur and heat through. Transfer to a chafing dish over a warmer and place within view of your guests. Pour the warmed brandy over the cherries and ignite. Ladle the flaming fruit over individual portions of ice cream. Serves six.

Forever and ever

Coconuts grow on palm trees of a particular variety that mature rapidly and produce nuts for seventy years. The seed of this hardy fruit barely needs planting; when the nut falls naturally from the tree, it cracks open and takes root within three years.

In tropical areas, coconut branches provide materials for building, clothing, baskets, and hats. Coconut fiber is used to make nets, ropes, brushes, and mats, and the fruit itself provides a sweet drink and a food rich in fat. For these reasons it is said, "He who plants a coconut tree plants vessels and clothing, food and drink, a habitation for himself and a heritage for his children."

Coconut oil is classified as a vegetable oil, which is a confusing designation. It is widely used in medicines, soaps, cosmetics, and suntan oil and as a substitute for natural dairy products in the manufacture of margarine and other foods. It is, however, a highly saturated fat and should be avoided by cholesterol-conscious people.

Extra coconut?

After you've sprinkled the top of your home-baked cake with fresh-grated coconut, you may find you have a lot left. Add it to your favorite muffin recipe (it will add sweetness and texture) or to pancakes, or mix it into yogurt, granola, or fruit salad.

The history of the coconut

Coconuts originated in Malaysia and floated across the sea in ships made out of their own tough shells to take root in South America. They are easily grown in tropical climates throughout the world, providing many useful products. From 26 to 29 billion coconuts are produced annually throughout the world.

Grow your own palm

Coconut palms can be grown at home by planting a whole coconut in a big pot of soil and keeping it warm. It will bring forth beautiful palm leaves, but no fruit.

COCONUTS

The coconut is not really a nut, although its rich, white meat has the taste and texture of one. The coconut actually belongs to the class of fruit known as "drupes," and the part of the coconut we eat is the drupe's seed—in fact, the largest seed of any fruit. This seed is encased in a rough hairy wrapping and contains inside its hard shell a delicious fluid known as coconut milk. Coconuts are exported to the United States from tropical countries.

Peak season. Available all year. Peak season is October–December.

Amount to buy. You can't buy *less* than one fresh coconut, which will provide enough meat for several cups of grated coconut.

Selection. A fresh, good-quality coconut is heavy and filled with milk, which sloshes when you shake it. Avoid cracked coconuts, coconuts without milk (these are spoiled), and those with wet or moldy "eyes" (the three small, soft circles at the top are called "eyes").

Storage. A whole unopened coconut can be stored at room temperature for about two months. Once cracked, however, it should be stored, covered, in the refrigerator; it will stay fresh there about a week. Fresh grated coconut meat can be covered with coconut milk and frozen.

Preparation and serving. Natives of tropical islands simply hack coconuts open with a machete. Extracting coconut meat from its hard shell in the kitchen, however, requires some labor. First, pierce the three "eyes" with a sharp instrument like an icepick or a skewer and strain the milk into a glass through a fine strainer or some cheesecloth. (Don't throw the milk out; it is a delicious drink, may be mixed with gin for a Coco Loco cocktail, added to curries, or blended into milk shakes. The milk should be refrigerated and used within twenty-four hours.) Then, tap the coconut all over with a hammer and break it open. This task is facilitated by heating the coconut in a 325°F (163°C) oven for 15 minutes, but no longer; overheating will destroy the flavor. Slide the knife between the shell and the meat to extract it. The dark skin that coats the white meat can be removed with a potato peeler or left on to protect your fingers as you hand grate. Fresh coconut meat can be eaten out of hand, or grated with a grater or chopped in the blender for use in cookies, cakes, and other baking. Fresh coconut is more flavorful and less expensive than packaged coconut, and it is free of the additives used to preserve it in cans. You can roast grated coconut by placing it in an iron skillet over medium heat for 3 to 4 minutes until it browns.

Dietary information. Fresh coconut is high in calories—346 in 3½ ounces (100 g) and high in saturated fat. It contains a small amount of vitamin A.

DATES

Dates are called "the candy that grows on trees"; these small, oblong brown fruits contain within their skins a sweet, sticky flesh loaded with natural sugar. The date was first cultivated in Iraq as far back as 2500 B.C. and has always been a popular food in the Middle East. Iraq still produces three-quarters of the world's supply, although dates are now grown and exported from most warm countries. About fifty years ago date orchards were introduced in dry regions of the United States, and California and Arizona are now leading producers among the states.

Peak season. Available all year. They are most abundant from September to May; peak season is November.

Amount to buy. Dates are sold loose by the pound in health food and specialty stores or may be purchased prepackaged in the supermarket in 8- and 16-ounce (227.2–454.4 g) containers.

Varieties. There are several varieties of dates, classified as "soft," "semisoft," and "dry," which describes the degree of softness and moisture contained in the ripe fruit. Another classification is based on the kind of sugar contained in the ripe fruit. Most soft varieties are invert-sugar dates and most dry varieties are cane-sugar dates. Invert sugar is a natural sugar, like honey. The leading commercial variety in the United States is the Deglet Noor, meaning "date of the light." A semidry variety, it is an excellent eating date, has a high cane-sugar content, and ripens late in the season. Other popular varieties are the Halaway, Khadrawy, and Zahidi; they are invert-sugar dates. Halaway and Zahidi are semidry, Khadrawy is soft.

Selection. Dates are sold fresh and dry, although it may not always be easy to tell the difference. Fresh dates are sold in a pressed mass in health food and specialty stores; they have been dried in the sun and contain no extra sugar or preservatives. Fresh dates are a plump and shiny fruit, ranging in color from yellow to golden brown. Their skins are smooth and their flesh pulpy. Avoid shriveled dates with visible crystals of sugar on the surface. Dried dates are usually those sold in cardboard or plastic containers. They are oblong, brown, cleanly separated from one another, and may have the pits removed. They are sometimes pasteurized to prevent molding, and may have been dried with the help of sulphur dioxide. Sometimes corn syrup is added to prevent them from drying out.

Storage. Fresh or soft dates should be stored in the refrigerator, where they will keep indefinitely. Dried dates can be stored at room temperature, but it is advisable to keep them refrigerated also. The lower the temperature, the longer dates keep their original quality. Dates should be stored covered, because they absorb odors from strong-smelling foods. They should not be stored near flour or cereals, which may be infested with weevils. Soft and semisoft varieties are more perishable than dry varieties.

Preparation and serving. Dates are 60 to 65 percent sugar, providing quick energy; they are thus a good substitute for sweets of refined sugar. They are delicious with cereal or mixed with fresh fruit salad.

An object of reverence

The date and the date palm have been regarded with reverence by various faiths. The Muslims held the date in deepest respect; they believed it came from a tree that also grows in paradise, where the date supposedly has the same delectable flavor it possesses on earth. Jews and Christians also give religious significance to the date; Jews carry branches of date palm to celebrate the founding of the Holy Land and Christians carry it to commemorate Palm Sunday.

The wondrous date palm

The date palm is a remarkable tree with some very human characteristics. It is covered with a fibrous hair, and if a leaf is cut off it will never grow another leaf in the same place again. Date palms are male and female, but unfortunately for the females there are very few males. The sexes refuse to grow close together in an orchard. Pollination must be done by hand, as bees shun the date palm. A good date tree bears 200 pounds of fruit a year; its leaves, trunk and fiber supply materials for building, fuel, baskets, and ropes. A coffee substitute can be made from roasted date pits, and vinegar and alcohol, as well as fermented beverages, are also made from dates.

Stuffed dates

Stuffed dates in an attractive box make an inexpensive and tasty gift. Remove the long oblong pit carefully, leaving the center of the date hollow. Stuff with nut meats, peanut butter, bits of marshmallow, grated coconut, almond paste, chocolate bits, or dried apricot. The sticky date will hold its stuffing with no help from toothpicks.

Feijoa

The feijoa is an interesting new addition to the family of unusual fruits. Besides New Zealand, a few scattered trees have been planted in Florida, California, and Hawaii, but there has been no extensive commercial production as yet. Feijoa trees are rather small, never growing much higher than 15 feet, with evergreen leaves from 2 to 3 inches long. They can survive quite cold winter temperatures, well below freezing.

Figs in antiquity

No fruit is mentioned more frequently in the Bible than the fig: its leaves provided Adam and Eve with the means for their first attempt at clothing; and its trunk, a hiding place for the infant Jesus from Herod's soldiers. The Buddhists, too, revere the fig, since it was beneath a species of fig tree that Buddha first received enlightenment.

Figs were well known in Egypt in 2000 B.C., as evidenced in their drawings and tombs. The Romans, who considered figs a sacred fruit of Bacchus, God of Wine, introduced them to western Europe. They were brought to the New World by the Spaniards in 1520.

Added to cake or cookie batters, they add texture and moisture to the final product, and they may be stuffed as a special sweetmeat. Delicious puddings are also made from pitted dates.

Dietary information. Natural and dry dates contain 274 calories per 3½ ounces (100 g). They are high in iron and potassium and other minerals and contain some protein, vitamin A, and some of the B vitamins.

FEIJOA

A dark green, or sometimes greenish yellow fruit with a waxy skin, the feijoa looks like a slightly elongated guava and is described, botanically, as a "pineapple guava." It is generally oval in shape, 1½ to 3 inches (3.8–7.6 cm) long, with a cuplike part at the stem end. It is grown mainly in New Zealand and is considered a great new taste treat. Feijoa trees grow to about 15 feet (4.56 m) in height, with evergreen leaves 2 to 3 inches (5-7.5 cm) long.

Selection. Select fruits that yield slightly to pressure, signifying ripeness.

Storage. Refrigerate when ripe and use immediately.

Preparation and serving. Cut the feijoa in two and use only the interior pulp. It can be scooped or spooned out and served as dessert, or combined with other fruits. It may also be stewed or made into jams and preserves.

FIGS

BLACK MISSION

DRIED FIG

Fresh figs have been providing a taste treat for humans for thousands of years. There is evidence that fig trees were cultivated long before recorded history. Their United States history is more recent. It started with the founding of the first mission in San Diego, California, in 1769, when a variety of fig was planted there. The fig was named the Mission, and it is still the leading black fig grown in California.

Unfortunately, fresh figs are extremely perishable and are a luxury in northern markets. Dried figs are available all year, but unlike dried dates which are similar to the fresh, dried figs are very different in form and taste from fresh figs. A soft, tree-ripened fig eaten out of hand, or peeled and quartered and bathed in cream, is a delicious experience.

Peak season. July through October.

Amount to buy. Fresh figs may be sold by the pound in areas where they are grown. In areas removed from their production points, they are generally sold individually. Figure two or three figs per portion.

Varieties. There are many varieties of figs, all differing in size, shape, color of skin, and color of flesh, but all equally good for eating fresh. They may be small, medium, or large sized, round, pear shaped, or egg shaped; their skin color may be yellowish green, dark brown to purple, or black, their flesh red, pink, violet, or almost white. Among the popular eating varieties are Black Mission, Brown Turkey, Brunswick, and Kadota.

Selection. Select fresh figs that are soft to the touch but not mushy. A slight bruise on the skin does not affect the taste of the fruit, but avoid figs with a broken skin or those with a sour, fermented odor, a sure sign of being overripe. Fresh figs are delicate and do not travel well, so it may not be easy to find good ones if you don't live in or near places where they are grown. Fresh figs should be ripened on the tree to reach their optimum flavor and quality, but they are often picked at the "mature-green" stage when they are to be shipped.

Storage. Ripe fresh figs should be stored in the refrigerator and used as soon as possible, within a day.

Preparation and serving. Fresh figs are excellent as a finger fruit or as a fruit salad ingredient or garnish. They may be peeled or not, according to the toughness of the skin. For most uses, you will probably want to remove the skin. Fresh figs make a fine appetizer served with thin slices of Italian ham (prosciutto), or as a dessert with cheese. In order not to disguise their natural sweetness, serve figs at room temperature or only slightly chilled.

Dietary information. Figs are a fine source of natural fruit sugar. Raw, fresh figs contain 80 calories in 3½ ounces (100 g), vitamin A, potassium, a small amount of protein, and other minerals and vitamins.

Figs for dessert

Fresh figs are delicious just as they are, but if you want to embellish them further, peel and slice them and serve with heavy cream. Or you might make a purée of fresh strawberries or raspberries, mix it with whipped cream, and serve it over slightly chilled fresh figs. Another lovely treatment is to peel and quarter the figs, sprinkle with brown sugar, and top with a combination of heavy cream, lightly whipped, mixed with an equal part of plain yogurt. Let this remain in the refrigerator for a couple of hours before serving so that the sugar and the figs and the cream marinate together.

The peculiar fig

The fig is really not a fruit in the strict botanical sense. It is a hollow receptacle with what appears to be seeds inside it. These seeds are actually the true fruits. These minute fruits ripen within the fig and never see the sun. Figs are pollinated through small openings in the top of the fruit.

However, one variety of fig, the Smyrna, is pollinated by a unique process known as "caprification." Caprifigs produce pollen, but their fruit is of little or no value for edible purposes. However, they do provide a home for a certain fig wasp, the Blastophaga. The fig growers bring these wasps, cozy and snug in their fig containers, to orchards that grow the female fig trees, the Smyrna, which produce edible figs. When the female Blastophaga, under the impression that she is still in the caprifig orchard, tries to enter the Smyrna figs to deposit her eggs, she leaves behind the pollen from the caprifigs that is necessary to fertilize the Smyrna. This wasp is the sole go-between for the male and female figs, which must exchange pollen in order to produce edible fruit.

Passionfruit

No one is quite sure how the purple granadilla came to be called "passionfruit," but one theory is that the name came from the early Christian missionaries to South America. On first seeing the flowers on the plant that bears the fruits, the parts of the flower were fancifully thought to resemble the instruments of the Crucifixion, the crown of thorns and nails, or to suggest the circumstances surrounding it.

The cultivation of the grapefruit

It is believed that Ponce de León first brought the grapefruit to Florida in 1513. It was recognized as a species distinct and separate from its wild parent, the pomelo, which still grows in the West Indies. The pomelo is a huge fruit and may weigh from 15 to 20 pounds. It has a coarse, acid flesh, and little juice.

Grapefruit is still occasionally referred to as "shaddock" or "pomelo." It was called "shaddock" in England for many years because it was confused with another fruit taken from the East Indies to Barbados by a sea captain named Shaddock in the late seventeenth century. Grapefruit is known as *pamplemousse* in French, which may have had its roots in "pomelo."

Grapefruit has made a contribution to the world of fruits in more ways than one. Crossed with the tangerine, it has parented the tangelo; crossed with the tangerine and Seville orange, it has produced a fruit unique for its ugliness, called, descriptively, the "ugli."

The United States continues to be the world's leading producer of grapefruit.

GRANADILLA

Granadilla, or the purple granadilla, also called "passionfruit," grows extensively in South America and is now being cultivated in California in increasing quantities. It is the size and shape of an egg, with a tough purple skin that becomes deeply wrinkled when ripe. The aromatic orange pulp has small black seeds that are edible.

Varieties. Besides the purple granadilla, there are sweet granadillas and giant granadillas. The sweet granadilla is not as well known as the purple, although its flavor is considered even finer. It is oval shaped, 3 to 6 inches long (7.6–15.2 cm) with tough, leathery, orange brown skin. The flesh is translucent and whitish. The giant granadilla is an oblong fruit measuring up to 10 inches (25.4 cm) in length. It is yellow green in color and resembles a thick zucchini. The inside is a mass of purple, sweet-acid pulp mixed with flat seeds. The flavor is inferior to the other two types. In the West Indies, it is called "watermelon."

Selection. The fruits are ripe when they yield to the touch.

Preparation and serving. All three types are interchangeable in use. When fresh and ripe, they are cut in two and eaten with a spoon, like melon. They may also be used in cakes and jellies or be blended into a beverage.

Dietary information. Purple granadilla is high in carbohydrates, potassium, and vitamin A and contains some phosphorus, calcium, and vitamin C. There are 90 calories in 3½ ounces (100 g).

GRAPEFRUIT

At one time the grapefruit was considered too sour for eating, but skillful cultivation has improved the flavor to the point where it is high on the list of breakfast priorities in countless homes. Its refreshing tanginess spiked with sweetness makes the low-calorie, vitamin-laden grapefruit an excellent eye-opener to help begin the day.

Peak season. Available all year from California and Arizona, from September through June from Florida and Texas. Usually most plentiful and inexpensive from January through April or May.

Amount to buy. Grapefruits keep well, so take advantage of specials and buy large amounts at one time. Half a grapefruit is generally an adequate serving.

Varieties. Grapefruits may be pale yellow, pinkish, bronze, or russet. The juicy flesh ranges from yellow to pink to deep red. They may have many seeds or few. No grapefruit (or orange, either) is absolutely seedless; citrus fruits are called seedless if they have five seeds or less. The two main types are the Duncan, which have numerous seeds, and the Marsh seedless, which have very few. The pink grapefruit is a hybrid, and many people consider it sweeter and more visually appealing than the white. These are known as Foster Pinks, Thompson or Marsh Pinks, and Ruby Red; the last two are seedless.

Selection. Grapefruits are tree ripened and are ready to eat when you buy them. The biggest grapefruits are not always the best; look for fruit that is firm, compact, well shaped, heavy for its size, and thin skinned. Avoid puffy, coarse, spongy fruits. The color of a grapefruit's peel is no indication of its taste; pink, yellow, bronze, or russet fruits can be equally delicious. Grapefruits are never artificially colored, and even the fruits with a greenish tinge that appear in the spring can be just as good to eat as those with bright yellow or pink skin. The thickness of the peel, however, can tell you a great deal about the quality of the fruit. Thin-skinned grapefruits are juicier than the thick-skinned varieties. If the grapefruit is pointed at the stem end, it probably has thick skin. Rough, ridged, or wrinkled skins are also evidence of thick skins, pulpy quality, and lack of juice. Superficial skin defects—scars, discolored patches, scratches—do not affect the quality of the fruit. Avoid grapefruits with soft, discolored areas on the peel near the stem end, water-soaked areas, or those with tender peels that break easily—all symptoms of decay.

Storage. Store, uncovered, in the refrigerator or in a cold room. Grapefruits will keep upwards of two weeks.

Preparation and serving. Grapefruit is usually cut in half and the segments loosened from the peel and separated from each other with a serrated knife. (The special grapefruit knife with a flexible curved blade is useful.) Prepared this way, it is eaten with a spoon as a breakfast fruit, appetizer, or dessert. Grapefruits may also be peeled, segmented, and eaten like oranges. This is a recommended method because the white membrane of the grapefruit, which contains nutritious substances and fiber, is also consumed. Grapefruit segments may be used in fruit salads and compotes, and grapefruits may be squeezed for their juice.

Dietary information. One pound (454 g) of grapefruit contains 87 calories, with about 50 calories in one-half medium-sized grapefruit. A 4-ounce (120 ml) glass of grapefruit juice contains 48 calories. It is high in minerals and very high in vitamin C; an 8-ounce glass (240 ml) of freshly squeezed grapefruit juice supplies more than the minimum daily requirement of vitamin C.

Broiled grapefruit

Cut the grapefruit in half and loosen the segments from the peel. Place grapefruit halves on a baking sheet and sprinkle them with a sweetener such as sugar, brown sugar, maple syrup, or honey. Dot them with butter or margarine and broil until the grapefruit is heated throughout, brown, and bubbly. Broiled grapefruit will add warmth to cold mornings. To serve it as dessert, add a spoonful of orange liqueur, rum, or brandy to each grapefruit half. Allow one half grapefruit per person.

Candied grapefruit peel

Grapefruit peel can be turned into a most pleasant sweet.

2 cups grapefruit peel
1 ⅔ cups granulated sugar
⅔ cup water
Additional sugar for coating

Remove peels from fruit with a sharp knife, cutting as close to the pulp as possible. (Save the fruit pulp for desserts.) Cut enough peels into strips ¼ inch wide and 2 inches long to make 2 cups. Place the strips in a heavy pan with 3 cups of cold water. Bring slowly to the boiling point and simmer for 15 minutes. Drain. Repeat this process four times, draining well each time.

Make a syrup of the 1 ⅔ cups sugar and the ⅔ cup water; boil for 1 minute, then add the cooked, drained peels. Simmer over moderate heat for 40 to 50 minutes, stirring occasionally. Pour the peels into colander and let drain about 15 minutes.

In a large bowl toss the well-drained peels and about ⅔ cup sugar to coat well. Spread the peels out on waxed paper to dry thoroughly. Cover loosely with waxed paper and let dry overnight at room temperature. Store in tightly covered plastic containers. Makes about ⅔ pound.

Growing them bigger

If you think that some varieties of grapes are bigger than they used to be, your eyes have not been deceiving you. In California and Arizona, several varieties of grapes are sprayed with a harmless, non-toxic product that stimulates plant growth. The spray material lengthens stems and delays maturity, giving the grapes time to increase in size. It is used on Perlettes, Thompson Seedless, Beauty Seedless, and Emperors. The treated grapes produce large, oval-shaped berries with firm flesh and a sweet, fine, mild flavor. The treated Thompson grapes are often 40 to 60 percent larger than the untreated ones.

Grape stuffing

To add an unusual fillip to poultry stuffing, mix two cups of seedless grapes with ¼ cup dry sherry, ¼ cup melted butter and 2 tablespoons of honey. Add this mixture to 4 cups of your favorite dressing recipe or a packaged brand in the proportion of two. Use 2 cups of the grape mixture for every four cups of stuffing.

GRAPES

CONCORD

FLAME TOKAY

MUSCAT

Grape growing is the world's biggest fruit industry, with grapes raised for table use, for raisins, for wine and juice, and for canning, the least important. Table grapes are those intended for use as a fresh fruit, and there are less than a dozen varieties produced extensively for table grapes. As a fresh fruit, grapes are unsurpassed for their appealing texture and sweet taste. Unlike some fruits, grapes will not improve in color, flavor, or quality after they have been harvested, and they will not ripen after leaving the vine.

Peak season. Available all year, with different varieties maturing at different times. The European-type grapes such as the Emperor, Tokay, Cardinal, Thompson seedless, and Ribier are grown in California and Arizona and are available from early June through April or May. The American-type grapes, like the Concord and Delaware, are available in the fall.

Amount to buy. The amount will vary according to your needs and the capacity of your grape eaters.

Varieties. The western, or European types are generally sweeter than the Eastern or American types, but the eastern varieties are as popular for eating as they are for use in jellies, wine, or grape juice. The skin of the western grape adheres closely to the pulp and the seeds are easily removed, whereas the eastern grape has a skin that separates easily from the pulp but whose seeds are difficult to pry away from the flesh. Listed below are some of the most important varieties:

CARDINAL. Large, dark red grapes, mild and delicious. Clusters are long and conical.

CATAWBA. Large, purplish red, American-type grape used mostly for wine and juice.

CONCORD. Dark purple, the principal American-type grape. Excellent for grape juice, jelly, or table use.

DELAWARE. Small, pink, tender-skinned American-type grape. Also used for wine.

EMPEROR. Large, red grapes with a cherrylike flavor. Clusters are large and very full.

FLAME TOKAY. Red, large, round grapes.

LADYFINGER. Pale green, large elongated grape.

MUSCAT. Greenish yellow, oval grape with a spicy flavor, used for wine.

PERLETTE. White, small, round- to olive-shaped seedless grape. Small to medium-sized, compact, tight bunches.

RIBIER. Large black round grapes, small to large bunches.

THOMPSON SEEDLESS. The all-American favorite; small, white, olive-shaped grapes, sweet and seedless.

Selection. Choose grapes that appear plump, have distinct color typical of their variety, and are firmly attached to the stem in well-formed, good-looking bunches. One foolproof method to use in buying grapes is to taste one in the store. White or green grapes are best when the color has a yellowish cast with a tinge of amber. Red varieties are the sweetest when the red color is predominant on most of the grape. Avoid wrinkled or leaking grapes, or grapes with bleached areas around the stem. Be wary of the grapes that are already packaged unless you plan to use them for cooking or in salads.

Storage. Store in the refrigerator. They will keep from three to five days, but use them as soon as possible while they are at their very best.

Preparation and serving. Wash grapes carefully and thoroughly under cold, running water just before serving. Grapes are generally eaten out of hand or combined with other fruits in fruit salads. Unless they are seedless, they must be halved and pitted before mixing with other fruits. Several varieties of grapes in a fruit bowl offer an eye-filling display of colors and a diversity of flavors. Grapes are a fine dessert served with cheese, and they are often used in sauces that accompany fish or poultry dishes.

Dietary information. Grapes are high in carbohydrates and contain minerals, vitamin A, and some vitamin C. There are 197 calories in one pound (454 g) of American-type grapes; 270 in a like amount of European type.

Viticulture

Grape horticulture is called "viticulture," after the botanical name for the grape—*vitis*. Although grapes grow wild, raising them is a delicate art. Grapes are sensitive to climactic changes and must be protected from cold, wind, heavy rain, and extreme heat. Grapes are not planted from grape seeds but are grafted. They need terraces, arbors, and trellises to support their climbing stems and leaves. Often grapevines are planted among other trees, which support them with their trunks and branches. The fruit, incidentally, is not the only part of the grapevine that is eaten; in Mideast cooking, tender grape leaves are wrapped around rice and meat stuffings. These little rolls are called *dolmas*.

Raisins

Raisins were no doubt discovered by accident, when someone let his grapes ripen too long on the vine. Raisins are sun-dried grapes, which have been used as a condiment and for commercial purposes since biblical times. Israelites paid their taxes to King David in raisins.

For fifteen hundred years, Armenia was the raisin capital of the world. Today California leads the world in raisin production. Raisins, like grapes, come in several varieties. Sultanas are seedless raisins; currants are small raisins, not to be confused with the fresh berry by the same name. Raisins contain iron and make a nutritious snack. They are also used in relishes, baking, sauces, and many meat recipes.

To use a guava

A ripe guava, served simply, can provide a pleasant and unusual dessert. Peel and slice the guava and sprinkle the slices lightly with sugar. Chill in the refrigerator and serve with cream.

The guava slices may also be sugared and baked in a 350° F oven for 30 minutes and served with cream. The standard open apple tart can be given a new look and taste by substituting guava slices for the apples.

What's in a name?

Often plenty. How much success the kiwi fruit would have had in the commercial world under its true name of "Chinese gooseberry" will ever be in doubt. The enterprising New Zealand businessmen who decided that the United States was a potential market for several New Zealand-grown fruits were not about to burden their export with the unimaginative, dreary-sounding Chinese gooseberry tag. And so they chose to identify it with their tiny native bird, the kiwi. A pert-sounding name for a pert-tasting fruit.

GUAVAS

Guavas are native to Mexico and South America but are grown extensively in Hawaii, Florida, and southern California. A member of the custard-apple family, they grow on small trees or bushes. They vary in size, shape, color, and flavor. They are round, from 1 to 4 inches (2.54–10.2 cm) in length, and have green or yellow skins, depending on the variety. The flesh when ripe is white, red, or salmon colored and has numerous small seeds embedded in it near the center of the fruit. Guavas are cooked or eaten raw.

Varieties. The most common varieties are pineapple and strawberry, so named because their flavor is similar to these fruits.

Selection. For cooking, use guavas that are firm to the touch. If you plan to eat them, choose fruits that give slightly to gentle pressure.

Storage. Ripe guavas keep well in the refrigerator for some time. If they are hard, they will soften and ripen when kept at room temperature and they may then be refrigerated.

Preparation and serving. Guavas may be puréed, baked, or eaten fresh, alone, or in combination with other fruits such as pineapple or bananas. They are widely used in jellies and preserves.

Dietary information. Pineapple guavas are very high in vitamins A and C. In 3½ ounces (100 g) of edible portion, there are 62 to 65 calories, depending on the variety.

KIWI FRUIT

The kiwi fruit is an unprepossessing, fuzzy little brown-on-the-outside, bright-green-on-the-inside fruit that may be as unknown to many Americans as pineapples were to fifteenth-century Europeans. In reality it is a Chinese gooseberry, similar in taste to the American gooseberry and quite delicious. A native of China, it was first introduced into New Zealand in 1906 and has been commercially cultivated only in that country. It was named for the tiny kiwi bird, native to New Zealand. The fruit is about 2½ to 3½ inches (6.4–8.9 cm) long and has a tender, soft skin. Kiwi fruit, like the papaya, is effective as a meat tenderizer. A slice of the fruit rubbed over a tough steak will tenderize the meat.

Peak season. June to March.

Amount to buy. One kiwi fruit will serve two.

Selection. The kiwi should be soft as a pear for best eating.

Storage. Ripen at room temperature and refrigerate.

Preparation and serving. Peel and eat out of hand or use in fruit salads or fruit compotes.

Dietary information. It is rich in vitamin C.

KUMQUATS

Kumquats are the babies of the citrus family. Shaped like large unshelled pecans, they are 2 to 2½ inches (5.1–6.34 cm) long. They are unusual in that the skin is sweet and the flesh is tart. They are never peeled; the whole fruit is edible. They make an attractive edible garnish on poultry and meat platters.

Peak season. Available fresh from November through February.

Amount to buy. They are generally sold in pint (480 ml) and quart (960 ml) baskets.

Selection. Look for plump, firm golden fruit without blemishes. Stems and leaves are often attached.

Storage. Kumquats will keep well for some time without refrigeration, but they may be refrigerated without damage.

Preparation and serving. Wash kumquats thoroughly before serving. Sliced thin and seeds removed, or quartered, they are delicious in fruit salads. Leave stems and leaves if kumquats are to be added to a fruit bowl. They are used for preserves, jellies, and candied fruit.

Dietary information. High in potassium, calcium, and vitamins A and C, 3½ ounces (100 g) of kumquats contain 65 calories.

LEMONS

The lemon is one of our most useful fruits, as indispensable as onions or parsley, although it is seldom consumed for its own sake. It can perhaps be best described as having "flavor power"; its freshness sharpens sweets, perks up bland dishes, and adds zest to the dull ones. From the tomato juice or wedge of melon that starts the meal to the soufflé and tea that ends it, almost every course can be improved with a dash of lemon.

Peak season: Available all year with the peak season from May through August.

Amount to buy. Keep a supply of lemons on hand at all times. They'll keep for weeks in the bottom drawer of your refrigerator. One good-sized juicy lemon yields about 3 tablespoons (45 ml) of lemon juice.

Pretty enough to eat

Native to China, kumquats were served at elaborate banquets in their native country complete with their own tree. They are still regarded as highly decorative for holiday dinners during the Thanksgiving and Christmas and New Year seasons, when they are available fresh. Kumquats are now produced in the United States, China, Japan, South Africa, Australia, and France.

Kumquats may be meeting some competition in the Lilliputian department, however. Coming up are limequats, orangequats, and cintrangequats, hybrids of kumquats with other citrus fruits. They are said to be basically the same as kumquats but have a greater resistance to cold.

The start of an industry

Lemons originated in Southeast Asia and today are grown in the United States, Italy, Greece, Spain, Argentina and Chile—in that order of major production. Lemons were first cultivated in the United States in California, and curiously enough it took the Gold Rush of 1849 to establish the great commercial lemon industry. Hordes of ambitious would-be miners flocked to the Golden State with visions of great wealth beclouding reality. Their numbers swelled the state's previous population tenfold. Food was scarce and astronomical in price. Undernourished, the miners fell prey to the inevitable scurvy because of a diet deficient in fresh fruits. They were willing to pay a dollar apiece for fresh lemons and oranges. Trees were planted to meet the demand, and by 1856 a new industry was born, a serendipitous event, to be sure. The fruit growers undoubtedly became richer than most of the miners.

To get the most juice out of a lemon

To increase the juice yield of a withered lemon, place it in hot water for half an hour or so before juicing it.

Before cutting the lemon, roll the whole fruit gently but firmly on a table, pressing it with the palm while rolling.

Juice a lemon quickly by holding the cut side against the palm of the hand and allowing the juice to run into the sauce. Properly held, the seeds will be trapped in your hand.

British "Limeys"

The lime has earned an enduring reputation as the fruit that prevented the British sailors from getting scurvy and was responsible for their nickname "limeys." Scurvy is a deficiency disorder resulting from a lack of vitamin C (ascorbic acid) in the diet. It was a serious problem in the past, when fresh fruits and vegetables were not available in the winter in many parts of the world. It was especially common among sailors when only non-perishable foods could be stocked for sea voyages that lasted for many months. In 1747 the Scottish naval surgeon, James Lind, treated sailors suffering from scurvy with lemons and oranges. The results were dramatic and years later the British navy began to distribute regular rations of lime juice during long sea voyages. This measure was largely responsible in preventing scurvy, which was the first disease to be definitely linked to a dietary deficiency.

Honey lime dressing

A piquant dressing for a fruit salad is made by mixing ½ cup honey with ¼ cup lime juice with one egg and ¾ cup pineapple juice. Cook over low heat, stirring, until mixture is thick and clear. Chill.

Varieties. Lemons differ in size, shape, and thickness of peel, but all are basically the same variety. Some have more seeds than others, but the consumer does not have much choice in this situation. There are also some sweet lemons, but these are grown mainly as a novelty.

The *citron* is an elongated variety of lemon grown mainly in Greece, Sicily, and Corsica. Citrons are large, knobby, and have less taste than lemons. They are used to make the candied lemon peel you use in your fruitcakes. The oil from the skin is used in perfume and some liqueurs.

Selection. Look for thin-skinned fruits, heavy for their size, as they are the juiciest. A good lemon has a rich yellow color, with reasonably smooth, slightly glossy skin, and is firm to the touch. Those that are lightweight and have rough, coarse skins have less juice. Lemons tinged with green have not been properly "cured" and will be very acid. Also avoid lemons with a dull, dark color, hardened or shriveled skin, and those with soft spots, mold and punctures.

Storage. Lemons will keep upwards of two weeks stored in the refrigerator.

Preparation and serving. Lemon juice is an indispensable ingredient in dressings, sauces, marinades, some soups, and fish dishes, and no self-respecting seafood platter would be served without lemon wedges as garnish. Lemon juice can bring a spark to bland foods for people on salt-restricted diets and it can replace caloric salad dressings for dieters. It is the prime ingredient in delicious pies, puddings, and soufflés and is effective in keeping freshly cut fruits from darkening. The peel of the lemon, known as the "zest," can be candied and used in many dishes. (In cutting peel for zest, use only the colored portion. The white below it is bitter.) Lemons are also used to make marmalade.

Dietary information. Lemons are high in vitamin C and contain vitamin A, some protein, calcium, phosphorus, and potassium. There are 27 calories in 3½ ounces (100 g).

LIMES

Limes are small fruits that look like green lemons, but they have thinner skins. Their acid taste, too, is subtly different from that of the lemon, although they are often used interchangeably. They are a must for marinating some fish dishes and for Key Lime pie, and indispensable for a variety of tall, cool summer drinks.

Peak season. Available all year. Peak season is June through September

Amount to buy. You will need more limes than lemons to make an equivalent amount of juice. There are about eight limes in a pound (454 g), and it takes about eight limes to yield 1 cup (240 ml) of juice.

Varieties. There are both acid and sweet varieties of limes, but only acid limes are grown in the United States. Acid limes are divided into Tahiti, or large fruit varieties, and Mexican, or small fruit with thin rinds. Most of the limes on the market are the Persian variety of the Tahiti type. They are large, with fine-grained pulp, light green of color, very acid, and highly flavored. When fully ripe, the skin is light orange yellow. Other limes range in color from light green to dark green. The

Florida Key lime, a Mexican variety, is distinguished by its light lemon yellow color, round-to-oval shape, and thin skin. The rind is smooth, leathery, and very thin.

Selection. Look for limes with glossy shine and good weight for their size. Avoid those with decayed spots, skin punctures and patches of mold. Some limes have a brownish irregular mottling of the skin surface; in its early stages this does not affect the taste of the fruit.

Storage. Store in the refrigerator until ready to use. Limes are less hardy than lemons and will keep for at least ten days.

Preparation and serving. Fresh lime juice is used in beverages and as a base for fruit punches, or it may be sprinkled over salads and melons. It is popular in sherbets, pies, and icebox cakes. Slices or wedges of lime can be used as garnishes for poultry and fish dishes.

Dietary information. There are 28 calories in 3½ ounces (100 g) of limes. They contain vitamin C, potassium, and other minerals.

LITCHI NUTS

L itchi, lychee, lichee, lichi—there are as many ways to spell the name of this delicious fruit as there are Chinese dialects. Originating in Asia, where it has been popular for two thousand years, it is now grown in Jamaica, Hawaii, Brazil, Florida, and California. The ripe fruit is a pearly white, jellylike pulp with a single seed enclosed in a roughly textured, coppery brown shell. Litchis have a uniquely rich smooth texture and a taste that is compared to that of a Royal Ann cherry.

Peak season. They are available fresh for only a short period in late June and early July.

Amount to buy. Fresh litchi nuts are sold by the pound. If you like them, buy in quantity because they come and go almost before you know they've been there. They can be purchased in Chinese groceries or food specialty stores.

Storage. They will keep well for two or three weeks in the refrigerator.

A capricious fruit

Before the mature litchi nut is picked, it has a bright scarlet warty skin and looks like an overgrown strawberry. After picking, the shell turns dark brown. When it is dried after maturing, the fruit changes from its smooth jellylike consistency and becomes brown, shrunken, and nutlike, rather like a large raisin. The outside becomes a thin, brittle shell. This is the form in which they are most familiar. Dried litchis are shipped to many countries throughout the world. They are delicious but not to be compared to the fresh. They are sold mainly in Chinese and Japanese shops.

Litchi nuts are also canned and in this form most closely resemble the fresh in taste, color, and texture.

The loquat tree

Loquats grow in clusters on small ornamental evergreen trees which may have been indigenous to China. They have been grown since earliest times in northern India and Japan, and are cultivated also in Indochina and the Mediterranean region. The trees thrive best in low, subtropical areas that are a few thousand feet above sea level. They are delicate and highly susceptible to damage from frost.

Sometimes the loquat is called the "Japanese medlar" because it resembles the medlar of Europe and Asia. The medlar is a tree that bears a fruit that resembles a crab apple.

Preparation and serving. Serve four or five chilled nuts on green leaves as a dessert or as a garnish on a fruit bowl. The fruits are taken directly from the pod. Shell removed, the fruit can be added to fruit cocktails or compotes.

Dietary information. There are 64 calories in 3½ ounces (100 g) of fresh litchis; 277 in the same amount of dried. They are high in potassium and vitamin C and contain other minerals.

LOQUATS

Loquats are a pale yellow or orange fruit with a somewhat downy surface and are about the size of a crab apple. The skin is thin and the juicy, firm, mealy flesh ranges from white to deep orange in color. The taste has been likened to apples, pears, or cherries (depending on who is tasting it) and is slightly tart. It is a pleasant fruit that is popular in Mediterranean countries but is not well known in the United States.

Peak season. Sometimes available in April and May.

Preparation and serving. Loquats are peeled and eaten fresh or stewed or are cooked into pies, jellies, or sauces.

Dietary information. There are 48 calories in 3½ ounces (100 g) of raw loquats. They are a fair source of vitamin A and potassium.

MANDARINS

The mandarin is a species of orange with skin that can be slipped off with as much effort as is needed to peel a banana. It is often called the "kid glove" orange because it can be peeled with gloves on. This type of fruit is often called a "tangerine," but this is not quite accurate because a tangerine is actually only one of many types of mandarin. All mandarins are distinguished by their zip-off skins and their neatly defined segments, which separate easily. Mandarins, as you might guess by the name, were originally cultivated in China. They have a unique taste, which is somewhat sweeter and drier than that of their closest kin, the orange.

The mandarin is a popular citrus fruit for snacking because of its easy-to-eat qualities. Japan, California, and Mexico are leading producers.

Peak season. November through January, with supplies of various types ending in May.

Amount to buy. Buy in quantity; they are a convenient snack food to have on hand and will keep well in the refrigerator.

Varieties. There are numerous varieties of tangerines and hybrids; all are yellow orange or red orange in color, with the typical loose-fitting skin. They come in many shapes, from slightly elongated to slightly flattened, some with necks and some without. Among them are the satsuma, small, sweet, almost seedless mandarins grown mainly in Japan; tangelo, actually a grapefruit-tangerine cross but resembling the tangerine; clementine, medium to large, with red-orange pebbled rind; Temples, believed to be a cross between tangerines and oranges, a heavy fruit with a sweet tart flavor and a slightly rough, red orange rind.

Selection. Select fruit that is heavy for its size, indicating generous juice content. Look for fresh, deep color, typical of the variety, and a bright luster. All mandarins have loose skins and therefore do not feel firm to the touch; a puffy appearance is normal for many varieties. A decayed fruit, however, will be extremely soft and may have a punctured skin. Avoid very pale or greenish-colored fruits.

Storage. Store mandarins in the refrigerator uncovered. They will keep for a week or slightly more. If they are held too long at cold temperatures, the skin may become pitted and the flesh discolored.

Preparation and serving. Mandarins are an ideal fruit for eating out of hand. They can be peeled and sectioned with no damage to hands and clothing, making them ideal for snacks, picnics, and lunchboxes. Tangerines are squeezed for juice, which is different in taste from orange juice. Mandarin slices or sections can be substituted in any recipe that calls for oranges.

Dietary information. Calories vary according to the type; there are 154 calories in 1 pound (454 g) of tangerines and 104 in the same amount of tangelos. One medium-sized tangerine, 2½ inches (6.4 cm) in diameter, contains about 35 calories. They are an excellent source of vitamin C and contain vitamin A and phosphorus, as well as small amounts of other minerals.

MANGOES

Until recently mangoes were familiar only to American travelers who had ventured into tropical lands. Now these large, oval fruits with soft, juicy, orange flesh and fragrant aroma are grown in Florida and are also imported into the United States. The delicious flavor of the mango is often described as a combination of pineapple and peach. A member of the sumac family (which includes poison ivy), the mango originated in India, where it is still a favorite fruit. It was planted in the Western Hemisphere in the eighteenth century in Brazil and the West Indies.

Peak season. Peak season is in June. Mangoes are available in some areas from January through August.

Amount to buy. Most of the mangoes in American markets are small to medium in size, and since a great deal of the mango consists of the peel and the large pit, one per person is a reasonable serving. A large mango, however, may serve two. About four medium-sized mangoes produce a quart (960 ml) of pulp.

Varieties. Mangoes vary in size and color. Some weigh as much as 4 or 5 pounds (1.8–2.3 kg); others are about the size of an egg. They may be kidney shaped, round, pear shaped, or long and narrow. The skin is usually green when immature and develops red and yellow areas as it ripens. Some mangoes are completely yellow when ripe. The large mangoes usually have a smoother pulp than the small ones.

The American tangerine is cultivated

The first instance in recorded history of citrus dates back to 2200 B.C. in China. But tangerines did not seem to have reached Europe until the beginning of the nineteenth century. They arrived from Tangier, in Morocco, which explains their name.

The tangerine was brought to America in the middle of the nineteenth century when the Italian consul at New Orleans planted it on the consulate grounds.

Sometime between then and 1893, the root stock was taken to Florida and a new era was begun for fruit eaters and fruit growers. The tangerine was given the name "kid-glove" orange by an early Florida grower, a Colonel Dancy, who also shared his name with one of the best-known, most popular varieties of the fruit. The Dancy tangerine has a lively, sweet-tart flavor with many seeds in a loose, easily peeled rind.

Chinese almond custard

A delicious way to employ the mandarin is atop a light, fragrant custard from China, its country of origin. Soften one envelope of unflavored gelatin in ⅓ cup cold water. Add ¾ cup of boiling water and stir in ⅓ cup sugar until it is dissolved. Add a cup of milk and 1 teaspoon almond extract. Mix and pour into a small mold, and chill until set. Peel and segment 2 mandarin oranges and squeeze the juice from enough mandarins until you have 2 cups of liquid. You may also use part mandarin juice and part water, sweetened to taste, and flavored with a drop of almond extract. Chill, and pour over the custard. Garnish with the mandarin segments. Serves 2.

How to eat a mango

Mangoes are a bit messy to handle. They are juicy and have large pits that cling tightly to the flesh, which makes the job of eating one somewhat of a challenge. James Beard, the well-known food expert, is a practical soul who suggests that to really enjoy a mango, one should eat it in the bathtub or, at the very least, in complete privacy. One method of eating it is to cut the mango in two, avoiding the pit as you would in an avocado. Then cut around the pit and remove it and spoon the flesh out of the shell. This is a fairly extravagant method, since a good deal of the flesh adheres to the pit, and it's a pity to waste that wonderful, juicy flesh. The most economical way (but not necessarily the most graceful) is to peel the skin and then eat the mango as you would a peach, not attempting to remove the stone.

Grow your own mango

You can grow a miniature mango tree in you own house by cleaning the stone from a ripe fruit and planting it, "eye" up, in a large pot of soil. Moisten with tepid water and keep it moist, but for one week out of every month allow the pit to dry out. A bunch of dark red leaves will appear after four to six weeks. The plant will grow eight inches in the first year. Like most indoor fruit trees, chances are slim that your mango will produce fruit.

Mango cream

A delicious Mexican custard from mangoes can be made in the blender. Peel, seed and chop 2 ripe mangoes and place in blender. Add the juice of 1 orange, 1/3 cup confectioners' sugar, and a pinch of salt. Blend on medium speed until the liquid is smooth. In a mixing bowl fold the mango purée into a cup of whipped cream. Chill and serve in small bowls, garnished with extra slices of mangoes. Serves 4.

Selection. Buy mangoes that are firm and let ripen at room temperature until the fruit gives easily to slight pressure. The skin color varies according to the species, but in general a ripe mango has more red and yellow areas than green. The mango must be eaten ripe; when it is immature it tastes acid and bitter, but when ripe it has flavor unequaled by any other fruit. Avoid mushy fruits with many black spots or those with a fermented odor.

Storage. Store at room temperature until ripe. Ripe fruit should be refrigerated and used as soon as possible.

Preparation and serving. The oil in the mango rind is irritating to some people's skins and produces a rash, so it is wise to avoid contacting the skin of the mango with your mouth. Mangoes can be peeled with a sharp knife and cut into sections by carving about the pit. Slices or cubes may be combined with other fruits in a fruit compote or served alone. Ripe mangoes can be used in purées, ice cream, or baked goods. Unripe ones may be poached or baked. When just mature, but not quite soft, they can be used in chutney, sauces, and for pickling.

Dietary information. Mango contains 66 calories in 3½ ounces (100 g), and vitamins A and C and small amount of minerals.

MANGOSTEEN

Mangosteen is an unusual fruit about the size of a mandarin orange, slightly flattened at each end. A cool, refreshing fruit, it is native to the Far East and is rarely exported. A thick, hard, reddish brown rind encloses five to seven segments, like those of an orange. The pulp is white and juicy with a sweet, tart flavor that is a cross between its relative, the mango, and a fresh litchi nut.

Serving and preparation. The rind may be removed and the fruit eaten out of hand or made into preserves.

Dietary information. There are 63 calories in 3½ ounces (100 g) and some minerals and vitamin C.

MELONS

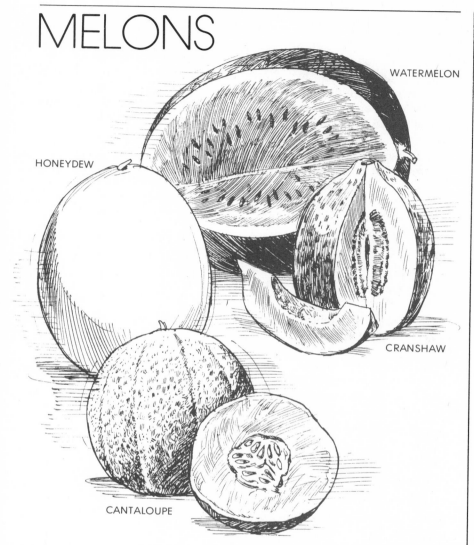

HONEYDEW

WATERMELON

CRANSHAW

CANTALOUPE

Melons are one of summertime's bonuses, along with fresh flowers from your garden and vacation time. A slice of chilled melon at breakfast can get your day off to a good start or provide a refreshing and taste-satisfying ending for a fine dinner. An enormous variety of colors and tastes and textures are tucked inside the profusion of melons that fill the fruit markets in summer, making the task of meal planning infinitely simpler.

The melons we know divide into two main botanical categories: the muskmelon or squash variety, which includes cantaloupes, casaba, cranshaw (or crenshaw), honeydew, honeyball, Persian, Santa Claus, and Spanish melons, among others; and the cucumber variety, whose best known member is the watermelon, which resembles a huge striped cucumber.

Selection. Selecting a melon that will always turn out to be exactly right—ripe, sweet, and juicy—is perhaps an impossible dream. There is absolutely no 100-percent infallible rule for determining quality in melons from the outside that will save you from ever making a mistake, but there are some identifiable characteristics of a good melon that can raise your batting average in the picking-a-good-melon department.

Early melons

Muskmelons probably originated in ancient Persia, a land where the fabulous fruits that grew in abundance were said to be sweeter and more succulent than those grown anywhere on earth. Golden juicy peaches, tart cherries, tender pink rhubarb, grapes, pears, and melons were some of the fruits for which the country was noted. The melons were called muskmelons because their aroma evoked the fragrance of the Persian perfume known as "musk."

A story is told of a medieval traveler to Persia who spoke of eating a melon, which, when opened, contained a tiny animal like an unborn lamb. "They eat these melons along with the little beasts," he chronicled. It seems that there actually is a melon known as a *baromez* (the Russian word for "lamb") that grows in the region. The meat of this melon is soft and flesh colored. A gullible medieval traveler might well have been convinced by his hosts that it was the delicate flesh of an unborn animal he was eating.

Melons were among the first fruits grown in early Egypt. They have been identified in pictures of Egypt dating back to 2400 B.C. Melons were known to the Greeks in the third century B.C. and a few hundred years later Galen, the Greek physician, wrote of the medicinal virtues of melons. They were brought to Rome around the beginning of the Christian era and became a favorite of the rich and powerful, who probably were the only ones who could afford them. It is said that the Emperor Tiberius ate a melon a day.

Columbus is said to have taken melon seeds (and lime trees) to the New World on his second expedition. During the late fifteenth century melons were introduced into France. Our American honeydew melon is descended from an old French variety called White Antibes Winter, which was brought to the United States about 1900.

Melon in the basket

A hollowed-out melon filled with a variety of nicely rounded melon balls and other fruits makes an attractive and edible centerpiece for a dinner party. Use any of the larger melons—casaba, Persian, watermelon, or honeydew. Place it on the side where it will rest the most firmly or cut a very thin slice from the bottom rind to give the melon a steady base. Cut a thick slice from the top side to create a wide-mouthed basket. Scoop out the seeds, and remove the flesh with a melon ball cutter. Place the melon balls in a bowl with other fruits of your choice. Flavor with sugar and orange liqueur, dark rum, or dry white wine. Mix and heap the fruit back in the hollow melon. Chill and serve. You may omit the liqueur, replace the fruit in the hollow melon, and fill to the brim with champagne or sparkling white wine. Serve in individual bowls or let your guests help themselves.

About cantaloupes

The cantaloupe grown in the United States is really the netted, or nutmeg, muskmelon, and not a true cantaloupe, but common usage has termed all muskmelons "cantaloupes." The true cantaloupe has the same pebbled, scaly rind but without netting and is grown only in Europe. The cantaloupe was named after the castle of Cantalupo, in Italy, outside Rome, where this Armenian melon was first cultivated in Europe at the country seat of a sixteenth-century pope.

To judge quality, look for symmetry in shape and color. A melon that is flattened on one side may be underdeveloped, or it may have been permitted to lie on the ground too long, which would spoil not only its shape, but its taste and texture as well. Uneven color indicates that the melon was not properly turned on the vine, and thus could not ripen evenly by exposure to the sun. Ripeness is the most important sign to look for. Melon sugar develops while the melon is on the vine, and if the melon is picked before the sugar is fully developed, it will never become sweeter, although storing it at room temperature may make its flesh softer and somewhat more juicy. (Honeydew melon is the exception; it will sweeten after leaving the vine.) However, no melon will ripen or improve once it has been cut open. It will merely dry out. Most ripe melons give off a warm, flowery aroma when you sniff the skin at close range. Other signs of ripeness are discussed in the individual melon entries that follow.

Storage. All ripe melons should be refrigerated and used as soon as possible. A cut melon may be stored in the refrigerator for an additional day or two. Cover it well with plastic wrap to keep it from drying and to protect other foods from absorbing its aroma.

Preparation and serving. Melons should be served slightly chilled, but not so cold that their subtle flavor is masked. Before serving, they should be cut open and the pulpy mass of seeds scooped out. They can be halved, quartered or sliced, depending on their size. A sweet, juicy melon needs no further embellishment except, perhaps, a wedge of lemon or lime. Sliced or cut in balls, they are wonderful in a salad with other fruits. There is no end to the variety of ways you can serve melon, but a succulent, sweet melon can stand on its own.

CANTALOUPE

This is the most popular of the melons. When fully ripe, it has a rough, netted skin and sweet orange flesh. The netting makes it resemble a large nutmeg, and it is sometimes called "nutmeg melon."

Peak season. June through August, although cantaloupes are available throughout the year. The Mexican varieties reach the markets in January, but the superior California type is harvested in the summer months.

Selection. Look for cantaloupes with a well-defined net tracery on their skins, an indication of a superior melon. The background skin color may range from a bright yellow green to a creamy yellow—*not* green. The cantaloupe should be almost round or football shaped without depressed or flattened areas and should have an indented scar at the stem end. If a cantaloupe is reasonably mature, the stem by which it was attached to the vine will slip easily and completely away. A ripe cantaloupe has a pleasant distinctive aroma and will yield slightly to finger pressure at the blossom end. A slight rattling of the seeds when shaken is sign of maturity, but this can be undependable, for the loose seeds could also be the last stages of maturity and the melon could be slightly sour. Actually, choosing a cantaloupe can require you to use all the body's senses: sniffing it, looking at it, feeling it, and listening to it. (The tasting comes later, when it may be too late.) Avoid melons that are heavily bruised or have strong, fermented odors. A mature, ripe melon may benefit from two or three days at room temperature before being served. Time and warmth will not make it sweeter, but they will soften the meat and make it juicier. Chill for a few hours before serving.

Dietary information. One-half of a 5-inch (12.7 cm) melon contains 60 calories. Cantaloupes are an excellent source of vitamins A and C and contain good quantities of calcium, phosphorus, iron, potassium, and magnesium.

CASABA

The casaba is a sweet, juicy, pumpkin-shaped melon with white flesh. The skin has deep, lengthwise furrows and may be light green to yellow in color.

Peak season. Casabas are best in September and October, but are available from July through November.

Selection. Look for melons that are golden yellow with a slight softening at the blossom end. Sniffing them will be of no help; the casaba has no aroma. Serve with a wedge of lemon or lime.

Dietary information. Casabas contain 27 calories in 3½ ounces (100 g). They are lower in vitamins and minerals than cantaloupes.

CRANSHAW

The cranshaw, a hybrid variety of muskmelon, has bright salmon-colored flesh with a delicate flavor and provides superb eating. Melons weigh between 7 and 9 pounds (3.2–4.1 kg), are round at the base and pointed at the stem end, and have rough, thick skins. Most are buttercup yellow when ripe; later in the season cranshaws may be medium to dark green instead of yellow. The best cranshaws are grown in California; good-quality cranshaws also come from Texas and Mexico.

Peak season. Cranshaws are available from July through October, but peak season is in August.

Selection. A ripe cranshaw has a tender blossom end that will yield to slight finger pressure. It has the quintessential melon aroma. Early cranshaws are best when their skins are bright yellow. Avoid those with sunken, water-soaked areas; they are starting to decay.

Dietary information. Cranshaws contain about 30 calories in 3½ ounces (100 g), vitamins A and C, and small quantities of minerals.

Gilding the lily

To dress up melons when an unadorned wedge is not quite enough:

Make small gashes in cantaloupe halves or quarters and dribble in a few tablespoons of port wine.

With a melon scoop, scoop out a line of melon balls down the center of a wedge of melon. Remove each ball and reverse it so that the rounded side is up, and place back in its cavity.

Fill cantaloupe halves with sweetened blueberries, strawberries, or raspberries.

Fill cantaloupe halves with ice cream and top with crushed berries and a crown of whipped cream.

Peel and section an orange and marinate in lime juice and a splash of rum. Add melon balls and mix. Divide into sherbet glasses and top with a scoop of lime or lemon sherbet.

Travels of the watermelon

Although watermelons are classified differently from the muskmelons, they are related. Both are members of the gourd family, which also can claim cucumbers and squash. Mark Twain was a great watermelon fancier. He called it chief of this world's luxuries and said, ". . . when one has tasted it, he knows what angels eat."

Watermelons originally came from Africa, and they have been cultivated in the Middle East and warmer parts of Russia for many centuries. Early in the Christian era they were taken to southern Europe by the Moors, finally arriving in China about a thousand years ago. They were then brought by European colonists to the Western Hemisphere and the Pacific Islands.

HONEYDEW

The honeydew is a large melon, from five to nine pounds (2.3–4.1 kg) with a smooth, cream-colored skin and pale green, watery flesh. The larger it is, the better. A small honeydew does not have thick meat and is seldom really good eating. Honeydew is the only melon that becomes noticeably sweeter after it is picked, and a properly chosen melon will improve on standing at room temperature.

Peak season. Peak season is June through October, although they are generally available all year.

Selection. Choose large honeydews that are creamy white or pale yellow, tender at the blossom end. Sniff the aroma, since a ripe one has a distinct and pleasing fragrance. The best ones have a fine, brown tracery of veins and a buttery skin color. Avoid a honeydew with a marked greenish white exterior unless you want to keep it as a centerpiece. It will never ripen in your home. An unripe melon that is white, smooth, and slightly waxy should be kept in a warm room, away from sunlight, for a few days. As it ripens, the sugar in it moves outward toward the skin, giving it a dull sheen and making it slightly sticky to the touch; this characteristic gave the honeydew its name. It is ready for eating when it develops a typical honeydew aroma and the stem and blossom ends become softer.

Dietary information. There are 33 calories in 3½ ounces (100 g) of honeydew melon. They contain some vitamin C.

HONEYBALL

Honeyball melons are much like honeydews but smaller and rounder with marked brown netting. When ripe, they are soft and sweet, with a fragrant aroma. Their flesh is a light white-green color, although some varieties have pink flesh.

Peak season. June to November.

PERSIAN

Persian melons resemble cantaloupes, but are the size of honeydews. They are round and have a fine network of veins and a green rind with a yellow tint when ripe. The flesh is thick, orange, and succulent. Look for the same characteristics as in choosing cantaloupe.

Peak season. June through October.

SANTA CLAUS OR CHRISTMAS MELONS

These muskmelons are oval and resemble small watermelons. Their flesh is pale green, sweet, and mild.

Peak season. December.

SPANISH

Similar in taste to a cranshaw, the Spanish melon has a dark green, corrugated rind. Test it for ripeness as you would a cranshaw.

Peak season. July through October.

WATERMELONS

Watermelons are the mammoths of the melon world, weighing anywhere from 15 to 50 pounds (6.8–22.7 kg). Their tough green rinds conceal red juicy flesh filled with water, sugar, and many seeds.

Peak season. June through August, although available from March through October.

Amount to buy. According to need. They are sold whole or in sections.

Varieties. Watermelons are oblong or round, which is the Mexican variety. The Mexican watermelon has a dark green, unstriped skin and a less fruity flavor than those grown in the United States.

Selection. When buying a whole watermelon, look for a symmetrical shape, a dull rather than a shiny surface, and, most important, a yellowish underside. But like a book, a watermelon can't always be judged by its cover. A less chancy procedure is to buy a portion of a melon already cut. Look for firm juicy flesh with good red color, and black, evenly-distributed seeds. The flesh should be wet and shiny, not mealy in appearance, with no white streaks or holes. Some shops charge more for cut melons, but the odds are in your favor for a good choice once you've seen the watermelon's insides.

There is a body of opinion that you can judge the quality of a watermelon by thumping its sides with the palm of your hand. If the sound is deep and resonant, the melon is fine. If the sound is hollow, the melon is overripe; a metallic sound signifies an underripe melon. Unless your ear is attuned to the various nuances of sound, however, you may have difficulty evaluating the quality of the thump, and there are those who claim that thumping will get you nowhere.

Storage. Watermelon should be purchased ripe and refrigerated immediately. It never benefits from being held at room temperature. It will keep in the refrigerator for three to five days. Always serve chilled.

Preparation and serving. Watermelon is a lovely thirst quencher, nibble, or dessert. It is too sweet for an appetizer. Don't use it in fruit salad or fruit cup. It loses its crispness and makes the fruit mixture watery. The rind may be pickled.

Pickled watermelon rind

A delicious pickle can be made from watermelon rind. You will need the rind of about half a watermelon for this recipe.

2 quarts 1-inch pieces watermelon rind (dark skin and pink flesh removed)
4 cups water
½ cup coarse salt
1 tablespoon whole cloves
2 cinnamon sticks, broken into pieces
1½ tablespoons whole allspice
2 cups white vinegar
4 cups granulated sugar
1 small lemon
3 cinnamon sticks

Place the diced watermelon rind in a large bowl. Place 2 cups of the water and salt in a saucepan and heat until the salt is dissolved. Add 2 more cups of the water and let cool. Pour the salt water solution over the watermelon rind and chill in the refrigerator overnight.

Drain the watermelon rind and rinse with cold water. Transfer to a saucepan, cover with hot water and bring to a boil. Reduce the heat and simmer for 10 minutes. Drain well. On a 6-inch square of cheesecloth, place the whole cloves, the broken cinnamon sticks and the allspice and tie the ends together to make a bag. Heat the vinegar, 2 cups of water, sugar, and spice bag to the boiling point in a large pot; reduce the heat to a steady boil and cook for 10 minutes.

Meanwhile, wash the lemon and cut the peel into thin strips. Add the lemon strips and drained watermelon to the vinegar mixture. Bring to a boil, then reduce the heat slightly and cook for about 45 minutes, or until the watermelon rind is translucent, stirring often. During the last 10 minutes of cooking, add the 3 whole cinnamon sticks to the watermelon rind. Discard the spice bag.

Pack the watermelon rind into sterilized jars, placing a whole cinnamon stick in each jar and leaving ⅛ inch head space. Work out the bubbles in the jar with a rubber spatula and add more liquid to fill the jars to the proper level. Close the caps tightly. Makes 3 half-pints.

A nectarine is a nectarine is a nectarine

And not a peach, although its history is so closely connected with that of the peach that it is understandable that so many people confuse them. They are practically first cousins, and even though there is little agreement among horticulturists about the history of the nectarine, many, Luther Burbank among them, felt that the nectarine was the elder. Nectarines are still found growing wild in north temperate climates. Their cultivation followed a route that began in Greece, then went to Rome, to Spain, and to Britain.

Historically, the early nectarine varieties were small, fast softening, and white fleshed, not suited to shipping long distances. But botanical know-how and skillful crossbreeding have changed this, and some horticulturists feel that the peach is in danger of being replaced by its relative, the nectarine.

Baked nectarines

The sweet, juicy nectarine is delicious when it is baked. Peel 6 nectarines by dropping them in boiling water for a minute, plunging them into cold, and slipping off the skins. Arrange them in a baking dish and preheat the oven to 350°. In a saucepan combine a cup of sugar, the juice and peel of 1 lemon, ½ teaspoon mace, nutmeg, or cardamom, and 1 cup port, dry red, or white wine. Bring the ingredients to a boil, stirring until the sugar is dissolved. Pour the wine mixture over the nectarines and bake them for 20 minutes, basting occasionally with the liquid in the pan. Cool in the dish and chill for 2 hours. Top with the syrup and whipped cream. Serves 6.

Dietary information. Watermelons are mostly water—92 percent. They are low in nutrients and high in natural sugar and contain 26 calories in 3½ ounces (100 g).

NECTARINES

Contrary to popular belief, the smooth-skinned nectarine is not a fuzzless variety of peach, or a cross between the peach and the plum. Actually, the nectarine is nothing more or less than a nectarine, a member of the rose family, closely related to peaches and almonds. Nectarines are one of our oldest fruits and were cultivated in China and Egypt before the birth of Christ. However, the new and better varieties, developed since World War II, have peach "blood" in their crosses in order to improve size and texture.

Nekter in Greek refers to the drink of the Gods; the nectarine, which gets its name from the Greek word, is indeed a fine fruit. Its bright, smooth, yellow red skin encases a meaty fruit that is smoother than the peach and has a delicious honey-sweet flavor. Nectarines must be picked mature, if not ripe, because they do not acquire more sugar once they are harvested. If you've found the nectarine to be a bland, uninteresting fruit, you've probably only tasted those picked before they are mature and shipped great distances. Some eastern and southern states grow nectarines, but most of them come from California.

Peak season. Available June through September, with peak season in July and August.

Amount to buy. There are from two to five nectarines in a pound (454 g), depending on the size. Allow one nectarine per person per serving; two if they are small.

Varieties. The modern varieties of nectarines are large in size and range in color from orange yellow with red areas to an almost entirely red fruit. The Le Grand, May Red, and Sun Grand nectarines are the most common varieties.

Selection. Select bright, plump nectarines with an orange yellow color between the red areas. But since most varieties of nectarines turn red before they are mature, you cannot judge maturity by the color. A ripe nectarine yields to thumb pressure. Bright fruits that are firm, or just moderately hard, will ripen within two or three days at room temperature. Avoid hard, dull, or shriveled fruits; they have been picked before they are mature and will never make good eating. Also avoid too soft or overripe fruits or those with cracked, punctured skins. Some nectarines have a russeting or staining on the skin; this does not affect their eating quality.

Storage. Store ripe nectarines in the refrigerator; they keep from three to five days. To ripen a mature nectarine at home, place it in a warm spot away from sunlight for several days, or until fruit yields to thumb pressure.

Preparation and serving. You can do anything with a nectarine that you can do with a peach. Before eating them out of hand, wash carefully. If you wish to peel them, first drop them in boiling water for a minute, although they may be eaten and served unpeeled. Slice nectarines and serve with cream and a jigger of sherry, or use them as a slight variation of an old favorite—nectarine shortcake. They may be pickled, brandied, spiced, canned, frozen, dried, and puréed. Nectarines may be used to flavor ice cream and puddings or baked in pies, cakes, and cobblers.

Dietary information. There are 267 calories in 1 pound (454 g) of nectarines. They are low in sodium, which make them suitable for reducing diets or for people who must limit salt intake. They are high in vitamin A and contain a significant amount of vitamin C.

ORANGES

Oranges are surely one of our most useful and valuable year-round fruits. Millions of people would find it difficult indeed to face the rigors of a new day without their morning glass of orange juice, and an even greater number of lunch boxes would look bereft without the familiar fruit nestling in a corner of it. And how many desserts and poultry preparations would be utter failures without the sweetness and juice of the little orange-colored globes!

But until the eighteenth century, when the rich upper classes in Europe began eating them, oranges, and particularly sweet oranges, were in the exclusive domain of kings, emperors, and titled nobility. By the nineteenth century they were within the reach of the middle class, although sweet oranges were still a special treat for special occasions until late in the century. Oranges did not become everybody's fruit until the present century.

Peak season. Fresh oranges are available the year round, with peak supply from December until March. Different varieties appear on the market at different times. Valencias, the most important variety, are shipped from Florida from February through June, and from California mainly from late April until November. California navels are available mainly from November through May. The Jaffa and blood oranges are in the markets from the middle of March until the middle of May. The Temple orange, a hybrid, is available from December until March.

Amount to buy. Oranges store well and can be purchased in large quantities, according to need. One medium orange yields 1/3 to 1/2 cup (80–120 ml) of juice. The rind of one medium orange yields 2 to 3 tablespoons (30–45 ml) of grated peel.

Varieties. Varieties of oranges are generally divided into sweet and sour. The sour, or Seville, oranges are used commercially, mostly for making marmalade. Of the sweet oranges, some are for juice and others are suited for eating. The common orange, such as the Valencia, is best for juice and for slicing. Others grown mostly for juice are the early Florida varieties—the smooth-skinned, seedless Parson Brown; the seedy Hamlins; and the Pineapple oranges. Especially meant for eating are the California navels, Florida Temples, and Jaffa oranges. The navels are almost seedless, with thick, easily peeled flesh that separates easily into segments. The bump or "navel" at the apex makes it easily identifiable. Temple oranges section readily, and have an excellent flavor. The Jaffa is a fine dessert orange, easily peeled and segmented.

A European delicacy

Oranges were considered a great delicacy when they appeared in western Europe in the sixteenth century. In England the orange was not eaten raw at first, but cooked into sauces, as were most fruits and vegetables at that time. Boiled turtle steak served with melted butter and orange juice was a gourmet treat. Later, the fruit was served raw or it was boiled with veal, mutton, and other meats. Oliver Cromwell once complained because his wife served one of his favorite meats without its proper orange sauce. She replied that thanks to England's quarrels with Spain, oranges were too expensive, and that he had better think carefully in the future and consider his food preferences when making political decisions. In both France and England oranges were grown in *orangeries,* greenhouses or enclosures for cultivating orange trees. Louis XIV built a beautiful *orangerie* at Versailles and filled it with many varieties of fruit trees and tropical plants.

Orange production

Orange trees do not need tropical climates. They do best where the trees are chilled by occasional night frosts. Florida, California, and Arizona—in that order—are the principal orange-producing states. Much of Florida's crop is turned into frozen orange juice. Texas and Mexico are now becoming increasingly important in orange production. Their varieties and seasons are somewhat similar to those of Florida.

Bathing oranges

The oranges we see in our markets have had a full measure of washing. On modern orange farms, oranges are picked with machines, then bathed in warm, soapy water, scrubbed with revolving brushes, rinsed, brushed again, rinsed with a borax solution, rinsed once more with clear water, and finally dried in an air tunnel before being crated.

Orange-colored oranges

The orange was not named for the color of its skin, for many varieties of oranges are green when ripe. As an example, Valencia oranges have a tendency late in the season to turn from a bright orange hue to a greenish tinge, particularly around the stem end. But the orange is the only fruit that may be artificially colored to match its name. Because consumers expect oranges to be orange, some producers treat them with ethylene gas, which decomposes the chlorophyl in the skin of the green fruit, giving it an orange pigment. Some fruits are dipped in or sprayed with a harmless vegetable dye solution at packing time. None of these processes have any effect on the quality of the fruit inside the peel, which is *always* orange: it is simply a means of giving the outer skin the conventional deep orange color that consumers are familiar with.

The name "orange" may have come from the old French word for gold, *auranja*, descriptive of the fruit's color and lovely taste.

Oranges Orientale

6 navel oranges
1 cup granulated sugar
¾ cup water
1 tablespoon lemon juice
2 tablespoons orange liqueur (Curaçoa, Grand Marnier, etc.)

With a sharp knife, remove the outer rind from three of the oranges. (Use the rind only, not the bitter white pulp underneath it.) Slice the rind into thin strips, julienne style. You should have a generous cupful of julienne strips.

Peel the remaining oranges and remove every bit of the white stuff under the peel of all. Carefully remove the center core and, ever so slightly, separate the sections at one end of each peeled orange so it will sit firmly on the plate. Place the six oranges on a serving platter.

In a saucepan, combine the strips of orange peel, sugar, and water. Bring to a boil, reduce the heat, and simmer slowly until the peel becomes tender and glossy (about 15 minutes).

When the syrup is thickened and the peel tender, add the lemon juice and orange liqueur, heat for a minute, and pour at once over the oranges. Chill. Serve each orange with the sauce and a generous crown of the candied rind. Serves 6.

The blood orange, or Ruby, is interesting because of the deep red color of the flesh.

Selection. Select firm, heavy oranges with bright-looking skin that is reasonably smooth for the variety. Avoid lightweight oranges because they are apt to lack flesh and juice. Very rough skin texture also indicates a thick skin and less juicy flesh. Avoid oranges with dull, dry skin and a spongy texture, and those that show signs of decay, as evidenced by soft spots, discolored, weakened skin areas around the stem end, and cuts or skin punctures. Some oranges have a brown stain on the skin known as "russeting," which may, in fact, indicate a good-quality orange.

The color of an orange is no indication of its quality because oranges are often artifically tinted to improve their appearance. If they have been colored, the producer must specify "color added." If you plan to candy the orange peel or grate it into batters or sauces, it is best to select oranges that have not been color treated.

Storage. Oranges keep well in a cool room or in the refrigerator for upwards of two weeks. Like all citrus fruits, oranges may develop a pitted skin and discolored flesh if they are stored too long in the refrigerator.

Preparation and serving. Oranges are eaten fresh by being peeled and separated into segments. Thin-skinned varieties may be cut into quarters and the juice and pulp eaten out of them, or cut in half and served with the segments loosened from the peel as you would serve grapefruit. Instead of orange juice in the morning, try eating a whole sliced orange—you will be getting additional nutrients. Oranges are used to flavor many desserts, and the peel, or zest, may be candied or added to a variety of baked dishes. Sauces, chutneys, relishes, mousses, gelatins, and sherbets are also made with orange juice as flavoring. Slices of orange are used as garnish, and orange segments may be added to fruit salads or cooked with chicken or duck. Duck à l'orange (duck with orange sauce) is a distinguished French dish.

Dietary information. Oranges are an excellent source of vitamin C. An 8-ounce (240 ml) glass of orange juice supplies more than the daily body requirements of this essential vitamin and contains about 105 calories. Both juice and pulp contain valuable nutrients, including iron. There are 66 calories in one orange, approximately 3 inches (7.6 cm) in diameter.

PAPAYAS

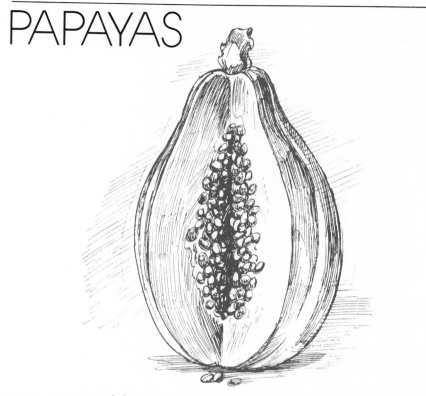

Papayas originated in tropical America and have become widely available in the United States comparatively recently. This delicious fruit has a smooth skin that ripens from green to yellow or orange. The flesh is orangy, sweet, and juicy, with a melon-like taste and texture, but softer and creamier. It contains a wealth of black seeds that look like shiny peppercorns or oversized caviar, depending on your frame of reference. The fruit varies in size from 5 to 10 inches in length (12.7–25.4 cm). It is cultivated in Florida, Puerto Rico, and Hawaii, but Hawaii is the main source of supply. In the Caribbean area the fruit is called *fruta bomba*.

Peak season. Available all year, with peak production in later winter and early spring.

Amount to buy. Figure on a half to a whole papaya per serving, depending on size.

Varieties. Papayas vary only in size—some may be large and shaped like a football, or small to medium and shaped like a pear. The latter are more usual in city markets.

Selection. Select papayas that are more than half yellow and yield to pressure between the palms, denoting ripeness. The fruit should be smooth, unshriveled, and free of bruises. Papayas are delicate and bruise easily. Avoid fruit that is too soft, with a fermented odor.

Storage. Green papayas may be ripened at room temperature away from sunlight. They will ripen in 3 to 5 days. When they are soft and mostly yellow or orange, refrigerate and use within a week.

Preparation and serving. Cut the papaya in half and remove the black seeds. Spoon out of the shell with a squeeze of lemon or lime juice, if desired. The fruit can be diced and used in fruit salads. It may also be

Good—and good for you

Before the papaya became well known in the United States as a delicious fruit, it was known for its special properties as a meat tenderizer and digestant. The papaya plant contains an enzyme, papain, which breaks down protein in much the same way as pepsin, which is an animal enzyme. The papain is found in the fruit, stem, and leaves of the papaya. In tropical countries, people bruise the leaves of the papaya and wrap them around meat they wish to tenderize.

The milky juice of the papaya, when chilled, is a delicious drink and is sold both fresh and bottled. Papaya juice has become an increasingly popular commercial item.

The seeds of the papaya are also edible. In a blender they can be cut to the size of coarsely ground pepper and added to salad dressing or used as a garnish, like capers.

Mexican milk shake

The *licuado* is a delicious Mexican milk shake that you can duplicate in your home if you have a blender, some milk, and a ripe papaya. Place a cup of cold milk and several chunks of peeled ripe papaya in the blender jar and blend until smooth. Sweeten to taste with honey or sugar.

Mistaken identity

Papayas are sometimes called "pawpaws," but pawpaws are never called "papayas." Actually, they are entirely different and completely unrelated. The papaya tree is a soft-stemmed tree of tropical America resembling a palm with a crown of spreading palm leaves. The pawpaw is a shrub or small tree of eastern North America that flourishes in a temperate climate. It belongs to the custard-apple family, a family of tropical shrubs, woody vines, and small trees that bears small edible fruits.

History

As with so many other fruits, the peach originated in China thousands of years ago. As early as 2000 B.C., Chinese poets wrote of the beauty of the peach and its blossoms. The peach was taken to Europe by way of Persia and for many years was known as the "Persian apple."

The Romans, ever alert for new foods, planted peaches in the parts of their empire that were sunny and mild. When the Spanish explorers made their expedition to the New World, they took with them the seeds of many plants, including peaches. Peaches soon grew wild over the southern part of the United States. These wild peaches are known as "Spanish" or "Indian" peaches and have little commercial value now.

Commercial peaches are carefully selected varieties crossbred from two groups: the so-called Persian peaches from Europe and others brought from China in more recent times. The Elberta peach, for example, is a cross between a Persian peach and a Chinese cling.

The peach child: a legend

The peach appears in many Oriental tales and legends. One charming Japanese folktale tells of an old woman who found a large, round object bobbing around in the pond where she washed her clothes. She fished it out and discovered it to be a huge peach, big enough to feed her and her husband for several days. When she brought it home and cut it open, they found a tiny boy instead of the peach stone. The poor couple raised the child with all the love they had and all the comforts they could afford. But they were richly rewarded. When the peach child grew up he invaded the Island of Devils, where he defeated the demons, seized their treasure, and brought it home for his worthy foster parents.

And they all lived happily ever after.

pureed and used to flavor sherbets, ice cream, and desserts. Green papayas can be peeled, seeded, and cooked as a vegetable.

Dietary information. The papaya contains 39 calories in 3½ ounces (100 g), vitamins A and C, potassium, and phosphorus.

PASSIONFRUIT *See* Granadilla.

PAWPAWS

The pawpaw (also "papaw") is often confused with papaya. It is a very different fruit, however. Indigenous to North America, the pawpaw is about 6 inches (15.2 cm) long and 3 inches (7.6 cm) in width, and weighs about 12 ounces (340.8 g). The yellow, creamy, many-seeded pulp has a sweet, bananalike flavor with a pungent odor. They are not universally admired; many people feel that a taste for them has to be acquired.

They are not picked until after the first heavy frost, then they are individually wrapped in tissue paper and stored in a cool place until soft. They are served and eaten like melon or papaya.

Dietary information. There are 172 calories in 3½ ounces (100 g) of pawpaw. They contain mostly water, some protein, vitamin A, a trace of minerals, and some of the B vitamins.

PEACHES

Peaches have always been a most popular fruit among consumers, ranking among apples, oranges, and bananas. They are most versatile, used for salads, baking, preserves, wine, brandies, snacks, and a variety of other preparations. A properly ripened peach is indeed a thing of beauty with incomparable flavor but unfortunately for people living great distances from peach orchards, its promise is too often not fulfilled. Peaches are often picked green and shipped thousands of miles, and while they may look big and beautiful with the proper blush on their downy cheeks when they arrive at the market, the flesh can be mealy and lacking in juice.

Peaches today are grown in many countries. They are produced commercially in almost every section of the United States. The greatest part of the national crop is used for canning. More than two thousand varieties of peaches are grown throughout the world.

Peak season. Peaches are available from May through October. Peak season is July and August.

Amount to buy. The number of peaches in a pound will vary according to size. Allow one peach per serving, or two if they are small. One pound (454 g) of peaches will yield 2 cups (480 ml) of sliced peaches.

Varieties. There are mainly two classifications of peaches: the freestone peach and the clingstone peach. As their name suggests, the freestone types have a pit that separates easily from the flesh and are the first choice for eating out of hand. In the clingstone types, the pit adheres tightly to the flesh; these are generally used for freezing and canning but they, too, can be delicious for eating fresh. There are innumerable types of both with varying tastes and flesh and skin colors. The Elberta was a great favorite, but it is being replaced by newly developed fruits that are superior in looks and flavor.

Selection. Choose peaches that are firm but will yield slightly to pressure. A blush on a peach is not alone a sign of edible quality, because some blush when green and others not at all. The skin color between the red areas should be yellow, or at least creamy. When possible, try to buy locally grown peaches in season. They may not look as wonderful as those shipped in, but they could have superior taste and juiciness. Avoid very firm or hard peaches with a distinctly green color, for they are probably immature and will never ripen properly. Don't buy peaches with large, flat bruises; the flesh beneath will be discolored, too. Decay in a peach begins as a pale, tan spot that expands and turns darker. An overripe peach may be a deep, reddish brown color and too soft, or even shriveled at the stem end.

Storage. Ripe peaches may be stored in the refrigerator for three to five days. If yellow peaches are firm and need to ripen a little, keep them at room temperature until they are ready to eat. Refrigerate when ripe. An immature peach will never ripen to your satisfaction. If you see signs of decay in a peach, use it immediately.

Preparation and serving. Peaches are delicious thoroughly washed, skins left on, and eaten out of hand. If you need to peel them, drop them into boiling water for a minute, then plunge them into cold water. The skins should slip off readily. If they are to be peeled and sliced and held for any length of time before using, sprinkle them with lemon juice to prevent darkening. To slice peaches, hold the peeled peach over a bowl and cut lengthwise wedges. If the peach is a clingstone variety, pry wedges loose from the stone with the blade of a knife. Sliced peaches can be served with cream, wine, or peach brandy. Whole or half peaches may be poached, baked, pickled, brandied, spiced, and canned, or made into pies, shortcakes, ice cream, and mousses. Frozen peaches are usually packed in a sugar syrup. Peaches may also be used as a garnish for main courses and cooked with ham or poultry. Peach Melba is a famous dessert created by the French chef, Escoffier, for singer Nellie Melba. It consists of poached peach halves over vanilla ice cream, topped with a sauce made from puréed raspberries and currant jelly.

Dietary information. Peaches are high in vitamin A and contain vitamin C, potassium, and other minerals. There are 150 calories in a pound (454 g); a peach about 2 inches (5.1 cm) in diameter contains 35 calories.

What happened to the peach fuzz?
Readers old enough to remember when peaches wore a fuzzy overcoat might wonder what happened to it, although they are not likely to miss it. There is a simple explanation: peaches are now de-fuzzed before shipping by a mechanical brushing process that employs soft, dry brushes. There is also another method that uses a waterbrush system.

Hydrocooling peaches is another common practice among some growers. The peaches are passed over a continuous chain conveyor and are subjected to a shower of ice water, which may contain a fungicide solution. The process reduces the temperature of the fruit and delays ripening and decay during shipping. The process is directed toward reducing marketing losses and bringing a better quality peach to the consumer.

Pears in the New World

The colonists brought European pears to the New World. At first the trees thrived. But about the time of the American Revolution, they began to die off from a disease called "fire blight," which was later found to be caused by bacteria that live in the bark. Although all high-quality European pears can be attacked by fire blight, the disease is less severe on the Pacific coast. For this reason, most of the pears grown in the United States are grown in California, Oregon, and Washington.

The Bartlett pear, called "Williams" in Europe, is the most important in the United States and in other western pear-growing countries. In Germany, France, and Switzerland, large quantities of pears are used for making perry, a fermented pear juice.

The wood of the pear is also used. It is a hard, dense wood that is used to a limited extent in furniture making.

Pears for dessert

A dessert of pears served in one form or another can bring a fine dinner to a smashing crescendo. The French have always known this: their *poires en vin*, fresh pears poached in wine; *poires Hélène*, that lovely concoction of poached pears over vanilla ice cream, topped with hot chocolate sauce; and *tarte aux poires*, delicious pear tart shiny with apricot glaze are popular dessert offerings on French menus.

But a fresh, ripe, juicy pear accompanied by a wedge of cheese served with knife and fork can hold its own in any competition. This has become a distinctively American custom, increasingly popular. The cheese can be any that pleases you: cream cheese, Brie, Fontina, Roquefort, a well-aged Cheddar, or any other favorite.

Sliced fresh pears may also be served, lightly sugared, with sour cream, sweet cream, or yogurt.

PEARS

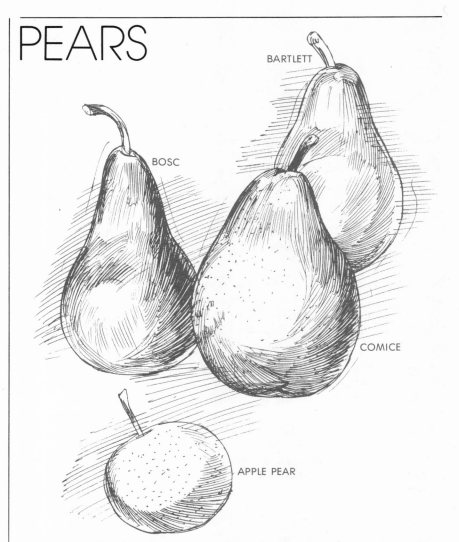

BARTLETT

BOSC

COMICE

APPLE PEAR

Pears have long been considered an aristocrat among fruits. There are literally thousands of varieties of pears grown throughout Europe and the Americas, although less than a dozen of them are of commercial importance. We are told that the genesis of this vast number of varieties goes back to nineteenth-century France, when it was the style for gentlemen farmers to hold contests to see who could raise the best species of pear—a distingué Gallic version of a county fair, one assumes. Scores of new pears came into being and then dropped from view, but some remained. From this horticultural caper came many of the fall and winter pears we have today.

The pear is one of the very few fruits, outside of bananas, that does not have to be tree ripened to be good. The pears you buy are seldom tree ripened. They are picked when full grown, but still green, and shipped. Most pear producers feel that pears develop a finer flavor and smoother texture when they are ripened off the trees; the starch converts to sugar and they become sweeter. It must be added that, like most opinions, this one is not endorsed by all pear connoisseurs.

Peak season. Available all year, with different varieties being harvested at different times. (See varieties.)

Amount to buy. Pears vary in size and are usually sold by the pound. There are about four medium pears in a pound (454 g). Allow one medium pear per serving.

Varieties: Following is a list of common varieties and peak season:

ANJOU. Medium to large, yellowish-green skin, globular in shape, with a short thick neck. Flesh is buttery and juicy. Spicy, sweet flavor. Excellent for eating fresh, general cooking. October through April.

BARTLETT. Medium to very large, bell shaped. Thin, clear yellow skin which may have a blush when ripe. Fine white flesh. Sweet and juicy. A most popular all-purpose pear eaten fresh, cooked, or canned. July through December. (The red Bartlett is like the yellow Bartlett, except for its bright red color.)

BOSC. Medium to large. Long, tapering neck and dark yellow skin with russet overtones and juicy yellow-white flesh with buttery texture. The Bosc is considered by some to be the finest winter pear. A wonderful dessert pear and may also be used in general cooking and for salads. October through March; peak supply in October.

CLAPP FAVORITE. Medium to large. Bell shaped with a clubbed stem end. Skin is greenish yellow, often blushed. Flesh is fine, juicy, and sweet. Good for eating fresh or general cooking. August through October.

COMICE. Medium to large. Almost round with a fairly thick, greenish-yellow skin, sometimes russeted. Flesh is fine grained, very juicy, with a sweet, aromatic flavor. A favorite dessert pear and for general cooking. October through March.

SECKEL. Small, heart shaped with dull brownish red skin. The flesh is granular but very juicy. Eaten fresh or cooked as a dessert. August to December.

WINTER NELLIS. Small to medium size, round in shape. Fairly thick green or yellow skin with russet mottling. Fine, buttery flesh with a rich, spicy flavor. Used for desserts and general cooking. October to May.

APPLE-PEAR. Also known as Japanese pear, Asian pear, Chalea, and Oriental pear, the apple-pear is a newcomer to the American market. It originated in the Orient. Shaped more like an apple than a pear, the fruit is still hard when ripe and has a delicious, juicy, firm flesh that tastes like a combination of pear and apple. However, it is not a combination of these two fruits, but a species of pear. It may be small and yellow with russet mottling or large with bright yellow flesh.

Selection. Select firm, unblemished fruit, but a slight scar or minor surface blemish will not affect the quality of the fruit. Avoid fruit that has bruises or rough scaly areas, or soft flesh near the stem. A pear is ripe when it responds to gentle pressure of the hands. Bear in mind that some varieties of pears are green and extremely firm even when ripe. All varieties should have typical color. Although pears ripen at room temperature, it is advisable to select pears that have begun to soften if you plan to eat them out of hand. Pears to be used for cooking are better when they are firm and slightly underripe.

Storage. Pears may need a few days more ripening time at home. Put them in a paper or plastic bag and keep in a cool place away from sun. Be sure to punch a hole in the bag. A ripe apple placed in the bag will hasten the ripening process. Pears are ready for eating when they yield to

The pear in history

Pears originated in Asia and nearby Europe centuries before the Christian era and have always occupied an important place in world gastronomy. Even the people of the Stone Age ate the juicy fruit of the pear tree. Homer sang the praises of the pear in his writings, calling them "a gift of the Gods." Marco Polo chronicled that the Chinese had brought cultivation of the pear to such a degree of perfection that the fruits were white on the inside, so succulent and delicate that they melted upon eating, and weighed ten pounds!

In the eighteenth century European fruit growers, especially those in Belgium and France, concentrated on improving the fruit. They crossed different varieties, and a Belgian priest developed the first of the pears having a soft, juicy pulp, now called "butter pears." He and other pear breeders developed many high-quality varieties that are still grown today.

Commercial storing

Most pears are picked when they have reached full size but are still hard and green in color. If they are to be kept for a long time, they are placed in cold storage at once at temperatures at or slightly below freezing. If they are not to be put in cold storage, they are held at 65 to 70°F, where they will become soft and juicy in a week or two.

Baked pears

4 large, firm pears
½ cup brown sugar
1 cup water
3 tablespoons apricot preserves
3 tablespoons lemon juice

Preheat the oven to 325°F. Wash the pears and cut in half lengthwise; do not peel them. You can do a tidy job of removing the core and seeds with a small melon ball scoop. In a small saucepan, boil together the sugar, water, apricot preserves, and lemon juice for 5 minutes. Arrange the pears, cut side down, in a buttered baking dish. Pour the boiling syrup over the pears and bake for 1 hour, or until they are tender, basting with the syrup from time to time. Let the pears cool in the syrup. They may be served warmed or chilled. Serves 4 or more.

slight pressure. After ripening, store them carefully in the crisper of the refrigerator. Pears bruise easily and they should not be stored on top of one another. The cold will keep them from ripening further. They will keep for three to five days.

Preparation and serving. Wash pears well before eating. If you insist upon peeling them, make the parings as thin as possible. Fresh pears may be added to fruit salads or served for dessert with cheese. Ripe pears with attractive yellow or rosy skins may be diced unpeeled. If pears are to be peeled and held for half an hour or more, sprinkle them with lemon juice to prevent their darkening. Pears are excellent for baking purposes; they may be used in pies, fruit tarts, puddings, cakes, and purées. They may be poached, baked, or broiled.

Dietary information. Pears contain a fair amount of vitamin C, some vitamin A and minerals. There are 61 calories in 3½ ounces (100 g).

PERSIMMONS

Known as "apple of the Orient" the persimmon is a large berry that originated in China and Japan. With its brilliant orange color and interesting shape, the smooth-skinned persimmon brings a wonderful burst of color to the fall fruit scene. Persimmons are lovely in a fruit centerpiece for the table and can be equally rewarding to eat. Larger than plums and usually seedless, persimmons have an unusual sweet, spicy flavor and most pleasing texture. They must, however, be eaten when they are soft and ripe. The astringent or puckery quality of which they are accused is present only when they are unripe. Persimmons reach full color *before* they are ripe, which is when they must be picked, because ripe persimmons are too perishable to ship. The misguided individuals who have eaten them while still unripe have a distorted idea of what this delicious fruit really tastes like.

Peak season. October to January.

Amount to buy. One persimmon for a serving.

Varieties. There is an American and a Japanese variety. The American variety, Hachiya, is slightly pointed in shape and a bright orangy red color; the Japanese variety, called Kaki, is the same bright color but flatter, looking something like a tomato.

Selection. Choose plump, glossy, deep-colored fruit with the green cap attached. Buy soft ones for immediate use and firm ones to ripen at home and use as desired. Avoid persimmons that are mushy, or with spots or broken skin.

Storage. Store ripe fruit in the refrigerator and use at once. Mature fruit will ripen best in a cool, dark place. Putting it in a paper bag with a hole in it and a ripe apple will speed the process. To ripen persimmons overnight, wrap the fruit in foil and place it in the freezer compartment of your refrigerator. Thaw at room temperature for several hours until soft. It must then be used immediately.

Preparation and serving. Persimmons should be washed, split, and served on a plate to be eaten with a spoon. The Japanese persimmon can be eaten out of hand; the American type may be a bit slippery. They do not need to be peeled first, but, if you prefer, plunge them into boiling water for a minute and then into cold. The skins will slip off easily. Persimmons can also be served in a bowl with cream, used as an ingredient in a variety of puddings, cookies, cakes and conserves, ice cream, custards, or sherbets. If the persimmon is frozen and served just slightly thawed, it makes an interesting kind of ready-made sherbet.

Dietary information. Persimmons are high in vitamins A and C and in potassium, phosphorus, and calcium. The Hachiya (American type) contains 127 calories in 3½ ounces (100 g); the Kaki has 77 calories in the same amount.

PINEAPPLES

The pineapple is a tropical fruit named for its obvious resemblance to a giant pine cone. When it is good—properly ripened on the plant until the flesh brims with sweetness and juice—it is a mouthwatering treat; and when it is bad, it is, to say the least, woody and tasteless. Unfortunately, many of the pineapples in northern markets are very different from the field-ripened fruit. However, within recent years, superior ripened fruits have been flown in from Hawaii. Their taste and texture more closely approximate the way pineapples are meant to be. The principal growing regions are Hawaii, Honduras, Mexico, the Dominican Republic, and Costa Rica, in that order.

Peak season. Available all year. Peak season is April through June.

Amount to buy. A small pineapple will serve two to three persons. A large pineapple can serve 8. The larger fruit may be a better buy because it has a greater proportion of edible flesh, and, since the cut pineapple will keep in the refrigerator for a few days, the larger fruit will not be wasted.

Varieties. There are many varieties of pineapple, among them the Sugar Loaf, and the Smooth Cayenne, which is the leading variety in the world.

Selection. Select a pineapple that is plump and fresh looking. Ripe pineapple may have an orange or yellowish skin (although the Sugar Loaf remains green even when ripe), and will yield slightly to finger pressure. Fresh, deep green crown leaves are a good sign, although the ease with which these leaves can be pulled out is not necessarily a sign of ripeness or quality. A fragrant pineapple aroma is a very good sign of a ripe fruit, as is a slight separation of the little spikes that protrude out of the eyes of the pineapple skin. Avoid fruit that is old looking, dry, with brown leaves, or those that have slight decay at the base with dark, soft watery spots, signs of overmaturity.

The pineapples that are shipped to markets are supposed to be picked at the peak of ripeness and flavor. Whether or not this is so is moot. An unripe pineapple will never get sweeter or riper after being harvested; it will merely soften and decay.

Storage. Storing pineapples after harvest may result in a change in shell color and softening of the flesh, but they will not become sweeter. Unlike bananas and pears, pineapples do not have a starch reserve and

Piña de Indies

Among the fruits growing in Hispaniola that were unknown to Columbus was the fruit that the natives called *anana*. This name had its roots in the name given it by South American Guaraní Indians—*naná*, meaning excellent fruit. But Columbus, observing its similarity in shape to a pine cone called it *piña de Indies*, pine of the Indies. In most European languages the fruit is *ananas*, but the Spaniards still call it *piña*, which is the basis of our English word, "pineapple."

The first pineapple groves were planted in Hawaii in 1813 from seeds brought to the island by Spanish seamen. The rest is history. However, today pineapple plants are grown from slips, crown, or suckers, and not seeds. But the tradition of the pineapple as a sign of welcome has survived since early times when the natives of the West Indies put pineapples or pineapple tops at the entrance to their huts as a sign of welcome. The Spaniards—and later the English and their colonists—picked up the tradition and carved pineapples on their gateposts and over their doorways. Even today, this custom is still referred to and occasionally featured in business promotions for some products.

Pineapple desserts

The pineapple can be as decorative as it is delicious, and there are no end of ways that both fruit and shell can be used to make a most attractive presentation.

One of the simplest and quickest pineapple presentations that is suitable for both a fruit platter or as individual desserts is to divide the pineapple lengthwise into four quarters, cutting right through the leaves so that each quarter will have its own plume. Trim away the core. With a sharp narrow-bladed knife, separate the pineapple from the shell in one piece. Slice the pineapple into ½-inch wedges, leaving them in place on the shell. Sugar lightly if the pineapple is not sweet enough. Place an unhulled strawberry or a pitted cherry on each pineapple wedge and secure with a toothpick. Serve chilled.

Pineapple fruit basket

Choose a large, well-shaped pineapple. Cut off the leafy top carefully and set aside. You will use this later to top your basket. With a sharp knife, remove all the meat from the pineapple, leaving a shell about an inch thick. Remove the tough core from the pineapple pieces. Cube the fruit and combine it with strawberries, blueberries, peaches, or raspberries sugared to taste and place back in the pineapple shell. Flavor with ¼ cup of orange juice or dark rum or Grand Marnier. Replace the top and chill well. You can use this as a table centerpiece and serve the fruit as dessert in individual bowls.

Small pineapples can be cut in half for individual portions, the meat scooped out and replaced in combinations with any other fruit in season.

Not for eating only

The plumy, graceful top of the pineapple can be rooted and makes a most decorative houseplant. Slice off the top of the pineapple about two inches below the leaves.

Trim off the rough outer pineapple skin and scrape out the fruit, leaving the hard, stringy core in the center, which will look like a little stump. Let the core dry out for a few days to safeguard against rotting. Insert the core in moistened, sterilized, fast-draining potting mix. Pineapples are a member of the bromeliad family, and require the same kind of treatment as all bromeliad plants. Keep the plant in a warm—about 65-70°F—location with lots of light. Mist the leaves every day. As the plant takes root, the leaves will grow out from the center.

thus have no material to convert to sugar. The best advice is to enjoy your ripe pineapple soon after you buy it. If your ripe pineapple seems a little hard, you can hold it at room temperature away from heat or sun for a day or two to soften a bit, then refrigerate it and use it promptly. To store pineapple, wrap it in plastic or aluminum foil to prevent its fragrant aroma from permeating other foods in the refrigerator. Refrigerate cut pineapple in a tightly covered container. It will keep for two to three days.

Preparation and serving. The rough, thorny skin of pineapples contain many eyes, which are also present in the surface of the flesh. To prepare a pineapple, cut off the crown and stem ends with a sharp knife. Cut the pineapple into horizontal slices a generous ½ inch (1.27 cm) thick. Cut off the skin and the eyes in the flesh of each slice. Remove the tough core with an apple corer or sharp-pointed knife. If the pineapple is sweet enough, it may not need any additional sweetening. Otherwise, sprinkle it with a bit of sugar and a couple of tablespoons (30 ml) of Grand Marnier or Cointreau and let it rest in the refrigerator for a few hours before serving. Another method of preparation is to cut off the crown and stem ends; set the fruit on its base and divide it lengthwise into 8 wedges. Remove the core from each wedge and pare the skin and eyes.

Pineapples may also be cubed, mixed with other fruits, broiled, sautéed, or cooked with meat and poultry dishes. It can serve as a salad or as an hors d'oeuvre combined with cheese chunks. If the pineapple is disappointing in flavor or texture, poach it in a sugar syrup. Do not add uncooked pineapple to gelatin desserts, as it contains an enzyme that prevents jelling.

Dietary information. Pineapple contains an enzyme that aids digestion. Pineapples are low in sodium and high in vitamin C and potassium, in addition to vitamin A and other minerals. There are 52 calories in 3½ ounces (100 g) of pineapple.

PLANTAINS *See* Bananas.

PLUMS AND PRUNES

GREENGAGE

SANTA ROSA

STANDARD

LARODA

DAMSON

ITALIAN PRUNE

P lums are a delicious fruit with a refreshing tart sweetness that can be enjoyed when they are eaten out of hand or in a wide variety of cooked preparations. There are thousands of varieties of plums in a wide range of shades and sizes, but mainly they come in three colors: blue or purple, red, and green on the outside and pink, yellow, or green on the inside. The small blue or purple plum is the prune plum, which is equally delectable fresh or dried; it is particularly sweet and has a freestone pit.

Peak season. A number of varieties of plums are in the markets from late May until September, but peak season is July and August. Fresh prunes are available from August through October.

Amount to buy. The number of plums in a pound (454 g) varies with the variety and can range from four for the large to twenty or more for the small. A pound will serve about four people and will yield about 2 cups (480 ml) of pitted fruit.

Varieties. There are two main types: the Japanese varieties and the European varieties. The Japanese varieties are medium to large in size and known for their juiciness. They come in a variety of shapes and

About plums and prunes

Plums were introduced to the New World by the colonists and were cultivated throughout the early colonies. Dozens of varieties are cultivated in the United States today, while Europe has only three or four. The leading plum producers outside of the United States are Yugoslavia, Germany, Turkey, and Japan. Much of the Yugoslavian crop is used to make a colorless plum brandy, *slivovitz*, with which guests to the country are always toasted.

Any plum that can be dried without having its stone removed and has firm, long-keeping qualities after it is dried out is a potential prune. The Santa Clara valley in California, where plum trees were originally planted, is still an important source for prunes.

Over 90 percent of United States plums are produced in California. They are derivatives of a Chinese plum, originally cultivated in Japan and introduced to California a little over a hundred years ago.

Was there a real Little Jack Horner?

Little Jack Horner, the nursery rhyme character famous for putting his thumb in a pie and pulling out a plum was, according to a legend, a real man named Thomas Horner, who was a steward to the abbots of Glastonbury Abbey. Skeptics might argue that the story is a convenient way of giving the nursery rhyme some validity, but be that as it may, the story goes that when sixteenth-century Henry VIII (he of the many wives) began to take over properties belonging to the Church, the abbot sent Tom Horner to the King with a pie containing the deeds to several estates. On the way, Tom, a greedy character and obviously no better than he should have been, opened the pie and extracted a deed to one of his master's properties. If true, this explains the use of the word "*plum*" in relation to its connotation as a sought-after and desirable prize.

It might be noted that the actual plum in Tom Horner's pie was as nonexistent as the plums in a plum pudding. The traditional Christmas pudding which goes under the name of plum pudding is full of all sorts of good things—except plums.

Poached plums

Any variety of plum or prune may be poached. Wash a pound of fresh plums. They may be halved and pitted or cooked whole. They do not need to be peeled. Boil together a cup of sugar with a cup of water, flavored with a teaspoon of vanilla extract and a pinch of cinnamon. Add the plums and poach gently until tender, basting with the liquid occasionally and turning them once during cooking time. Watch the plums carefully; the fresh prune variety can reach the proper degree of tenderness in 6 or 7 minutes. Cool in the syrup and serve warm or chilled. Serves 4.

Baked prunes

Italian prunes are firm and bake very well. Split and pit a pound or more of prunes and place them in a shallow buttered baking dish, overlapping each other. Sprinkle them with brown or white sugar, dot generously with butter or margarine, and bake at 350°F for 20 to 25 minutes, or until tender. Serve warm.

colors, but they are never blue or purple. European varieties are always blue or purple, and round or oval in shape. They are smaller, milder, and with a firmer texture than the Japanese varieties.

Although all prunes are plums, not all plums are prunes, even though plums are called *prunes* by the French. There are more than a dozen leading varieties of plums grown under more than two hundred different names. Among them are Santa Rosa, Beauty, Formosa, and Red Beaut, which are red to crimson with yellow to amber flesh; the Italian prune (which really isn't Italian) is a small, blue purple freestone; Greengage (named after Sir William Gage who brought it from France to England) is a fine fruit with thin green skin; Eldorado is reddish-purple; and Laroda, President, and Standard are dark purple to black with yellow-green to amber flesh. The small Damson plums (named after Damascus) are used mainly for preserves.

Selection. Choose plums that have a good color for the variety and are at the firm-to-slightly-soft stage of ripeness. Plums that were picked before reaching the mature stage will not ripen after picking. They should be soft enough to yield to slight pressure. Plums should be purchased a little softer than other fruits with stones or they will be too hard and sour for good eating. Avoid plums with breaks in the skin, punctures, or discolorations. Do not buy any that are sticky or too soft.

Storage. Store firm plums in a cool dry place to soften, or if fully ripe and ready for eating, in the refrigerator. They will keep from three to five days.

Preparation and serving. Wash plums well before serving. They can be eaten out of hand, combined with other fruits for fruit salad, and baked in tarts, cakes, puddings, and pies. Plums make excellent preserves and jellies and can be canned or poached. Fresh prunes cook very quickly; they must be watched carefully or they can become mushy.

Dietary information. Plums are high in vitamin A and contain vitamin C and other minerals. Prunes, both fresh and dried, are high in iron and other minerals. Prunes and their juice are known for their laxative qualities. Fresh plums contain approximately 213 calories in 1 pound (454 g). There are 119 calories in 3½ ounces (100 g) of cooked, unsweetened, dried prunes.

POMEGRANATES

The word "pomegranate" literally means "apples with many seeds," which is a reasonably good description of this colorful autumn fruit. About the size of a large apple, it has a hard rind and varies in color from yellow to deep red. Its insides are composed of many tiny seeds encased in a shiny crimson pulp, surrounded by a spongy, soft membrane, which is quite bitter. The seeds, flesh, and juice are edible. There are few ways to prepare a pomegranate and it is not the most nutritious of fruits; its shiny red pulp, however, is delicious, especially to those who relish a challenge along with eating a fruit.

Peak season. Available in September to early December; peak month is October.

Amount to buy. One large pomegranate will serve one or two.

Varieties. The Wonderful or Red Wonderful is the principal commercial variety. It is large and glossy and has a deep red or purple color.

Selection. Select a large pomegranate if possible, as it will have juicier and better developed kernels. However, regardless of size of the fruit, all pomegranates have approximately the same number of seeds. Choose fruit with an unbroken rind and no sign of decay, heavy for its size, and with a fresh, not dried out appearance.

Storage. Store ripe pomegranates at room temperature away from sunlight or in the refrigerator. They will keep for several days. The seeds may be removed, placed in an airtight container and frozen for an indefinite period of time.

Preparation and serving. Pomegranates are served fresh as a dessert or as a nibble. Since no one has yet devised a perfect, graceful, foolproof—or, perhaps, spotproof—method of eating a pomegranate, it might better be saved for occasions that are not shared by too large an audience. Start with a sufficient supply of paper napkins. You can cut the pomegranate in half and pry the seeds out of the shell with a spoon; or you can quarter the pomegranate and dig into the seeds with your teeth, leaving the white core. Both seeds and pulp are edible, but some people prefer to just suck the flesh from the seeds and discard the seeds. However, the seeds do have an agreeable nutlike texture. The juice is delicious. You may squeeze the juice out of the seeds in a juicer, freeze it, and use as desired. A few shiny, crimson pomegranate seeds added to a French dressing or sprinkled over a salad add sparkle and texture.

Dietary information. Pomegranate pulp and seeds contain 63 calories in 3½ ounces (100 g) and small amounts of potassium and other minerals.

The mysterious pomegranate

The pomegranate has been surrounded by a cloud of myths and legends throughout the ages. Certainly the fruit is as old as stories of the Garden of Eden and is described in the most ancient of Oriental literature. In the Old Testament, King Solomon sang of "an orchard of pomegranates." Moses described the promised land as a "land of wheat and barley, and vines and fig-trees, and pomegranates." We find the fruit playing an important role in the Greek legend of Persephone, a lovely young maiden who was carried off by Pluto to his gloomy subterranean world. According to the legend, if she had not been tricked into eating a pomegranate, the world might not have had to endure the cold, dark months of winter. In China the pomegranate was a fertility symbol, and in Christian art it is a symbol of hope. Great honor was paid the fruit by Muhammad, who said, "Eat the pomegranate, for it purges the system of envy and hatred."

Another aspect of the pomegranate

Aside from its importance as a religious and artistic symbol, the pomegranate has some real value in today's world, in addition to its being a table fruit. It is a source of chemicals for tanning leather and treating tapeworm infection. The flowers are used to make a strong red dye. Pomegranate juice is the chief ingredient of grenadine syrup. Grenadine syrup (which may also be made of red currants) is a popular flavoring for wines, cocktails, carbonated beverages, preserves, and confectionery.

The pomegranate tree is extremely ornamental with its distinctively vivid, orange red flowers and glossy leaves. The pomegranate is grown in many subtropical areas. In the United States it is grown in some southern areas, but all commercial production is in California.

PRICKLY PEARS

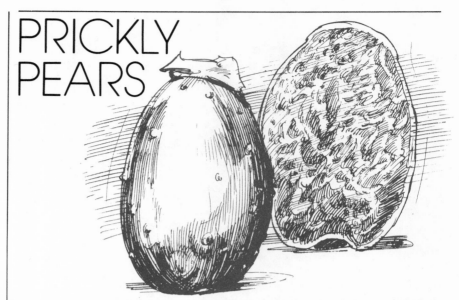

Prickly pears are the delicious fruit of a species of cactus and are most abundant during fall and early winter. They are also known as "Indian figs," "barbary figs," and "tuna." The skins range in color from yellow to crimson and have sharp spines. The plants have been widely grown in the Mediterranean countries, Australia, and elsewhere as a source of food.

Peak season. September to December.

Amount to buy. Figure on one or two per person.

Selection. Select pears that are firm but not hard, with a bright, fresh appearance. They are red when ripe.

Storage. Ripen at room temperature. When ripe, store in the refrigerator. They will keep for a few days.

Preparation and serving. Most prickly pears in the markets have already been de-spined, but, if not, remove the spines by singeing over a gas flame. Peel and slice or cut into pieces for eating or for including in fruit salads.

Dietary information. Prickly pears contain 42 calories in 3½ ounces (100 g), a fair amount of vitamins A and C and potassium, and small amounts of other minerals.

PRUNES *See* Plums and Prunes.

QUINCE

Quince is an autumn fruit that cannot be eaten fresh but is delicious when cooked or made into jellies or preserves. The quince is a hard, yellow-skinned fruit with a slightly wooly surface. It may be round or pear-shaped, resembling an apple with an irregular stem end. Like the pomegranate, the quince is rich in symbolism. The ancient Romans believed in the power of the quince to ward off the evil eye. In former times quinces were eaten and exchanged by lovers as tokens of devotion; to dream of quinces meant success in love.

Peak season. September through November.

Amount to buy. One per person if you plan to bake them. There are about three medium-sized quinces in 1 pound (454 g), which will yield 1½ cups (360 ml) of chopped fruit. For pies, buy them in the same quantity as apples.

Selection. Choose large, firm, smooth quinces with bright yellow color. They are hard when ripe. Avoid the small, knobby ones, as they are wasteful.

Storage. Store in the refrigerator. Handle them carefully, for, like pears, they bruise easily. They will keep for a long time.

Preparation and serving. Quinces are used for candy, marmalade, jelly, and preserves, and they may also be poached or baked. To prepare the fruit, pare them, cut into sections and remove the core. Poaching will take about 45 minutes, baking, an hour or more. Quinces require a good deal of sugar to sweeten them.

Dietary information. Quinces are moderately high in vitamin C and potassium, and they contain calcium and phosphorus. There are 57 calories in 3½ ounces (100 g), but since they require a good deal of sugar in cooking, the end product can be highly caloric.

SAPOTE

Sapotes are also called "Mexican custard apples" and "marmalade plums." The white sapote, common in tropical markets, is sometimes available in commercial markets in the United States. It is grown in limited quantities in southern California. It looks like a green apple but does not have an indentation on the blossom end.

Varieties. There are four principal varieties: sapote, black sapote, white sapote, and yellow sapote. The white sapote is known as the "peach of the tropics."

Selection. Choose firm sapotes, free of bruises, with color that ranges from green to yellow green.

Storage. Allow to ripen and soften at room temperature and then refrigerate. They will hold from three to five days.

Preparation and serving. Wash well and eat out of hand, as you would a peach or plum. The sapote does not need to be peeled. It may also be made into preserves or jams.

Dietary information. There are 125 calories in 3½ ounces (100 g) of sapote. The fruit contains a fair amount of vitamin A, a small amount of vitamin C, and other minerals.

Baked quince

Peel three large, ripe quinces and cut them into eighths. Arrange them in a buttered casserole in a single layer. In a small saucepan, combine 1½ cups of sugar with ¾ cup water and a pinch of salt and bring to a boil. Pour the syrup over the quince slices and bake in a 325° F oven for 1¼ hours, or until the fruit is tender but not mushy. Cool, then serve with sour cream or yogurt. Serves 4 to 6.

Variation: Wash the quinces well, and rub with butter or margarine. Bake in a 350° F oven for 45 minutes, or until softened and almost done. Cut a slice off the top, hollow out the shell, leaving a thick rind, and reserve the fruit. Make a mixture of the fruit with some bread crumbs, chopped nuts, grated lemon peel, and enough brown sugar to sweeten. Stuff the shells with the mixture and bake for 15 to 20 minutes longer, or until tender. Serve warm or chilled, topped with sour cream or yogurt.

A Mexican fruit

The sapote, a custard apple, is one of the principal fruits of Mexico and is grown in many citrus areas in limited quantities. The fruit grows in clusters that are large and greenish yellow.

Custard apples are a common name for a family of shrubs, woody vines, and small trees of the tropics that bear small, juicy edible fruits. Sapotes and cherimoyas are both members of this family.

The tamarind tree

The tamarind is a tropical evergreen tree that may grow as high as 70 or 80 feet. It bears elegant foliage and purplish or orange-veined flowers. It is generally considered native to eastern tropical Africa; the name in Arabic means "Indian date" and indicates that it entered medieval commerce from India, where it is used not only for its pulp, but for its seeds, which are astringent; its leaves, which furnish a red or yellow dye; and its timber.

The pods of the tamarind are very similar to those of the carob tree, which is native to the Mediterranean. Both trees are in the same family. The large red pods of the carob have been used for food for animals and humans since prehistoric times. Carob pods are also known as "locust bean gum" and "St. John's bread"—the latter from the belief that they may have been the locusts eaten by John the Baptist in the wilderness.

A crossbreed

Fruits are often crossbred to produce superior-looking products. Something must have gone awry with the ugli to have had such an extraordinarily miserable-looking product result. The ugli is said to be a blend of tangerine, grapefruit, and Seville orange, but this has not been confirmed. It was discovered in 1915 or 1916 in Jamaica, and the good-tasting but ill-endowed fruit has been on the market ever since, pleasing people with its good flavor and what could be euphemistically described as its distinctive appearance.

TAMARIND

Tamarinds are flattened cinnamon-brown pods, 3 to 8 inches (7.6–20.3 cm) long. They grow on the tamarind tree that is cultivated widely throughout the tropics for its fruit, fragrant flowers, shade, and timber. Within the tamarind pod are several oval seeds surrounded by a juicy, acid pulp, which is used as an ingredient in chutneys, curries, and medicines and for preserving fish. A refreshing drink is made by adding sugar and water to the pulp. Tamarind is grown in the West Indies and Florida especially as a flavoring for guava jellies. The pod has been an article of commerce since medieval times. Tamarinds are sometimes available in Latin American specialty stores.

Dietary information. Tamarinds are high in calories—239 in 3½ ounces (100 g)—and contain calcium, phosphorus, potassium, and small amounts of protein, iron, and vitamin C.

TANGELO *See* Mandarins.

TANGERINES *See* Mandarins.

UGLI FRUIT

Ugli fruits are about the size of a grapefruit with an extremely thick, knobby rough peel that doesn't seem to fit the pulp very well, like a size 14 grapefruit wearing a size 18 skin. The skin has light green blemishes that turn orange when the fruit is mature. It is imported from Jamaica, but a few are grown in Florida. One would have to admit that the ugli fruit is aptly named, but in spite of this it is a juicy, delicious fruit, sweeter than grapefruit, and more nearly resembling the orange in flavor. It is almost seedless. It may be that it has become popular not only because of its fine flavor, but because it is so unconscionably ugly.

Peak season. October to February.

Preparation and serving. It is stored and used as other citrus.

NUTS

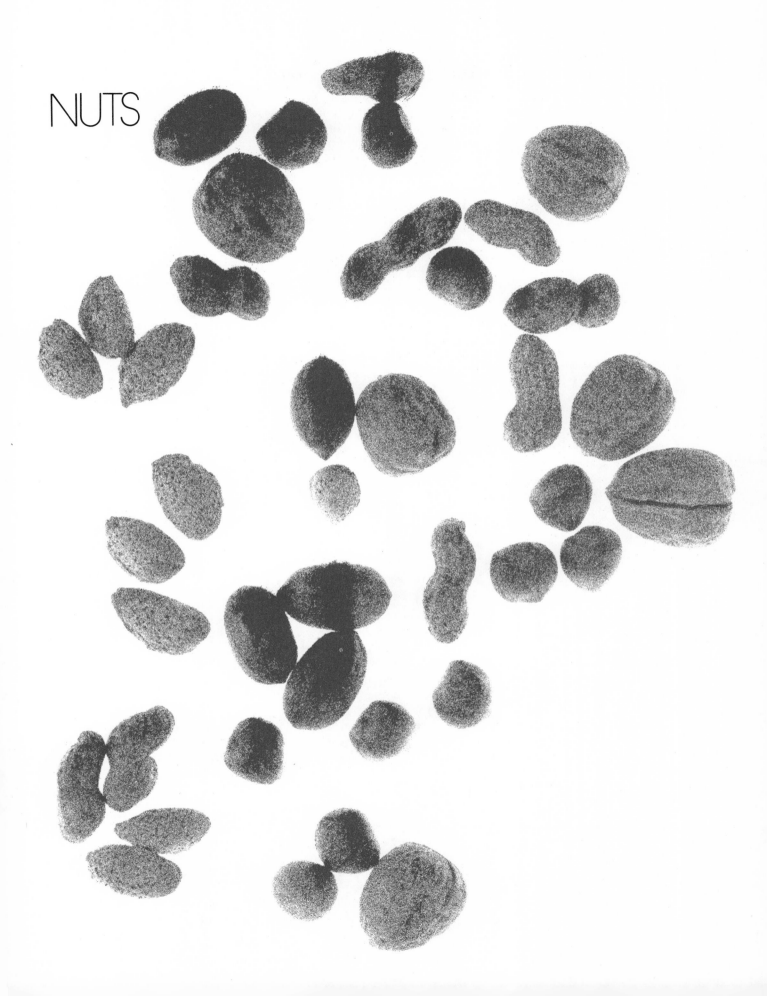

Ancient provender

Nuts have served humans well as food for thousands of years. Archaeologists have found traces of nutshells in ancient caves, and the Old Testament relates that Jacob sent gifts of almonds to Joseph. Nuts were a favorite food of the Queen of Sheba, and the Greeks and Romans enjoyed many varieties, especially hazelnuts and chestnuts.

Pre-Columbian cave drawings and artifacts reveal that the Indians of North and South America ate the nuts from trees that grew wild in the forests, and the first European settlers learned a great deal about cultivating nut trees from friendly Indian tribes. In the colonies, "nutting" was more than a social activity. Every autumn groups of settlers gathered together in nutting parties to reap the harvest of the wild trees for use throughout the winter and spring. The nuts, stored in tubs and baskets in root cellars and sheds, often lasted until the next nutting party the following fall.

Waste not, want not

In Colonial times, no part of a nut was discarded. The hard shells of some varieties were added to fireplace logs to give extra warmth. Softer shells were used to augment animal food.

Today nut hulls and shells are used commercially in scores of different ways. Coconuts provide coir, the husk fiber used in making mattresses, brushes, mats, and cordage, and copra, the dried meat from which oil is extracted. Hulls are pulverized into garden compost containing many valuable nutrients, and pulverized shells are made into fine cleaners for removing oil and metal cuttings from machinery.

For the cholesterol-conscious

The fat in peanuts, almonds, pecans, and walnuts is polyunsaturated, with walnuts the highest of all in polyunsaturated fatty acids. Consequently, these nuts are recommended for people who are concerned with cholesterol. Cashews and macadamia nuts, on the contrary, contain saturated fat and should be avoided. Coconut, which really isn't a nut (but sounds like one) is completely outside the pale for people with a cholesterol problem, since its oil is extraordinarily high in saturates.

In the unlikely event that you are ever the victim of a shipwreck, make a wish that you'll find yourself marooned near a grove of nut trees, for this happy accident could keep you from starving to death. Nuts come close to being an all-purpose food. They supply many of the body's nutritional requirements, they store well, and they can be eaten, just as they come from the shell, without danger of contamination or the need of preparation. There are not too many other fresh foods that can make these claims.

Botanically speaking, a nut is the dry fruit or seed of a plant or tree. Characteristically, it grows inside a fibrous protective hull. At maturity, the hull opens to release the fruit, which consists of a dry inner shell that surrounds the edible meat. When we talk about nuts, we mean either the entire in-shell fruit or only the edible portion, which is also called the "nutmeat" or "kernel."

Nuts are an important fresh food. They are high in protein, and, for people who prefer not to eat meat, nuts can supply all the protein the body needs for a balanced diet. In fact, nuts are the food staple in parts of the world where there are prohibitions against eating meat. Nuts also supply iron, potassium, thiamin, niacin, phosphorus, and a few vitamins. Most people have no difficulty digesting them. In addition, nuts come "prepackaged," in the wrapping that nature provided.

In case you're beginning to conclude that nuts are an almost perfect food, you should be aware of their one fatal flaw. Most varieties have an extremely high fat content, and for the calorie conscious a diet augmented with large amounts of nutmeats is sure to add unwanted pounds.

How nuts grow. Most of the nuts consumed, particularly in the United States, are commercially grown in orchards. Nut trees tend to grow slowly, and, with the exception of the almond and the dwarf varieties, they are very tall at maturity. Trees are generally long lived, and given proper conditions they will thrive, and often continue to bear fruit, for as long as seventy-five or a hundred years.

Selection. Although some specialty shops sell nuts in bulk, they are more often marketed in transparant plastic wrappings. Judging nuts for freshness, even inside their wrappings, is a fairly simple matter. If they are unshelled, make certain that the shells are shiny and well shaped. Avoid bags containing grayish, dusty-looking nuts with cracked shells. If you're buying shelled nuts, select bags containing firm, plump-looking kernels with no sign of the dryness or withering that means they've been on the grocer's shelf too long.

It is always less expensive to buy nuts in shell than shelled kernels. If you buy the kernels, you're paying someone for having cracked the shells and removed the nutmeats, although it's sometimes worth the extra cost. One pound (454 g) of in-shell nuts produces about 6½ to 7½ ounces (185–213 g) of shelled walnuts, almonds, or pecans.

Storage. For peak flavor, nuts should be kept in the shell until they are to be eaten or used in cooking. However, both in-shell and shelled nuts can be stored successfully. If you're planning to store nuts for longer than a few weeks, don't shell them. In-shell nuts will keep better.

To store shelled nutmeats, place them in a covered container in the refrigerator, or, if you plan to keep them for more than a week or so, put them in an air-tight, moistureproof plastic bag in the freezer where they can be kept for months. Because nuts contain a large amount of fat, they sometimes become rancid after a long period of time, but the odor and flavor will tell you at once whether they have turned.

Many varieties of unshelled nuts will keep well for months in a basement or any other cool area. If they are to be kept for a longer period, place them in plastic bags in the freezer, where they will remain fresh for a year or more.

ALMONDS

The almond, a member of the rose family and closely related to the peach, is scientifically a stone fruit, and an almond kernel looks very much like the pit of a peach. There are two kinds of almonds. The sweet variety is the one we eat; the oil of the bitter almond is used to make flavorings. Fresh almonds have a thick outer hull containing the oval yellowish-tan shell that holds the edible seed. Almond trees are delicate and subject to frost injury, so they do best in warm climates. In the United States, California produces the largest quantities. Chopped, slivered or ground almonds are used in cookies, cakes, and tortes. Whole almonds are delicious just as they come from the shell, salted as an accompaniment to apéritifs or sugared as a dessert nut. Calories—about 65 per twelve nuts.

BRAZIL NUTS

The huge trees that bear Brazil nuts grow wild in the forests of the Amazon region of South America. The seed pods of the gigantic trees contain anywhere from one to three dozen of the large, hard-shelled, three-sided nuts. The density of the Amazon jungles makes harvesting extremely difficult, and as a result Brazil nuts usually command a high price. Brazil nuts—the meats of which are firm, white, and slightly oily—are best eaten raw. The large kernels are often slivered and used as a garnish for cakes. Calories—about 97 per four medium nuts.

Some helpful hints

To blanch shelled almonds, pour boiling water over the nutmeats and let them stand for about 5 minutes. Then place them in cold water for a few minutes, and drain. The skins will slip off easily. Blanched almonds can be stored in a covered jar in the refrigerator.

Nuts can be shredded more easily if they are at room temperature.

Hard-shelled pecans will be easier to crack if they are rinsed first in boiling water.

Nuts are excellent natural "extenders" for many dishes. Add them to hamburger, to meat loaf and to rice casseroles.

Try hazelnuts or pecans in poultry stuffing instead of chestnuts.

Before cooking chestnuts, make a crisscross cut on the flat side, or cut a circle around the crown so the shells can be removed more easily.

Try puréed chestnuts as a different hot vegetable.

Add chopped almonds or walnuts to chicken salad.

If toasted nuts become limp, they can be refreshed by placing them in a 150°F oven for a few minutes. They'll come out tasting like freshly roasted nuts.

A nut that really isn't a nut

Botanically, almonds are not nuts at all. They are a stone fruit like peaches and plums. What we eat is the pit, or seed. This explains why almonds are firmer and crisper, even harder, than true nuts like pecans and walnuts.

Spanish missionaries brought almonds to the New World along with the word of God. They are now the most widely known, grown, and eaten of all nuts. Almond trees are medium sized, larger than most peach and apple trees, and smaller than pecan trees. The beautiful pink or white blossoms make an almond orchard a fairyland in late February or early March.

How to pronounce the word? The growers pronounce "almonds" to rhyme with "ham," whereas many nongrowers pronounce it to rhyme with "palm." But "am-ond" or "ah-mond" growers don't mind how the public pronounces the word as long as it buys them.

Cocktails and . . .
Roasted almonds
Place 1 pound blanched almonds and 2 tablespoons cooking oil in a shallow pan or skillet in a 350°F oven for about 30 minutes. Shake the pan from time to time. When the nuts are brown, remove from the oven and drain on paper towels. Sprinkle with salt, garlic salt, or hickory salt.

Nut canapés
Sprinkle chopped nuts generously on buttered toast rounds. Heat in a hot oven until the nuts are brown.

A magical nut
The hazelnut figures in many old tales and superstitions. Hazels were often symbols of love, and to court someone under a hazel tree was to make sure that the wooing would be successful and the love returned. Forked branches from the hazel tree were used by dowsers as divining rods. They believed that the branch would twist if water or some subterranean treasures lay beneath the surface. They tested the rod by immersing it in water, and, if it made a sound like the squeal of a pig, it could be trusted.

The hazel is a small tree, never growing taller than twenty feet. First catkins form, and then the nuts develop. Like acorns, they grow in little cups. When the nuts are fully ripened, the husks turn brown and the nuts fall to the ground. Hazel trees can produce nuts until they are about fifty years old.

CASHEW NUTS

Cashew trees are believed to have originated in Brazil and now grow in practically all hot, humid countries. This tall, spreading evergreen tree bears clusters of a pear-shaped fruit called "cashew apples," which are soft and juicy and eaten as a hand fruit. The kidney-shaped nut grows at the end of the fruit stalk. There is a very good reason why all cashew nuts commercially available are already shelled and roasted. In its natural state, the cashew-nut kernel is enclosed in a double shell. Between these two shells is an oily liquid that would severely burn the mouth and lips of anyone attempting to bite into it. However, after the nuts are shelled they are roasted, and any oily substances remaining are destroyed by the heat. The roasted nuts can then be eaten without danger.

Cashew nuts have a fine texture and a distinctive, slightly sweet flavor. They can be eaten plain or salted. Calories—about 176 per twelve nuts.

CHESTNUTS

Since the early decades of the century, when all the native chestnut trees were destroyed by blight, the United States has had to import chestnuts from southern Europe. The green, prickly burr of the chestnut tree contains two to four shiny, round edible nuts. Chestnuts can be eaten raw, but most people prefer them boiled or roasted. Chestnuts are an excellent addition to poultry stuffings and are traditionally combined with Brussels sprouts and red cabbage. They are often used in desserts, either preserved in syrup (*marrons glacés*) or puréed. They contain less fat than any other nut. Calories—about 56 per six nuts.

HAZELNUTS

Originally, the European variety of this nut was called "filbert," and the American variety "hazelnut," but the names are now used interchangeably. Turkey is the world's largest producer of hazelnuts, which grow in clusters close to the stem of the hazel tree. The outer husks contain the thin, round shell that holds the edible kernel. The nuts are bleached after being harvested, and when they reach the market they are the lovely light brown color we call "hazel." Hazelnuts, sweet and firm, are used in cakes, tortes, and soufflés, as well as in poultry stuffings. Calories—about 97 per twelve nuts.

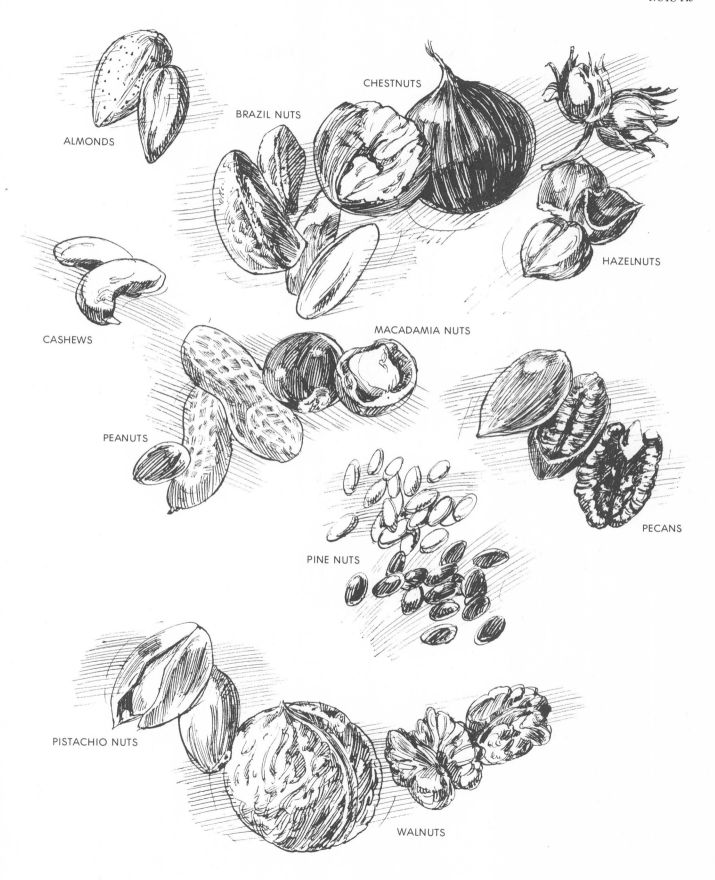

ALMONDS

BRAZIL NUTS

CHESTNUTS

HAZELNUTS

CASHEWS

MACADAMIA NUTS

PEANUTS

PECANS

PINE NUTS

PISTACHIO NUTS

WALNUTS

MACADAMIA NUTS

Macadamia trees once grew only in Australia, but they are now being raised commercially in Hawaii and California. These lovely evergreen trees, which grow as high as 60 feet (18.3 m), bear thick husks that surround the hard-shelled, round nuts, which in turn contain the sweet, white kernels. The shells are so difficult to crack that macadamias are always marketed shelled, either in tins or jars. The flavor of the kernels is somewhat like the Brazil nut, but milder and more delicate. Macadamias are used as cocktail or dessert nuts. Calories—about 196 per twelve nuts.

PEANUTS

Botanically, peanuts are not nuts at all but rather legumes closely related to peas and beans. Also known as "goobers," they grow beneath the surface of the soil, and only the lovely yellow flowers of the low-growing plants show above the ground. There are several varieties; the Virginia, Spanish and runner are the most common. Peanuts are made into peanut butter, a mainstay of lunch-box sandwiches for people of all ages. The oil that is pressed out of crushed peanuts is a popular cooking oil used in the manufacture of margarine and other products that require cooking oil. Peanuts have the softest shells of any nut. They are probably the most popular of all cocktail nuts, and are also used in candies and baked goods. Calories—about 420 per ½ cup (120 ml).

PECANS

Pecan trees, initially cultivated by the American Indians, are the first nut trees to have been grown commercially in the United States. Pecans grow in clusters, and their thin husks often split when the nuts are ripe. The shell is smooth, light brown, and generally oval in shape, although some are round. Pecans are usually polished before they are marketed to improve their appearance. The most highly prized are the large paper-shelled nuts that are grown throughout the southern part of the United States. Pecans are used as cocktail and dessert nuts and in baking. Pecan pie rates close to apple pie as one of America's favorite desserts. Calories—about 104 per twelve halves.

PINE NUTS

These delicate little nuts are also called "pinyons," "pinoleas," "pignolias," "piñons," and "Indian nuts," depending on the country of origin, for they are grown almost everywhere in the world. They are the edible seeds of various species of pine trees and are contained in the pine cones. The pine nuts grown in the United States are very small, usually no larger than the seed of an orange or lemon. Those that grow in some South American countries, however, can reach a length of 2 inches (5.1 cm). Pine nuts have soft, easily cracked shells and a sweet delicate flavor that combines well with rice, meat, and vegetables. Calories—about 95 per 2 tablespoons (30 ml).

PISTACHIO NUTS

Pistachio trees are evergreens that grow in tropical climates. The pistachio nut is actually the stone or seed of the red fruit of the pistachio tree. The fruit, usually about ½ inch (1.27 cm) long, grows in bunches. The nuts have a double shell; the outside one is red, but it is removed before the nuts are marketed. The inside shell is smooth and thin and, in most varieties, is grayish white in color; the oval kernel is pale yellowish green. The familiar red-shelled pistachios you see around have been dyed solely for eye appeal. The partially open shells in pistachio nuts are also not an accident of nature; the processor has had the shells cracked to make it easier for the consumer to extract the delicious little green kernels lurking inside. Pistachios are used as cocktail nuts and as a flavoring in cooking and for candies and ice cream. Calories—about 40 per twelve nuts.

WALNUTS

The variety of walnuts we know best is the English, or Persian walnut. It is believed to have originated in the Middle East and was eventually brought to Great Britain by the Romans. The walnut family also includes black walnuts, hickory nuts, and butternuts. Today the United States is the leading world producer of English walnuts. They are also cultivated in France, Italy, and mainland China.

Walnut trees flourish best in a temperate climate. The walnuts grow in clusters, with a husk covering the shell of each nut. The husks open as the walnut ripens and the nuts fall to the ground. After being harvested, the ridged tan shells are washed and polished. The inside of the kernel should be clear and white. If the kernel is rubbery or a dingy gray, the nut has passed its prime.

Walnuts are sold both in shell and out of shell, either salted or plain, chopped or in halves. Walnut meats are used in all manner of recipes, in salads, and in baking and candy making, as well as eating out of hand. They are the highest of all nuts in polyunsaturated fat content. Calories—about 100 per 12 halves.

A luxury item

Pine nuts are costly, less because of their rarity than the arduous task of extracting them from the pine cone and then removing their hard shell. Consequently, they are used sparingly for cooking and rarely for nibbling. They are popular in Mideastern cooking, in the rice stuffing for grape-leaf *dolmas*, and are a must for the delicious Genoese pasta sauce known as *pesto*, made with fresh basil, garlic, grated cheese, butter, and olive oil ground into a mouth-watering sauce. The traditional recipe did not call for pine nuts, but they have now become an essential ingredient, adding a special flavor.

A noble tree

Walnuts have been cultivated since the most ancient times, and walnut trees occupied a major portion of King Solomon's extensive garden outside of Jerusalem. In the time of Christ, cloth was dyed from the brown dye produced by the nuts. This same dye, called "tincture of Juglans," was used for many centuries as a stain for the skin.

In ancient Rome walnuts were thrown at bridal couples (shelled, it is hoped) much as rice is thrown now. The English walnut did not find its way to England until the seventeenth century, and, as a sign of how highly it was regarded by the Anglo-Saxons, they attached the name "English" to it.

Unlike pecans and other nuts, walnuts are difficult to shell in complete halves. They break so easily in the shelling process that they are generally sold in pieces or mixed halves and pieces.

DAIRY PRODUCTS

A bewildering and beguiling array of manufactured milk products are huddled together on the refrigerated dairy shelves of today's large supermarkets. Although all of these products are created from one main ingredient, milk, the various ways in which it is handled and treated give consumers a wider choice of dairy supplies than they have ever had before: whole milk, low-fat milk, skim milk, sweet cream, sour cream, yogurt, cheese, buttermilk, and butter, in addition to flavored and "imitation" versions of these products. Many of these products seem at first glance to be similar, but there is a wide variance in their chemical composition and calorie content, and in the various ways in which they can contribute to our eating and cooking, which this chapter will explore.

MILK

Milk and milk products supply 20 to 30 percent of the total protein in the American adult diet. Milk has been called a "perfect food" because it is responsible for the growth and development of young mammals during the period when they lack the teeth to hunt, forage, or chew. It provides proteins and fats and is a reservoir of calcium, a bone-building mineral not present in large quantities in most other foods.

Cow's milk is also a source of vitamins A, D, E, and B, and it contains traces of many minerals, such as potassium, chlorine, phosphorus, sodium, magnesium, and zinc. It lacks iron, however, and any adult who depended solely upon milk products would develop an iron-deficiency anemia.

But not all physicians and nutritionists agree about the value of milk in the adult diet. Some contend that adults do not need large amounts of calcium in their diets. They maintain that it is mother's milk that is the ideal food and that cow's milk was meant for calves and not humans. Milk, too, is high in saturated fat (milk fat) and contains cholesterol. However, people who must restrict saturated fats and cholesterol in their diets can drink skim milk with safety.

There are also situations in which people cannot digest milk because they suffer from lactose intolerance. This is due to the lack of an intestinal enzyme that converts the main carbohydrate in milk, lactose, into a form that the body can absorb. This enzyme, lactase, is usually present in the intestines of both infants and adults. But in some areas of the world, such as West Africa and parts of Asia, many adults lack the enzyme. While they are able to tolerate only very small quantities of fresh milk, large amounts producing gastrointestinal complaints, they have no trouble with fermented milk products because the lactose in them has already been broken down by the fermentation process.

But in spite of medical controversy and human idiosyncrasies and allergies, milk is consumed and tolerated well by millions of people. Strict government regulations surrounding the production and distribution of milk has made it a safe and nutritious product.

Pasteurization and homogenization. Almost all milk today is pasteurized. Pasteurization is a heat-then-cool process, discovered by Louis Pasteur in 1860, that destroys from 95 to 99 percent of the bacteria in milk without greatly altering its flavor or composition. The law now

The milch cow

A good cow produces ten times her own weight in milk in a single year. Exceptional cows may produce as much as twenty-five times their own weight in milk. Cattle are bred and selected for their ability to produce quantities of milk, rich in milk fat. Milk varies slightly in taste and composition according to the breed and what the cow is fed. Jersey cows, for example, produce milk containing 6 percent milk fat; other breeds, such as the Holstein, produce milk with less milk fat.

Milk from many mammals

All mammals produce milk to feed their young. Although all milk has the same nutritious elements, the amount of protein and fat varies according to the stage of development of the animal's young at the time of birth.

Human milk is closest in composition to that of equine animals. On the other hand, porpoise and seal milk contain the most fat and protein. The camel produces a sweet, fat-free milk, while yak's milk, by contrast, is richest in milk fat.

The milk of most mammals may be safely ingested by most other mammals. Although mother's milk is usually thought the ideal food for the human baby, babies throughout the world are weaned on the milk of other animals. Throughout history adults, too, have drunk the milk of any mammal that allowed them to tap it. The Roman historian Pliny praised camel's milk, claiming it to be the sweetest. Ancient Scythians enjoyed the cream of mare's milk (which contains four times the vitamin C found in cow's milk), and in colder climates reindeer have provided inhabitants with milk and milk products.

What is whey?

Those who, as children, read the charming nursery rhyme about Miss Muffet, her curds and whey, and the spider probably wondered exactly what Miss Muffet was eating that tempted the spider so. Whey is the watery part of the milk that remains when the protein, casein, and fats are removed. Curds are the milk solids left when the whey is removed and milk has coagulated. At one time whey was thought to have medicinal properties, and people with ailments visited "whey houses" in England. In Poland and Russia, people still drink carbonated beverages made from fermented whey. Whey is also the base of ricotta and other "whey" cheeses.

The alternative milkshake

The milkshake can be more imaginative, more nutritious, and less caloric than the usual blend of milk, syrup and ice cream. Try blending 1 cup milk with ½ teaspoon vanilla and 1 tablespoon honey. To this basic mixture add chunks of your favorite fruit and liquefy in the blender. Sprinkle with nutmeg or cinnamon and serve. You may also try blending a quart of milk with ⅓ cup peanut butter and 2 tablespoons honey for "peanut milk."

Make your own diet milk

A quart of skim or partially skim milk costs as much as whole milk—although skim milks lack cream, one of milk's principal ingredients. You can easily make your own diet milk at a lower cost, by combining 3 cups reconstituted nonfat dry milk, 1 cup ordinary milk, a little honey and 2 tablespoons nonfat milk powder. This mixture will provide you with the sweet, rich taste of whole milk without the added fat and calories.

requires pasteurization of milk to ensure its freedom from germs that spread disease and also cause the product to spoil. Prior to 1908, however, when milk pasteurization became mandatory, the process was illegal and was used by unscrupulous dairy farmers to extend the life of milk past its proper period.

Immediately before or just after milk is pasteurized, it is homogenized. Homogenization is a process in which the milk is pumped, under high pressure, through a small opening in a valve that breaks up the fat particles and distributes them evenly through the milk. This prevents the milk and cream from separating, thus adding body and a richer flavor. The process was invented in France and became popular about 1932; today almost all whole milk and most cream is homogenized. The disadvantage of homogenized milk is that it curdles easily when heated and custards made with it take longer to cook. Some people prefer the nonhomogenized type, although it is difficult to find.

Milk grades. Milk production is carefully supervised by governmental agencies to make sure it is produced under sanitary conditions and is of top quality. Government inspectors visit dairy farms regularly. They examine the cows and check all equipment used for milking, handling, and storage. Grades are given according to the standards of milk production and the purpose for which the milk is to be used. All the milk we buy in containers is Grade A, the highest quality; Grades B and C are used to manufacture cheese, ice cream, and other dairy products.

TYPES OF MILK

WHOLE MILK is fresh, fluid milk that contains between 3.25 and 4 percent milk fat and at least 8.25 percent milk solids. Standards for the composition of whole milk vary slightly from state to state. Most milk is fortified with vitamin D, and sometimes vitamin A. The information about the vitamins that have been added always appears on the milk carton.

SKIM MILK is milk from which some of the fat has been removed. Dairy farmers of former years scorned the thin, watery milk that remained after they skimmed the cream from it for their butter making. They regarded it as unfit for human consumption and fed it to their pigs. How times have changed! Now skim milk is the milk of choice for people who must restrict fat and cholesterol in their diets, or for those concerned with calories. Although skim milk has lost some fat-soluble vitamins, it contains all the protein, calcium, and B vitamins of whole milk. Skim milk can be used successfully in place of whole milk in cooking and baking.

Two kinds of skim milk are sold: partially skim milk, also called "low-fat milk," and skim milk. Partially skim milk looks and tastes more like whole milk. It contains 2 percent fat, and skim milk contains 1 percent. Both kinds of skim milk are usually labeled "fortified," which means that some of the vitamins that were removed with the fat have been replaced.

RAW MILK is whole milk that has not been pasteurized or homogenized. There are people who feel that pasteurization not only destroys the natural taste of milk, but also vitamin C, thiamine (one of the B vitamins), and the useful bacteria along with the bad. Certified raw milk is available from some dairies. The certification means that it has been government inspected and has met the most rigid sanitary standards. This is essential, for improperly produced raw milk can be a source of serious diseases, such as typhoid fever, diphtheria, and tuberculosis.

Raw milk is sold in health-food and specialty shops, but because of the small amount produced and the special care that must be taken to produce it, the cost is about double that of pasteurized milk.

GOAT'S MILK is said to be closer in composition to human milk than cow's milk. It is easier to digest than cow's milk because it forms smaller curds in the stomach. Some people who are allergic to cow's milk can tolerate goat's milk. It contains a tiny amount of iron—a bit more than the negligible trace that is present in cow's milk, but basically, the same nutrients are present in the milk of both animals.

Mass marketing of goat's milk is not practical, due to the limited amount of milk the goat can produce and the fact that goats are difficult to raise. Goat's milk is sometimes available in health-food and specialty shops, and it costs more than cow's milk. It is also used in cheese making.

BUTTERMILK was traditionally the liquid that remained in the churn after the butter was made. It was rich, frothy, and studded with flecks of real butter. But real buttermilk is now a memory, available only if you live on or near a dairy. Today commercial buttermilk is made by artificially fermenting whole milk or skim milk with a "starter" of lactic-acid bacteria. Gelatin is sometimes added to buttermilk to give it a smoother consistency, and it may be adulterated with artificial coloring as well. Particles of butter may also be added to make the buttermilk more authentic. Buttermilk is lower in fat and calories than whole milk. It may be substituted for sour milk in any baking recipe.

SWEET CREAMS

CREAM is the fatty part of whole milk that rises to the top of non-homogenized milk on standing. In dairies it is separated from the milk by mechanical separators. A thick, rich white liquid, cream is used in coffee, sauces, and desserts and is whipped for a topping for fruits and sweets.

Cream is classified "light" or "heavy" according to the amount of milk fat it contains. Like milk, it is always pasteurized and sometimes homogenized. Light cream contains from 18 to 30 percent fat, and heavy cream, or "double cream," usually used for whipping, about 36 percent. In general, the thicker the consistency of the cream, the greater its fat content, although thinner cream may have a high fat content as well. Since the consumer tends to judge the cream by its thickness, creameries try to increase the viscosity by holding the cream a day or two at low temperatures.

HALF-AND-HALF is a mixture of milk and cream, used to impart the rich taste of cream to coffee with fewer calories than cream. It contains about 12 percent fat.

NONDAIRY COFFEE CREAM under various trade names has become a widely distributed product. It is usually bought by people who are under the impression that since it contains no dairy products (i.e., cream), it is unsaturated and low in calories. The ingredient list printed on the car-

Blancmange

One of the easiest and most versatile milk custards to prepare is a "blancmange." Boil 2½ tablespoons cornstarch with 2 cups milk, then cool. As the milk cools it becomes a soft pudding. Flavor with any ingredient you fancy: puréed fruit, chocolate, almond, vanilla, or coconut, and sweeten with honey or sugar to taste. Refrigerate.

Whip your own

Whipped cream is simple to prepare at home and infinitely better and purer than the prepackaged product. Why settle for a synthetic substance that "tastes like fresh," when with little effort it *can* be fresh? Use heavy whipping cream, at least a day old. After whipping, it will expand to double its volume. You can whip with either an electric or a hand beater, not a blender. Make sure that the beater, the bowl, and the cream are well chilled. Whip 1 cup of cream until it stands in peaks. Watch it carefully, particularly if your kitchen is warm, and don't overwhip, or it could churn into butter. The whipped cream will keep for an hour or two in the refrigerator. Just before serving, sift on 3 tablespoons of confectioner's sugar, add ½ teaspoon vanilla, and fold them in, using a rubber spatula. We call this "whipped cream," but the French call it *crème Chantilly*.

European imports

The thick, fresh clotted cream known as "Devonshire cream" can be read about in English Victorian novels, but to taste it you must make it yourself.

First scald whipping cream in a double boiler. Heat the cream to 170° to 190°F and keep it hot until the top of the cream becomes thick, crusty, and wrinkled, stirring occasionally. When the cream is ready, cool it rapidly by placing the pot in cold water. Then refrigerate, or leave it in a cool place for 24 hours. Spoon the thick, delicious cream over strawberries.

Crème fraîche is the nutty-flavored cream the French use to enhance fruits and desserts. Unlike American whipped cream, crème fraîche is made from thickened, slightly ripened cream; to those unaccustomed to the unique flavor, this Gallic delicacy may seem spoiled. To make your own crème fraîche stir 1 ½ teaspoons buttermilk into 1 cup whipping cream and heat gently to lukewarm—not more than 85°F. Pour the mixture into a bowl covered with a single thickness of paper toweling and allow to stand at a temperature between 60° and 85°F until it has thickened. This will take from 8 to 24 hours, depending on the temperature. Every 8 hours or so, it should be checked and stirred. As soon as it has thickened, refrigerate, covered.

Bake with buttermilk

Try substituting buttermilk for milk the next time you bake biscuits, muffins, bread, or coffee cake for a subtle difference in flavor.

ton may mention "vegetable oil," along with the chemicals and artificial flavorings that have gone into it. In most cases this vegetable oil is coconut oil, which is the most highly saturated of all oils, so the buyers would be better off using whole milk in their coffee. There are one or two nondairy cream products that are made with liquid polyunsaturated oil (corn, cottonseed, soybean, safflower), but make sure you know what you are buying. If in doubt, write the manufacturer for information about exactly what kind of oil is used.

Buying. Although some areas still distribute milk in glass bottles, most milk is now packaged in disposable, plasticized paper containers that range in size from 8 ounces (240 ml) to a gallon (4.4 l). Buy only as much as you can use; large containers can save you money, but only if the entire amount can be consumed by your household before it spoils.

Modern dairy methods ensure the delivery of fresh milk to retail stores, but usually the milk is about three days old before it finally arrives. Methods of informing the consumer of the age of the milk vary throughout the country, but most containers show either a pasteurization date, which tells when the milk was pasteurized, or an expiration date, which specifies the last day the milk may be legally sold. Sale should be within sixty-eight hours after the pasteurization date; milk purchased as far before the expiration date as possible will be the freshest. Watch dates carefully to be sure you are not buying a product after the expiration date has passed.

Storage. Milk and cream keep well under refrigeration, but every moment of exposure to heat and light decreases their lives. Keep them in the refrigerator as much as possible; after filling the glasses or pitcher, return them to the refrigerator at once. Once they have been poured into a pitcher or glass, don't pour the unused portion back into the refrigerated container. Store it separately in a jar because the exposure to light and warmth has automatically made it less fresh than what is in the container.

Your nose will tell you at once when milk begins to sour. Slightly sour milk will also "feather" when added to hot beverages. The color of milk varies naturally from bluish white to creamy yellow, according to the diet of the cow, and is no indication of its quality or freshness.

Milk should be used within three to five days after purchase and cream even sooner, if possible. Buttermilk, because it is fermented, will keep longer in the refrigerator. Buttermilk may separate if it gets warm, but stirring will return it to its original consistency.

FERMENTED MILK PRODUCTS

Fermentation, or the slow souring of milk, has been used by the peoples of eastern Europe and Asia Minor since biblical times to preserve milk that would otherwise spoil for lack of refrigeration. Milk ferments when certain bacterial organisms grow in it. They change the lactose into lactic acid, which acts as a preservative and transforms the milk into a slightly acid, semisolid curd. Fermented milk products are made by inoculating fresh milk with various types of bacterial cultures, known as "starters," and encouraging these cultures to grow by heating the milk to a specific temperature. Milk will also "ripen" or sour naturally if it is simply allowed to stand in a warm spot.

Fermented milk from cows, goats, buffalo, reindeer, mares, and ewes is eaten in varying forms throughout the world. It is easy to digest and destroys some disease-causing bacteria in the intestines. A variety of fermented milk products are now manufactured on a large scale for the commercial market.

SOUR CREAM has always been a favorite milk product in Central European and Slavic nations. In earlier times, it was made by letting heavy sweet cream sour naturally in a warm spot behind the stove. Now sour cream is made by inoculating sweet, pasteurized cream that has an 18 to 20 percent fat content with a lactic-acid culture and exposing it to heat and pressure. Chemical additives are often added to give the cream a heavy body and smooth appearance. Sometimes called by more elegant names, "salad cream" or "Hampshire cream," sour cream is used in salad dressings, as a spread, in sauces and dips, and as a topping for vegetables and other cooked foods. One of its most popular nesting places is atop a baked potato, sprinkled with chives.

A less caloric version of sour cream called "sour half-and-half" is now available in some markets. The conventional half-milk and half-cream mixture, which has been treated with a culture, makes an acceptable substitute for sour cream. The "imitation" sour creams sold in dairy departments, highly touted as containing no dairy fat, are generally made with coconut oil. While it is true that they do not contain dairy fat, they are saturated and not recommended for low-cholesterol diets.

YOGURT is the pungent, custardy product that results from milk being fermented with special bacterial cultures. Yogurt is a staple in the diet of peoples of many countries and has recently become enormously popular in the United States as well. An excellent source of protein, vitamin B and calcium, and comparatively low in calories, yogurt has the added virtue of being easily digested by many people who have difficulty digesting regular milk.

Yogurt is made from either whole milk or skim milk. The low-fat yogurts are clearly identified as such by the manufacturer; it can be assumed that those not so marked are made from whole milk. Yogurt can be bought plain (unflavored) or in a wide range of flavors. The fruit-flavored yogurts are the highest in calories. Yogurt made from goat's milk is also available in health-food or specialty stores.

Yogurt is a most versatile product. It can be eaten for breakfast with fruits and cereal, as a dessert, and substituted for sweet or sour cream in breads, cakes, or cookies, using an equal amount of plain, unflavored yogurt. It can replace cream in sauces, salad dressings, and cooked meat and poultry dishes.

KEFIR differs from yogurt in that it is more liquid in consistency and is fermented by both alcoholic- and acid-type organisms. Long popular in Asia, where it is made from the milk of mares, goats, or cows, kefir is now available in some American health-food stores.

Buying and storing. Yogurt and sour cream are sold in plasticized paper containers of varying sizes; in most areas these have the expiration date stamped on the top or bottom. Always check the expiration date to be sure you are buying a fresh product. See that the container you have selected has a tight-fitting top that has not been tampered with.

Both yogurt and sour cream have a long life in the refrigerator—a week to ten days. As they get older, they may separate, the liquid whey

A secret cure
The first Frenchman to eat yogurt was King François I, who suffered from an intestinal complaint no French doctors could cure. Word arrived in France that a Jewish doctor from Constantinople had cured similar disorders with a miraculous concoction of milk. The doctor was sent for and promptly arrived with his own flock of sheep. He cured François I but would not reveal his secret formula. Today we know it was yogurt—still useful for aiding digestive problems.

Many monikers
What we call "yogurt" is eaten under many different names in different lands. In Armenian yogurt is *matzoon*, and in Russian *kumyss* or *kefir*. In Egypt it is called *leben*; in Bulgaria, *naja*; in Italy, *gioddu*; in Greece, *tiaourti*; and in India, *dadhi*. The type of milk used to make yogurt and its texture also varies from place to place. In Greece, for example, yogurt made from cow's milk is deemed inferior to that made from goat's or lamb's milk. Genghis Khan is said to have eaten a yogurt of mare's milk and yak's milk.

Homemade yogurt
Yogurt is easy to make, and making it at home is more economical than buying it. Heat 1 quart whole or skim milk in a heavy saucepan until it is hot (about 180°F). (For a thicker, creamy-textured yogurt add ¼ cup nonfat dry milk solids to the milk before heating.) Cool the milk until lukewarm, covering to protect it from contamination. Stir in ⅓ ounce dry culture or 1 tablespoon natural, fresh yogurt (health-food stores sell the powdered culture). Pour the cooled mixture into a sterilized quart jar and cover with plastic wrapping. Place in a warm spot so the culture you've added will ferment the milk. A pan of medium-hot water over a pilot light on the stove, or your oven, if it has a pilot light, can serve as an incubator. The temperature should be about 110°F. The yogurt must remain undisturbed while it is forming; it should thicken in about five hours. Once the yogurt is set, place it in the refrigerator, where it will thicken more. Sweeten or flavor to taste.

Yogurt, Indian style

A delicious and refreshing yogurt drink from India is called *lassi*. Blend 1 cup yogurt, crushed ice, honey to taste, and 2 tablespoons rose or orange water in the blender. For another Indian treat mix 1 cup yogurt with 1 teaspoon curry powder for an interesting, low-calorie dip for raw vegetables.

Clarified butter

Clarified butter is butter that has been rid of its milky residue. It is that milky residue that turns dark and bitter when butter is overcooked. To clarify butter, cut it into small pieces and melt it over moderate heat. Skim off the foam that rises to the top, then pour the clear yellow liquid off the milky residue that coats the bottom of the pan. The clear liquid is clarified butter, which will keep for weeks in a covered jar in the refrigerator. It is used in French cooking for foods that must be delicately sautéed.

In India clarified butter is called *ghee*, and it has been an essential cooking ingredient in India since ancient times. It is also widely used in Africa. Butter is made fresh in India every day, usually from buffalo milk, but the Indians prefer *ghee* to solid butter, probably because it keeps better and does not turn rancid quickly, even in India's intense heat.

emerging from the solid curds. This does not mean that the product is bad; it may be reconstituted by stirring. Once the product has separated, however, it will not blend as well in gravies and sauces.

BUTTER

All butter is made from fresh or soured cream. By law, it must contain at least 80 percent fat. The remaining 20 percent consists largely of water with some milk solids. Small amounts of salt, for flavor and preservative action, and artificial coloring are sometimes added. Butter is the least nutritious of dairy products. It supplies vitamin A and fat (which is saturated) and little else. However, its taste, and the delicate, distinctive flavor it brings to baked and cooked foods, makes it an essential kitchen ingredient in many homes.

Grades and varieties. United States grades of butter are determined by flavor, body, color and butterfat content, and the amount of salt added. The best quality is U.S. Grade AA or U.S. 93 Score. It is made of top-quality sweet cream and has a pleasing aroma and creamy texture. U.S. Grade A is close in quality to Grade AA. The lower grades are made from soured cream and may have an acid or even musty taste and poor texture.

Salted butter contains about 2 percent salt. Unsalted, or sweet, butter is more delicate in flavor, and many people treasure it for use as a table spread and in the preparation of certain baked foods. Since salt acts as a preservative, sweet butter will not keep as well as salted butter, but households that use butter fairly quickly will have no problem with the unsalted variety. Since salt may also mask a rancid flavor, some people feel they are more assured of freshness when they buy sweet butter.

Whipped butter is butter, either salted or sweet, with air beaten into it. This makes it soft and easy to spread. Whipping increases not only the volume, but also the price. You can make your own by whipping regular bar butter in your blender.

Buying and storing. For assurance of quality, buy Grade AA. Butter is sold in packages of 1 pound (454 g) and 8 ounces (227 g) and may be divided into individually wrapped sticks of 4 ounces (113.5 g). Butter sold in undivided one-pound blocks is often cheaper than cut butter, because less packaging is involved.

Store butter in the refrigerator in a tightly covered container or in its original wrapper. If uncovered, it will absorb flavors of other foods. Well-wrapped butter can be stored in the refrigerator for up to two weeks. For easier spreading, bring cold butter to room temperature before using.

Fresh creamy butter made with pasteurized sweet cream can be frozen safely at 0°F (−17°C) or below for up to six months. It must be wrapped with moisture-proof freezer wrapping and tightly sealed. When ready for use, it should be thawed slowly, in the refrigerator.

*Calories and Fat in Dairy Products

Dairy products	Percentage of fat	**Calories
Milk products		
Butter (salted or unsalted)	80	1,625
Buttermilk		
cultured skim milk	1	85
cultured whole milk	3½	158
Cream		
light	18–30	505–690
heavy	36–40	840
half-and-half	12	320
sour cream	18–20	506
sour half-and-half	12	320
Eggs (medium-size)	5.5	75
white	.1	15
yolk	5.4	60
Milk		
whole	3.5	152
low-fat	2	110
skim	1	85–95
goat's	4	160
Yogurt		
whole milk	3.5	152
low-fat milk (plain)	2	122
low-fat milk (with fruit)	2	250
Cheeses		
Cottage cheese		
low-fat, uncreamed	1	180
low-fat, pot style	2	200
creamed	4	230–247
Cream cheese	33–50	800
Farmer cheese	8	240
Gjetost	31.5	1,080
Mozzarella		
part skim	16.8	630–672
Neufchâtel	24	560–585
Ricotta	13	400
part skim	8.2	250

*Figures are from United States Department of Agriculture and Geigy Scientific Tables, 7th ed.
**Figures are for quantities of one 8-ounce cup (240 ml).

The value of butter

Like many other foods, butter was originally looked upon not as a food, but as medicine. Ancient Greeks and Romans did not eat it; they used it as a hair oil and as ointments to treat skin injuries (as we still use it for burns). The Romans thought the soot of burned butter would cure sore eyes. The Hindus valued their cows according to the amount of butter obtained from their milk.

Many years ago in Scotland and Ireland, the amount of butter people possessed was an indication of their wealth, and casks of butter were buried with their owners when they died. The French have always valued butter but for a practical reason: the rich flavor it adds to foods. The French still load their sauces with butter, and use about 5 pounds of it for every pound of margarine.

Butter or margarine

It is crucial for cholesterol-conscious people who are substituting margarine for butter to check the label of the product they buy. Just as all butter is not the same, neither are margarines. No one should be misled by the fact that a margarine is advertised as being made from 100 percent corn, soybean, or safflower oil. The statement may be true, but it is meaningless unless the oil is in liquid form. Many margarines, especially the less expensive ones, contain large amounts of vegetable oils, but they have been partially saturated during processing. Food labeling requires that the ingredients be listed in the order of their quantity in the product, with the predominant ingredient appearing first. The best margarines list liquid vegetable oil first and name the type (safflower, corn, or soybean) as the first ingredient.

Thin man's cheesecake

Cheesecake is generally so rich, so delicious, and so fattening that most people feel they are committing a venal sin while enjoying every bite. Cheesecake is made from no less than three fat-packed dairy products: its traditional ingredients are eggs, sour cream, and cream cheese, used in varying proportions.

A less caloric version of cheesecake can be made by substituting cottage cheese or a combination of Neufchâtel and cottage cheese for the cream cheese called for in your favorite recipe. You might also substitute yogurt for the usual sour cream. Some cooks use ricotta instead of cream cheese to create a drier cake with a different texture. This thin man's cheesecake will please your tastebuds without damaging your waistline.

Warm or cold?

Fresh cheeses are the only cheeses that should be served directly from the refrigerator. All other cheeses should be brought to room temperature to reveal their subtle, characteristic flavor. Remove the hard cheeses an hour before serving, but keep them wrapped so that cut surfaces do not dry out.

Cottage cheese for every meal

Cottage cheese—high in nutrition, low in calories—makes a good breakfast food, guaranteed to keep you zipping along until lunch. Mix it with raisins, cinnamon, a little honey or molasses, or top it with your favorite fresh fruit. For lunch, dig into the cottage cheese again, with cucumbers and tomatoes, salt and pepper, or spread it on your favorite flatbread for a low-calorie sandwich. For dinner, try cottage cheese in salads, or substitute it in recipes that call for other kinds of cheese. Cottage cheese is so versatile you will find ways to use it to fit into every meal.

CHEESE

The first cheese came into the world by accident. Legend has it that a traveling horseman placed his supply of milk in a saddlebag made from an animal's stomach, and when he arrived at his destination he found that the contents of the bag had turned into a semisolid, fermented substance, or cheese.

It is unlikely that the horseman understood that milk becomes cheese because of the clotting action of its principal protein, casein, when it comes in contact with an enzyme called "rennet." Rennet is found in the stomachs of suckling mammals. All cheese is made by heating milk with rennet or other clotting enzymes made of vegetable matter, which induces milk to coagulate. Once the milk has separated into curds (soft, white lumps) and whey (the watery liquid that remains when the curds have been removed), the curds are drained, pressed into molds, and allowed to ripen through the action of harmless bacteria that are added. The flavors intensify as the cheese ages. Cheese contains most of the nutrients of milk and is a good source of protein.

In many cases, the formulas for making cheese were passed along from one generation to another as family secrets. Similar cheeses were created simultaneously in different places; consequently, similar cheeses often have different names. Cheeses, like people, tend to migrate, and the same cheeses are now made in many countries, with only slight variations in taste and quality. English Cheddar, for example, is very much the same as the Cheddar made in the United States and Canada. There are a number of North American versions of European cheeses—mozzarella, Limburger, and Port Salut among them.

Cheeses fall mainly into three divisions: natural cheeses, process and blended cheeses, and fresh or uncured cheeses, such as cottage cheese and cream cheese, which are highly perishable.

NATURAL CHEESES

Natural cheeses are made directly from milk solids, although sometimes whey is used. The milk comes from cows, goats, or ewes and is usually whole milk, but in some cases skim milk or cream is used. Cheeses are categorized according to the method by which they are ripened or cured. Cheeses come soft (Brie, Camembert), semisoft (Bel Paese, Muenster), hard (Edam, Gouda), and very hard (Parmesan, Romano). Some may be ripened so as to produce a blue-veined mold (Roquefort, Danish blue).

PROCESS CHEESES

Cheeses that are not natural are known as "process cheese." Process cheese is a blend of fresh and aged natural cheeses that has been melted, pasteurized, and mixed with an assortment of emulsifiers and stabilizers to form a smooth, plastic mass that can be rolled flat or packed into blocks. Sometimes coloring and flavoring are added. Unlike natural cheese, which improves in flavor as it ages, the flavor of processed cheese remains constant; pasteurization has prevented further ripening. Process cheeses have no rind. They spread and melt easily and are often packaged conveniently presliced or as spreads. Their major drawback is the amount of chemicals used in their manufacture and their rather bland taste. The most popular process cheese is American cheese, which is made from Cheddar or Colby.

Storing natural and process cheeses. Cheese should be stored in the refrigerator. How long it will keep depends on the kind of cheese and how carefully it has been wrapped. To protect the cut surface from drying out, cover tightly with waxed paper, foil, or plastic, or store the cheese in a container with an airtight lid. Cheeses that have a strong odor, such as Limburger and Liederkranz, should be stored in a tightly covered container. Cheddar, Swiss, and other hard varieties will keep for several months unless mold develops.

If any surface mold develops on hard natural cheeses, it should be trimmed off completely before the cheese is used. However, mold is an important part of mold-ripened cheeses such as Roquefort and blue and it can be eaten. If mold penetrates the interior of cheeses that are not mold ripened, such as Cheddar and Swiss, you have the choice of either cutting away the moldy parts or discarding the cheeses.

Cheese that has become dried out and hard may be grated. Four ounces (113.5 g) of cheese will make 1 cup (240 ml) of grated cheese. Store in a tightly covered jar in the refrigerator and use for topping and seasoning.

Freezing is not recommended for most cheeses because they become crumbly when frozen and thawed. But you can freeze small quantities of Gorgonzola, blue, or Roquefort for use in salads or salad dressings or where a crumbly texture is desirable. The following may also be frozen in pieces of 1 pound (454 g) or less and not more than an inch (2.54 cm) thick: brick, Cheddar, Edam, Gouda, Muenster, Port Salut, Swiss, Provolone, mozzarella, and Camembert.

To freeze, wrap cheeses tightly in freezer wrap, freeze at 0°F (−17°C) or below. They will keep up to six months. When ready to use, thaw slowly in the refrigerator.

FRESH CHEESES

Fresh cheeses are not allowed to ripen at all. They must be used soon after they are made. Unripened natural cheeses include the following:

COTTAGE CHEESE. One of the most popular fresh cheeses is cottage cheese, also known as "pot cheese," "baker's cheese," "smearcase," and "crowdie." It is a soft, white, acid-tasting cheese made from skim milk that has been curdled by the action of a lactic bacteria.

Cottage cheese is sold in two curd sizes: large curd, sometimes called "country" or "California style," and small curd, also called "old-fashioned" cottage cheese. If not specified on the container, the curd is small, its traditional form. There is no difference in the taste between the large and the small curds. The large-curd cottage cheese is a little moister, but the choice is a matter of preference.

Cottage cheese is available in special diet brands (uncreamed, no salt added), low fat, and "creamed," or mixed with added milk or cream for a richer taste. Pot cheese differs slightly from cottage cheese in that it contains less moisture and is never creamed. Farmer cheese is cottage cheese dried and pressed into blocks so it can be sliced. It is somewhat higher in fat content than cottage cheese and can sometimes be used as a

History of cheese

The history of cheese making goes back four thousand years. Earthenware cheese pots were found in the tomb of an Egyptian king who lived in 3200 B.C. As an indication of how highly cheese was regarded, conquering tribes demanded cheese as a tax from the Egyptians. In Greek mythology the Gods bestowed cheese making upon the human race as a divine gift. The Greeks liked cheese so much they even invented a word for a cheese lover—*tyrophile*. The Romans, too, were tyrophiles, Latin style, and obtained new varieties of cheese from all parts of the empire; they brought the art of cheese making to England during the first three centuries of the Christian era.

Nowhere, however, did the art of cheese making develop as it did in France. Many new cheeses were invented in monasteries in the Middle Ages, when the church imposed numerous fast days on its clergy. Forced to make delicious food out of simple ingredients, the monks developed incredible recipes for cheeses that are still produced and eaten today.

Cheese came to America on the *Mayflower*, and for many years cheese making was largely a home industry. The first cheese factory was built in New York State in 1851. For a while New York was the leading cheese manufacturer in the country, until the cheese industry moved to Wisconsin. Now many cheeses that originated in other parts of the world are made in America.

Cheese for dessert

In France cheeses of excellent quality are served before a sweet as part of the dessert. Said one French sage, "A dessert without a cheese is a beautiful woman with only one eye."

Fertile and organic eggs

There is an ongoing controversy about the relative nutritive values of eggs from free-ranging chickens that are allowed to scratch for their own food and socialize at will with roosters, and those from hens leading a monastic life and dining on commercial feeds. Weighty and unequivocal pronouncements are made by both experts and self-appointed experts in support of each.

"Are the chicken hormones found in the fertile egg beneficial to humans?" "Does the egg from the hen that runs loose in the garden have a superior flavor and more nutrients than the one produced in the chicken factory?" "Can the chemical additives in the commercially prepared feed persist in the egg and present a health hazard to humans?" Both "aye" and "nay" answers ring out loud and clear to these and similar questions.

People who would answer the above questions affirmatively can find organic and fertilized eggs in some specialty and health-food stores, in limited supply. They are usually smaller in size and higher in price than the eggs that are commercially produced on large poultry farms.

Eggsotic trivia

In our society, the word "egg" means "chicken egg," although duck, goose, and quail eggs are available from time to time in specialty stores. All bird's eggs are nutritionally the same and are said to taste very much alike, although goose and duck eggs are oilier than hen's eggs. For some reason, duck, goose and turkey eggs are all higher in calories than chicken eggs. In France lapwing eggs, prized for rarity more than flavor, are available in season. (The lapwing is a member of the plover family.) Turtle's eggs, with their rubbery white shells, are considered a great delicacy in many places, but the legal sale of them is often banned because of the rapidly decreasing number of sea turtles. But you would be hard put indeed to find a peacock or ostrich egg anywhere in the modern world. A pity, too, because one ostrich egg provides eighteen servings of scrambled eggs. Think of the saving of time and effort in having to break only one eggshell!

substitute for cream cheese.

When buying cottage cheese, check the container to make sure that the lid is securely fastened and that the expiration date is in the future. It should be refrigerated, covered, and used within three to five days.

CREAM CHEESE is made from cream, plus milk and water. It is given its characteristic smooth texture by the stirring of the curd, which is then heated for an hour. Chemical additives may be used to make the cheese more concentrated and cohesive. Cream cheese combines well with other ingredients—jelly, olives, and dates, to name a few—and in dips and sandwiches.

Cream cheese should be refrigerated covered or tightly wrapped and used within two weeks or it will develop a sharp, rancid taste.

Cream cheese is high in fat (see Table, p. 159), and unlike other cheeses it does not contribute much in the way of protein.

NEUFCHÂTEL is a type of cream cheese that originated in France. It is made with more milk and less cream than cream cheese; consequently, it has less fat and fewer calories. In France, Neufchâtel is sometimes ripened and molded into whimsical shapes, but it is always sold fresh in this country.

GOURNAY, a French cheese, is a member of the Neufchâtel family. This soft cheese is flavored with either pepper or garlic and herbs. It is packaged in 5-ounce (142 g) foil containers and is marketed under such trade names as Boursin, La Bourse, and Tartare Provençal. It must be refrigerated, tightly closed, and will keep for up to ten days or two weeks. It becomes bitter when aged.

PETIT-SUISSE is a very soft, creamy, unsalted cheese with a slightly sour flavor, that comes from France. Made with whole milk and heavy cream, it is excellent for desserts served with sugar, strawberries, and preserves.

WHEY CHEESES are made from the part of the milk that is usually drained off in other cheese-making processes. When whey is reduced and coagulated, it achieves the consistency of heavy cream. Some of the most popular whey cheeses are listed below.

RICOTTA. The best-known whey cheese is ricotta. Resembling cottage cheese in color and texture, it has a slightly sweeter, richer taste. It can be eaten like cottage cheese, or used in many Italian pasta dishes and sweets. Sometimes it is dried, and in this state it can be grated. First made in Italy, ricotta is now widely available and can be purchased from Italian specialty stores. It is also sold in pound (454 g) containers in some supermarkets, and is available both whole and partially skimmed. Like cottage cheese, it is perishable and should be used within three to five days.

MYOST. This whey cheese, which originated in Scandinavia, is made from cow's milk or goat's milk. The goat's-milk product is called "Ghetost." When small amounts of buttermilk, whole milk, or cream are added to the whey, the cheese is called "Primost." All three cheeses are light brown in color, with a buttery consistency and a mild semisweet flavor. Some manufacturers add brown sugar, cloves, or cumin to Myost. It may be purchased in cheese specialty stores and will keep well in the refrigerator, wrapped in plastic. These cheeses are suitable for snacks or as dessert cheeses.

MOZZARELLA. Originally mozzarella (also called *scamorza*) was made in Italy from buffalo milk, but it is now produced everywhere from the pasteurized milk of cows. The rubbery texture of this bland, mild-tasting cheese is created by placing the fermented curd in hot water, then pulling and kneading it until it is smooth. Mozzarella is used for melted-cheese sandwiches and for toppings on pizzas, lasagna, and casseroles. It may also be eaten uncooked.

Mozzarella can be bought fresh from the pot in Italian specialty stores and in many supermarkets. It can be made either from whole or partially skimmed milk, which will be indicated on the label.

It is not as perishable as some of the soft, ripened cheeses, such as Brie or Camembert, and will keep well in the refrigerator tightly wrapped.

FETA. A salty, crumbly, dry fresh cheese originally made in Greece, feta resembles farmer cheese in color and texture. It may be domestic or imported and is made from either goat's or sheep's milk. It has a sharp, salty taste because it is pickled in a concentrated salt solution (brine). Excellent crumbled over salads or as a snack, doused with olive oil and accompanied by olives, peppers, and sliced tomatoes, it can be purchased in tins or glass jars in the supermarket or from cheese specialty stores. It will keep indefinitely if refrigerated in a covered jar filled with a solution of salt water.

EGGS

With its rich assortment of protein, fat, vitamins, and minerals all done up in a container that can also double as a cooking pot, the egg represents as tidy a job of food packaging as was ever devised. It is also the most versatile performer of all foods. It can be fried, baked, scrambled, boiled, poached, coddled, or added raw to enrich an eggnog. It can bring airy lightness to a cake or a soufflé, act as an emulsifying agent in mayonnaise or salad dressing, or thicken a sauce or a soup without distorting the flavor.

The egg also chalks up an impressive record on the nutritional scoreboard. Eggs contain amounts of every mineral and vitamin except for vitamin C. But the egg yolk is extremely high in cholesterol and saturated fat, which makes cholesterol-conscious Americans unhappy and has led to a decrease in egg consumption nationally. A large egg contains about 75 calories, to which the yolk contributes 60 and the white 15. All of the fat is concentrated in the yolk; the white is pure protein.

Egg grading. Eggs are graded according to size and quality. The size classification is based on the minimum weight of a dozen eggs; the legal range of weights varies from state to state. There are six classes: jumbo, weighing 30 ounces (852 g) per dozen; extra large, 27 ounces (767 g) per dozen; large, 24 ounces (682 g) per dozen; medium, 21 ounces (598 g) per dozen; small, 18 ounces (511 g) per dozen, and peewee, 15 ounces (420 g) per dozen.

Egg cooking

Eggs are delicate, and for best results they must always be cooked slowly, over gentle heat, or they will toughen and dry out. This pertains to omelets and scrambled or fried eggs.

Unflattering appraisals of a person's ability in the kitchen is often expressed by the statement, "She (or he) can't boil an egg." Actually, boiling an egg can be a tricky business, but not if you have a kitchen timer or can, at the very least, tell time.

Soft-cooked. Place eggs in a saucepan and add water to cover them. Place over moderate heat and bring the water slowly to a boil. Cover the pot at once and remove from the heat. Soft-cooked eggs should remain in the pot for 2 to 3 minutes, depending on how you want them.

Medium-cooked. Proceed as above but allow the eggs to remain in the covered pot for 4 to 5 minutes if they are large; 6 minutes if they are extra large.

Hard-cooked. If hard-cooked eggs have tough whites and the yolks are surrounded by a dark ring, it's because they were hard boiled instead of hard cooked. Cover eggs with cold water and slowly bring to a boil. Reduce the heat to a slow simmer and set your kitchen timer for 10 minutes. Remove the eggs at once and plunge them into cold water to stop further cooking. Peel the eggs immediately and refrigerate, covered.

Cakes with many eggs

Cookbooks were quite rare in this country until the mid 1800s (a shortage that has been amply compensated for in the last few decades), and most recipes were handed down from mother to daughter in laboriously handwritten notebooks. The large number of eggs that went into some of the cake recipes of that time is astonishing until you realize that baking powder did not appear on the culinary scene until 1856. Up until then, eggs were the only leavening agent for cakes, and the sole tool to beat them with was a hickory rod. Eggbeaters were introduced to the New England and pioneer housewives in 1870 when Yankee peddlers began to sell their wares. This newfangled gadget probably caused more of a stir than the food processors of today.

Good eggs and bad eggs

For centuries people have believed eggs possess both good and evil powers. In many cultures the egg was regarded as a symbol of fertility; German and Slav peasants annointed their ploughs with a mixture of eggs, flour, and bread on the Thursday before Easter to ensure a good harvest. In the seventeenth century French brides traditionally broke eggs on the door sills of their new homes before entering them—an insurance policy for domestic bliss. In Christian nations the egg is a symbol of Christ's rebirth; thus, the colored Easter egg we still hunt today.

Conversely, the empty shells of eggs were deemed unlucky in some places. Romans destroyed vacant egg shells, and for ages people believed that witches inscribed their evil spells in empty shells and flew about in them. In Europe it was believed that it was bad luck to take eggs in or out of the house after dark.

Today we still refer to our friends as "good eggs" and our enemies as "bad eggs."

What an agile man!

How did the concoction of eggs known as an omelet get its name? Legend has it that the king of Spain was overcome with hunger pangs while hiking in the countryside and dropped into a peasant's hut for lunch. The loyal peasant set to work with great speed and soon presented the king with a treat he'd never tasted before—a dish of beaten eggs cooked in oil. Much pleased with the cook, the king exclaimed, "Quel homme leste!" —which in French means, "What an agile man!" Thereafter, homme leste (sounds like "omelet") became the official name of this special peasant recipe. It's a lovely story, but it has some holes in it: Why was the king of Spain speaking French and why is the omelet called tortilla in Spanish?

A still questionable—but more likely—explanation for the genesis of the word "omelet" is offered by an account of the Roman merchant and famed gourmet, Apicius, who lived in the first century A.D. His interest in food and his appetite for exotic dishes were prodigious. He was inordinately fond of a dish made of eggs with honey and pepper, which he called ovemele, "egg honey."

The size of the eggs is no reflection on the quality. If medium-sized top-quality eggs are notably cheaper than large eggs, you can save money by buying the medium sized. However, if you are using them in baking, you may need to use more of the smaller ones. It takes four to five large eggs to make a cup; six medium sized, and seven small for the same amount.

There is also a voluntary government inspection program for eggs. The three grade marks are U.S. Grade AA (or Fancy Fresh Quality), U.S. Grade A, and U.S. Grades B and C. Many state grade standards are the same as the U.S. grades. Grades AA and A are first quality, with a higher proportion of thick white and a firm yolk. They are both recommended for frying, poaching, and boiling. Grades B and C are less expensive and are completely acceptable for baking and cooking.

Selection. When the grade is marked on the egg carton, select Grade AA (Fancy Fresh Quality) or A for table use. Examine the eggs to be sure there are no cracked ones, because bacteria can seep through the crack and set up housekeeping inside the egg. This can be dangerous unless the egg is very well cooked. Bacteria is destroyed if the egg is boiled for 10 minutes or baked in a cake for at least an hour, but to be safe, stay away from cracked eggs even when they are offered at bargain prices. Do not buy eggs from nonrefrigerated counters, since any time out of the cold diminishes the life of an egg.

Egg-carton dating practices vary from state to state; some specify the last date on which the carton should be sold, while others note the date the eggs were inspected. You should purchase eggs within ten days after inspection, and make sure you are not buying eggs whose expiration date has passed.

The eggs sold in the average supermarket may or may not be completely fresh when you buy them. They may have been shipped some distance and held in refrigerated units for some time, giving the flavor time to deteriorate. Usually eggs arrive at the market within one or two days after they are laid, but they may not be put out for sale immediately, in favor of first selling those already on the shelf. Smaller markets that receive daily egg deliveries are a good source for fresh eggs, and, if you live near a farm, you can buy the freshest of all.

There is no difference in nutrition or flavor between a white and a brown egg of the same grade. Exactly the same thing is going on inside the shells of each. The color of the shell is due simply to the pigment produced by the hen. In some parts of the country brown eggs command a premium price; in other places, it is the white. Buy the eggs that offer the best value and never mind the color of the shell.

To judge freshness. There's no room for doubt when an egg has gone bad. You couldn't possibly miss the unpleasant "rotten egg" odor that seeps out even through the shell. But what about the eggs that have been in your refrigerator for a while? Are they all right to use in the cake, or will you have to buy fresh ones? There's a very simple way to test for freshness. Place the egg in a bowl of cold water. If it floats to the top, it is stale or bad. A fresh egg will lie on its side or stand on end in the water.

The reason for this is simple. The shell of the egg is porous and lined with a delicate membrane that separates from the large end of the shell to form an air chamber. The fresher the egg, the smaller the chamber. Thus a fresh egg feels heavier than an old egg and will sink in a bowl of water. The shell of a fresh egg should also feel slick to the fingers. Egg shells develop a rough texture from exposure to the air, so the rougher the shell, the older the egg. Never use a doubtful egg, or one that is cracked, or one that has any odor or discoloration.

Once a fresh egg is broken, it displays a clear white and a gleaming yolk, which stands up firmly in the middle of the white. A yolk that breaks easily is another sign that the egg is aging. When cooking, break each egg required into a separate bowl before adding it to the other ingredients in order to avoid ruining whatever you are making with an unexpected bad egg.

Storage. How long eggs will keep in the refrigerator is variable, depending on their freshness and quality when you bought them. For instance, young hens lay eggs with harder shells, which, being less porous, will keep the egg fresh longer. Fresh eggs will generally keep well in the refrigerator for six weeks or longer, however. Store them in the coldest part of the refrigerator, with the large side down. Always remove them from the refrigerator at least 45 minutes before using them. Eggs cannot be beaten to full volume when they are cold; they must be at room temperature.

If you use part of an egg, you can store the remaining yolk or white in the refrigerator. Store the unbroken egg yolk in a covered container with just enough cold water to cover, to keep it from getting hard. Use within three to four days, first draining off the water. Store the whites in a covered container and use within four days.

Egg whites can be frozen in a moisture-proof container. After thawing, they can be used exactly as if they were fresh. A single egg white can be frozen individually in a plastic ice-cube tray. One egg white fits nicely into a single ice-cube compartment. When frozen, transfer to a plastic freezer bag. In this way you can thaw only as many as you need for a recipe.

Egg yolks freeze best when you add salt or sugar to them. For yolks to be used in desserts, gently stir 2 tablespoons of sugar or corn syrup into a cup of yolks. (About twelve large yolks make a cup.) If you plan to use them for main-dish cooking, gently stir 1 tablespoon of salt into 1 cup of yolks. Transfer to a moisture-proof container and store in the freezer.

It might be noted that, in the case of hard-boiled eggs, fresher is not better. Eggs should be at least three days old before being hard cooked. Fresher than that, they turn greenish and are difficult to peel. Shelled, hard-boiled eggs can be stored, covered, in the refrigerator for two days. After that, they become tough.

Equivalents. It probably would make better sense if recipes specified the volume of eggs needed—¾ cup (180 ml), ½ cup (120 ml), and so on—instead of the number of eggs, since they vary so widely in size. Most recipes are based on medium-sized or large eggs, and generally the difference is not critical. But there is a difference. Two large or three medium-sized eggs are needed to give you ½ cup (120 ml). Depending on their size, four to seven eggs are needed for 1 cup (240 ml); from eight to twelve for 1 cup (240 ml) of egg white; from twelve to sixteen eggs for 1 cup (240 ml) of egg yolk. The yolk of an egg is about 1⅓ tablespoons (20 ml); the white, about 2 tablespoons (30 ml). If you decrease a recipe and need only a portion of an egg, beat it slightly and measure about 1½ tablespoons (22.5 ml) for half an egg and about 1 tablespoon (15 ml) for a third. Four ounces (113.5 g) of beaten egg is the equivalent of two large eggs and make an adequate serving for one person.

Ancient eggs

Most people like their eggs fresh, but a special treat for Chinese people is a preserved duck egg—the hundred-year-old egg. The eggs are preserved by coating them with a mixture of lime, salt, ashes, and tea and letting them cure for one hundred days; you can see that the egg is far younger than its name. Its inside is dry and firm, with a cheesy, pungent taste and sulfuric odor. The Chinese eat them for appetizers, and they are imported from Taiwan to Chinese specialty stores in America.

Beating egg whites

Many recipes for soufflés, cakes, and other confections call for beaten egg whites. Egg whites incorporated into a mixture add lightness and volume, causing it to rise in the oven. Beating an egg white into snowy peaks is easy when you know the secrets. Egg whites will not beat properly if they contain a single particle of yolk, or if the bowl you beat them in, or the beater, is moist or greasy. Eggs separate more easily when chilled, but beat better at room temperature. For maximum volume, let the egg whites come to room temperature before beating. Use a stainless steel, copper, or glazed pottery bowl—not aluminum—and beat with a balloon whisk or electric or hand beater. As air is incorporated into the whites, they will become foamy. At this stage add a small pinch of cream of tartar or salt. (Sugar is beaten in very slowly, a little at a time, after the egg whites begin to peak. The usual amount is 2 tablespoons of sugar to one egg white for a meringue.) Properly beaten whites stand in stiff peaks and are moist, not dry or granular. Fold the beaten whites into the batter as soon as possible, because they sink rapidly.

Stubborn stains

To get rid of egg-yolk stains on cutlery and china, soak the pieces in *cold* water before washing them. Trying to remove the coagulated yolks with hot water will only make them firmer and more resistant to your efforts.

MEAT AND GAME

Meat accounts for about a quarter of the average American family's food budget. The most expensive item in that budget, meat has more time and care spent on its purchase and cooking than is spent on any other. A fine source of essential nutrients, meat supplies, in one 3½-ounce (100 g) serving, over half of an adult's daily protein needs, as well as high degrees of iron, copper, phosphorus, calcium, and three of the B vitamins—thiamine, riboflavin and niacin. With calorie counts that range from under 200 to over 500 for a 3½-ounce (100 g) serving, meat is a good choice in either a low- or high-calorie diet.

But it is in enjoyment that meat really gives us our money's worth. One of the greatest goads to appetite is the smell of meat cooking. For the eye, there are few greater pleasures than the sight of a steak still sizzling on a hot platter, a roast cooked to a handsome brown, or a succulent stew. As for taste, there is almost no limit to the variety of flavors and textures meat can offer in the hands of an adventurous and ingenious cook.

No wonder meat is the favorite food of millions of Americans. We consume an average of 120 pounds (54.5 kg) a person a year, making the meat industry the country's third largest business, right after automobiles and steel.

Inspection and grading. All meat that crosses state lines must be federally inspected to be sure the meat comes from healthy animals and sanitary packing plants. The small proportion of meat that stays within state borders receives equally careful state inspection. The state inspection stamp is usually in the form of the state as it appears on the map, with the name of the state and "Department of Agriculture" on it. The federal stamp is round and purple and says "U.S. Inspected and Passed." It bears the number officially assigned to each packing plant.

Meat is graded for the qualities that affect flavor, juiciness, and tenderness, but the nutritive value is the same in all grades. Grading is voluntary, at the request of the meat packer, who pays for it; a large proportion do request it. Some large supermarket chains and companies who buy meat to sell under brand names do their own grading. Government-graded meat will always carry the letters "USDA" (United States Department of Agriculture), in addition to the grade designation.

The grade is stamped along the entire carcass with a roller stamp so it will appear on as many cuts as possible. If you want to know the grade and can't see it on the meat displayed, ask the butcher to show it to you on a larger section of the carcass.

Storage. Meat should be stored so as to retard the growth of bacteria, which thrive on warmth and moisture. It is the growth of bacteria that produces an off-taste and smell and ultimately causes the meat to spoil. Therefore, stored meat should be kept cold, and air should be able to circulate around it.

After purchase, meat should be taken out of the store packaging, wiped or patted dry on paper towels, loosely wrapped in fresh foil, plastic, or waxed paper, and stored in the coldest part of the refrigerator—usually the top shelf, where cold air comes from the freezer section. (Check side-by-side models and those with freezers on the bottom with a thermometer to locate the coldest part.) Meat storage bins are usually no cooler than the rest of the refrigerator, unless they are especially rigged to provide extra cold. The meat should not be crowded or piled one piece on top of the other.

Aging

Aged meat has a characteristic firm texture and full flavor produced by the action of enzymes. As a rule, only ribs and loins of top-quality beef, lamb, and mutton are aged.

Aging takes place in a large, refrigerated room kept at 34–39°F. The slabs of meat are hung well apart so air can circulate freely around them. The humidity in the room is kept to a minimum by fans that circulate the air constantly. The meat is hung for 2½ to 3 weeks.

Aging is usually done by the wholesaler, who sells the meat to clubs, hotels, and restaurants. Unless you are lucky enough to know a butcher who offers well-hung cuts at premium prices, you will find it difficult to obtain aged meat for home use.

Retail cuts of meat cannot be aged successfully at home because the necessary conditions of temperature and humidity cannot be reproduced there. Furthermore, there is some shrinkage—about 2.25 percent—and some waste during the aging process, since mold forms on the outside fat that must be cut off and discarded. For this reason, it is only practical to age large quantities of meat. However, meat is up to 2 weeks old by the time it reaches the consumer, which is long enough for some tenderizing to have taken place.

Naming the cuts

The National Livestock and Meat Board based in Chicago is not, as you might think, a government agency. It is a nonprofit service organization supported by and representing all segments of the livestock and meat industry, and acting as its lobby in Washington. One of their most laudable programs is the recent one to standardize the nomenclature for meat cuts across the country. Under this program cuts of meat are beginning to be called by the names intended to indicate the part of the animal they come from, instead of something cute, regional, or misleading.

What to do if your steak catches fire (and still keep it edible)

It is the fat that catches fire, so pour off any fat that accumulates as the steak cooks and it won't catch fire. But if it *has* caught fire, do the following:

1. Tear off a large piece of aluminum foil, preferably heavy-duty.

2. Put on a pair of asbestos-lined gloves. If they are not handy, pick up a couple of wooden spoons or any long, blunt object that will not pierce the foil.

3. Drop the foil over the flaming pan, and with your gloved hands or the spoons press the foil down around the steak, taking care not to pierce the foil. This usually smothers the fire. Cut off any charred bits and put the steak in a clean pan to complete cooking.

4. If the fire still doesn't go out after you have done the above, remove the steak to a platter, or the counter if it is fireproof, and smother whatever is still flaming with a piece of foil.

Never use water to put out a grease fire. The oil will float on top of the water and continue to burn. As a last resort pour quantities of salt over the flames; this can usually be rinsed off and the steak will still be edible, if a little worse for wear.

Higher mathematics

Counting the calories in a stew or meat loaf is difficult, but it can be done if you must. Starting with lean meat and your favorite calorie counter, measure each ingredient and count its calories. (Dry wine, dried herbs, and water don't count.) When you have the total calories for the dish, divide it by the number of servings or slices and you will have your count, as well as a nice change from the usual diet fare.

Large pieces of meat—roasts, steaks, and chops—can all be stored for up to 4 days. Ground meat—beef, veal, lamb, or pork—should be used on the day purchased, certainly within 24 hours, since the many small surfaces invite bacterial growth. Restaurants known for exceptional hamburgers grind several times a day so the meat is cooked promptly, once ground. Ground meat should be used quickly to preserve flavor as well as for safety, whether it is to be used for hamburgers, meat loaves, or patties.

Variety meats, once known as "innards," are perishable and should be used within 24 hours of purchase.

Preparation. Meat need not be washed before cooking, but it should be wiped dry with a paper towel if it is to be browned, since moisture on the surface will prevent browning.

There are several other ways to treat meat before it is cooked:

Butterflying. With a sharp knife, carefully split a chop or piece of meat down the center, almost but not quite through, then open out sides like butterfly wings. Your butcher will usually be willing to do this for you.

Larding or barding. These are both methods of adding fat to lean meat to supply juiciness and flavor. To lard is to draw strips of salt pork or bacon (called "lardoons") through a piece of meat with a larding needle. The lardoons should be cut into strips about 2 inches (5.1 cm) long by ¼ inch (0.6 cm) and should be inserted in the meat about 1 inch (2.54 cm) apart.

To bard is to cover a piece of very lean meat with fat bacon or sheets of pork fat before cooking.

Marinating. Add flavor and tenderize meat by letting it stand for several hours, or even a few days, in a mixture of wine, vinegar, or lemon juice (their acid helps break down tough fibers and therefore makes the meat more tender), and oil and seasonings.

Tenderizing. The tough fibers in meat can also be broken down, and the meat made more tender, by adding a chemical tenderizer, scoring the surface of the cut with a sharp knife, or by placing the meat between two sheets of waxed paper and pounding it with a mallet.

Cooking methods and terms.

Barbecuing. In present-day usage, a method of broiling meat after the application of flavoring either through marinating or by brushing on a seasoning or sauce before or during cooking. While a barbecue generally takes place outdoors over an open fire, a similar result can be produced in a home oven.

Braising. A process in which the meat is first browned on all sides, the excess fat poured off, then cooked until tender in liquid, often in as small an amount as ½ cup (120 ml) or so, just enough to cover the bottom of the pot. The liquid can be red or white wine, sherry, Vermouth, stock, beer, tomato juice, or even water. After the liquid is added the pot should be covered tightly and the meat simmered very gently, either on top of the stove, or in a 300° to 325°F (149 to 163°C) oven. See also Stewing (page 170).

Broiling. Cooking meat by direct exposure to the source of heat, such as a charcoal fire or gas flame. High heat cooks the meat quickly so that juices are not lost, making it possible to cook smaller pieces of meat by dry heat than is possible in roasting. However, broiling is not recommended for thin cuts of meat since they will dry out and toughen.

Meat that is to be broiled should not be salted until after it is cooked, since salt brings moisture to the surface and prevents browning.

To broil meat in the broiling unit of a stove, preheat the broiler and rack for 10 minutes. Place the meat on a greased rack in the broiler pan 2 to 5 inches (5.1–12.7 cm) below the heat (thicker cuts further away from the heat than thin ones). Cook until brown on one side, then turn with tongs, and brown on the other side. Test for doneness by making a small incision in the meat with a sharp knife.

Broiling meat on a rack over the source of heat is also called "grilling." The meat is placed on a rack 2 to 8 inches (5.1–20.3 cm) above the heat, depending on the thickness of the cut and the degree of heat. Cook on one side just until a spot or two of blood appears on the surface of the meat, then turn with tongs and cook on the other side until juice appears. This method will result in rare meat; cook each side a little longer for medium to well-done meat.

Panbroiling. A way of cooking meat uncovered in a heavy skillet with no fat or liquid. It is a good way of cooking a piece of meat too thin to be broiled by direct heat. To panbroil, scatter some salt on the pan or grease it lightly, then heat the pan until it is hot but not smoking. Brown the meat on one side until juice just begins to moisten the surface, then turn with tongs and brown on the other side. Pour off fat as it accumulates.

Panfrying. Another way of cooking meat that is too thin to be broiled, this process is also called "sautéing." Heat a small amount of fat, just enough to cover the bottom of the pan, until hot but not smoking. Add the meat and turn it frequently; thin cuts are usually done by the time they are brown on both sides.

Roasting. Meat cooked by dry heat—that is, without liquid. Roasting is most usually done in the oven, but it can also be done on a spit, such as a rotisserie, or, more exotically, in a pit dug in the ground. Because no liquid is used, only large, well-fatted pieces of meat should be cooked by this method, since only they contain sufficient juice to remain tender.

Meat that is to be roasted should be at room temperature, so take it out of the refrigerator 1½ to 2 hours before cooking. Preheat the oven to the temperature called for, then place the roast in a shallow roasting pan on a rack, so the dry heat of the oven will go under the meat as well as around it. Standing rib roasts do not need a rack because the arch of the ribs acts as a rack, keeping the meat out of the pan juices. Insert a meat thermometer in the thickest part of the roast, not touching any bone. Roast fat side up, uncovered; do not baste.

There are two schools of thought about roasting. One way is the *continuous low-heat method,* which is to cook the meat at the same low temperature all the way through. The other is the *searing method,* which is to place the meat in a hot oven to sear it for 15 to 20 minutes, and then to turn the heat down for the rest of the cooking. Some cooks claim that there is less shrinkage with the low-heat method, and the roast cooks more evenly all the way through. Proponents of the searing method say this way crisps the outside and the browned bits in the pan make good gravy. The searing method also offers slight variations in doneness, so different tastes can be satisfied.

Beefalo, a new animal

This cross between buffalo and beef did not meet with much success when it was introduced in the East a few years ago, but it is growing in popularity in California. Domestic cows are artificially inseminated with semen from a crossbreed three-eighths buffalo and five-eighths beef, and the "beefalo" is the offspring produced. The producers of beefalo feel it will eventually catch on and be an interesting addition to our choices of meat. Enthusiasts claim it is delicious—tender, juicy, and slightly beefier than beef. It is higher in protein and lower in fat than beef, and it could, when it is produced in large enough quantities, be cheaper than beef because it does not need as much grain in its food.

Kosher meat

"Kosher" means that a food is allowed to be eaten or used according to the dietary laws of Judaism. To be kosher, the animal must first be ritually slaughtered—that is, as humanely as possible—by a qualified person. The one who does the slaughtering is a learned, pious man, whose duties include examining the internal organs afterward to make sure there is no sign of disease. Second, the blood of the animal must be removed by salting and washing.

Only the forequarter of beef may be used, and the foresaddle of veal and lamb. Pork is not allowed at all. Game animals are not allowed because they are killed by being shot. In Switzerland, however, deer are raised to be slaughtered ritually, and therefore qualify as kosher.

Kosher meat must be consumed shortly after the animal has been slaughtered.

The best way to cook standing ribs of beef

A 2-7-rib roast (4½-12 pounds)
2 teaspoons salt
1 teaspoon freshly ground black pepper

Take the roast from the refrigerator 2½ hours before starting to cook. Preheat the oven to 500°F. Sprinkle all sides of the roast with the salt and pepper, rubbing it in well. Put the roast, ribs down, in a roasting pan and cook at 500°F for 5 minutes for each pound of roast, for rare beef.(For example, a 6-pound roast should be cooked for 30 minutes to be rare.) Then turn off the oven and *do not for any reason open the oven door for 2 hours*. Repeat: *DO NOT OPEN THE OVEN DOOR FOR 2 HOURS*. The roast is then ready to serve, or it can be kept in the oven for as much as 4 hours, when it will still be warm and juicy. If your roast weighs more than 6 pounds, put 2 cups of water in the bottom of the roasting pan so the fat that drips off the roast does not burn and smoke up your kitchen.

How porterhouse steak got its name

In the early 1800s when the country was young, the inns and taverns in New York's dockside area were called "porter-houses," serving a meal and a glass of porter or ale to sailors and travelers. The proprietor of one of these establishments, short of food one night for a special customer, sliced a steak off the family short loin roast and grilled it. A great success with the customer, the steak soon became a favorite in the dockside community and was called a "porterhouse steak" to differentiate it from steaks purveyed elsewhere.

Roasts should be allowed to "rest" for about 10 minutes after being taken out of the oven, or off the spit, before carving. This permits the juices to settle.

Pot roasting. Large cuts of meat that are too tough for dry roasting may be stewed. The liquid—wine, stock, water, juice, or any of these in combination—should come about a third of the way up the side of the roast. See also Stewing, below.

Stewing. A method of cooking meat, cut into cubes or left in a chunk, in enough liquid to barely cover the meat. Similar to braising except that the meat may or may not be browned, and more liquid is used.

The three processes in which meat is cooked in liquid—braising, pot roasting, and stewing—all require that the cooking liquid be brought to a boil, then reduced to a simmer. "Simmer" is hard to define; *Larousse Gastronomique* probably does it best when it describes simmering as "the slight quivering of a liquid just before it comes to the boil." There should be movement, but no violent activity on the surface of the liquid, nothing more than an occasional gentle plop or the breaking of a bubble.

It is hard to maintain a simmer. Often the liquid goes from simmering to doing nothing at all. Then, when the flame is turned up a hair, it goes into a gentle boil. A pierced metal or asbestos plate that goes on top of the burner will often help to produce the low heat required for slow, even cooking. Another alternative is to cook the dish in the oven. Temperatures vary from oven to oven, so you will have to experiment with your oven within the range of 300 to 325°F (149 to 163°C) to find the right temperature to maintain a simmer.

BEEF

I n Henry VIII's time, when an Englishman said "meat" he meant "beef." This is still true in some parts of the world, for beef is certainly the most popular of all meats. Because of the demand for beef, much research has gone into the breeding of good beef cattle. Today's animals, with short legs and necks and compact bodies, yield a higher proportion of meat to bone and are a far cry from the long-legged, muscular cattle of 200 years ago. The best grades of beef come from two-year-old cattle whose last months have been spent in dry lots or pens. Fed on corn and other grains to give their meat superior flavor, and allowed little or no exercise, they are fat, lazy, and tender. Lower-quality beef is range fed: the animal roams the pasture and feeds mainly on grasses and hay. Meat from range-fed cattle tends to be stringier and less marbled with fat, since the cattle have been more active.

Grades of beef. There are eight grades of beef, but the only ones we are likely to see on the retail market are the first four: Prime, Choice, Good, and Standard. The others—Commercial, Utility, Cutter, and Canner—go into hamburger or processed meat products. While this meat is perfectly good, it is from older animals, and not as flavorful or tender as the higher grades.

Prime. Prime beef is the highest grade of beef, and the meat is marbled with the greatest amount of fat. From pen-fattened, grain-fed animals, Prime beef is expensive, and most of it goes to fine restaurants. However, grading procedures were changed in 1976, requiring less marbling in Prime and Choice beef. As a result, 2 percent more beef now qualifies as Prime, and there is a little more for the retail consumer.

Choice. This grade of beef is the most widely available grade. Since grading specifications were changed in 1976, the amount of graded beef marked Choice has gone from over half of the total supply to two-thirds. This means that some Good grade with less marbling is being upgraded into Choice, and the range of quality is wide and uneven. For the best value in Choice, look for lacy marbling and a fair amount of outside fat.

Good and *Standard.* These grades will continue to be popular in some areas, and in cut-rate steak houses all over. These grades of beef are good for dieters because of their lack of fat, but for the same reason they are not suitable for roasting or broiling.

How to choose your cut. Meat is muscle, and the less work the muscle does, the more tender the meat. In humans, the long muscles that go from the shoulder blades to the lower back work hard keeping the person erect. In four-legged animals, these same muscles just lie there with hardly any work to do and, as a result, produce the most tender meat. The cuts from this section are the *rib, loin,* and *sirloin.*

Look for firm, fine-grained, rosy flesh and creamy white fat. Good marbling (flecks and streaks of fat in the flesh), is important to the consumer buying expensive cuts to roast or broil. The more marbling, the more tender, juicy, and flavorful the meat.

The muscles at each end of the animal are working muscles, and they are less tender, and not generally suited for roasting or broiling. However, they are just as nutritious, and less expensive, and they can be tender and delicious if they are cooked in the right way. The cuts from these busy parts, and the belly, are the ones for all those good things like pot roasts, braised meats, stews, and of course hamburger. The main cuts are *chuck, shoulder, brisket, plate, flank,* and *round.*

The *rib* section is from the shoulder to the end of the ribs, and this is where the tenderest roasts come from. The *short loin* section is from the end of the ribs to the hipbone, and this is where the tenderest steaks come from—club, T-bone, and porterhouse.

Sirloin steaks and roasts come from the *sirloin* and *hip* section, which is the part from the hip to the ball joint of the leg. They are not quite as tender as rib or loin.

The French way with tenderloin

In France the tenderloin is always removed whole from the loin of beef. What is left of the loin is called the *faux filet,* or *contre-filet.* The tenderloin is cut into steaks called *filet mignon* (nearest the ribs), *tournedos, filet* steak, *Chateaubriand* (the thickest part), and *biftek.* In this country the tenderloin is usually left in; it appears as the extra tender little piece of meat in our T-bone, porterhouse, and sirloin steaks.

That famous Japanese beef

Japanese black cattle from the Kobe and Matsuzaka areas are celebrated for having the finest flavor and texture of any beef. The superior juiciness and tenderness of this beef is attributed partly to the fact that in the last stages of fattening, the cattle are given a bottle of beer a day. Kobe cattle are also massaged once a day by some farmers with a bundle of soft rice straw. Matsuzaka beef producers claim that another reason their beef is so good is that they choose only *virgin* female calves to raise as beef cattle.

Watering stock

The phrase comes from the days when there were cattle ranches up the Hudson from New York and the stock was driven to New York for slaughtering. The story goes that the cattle were encouraged to eat large quantities of salt along the way and were kept away from water. Just before reaching market they were allowed to drink all the water they wanted. Arriving in New York bloated and heavy, this "watered stock" brought extra profit to wily ranchers.

To carve a roast beef

Start with proper tools: a sharp knife honed to perfection and a two-pronged carving fork. Bear in mind that meats are more tender when carved across the grain than when cut with the grain.

Place the roast beef, meat side down, resting on the larger end. You might need to remove a bottom slice so that the roast will lie steady on its base and not rock. Slice the meat across the top of the roast. Slices may be thin or thick, according to your preference. Separate each slice from the rib bone by inserting the tip of the knife at the edge of the rib bone and cutting vertically. Lift each slice to a platter after it is cut and proceed with the next.

CUTS OF BEEF

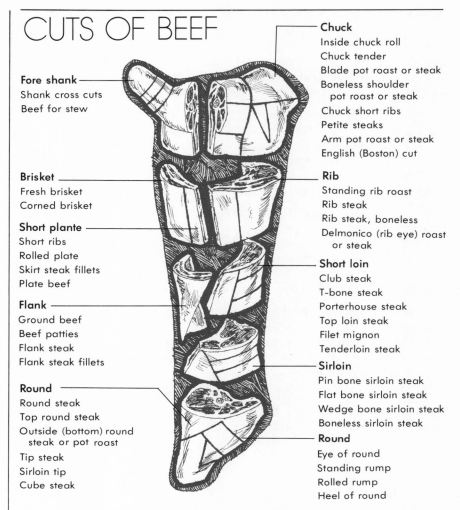

Fore shank
Shank cross cuts
Beef for stew

Brisket
Fresh brisket
Corned brisket

Short plante
Short ribs
Rolled plate
Skirt steak fillets
Plate beef

Flank
Ground beef
Beef patties
Flank steak
Flank steak fillets

Round
Round steak
Top round steak
Outside (bottom) round
    steak or pot roast
Tip steak
Sirloin tip
Cube steak

Chuck
Inside chuck roll
Chuck tender
Blade pot roast or steak
Boneless shoulder
    pot roast or steak
Chuck short ribs
Petite steaks
Arm pot roast or steak
English (Boston) cut

Rib
Standing rib roast
Rib steak
Rib steak, boneless
Delmonico (rib eye) roast
    or steak

Short loin
Club steak
T-bone steak
Porterhouse steak
Top loin steak
Filet mignon
Tenderloin steak

Sirloin
Pin bone sirloin steak
Flat bone sirloin steak
Wedge bone sirloin steak
Boneless sirloin steak

Round
Eye of round
Standing rump
Rolled rump
Heel of round

Nestled against the backbone, lying under the main loin muscle and running into the sirloin, is the *tenderloin*, the laziest muscle of all, and the most tender. When T-bone, porterhouse, and sirloin steaks are cut, the tenderloin appears as a round nubbin of extra tender meat. It is largest in the porterhouse, which is why that steak is considered the best of all. When the tenderloin is removed intact, it is sold either whole or cut up into filet mignon steaks. Shell or strip loin steaks are T-bone and porterhouse steaks after the tenderloin has been removed.

BEEF ROASTS

Allow 12 ounces (340.8 g) per person for meat with bone in it, and 6 to 8 ounces (170.4–227.2 g) per person for boneless meat. Buy at least 2 ribs for a rib roast; anything smaller will dry out during roasting.

Standing rib roasts. *First cut* is the best of the rib roasts, next to the loin. It has the largest amount of the tender eye. *Center cut* is a good buy, but it has more fat and some less tender muscles above the eye. *End cut* is the largest of the rib roasts, still with large eye but more fat.

Rolled rib roast. Boned and rolled rib roast. Buy at least 4 pounds (1.8 kg) after trimming.

Rib eye roast (Delmonico). The boneless eye of the rib roast. Buy at least 4 pounds (1.8 kg).

Tenderloin or filet. A long, tender muscle under the loin, this cut can be roasted whole or cut into individual filet mignon steaks.

Sirloin. Sometimes called "top sirloin butt," this is a good roast, but it is more often cut into steaks.

Borderline cuts for roasting. There are a few cuts—less tender but some say more tasty—that can be oven roasted, but only if they are Prime grade. They should be cooked only to medium rare, not well done, or they will be dry, and they should be served thinly sliced. They are *sirloin tip, top round, rump (and boneless rolled rump),* and *eye round*.

ROASTING BEEF TIMETABLE

New since 1977, when there was a salmonellosis scare, is the recommendation that all beef be cooked to an inner temperature of 145°F (63°C) (medium rare), so that there is no danger of food poisoning.

To Roast by the Continuous Low-Heat Method
Place roast uncovered, in oven preheated to suggested temperature.

Cut	Weight in pounds	Approx. minutes per pound	Oven temperature	Meat thermometer temperature
Standing ribs				
Medium rare	5 to 8	20 to 22	300°F	145°F
Medium	5 to 8	23 to 25	300°F	155 to 160°F
Well done	5 to 8	27 to 30	300°F	165 to 170°F
Rolled rib roast	4 to 6	Add 6 to 8 minutes per pound to above times, and watch the thermometer carefully. Use the same oven temperature.		
Rib eye (Delmonico)				
Medium rare	4 to 6	14 to 16	350°F	145°F
Medium	4 to 6	16 to 18	350°F	155 to 160°F
Well done	4 to 6	18 to 20	350°F	165 to 170°F
Tenderloin				
Medium rare	4 to 6	8 to 9	450°F	145°F
Sirloin	8 to 12	Roast, uncovered, for the same time at the same temperature as standing ribs.		
Sirloin tip and Top round		These should be roasted only if top (Prime) grade (borderline roast).		
Medium rare	3 to 5	30 to 33	300°F	145°F
Standing rump		This and the rolled, boneless version should be roasted only if top grade (borderline roast).		
Medium rare	5 to 7	23 to 25	300°F	145°F
Rolled rump	4 to 6	Add 5 to 8 minutes per pound to roasting time for standing rump, but watch the meat thermometer.		
Eye round		This should be roasted only if top (Prime) grade (borderline roast).		
Medium rare	3 to 6	14	350°F	145°F

Tenderized beef

Beef is sometimes treated before cooking to increase tenderness. Some tenderizing treatments are applied before the meat is sold and others are applied at home. There is no general agreement about the success of these procedures; some people find them satisfactory and others claim that they give the flavor and texture of the meat an unpleasant quality.

Tenderized beef is now available in some markets. The beef is from animals that have had papain, a food enzyme from the papaya fruit, injected into their circulatory systems before being slaughtered. This process makes it possible, it is claimed, to treat ordinarily tough cuts such as blade, arm, and leg, as if they were loin, rib, or sirloin. This beef is marketed under a national brand name and is called "tendered beef." Or powdered or liquid tenderizers can be bought for home use.

The other method of tenderizing is to cut or break connective tissues and muscle fibers. The markets do this by putting thin steaks such as sirloin tip or round steak through a machine that scores the surface. The meat is then sold as "minute" or "sandwich" steaks. In your own kitchen, you can tenderize round steak or flank steak by pounding them with a mallet to break the tough tissues.

Tips on roasting

• A shallow pan is better than a deep one for roasting because it allows heat to circulate around the roast.

• Placing the roast on a rack in the baking pan keeps the meat up from the drippings and increases the circulation of heat. A rack is not needed for a rib roast, since the rib bones will serve as a rack.

• For easier slicing, allow the roast to rest for 15 or 20 minutes after removing from the oven before carving.

Beef gravy

Roast beef may be served with the natural pan juices—*au jus*—or a thickened brown gravy made from the drippings. For the latter, skim the fat from the drippings in the roasting pan and reserve them. Add 1 cup of water or beef stock to the pan juices and bring to a boil over moderate heat, stirring to loosen the brown particles at the bottom of the pan. Measure the amount of pan drippings; for each cup of drippings measure 2 tablespoons of fat, 2 tablespoons of flour, and ½ cup of water, milk, or stock.

In a heavy saucepan, over moderate heat, heat the fat. Add the flour and cook until bubbly. Gradually add the water, milk, or stock, and pan drippings. Cook, stirring constantly with a wire whisk, until smooth and thickened. Season to taste with salt and pepper.

Use the hot gravy to warm up leftover rare roast beef. It will heat up the meat without making it look like pot roast.

The Hamburg hamburger

The hamburger on a bun is a distinctly American idea that has probably been as basic an item of nourishment for Americans as the potato in Ireland during the nineteenth century. The name comes from the German city of Hamburg, whose inhabitants were fond of shredded raw meat, which we now call "steak tartare." When they emigrated to the United States, they brought their food preferences with them.

Initially the hamburger was called a "hamburg steak" and was served like any other steak, not tucked between pieces of bread. It was an inspiration on the part of some enterprising food merchant to put the hamburg steak into a bun at the St. Louis Exposition in 1904, and the rest is history, etched in mountains of mustard, catsup, and pickle relish.

In the beginning, hamburgers were made of scraps of beef or fourth-rate cuts of meat. Today whole carcasses are butchered for the sole purpose of keeping up with the demand.

To Roast by the Searing Method

Place roast, uncovered, in preheated 450°F (232°C) oven for 20 minutes. Turn oven down to 300°F (149°C) and continue cooking according to timetable below. Count the minutes per pound from the time the roast is put in the oven, and watch the meat thermometer.

Cut	Weight in pounds	Approx. minutes per pound	Oven temperature	Meat thermometer temperature
Standing ribs		Sear at 450°F for 20 minutes, turn down to:		
Medium rare	5 to 8	18	300°F	145°F
Medium	5 to 8	20 to 22	300°F	160°F
Well done	5 to 8	25 to 27	300°F	170°F
Rolled rib roast	4 to 6	Add 6 to 8 minutes per pound to above times, and watch the meat thermometer.		

STEAKS

Allow 8 to 12 ounces (227.2–340.8 g) per person for bone-in steaks, 6 to 8 ounces (170.4–227.2 g) for boneless. These are steaks that may be broiled, panbroiled, or panfried.

Rib steak. Steaks cut from the small end of the rib section, the first-cut rib section, with or without bone.

Delmonico. The eye of the rib, boned, trimmed and cut into steaks.

Club steak. First steaks past the ribs, in the loin section.

T-bone. From the middle of the loin, containing some tenderloin.

Porterhouse. The best of the loin steaks, with the most tenderloin.

Shell steak, strip loin. T-Bone and porterhouse steaks without the tenderloin. They can be boned and trimmed and are sometimes called "New York" or "Kansas City steaks."

Filet mignon. Small steaks cut from the whole tenderloin

Sirloin steaks. From the hip section. The *pin bone*, closest to the loin, is the most tender, but it has a lot of bone.

The *flat bone* has less waste than the pin bone, while the *wedge bone*, farthest from the loin, is the least tender. They can all be boneless.

London broil. Originally flank steak broiled and served in thin slices, cut on a sharp diagonal to make a larger slice. Now it is often a piece of round, sirloin or chuck, 1½ to 2 inches (3.8–5.1 cm) thick. Broil or panfry to medium rare and serve in very thin slices, cut on the diagonal.

Cube steak, minute steak, petite steak, sandwich steak. These thin little steaks are best panfried.

Other steaks for broiling. There are some steaks that can be broiled only if they are Prime or top Choice grade. They are *blade chuck, top round, eye round, skirt fillet,* and *sirloin tip*. They can also be helped with a little tenderizer. The ones without much fat might better be panfried in some fat.

GROUND BEEF

One pound (454 g) of ground meat makes 3 to 4 patties, or 2 half-pounders (227.2 g). Allow 1 to 2 patties per serving.

Ground round is the leanest; *ground sirloin* next leanest and most expensive; *ground chuck* is less lean than either, but it is less expensive and considered by some to be the most flavorful. A few stores have begun to label ground beef according to the fat-lean ratio, a fine trend.

Packages labeled "hamburger" or "ground beef" are not good buys, even though the price may be attractive. This ground beef from un-specified sources not only contains excess fat, but sometimes water, too. The amount of weight lost in cooking cancels out the savings in cost.

Timetable for Broiling Beef

Do not try to broil steaks less than 1 inch thick (2.54 cm); they will be dry and tough. Instead, panbroil or panfry them (see page 169).

Steaks	Thickness in inches	Distance from heat in inches	Approx. minutes per side for		
			Medium rare	Medium	Well done
Rib, delmonico					
Club, T-bone	1	2	5	6	7
Porterhouse	1½	3	8	9	10
Shell	2	4	16	17	18
Strip loin					
London broil					
Sirloin	1	3	9	10	11
	1½	4	12	13	14
	2	4	20	21	22
Filet mignon	1 to 2	3	6 to 7	8 to 9	not recommended
Blade chuck Top round Eye round Skirt fillet Sirloin tip	These steaks should only be broiled if they are top quality or have been tenderized (borderline steaks).				
Cube Petite Sandwich	Panfrying (see page 169) is best for these little steaks. Cook uncovered for 2 to 3 minutes per side, turning frequently. Be careful not to over-cook; the meat is done as soon as blood rises to the surface and the meat becomes just slightly stiff.				

THE LESS TENDER CUTS

The cuts from the front, rear, and belly of the animal are the ones for braising, pot roasting and stewing (see page 170). Even though some of them are called "steaks" and "roasts" and other tender-sounding names, they do not lend themselves to broiling or dry oven roasting. They need to be cooked with some moisture to make them tender.

Salisbury steak

An item called "Salisbury steak" was frequently seen on restaurant menus until recently, but, like the dodo bird, it appears to be a vanishing species. Salisbury steak was simply a hamburger without the bun. It is credited by some authorities to a Dr. J. H. Salisbury, who, around the turn of the century, recommended ground steak three times a day for a long list of ailments. However, the status of hamburger has risen so appreciably that it is no longer necessary to gussy it up under another name. It is featured by even the grandest restaurants with no attempt to conceal its identity, except, perhaps, to describe it as "ground sirloin."

Carne alla Genovese

This is a delicious preparation. The meat is served with a topping of a thick puree of vegetables. Allow from 3 to 4 hours for slow, gentle cooking.

1 eye round roast (4½ to 5½ pounds)
¾ cup water, approximately
2 large onions, peeled, with cross cut at bottom
1 large carrot or 2 small ones, scraped
½ cup dry white wine
Salt and freshly ground pepper

Trim the meat of excess fat and place in a heavy casserole or Dutch oven. Add water to the depth of 1 inch. Add the onions and carrot, then cover the pot and place over medium heat. When the water reaches a boil, lower the heat and simmer slowly, covered, until the water has evaporated (this step could take 2½ to 3 hours), turning the meat and vegetables from time to time.

When the water has evaporated, add the wine and salt and pepper to taste. Cook until the wine has evaporated and the meat and vegetables are soft and tender. Keep the meat warm in a 250°F oven while you mash the vegetables—or, better still, put them through a blender. Taste and correct the seasonings.

Slice the meat, cover each slice with a topping of pureed vegetables, and run under the broiler before serving.

Serve with hot, fluffy rice. Serves eight to ten.

This sauce is an excellent accompaniment to macaroni.

The versatile meat loaf

Few foods can be fashioned and served in as many different ways, and be as ready for unexpected emergencies, as a meat loaf. You can mold it into an oval on a flat pan or sharply angle it in a loaf pan, or present it in a perfect circle by baking it in a ring mold. You can make individual meat loaves by baking them in small muffin tins or present it like a layer cake with a good stuffing between two layers. It can be the focal point of a hot dinner accompanied by a steaming pasta, or as a cold supper accompanied by crisp vegetable salads. As a ring mold, the center can be filled with green peas, creamed mushrooms, or any other vegetable you choose. It can be baked in a brown gravy, a tomato sauce, a creamy mushroom sauce, or a thin layer of chili sauce or catsup. Slices of cold meat loaf topped with a spicy Dijon mustard make a delicious sandwich for a lunch box or a picnic. And an unexpected visit from friends over a weekend will find the hosts who have a large meat loaf in the refrigerator cool and unperturbed.

The same broad spectrum of choices looms in putting the meat loaf together. It can be made from chopped beef, chopped beef and pork, or chopped beef, pork, and veal. Always there is the incontrovertible fact that, by grinding meat, it can be made to seem more than it really is. And it can be further stretched by adding soft bread crumbs soaked in milk or stock, finely grated raw potato or carrots, cooked and ground soybeans, dry processed cereal, or wheat germ.

You will never, of course, store uncooked ground meat in your refrigerator longer than 24 hours, so if you have miscalculated your buying and find yourself with more ground meat than you can use (and are reluctant to freeze it), turn it into a meat loaf. It will keep nicely in your refrigerator after it is cooked and will give a good account of itself for meals or nibbles.

Timetable for Braising, Pot Roasting, and Stewing Beef

Cook covered, on top of the stove, or in a preheated 300 to 325°F oven. *See also* Stewing (page 170).

To braise

Cut	Thickness in inches	Approx. cooking time
Chuck steak Skirt steak Round steak	1 to 1½	1½ to 2½ hours, or until tender

To pot roast

Cut	Weight in pounds	Approx. cooking time
Chuck roast Round roast Sirloin tip Rump Heel of round Brisket	3 to 5	2½ to 3½ hours, or until tender
Rolled plate	5 to 8	3½ to 4½ hours, or until tender

To stew

Cut	Amount in pounds	Approx. cooking time
Any cuts from the cuts to stew	2 to 4 boneless	1½ to 2½ hours, or until tender
	4 to 6 with bone	2½ to 3½ hours, or until tender

Cuts to braise. Allow 6 to 8 ounces (170.4–227.2 g) per serving for bone-in cuts, 4 to 6 ounces (113.6–170.4 g) for boneless.

Blade chuck steak
Arm chuck steak
Shoulder chuck steak

Chuck fillet steak
Skirt steak
Round steak

Cuts to pot roast. Allow 6 to 8 ounces (170.4–227.2 g) per serving for bone-in cuts, 4 to 6 ounces (113.6–170.4 g) for boneless.

Blade chuck roast
Arm chuck roast
Shoulder chuck roast
Chuck fillet roast
Inside chuck roll
English-cut roast (chuck)
Boston-cut roast (chuck)

Cross-rib roast (chuck)
Brisket
Rolled plate
Top-, eye-, bottom-round roasts
Sirloin tip roast
Rump roast
Heel of round

Cuts to stew. Allow 6 to 8 ounces (170.4–227.2 g) per serving for boneless cuts; 8–12 ounces (227.2–340.8 g) for bone-in cuts; 12 ounces to 1 pound (340.8–454 g) for very bony cuts such as short ribs, or cuts with a lot of fat as well as bone.

Bottom round	Rolled plate
Chuck, any part	Rump
Flanken	Shank (shin)
Neck	Short ribs
Oxtails	Top of rib

Cuts to boil. Allow 6 to 8 ounces (170.4–227.2 g) per serving for boneless cuts; 8 to 12 ounces (227.2–340.8 g) for bone-in; 12 ounces to 1 pound (340.8–454 g) for very bony cuts such as oxtails or cuts with a lot of fat as well as bone.

Brisket	Oxtails
Heel of round	Shank (shin)
Neck	Short ribs

LAMB

4- TO 6-WEEK-OLD BABY LAMBS

6-MONTH-OLD LAMB

The many sides of lamb

Traditionally lamb is eaten during religious festivals like the Christian Easter and the Jewish Passover. It is a symbol of peace and love; in Italy a white baby lamb may be presented to a young girl at Easter by a suitor. In ancient times, lambs were used for sacrifices to placate or charm a hostile god.

In Egypt a ceremonial lamb is roasted on the spit, its mouth stuffed with a piece of sweetmeat, its head turned toward Mecca. It is a modern "sacrifice," performed for many occasions: the birth of a child, a death in the family, or to commemorate religious or festive occasions. The meat of the lamb is carved and distributed to the poor.

The lamb is associated with spring and for many years was considered seasonal. This is no longer so. Now "spring lamb" refers simply to the meat of a young animal.

A geography of dishes

Lamb is not subject to dietary taboos; its meat is eaten all over the world, and in some parts of the world, like the Mideast, it is a basic food. From this part of the world come the shish kebab (from the Turkish word *sis,* "sword or skewer" and *kebab,* "lamb" or "mutton"). In the Arab countries, the Bedouins have the "Musaf," a feast of lamb and rice during which the guest of honor is fed the eye of the animal, a most delectable morsel.

Ground lamb lends itself to many preparations of which *moussaka,* a mixture of meat, eggplant, and spices, is a mouth-watering example.

The populations of Australia, New Zealand, and Great Britain are also large consumers of lamb and mutton. Specialties like Lancashire hot-pot, a kind of savory pie in which oysters are included; the well-known shepherd's pie, and the unusual mutton and barley broth of Scotland are only a few of the many dishes from the United Kingdom containing the robust presence of mutton.

The cuisines of France and Italy list an array of lamb recipes that range from sophisticated crown roasts and tenderly braised chops, to the peasant *navarins* and *cabassoles* (stews) of the Lyons and Larzac regions, and the *spezzatini* (dry stews) of the mountainous regions of Italy.

Broiled leg of lamb

1 leg of lamb (6– 7 pounds)

Marinade

1 cup vegetable oil

¼ cup lemon juice

1 teaspoon salt

½ teaspoon freshly ground black pepper

2 tablespoons chopped parsley

1 teaspoon oregano

½ teaspoon basil

2 bay leaves, crumbled

3 onions, thinly sliced

3 cloves garlic, sliced

Seasoned salt (such as Lawry's)

Have the leg boned and butterflied by the butcher.

In a large, shallow enamel or glass dish, combine all the marinade ingredients except the seasoned salt, and mix thoroughly. Marinate the meat in this mixture overnight, turning a number of times.

Preheat the broiler for 15 minutes. Place the meat (which must be at room temperature) on the broiler rack and sprinkle lightly with seasoned salt and a little of the marinade, liquid only. Place the broiler rack 4– 5 inches below the heat and broil for 15 minutes.

Turn the meat with tongs and sprinkle again with marinade and seasoned salt; broil for an additional 10 to 12 minutes. A slight cut in the thickest part of the meat will show if it has reached the proper shade of pink or needs an additional 2 to 3 minutes.

When done, remove immediately and slice against the grain in ¼ -inch slices. Serves 8.

Beautiful lamb

Fewer lamb carcasses are condemned by federal inspectors than any other meat inspected under federal regulations. This is an indication of unusually good health in the animals and commendable care in their raising.

New York City is the major market for lamb, although it is found in metropolitan areas on both coasts and around the Great Lakes. Descendants of Mediterranean settlers have preserved their liking for lamb, but the preference does not seem to have survived the shift from coastal cities to inland regions. Lamb is not seen as much in the Midwest, the South and mountain states, except in the immediate vicinity of shepherds and their flocks.

L amb provides many of the most glamorous cuts of meat: rack of lamb, saddle of lamb, Frenched rib chops, and roast leg, with a huge paper frill on the end bone. Although much of the animal provides expensive cuts for roasting and broiling, there are other less-costly cuts that are wonderful braised or in stews. Other nations have always taken full advantage of the robust taste of lamb and its possibilities. The Greeks use ground lamb for their *moussaka* and *dolmas*, and there is curried lamb from India, *couscous* from North Africa, and the beautiful spring lamb stew from France, *navarin printainier*, just to name a few.

Lamb goes to market at 6 to 8 months, and should have bright pink, well-marbled flesh; waxy, creamy white fat; and young bones that are moist and red at the joints. Size is a clue to youngness, too. The whole leg should not weigh more than 9 pounds (4.1 kg) at the very most, or it is too big for lamb and has to be called "mutton." There is nothing wrong with mutton, as long as it is marketed as such. Mutton is not only older, but stronger in taste and less tender than lamb, and needs slightly longer cooking. Mutton should also be cheaper than lamb.

The outer, parchment-like skin that covers the fat of lamb, called the "fell," may or may not be left on the leg for cooking. Some say leaving it on makes for stronger flavor and helps keep the leg in shape. The fell should be removed from lamb chops and other cuts before cooking.

Lamb grading. Lamb is graded Prime, Choice, and Good. There are also lower grades we don't see on the retail market. Most of the lamb we see is Prime and Choice, and Choice is so good that at least one supermarket that specializes in Prime beef buys Choice lamb because the management feels the higher price for Prime is not warranted by the difference in quality. Lamb is graded for the amount of fat marbling in the flesh and signs of youthfulness, both of which qualities you can see for yourself.

LAMB ROASTS

Allow 12 ounces to 1 pound (340.8–454 g) per person for bone-in roasts, and 6 to 8 ounces (170.4–227.2 g) per person for boneless.

Full leg. This is the leg with the sirloin or hip section left on. The whole leg can be roasted as is, or boned and tied, or boned, butterflied, and flattened to broil. When it is prepared for broiling it is often marinated first, more for flavor than for tenderizing.

The leg is also found cut into *shank half* and *sirloin* (or butt) *half*. Of the two, shank half costs more, has more meat on it, and looks better, showing the round end of the leg bone. The sirloin, or butt, half is bonier and hard to carve. For easier carving, ask the butcher to crack the bones for you. It is also possible to buy the whole leg and have the sirloin end cut off as steaks.

Loin. The loin makes a fabulous and expensive roast, containing the tenderloin. When both sides of the loin are used, it is a *saddle of lamb*.

Rib or rack. This is a very tender and elegant roast, but there is not much meat on it; one rack is barely enough for 3 people. When the lamb's 2 racks are fastened together in a circle, with the rib ends trimmed and the back bones cracked for carving, it is a *crown roast*. The center can be filled after cooking with a hot green vegetable, a meat stuffing, or just crisp watercress or parsley. Allow 2 ribs per person.

CUTS OF LAMB

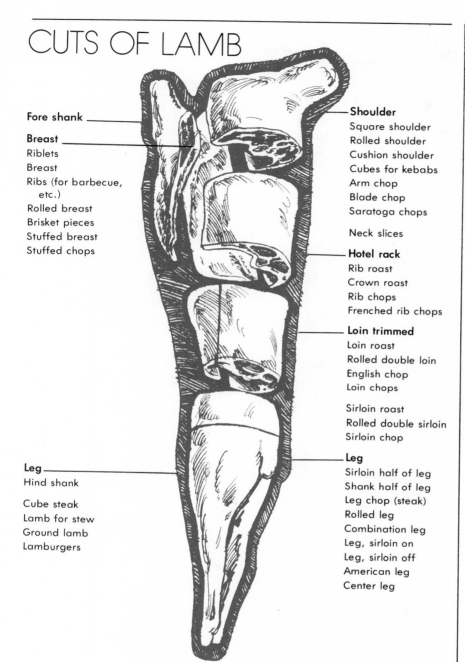

Fore shank

Breast
Riblets
Breast
Ribs (for barbecue, etc.)
Rolled breast
Brisket pieces
Stuffed breast
Stuffed chops

Leg
Hind shank

Cube steak
Lamb for stew
Ground lamb
Lamburgers

Shoulder
Square shoulder
Rolled shoulder
Cushion shoulder
Cubes for kebabs
Arm chop
Blade chop
Saratoga chops

Neck slices

Hotel rack
Rib roast
Crown roast
Rib chops
Frenched rib chops

Loin trimmed
Loin roast
Rolled double loin
English chop
Loin chops

Sirloin roast
Rolled double sirloin
Sirloin chop

Leg
Sirloin half of leg
Shank half of leg
Leg chop (steak)
Rolled leg
Combination leg
Leg, sirloin on
Leg, sirloin off
American leg
Center leg

Lamb in the Mideast

Lamb has always reigned supreme in the Mideast. Many ancient recipes from this part of the world list "meat" among the ingredients without specifying which kind. It was a general term standing for lamb, mutton, or occasionally kid or goat. Cattle are rarely bred in the Mideast, so it is not surprising to encounter so many ways of preparing lamb.

When a baby lamb is needed for a special occasion, it is generally killed the day after it is born. Often it is roasted on a spit over an open fire, and sometimes it is stuffed with a mixture of rice, almonds or nuts, currants, and spices. In some parts of the coastal region of Syria, lamb is simply boiled in sea water.

Chelo kebab is a favorite dish of the Iranians. To prepare it, the lamb is marinated, roasted over an open fire, and served with a mound of rice *(chelo)* nestling a raw egg yolk in its shell. The diner mixes the egg yolk with the rice. Other accompaniments for this dish are yogurt and a bowl of sumac, a nonpoisonous relation of our tree.

Ground lamb is the basis for many delicious appetizers like the spicy little *sfeeha* from Syria, the *dolmas* from Turkey, and the *chawarma,* the giant *kebab* whose slices are wrapped in pita bread and served hot. This snack was introduced to New York by enterprising newcomers from Greece and other parts of the Mideast. It has become very popular and is sold under the name of "gyro sandwich."

The pastoral region

September is the time when one encounters on the *tratturi*, the trails of the scenic Apennine mountains of Abruzzi in central Italy, the shepherds with their herds and woolly dogs descending toward the valleys. They are on their way to the plateaus of Puglia, in the south, where a milder winter and greener pastures await them. The return of the herds in the spring coincides with the first blooming of the jonquils.

It is the best time to eat lamb. Many Roman restaurants will advertise their baby lamb from Abruzzi as the best. The baby lamb is sometimes cooked whole or cut in half. Either way, it is baked with one or two garlic cloves, a sprinkle of rosemary, and a touch of fresh mint.

The people of Abruzzi have many interesting ways of preparing lamb; one recipe calls for "burning your fingers—a *scottadito*." The pieces of meat, broiled on burning coals, are small and bony and the diner picks them up with the fingers. Another dish, *maccheroni alla chitarra*, calls for macaroni served in a sauce made from a ragoût of lamb.

A casserole called *alla Guardiese* is reminiscent of the one described by Colette in her book *My Mother's House*. Both these dishes are flavored with an incredible number of garlic cloves. Colette remembers how the pungent smell would permeate the house, and this tantalizing aroma was only the prelude for a memorable feast of divinely flavored lamb.

The famous Italian cooks brought to France in the fifteenth century by Catherine de' Médici came from Abruzzi, which had been dominated by the French. One may speculate on whether it was the French or Italians who originated Colette's casserole.

Shoulder. There is a lot of bone in this roast and quite a bit of fat. It can be boned and rolled, or boned and made into a *cushion* for stuffing. These roasts may also be braised.

Breast. Unboned, the breast can have a pocket cut in it for stuffing. Boned, it can be rolled and tied, with or without stuffing. The breast may also be braised.

Timetable for roasting lamb. Many Americans have come to like their lamb really rare, as the French do, but the old way, well done without a trace of pink and rather dry, still appeals to some. And there are all the degrees in between.

To Roast by the Continuous Low-Heat Method

Roast, uncovered, in preheated 325°F (163°C) oven to internal temperature desired.

Cut	Weight in pounds	Approx. cooking time per pound	Meat thermometer temperature
Leg	6 to 9		
Shank half	3 to 4		
Butt half	3 to 5	12 to 13	rare 130 to 135°F
Loin	2 to 2½	14 to 16	medium rare 140 to 145°F
Saddle	4 to 5	18 to 20	medium 150 to 160°F
Rib	2½ to 3	25 to 30	well done 165 to 170°F
Crown			
Shoulder	4 to 6		
Cushion	3 to 5		
Breast	2 to 3		
Rolled breast	1½ to 2		

For boneless roasts, add 3 to 4 minutes per pound for each degree of doneness.

To Roast by the Searing Method

Preheat oven to 450°F, roast, uncovered, for 15 minutes. After 15 minutes, turn oven down to 325 to 350°F. Figure cooking time when roast is placed in oven.

Time	Temperature
10 to 12 minutes per pound for rare	130 to 135°F
12 to 14 minutes per pound for medium rare	140 to 145°F
14 to 16 minutes per pound for medium	150 to 160°F
16 to 18 minutes per pound for well done	165 to 170°F

LAMB TO BRAISE AND STEW

Allow 8 ounces (227.2 g) per serving for boneless cuts, and 12 ounces to 1 pound (340.8–454 g) for bony ones.

To braise. Lamb *shanks* weigh nearly 1 pound (454 g) apiece, and you need 1 shank per person. They are delicious braised, and can be varied with different liquids and seasoning. *Neck* slices are inexpensive, but they have a lot of bone in proportion to meat. *Breast*—plain, stuffed, or rolled—has good flavor. Boned *shoulder* roasts can be braised as well as roasted. *Arm* and *blade* chops are better braised than broiled.

To stew. Cubes of *shoulder* or *foreshank* are the best cuts for boneless stew, but bones give flavor. *Neck* makes the best bony stew. *Breast* chunks or *riblets* make good stews by themselves, but they haven't much meat on them. A few bony pieces can be added to an otherwise boneless stew for extra flavor.

Timetable for Braising and Stewing Lamb

To braise

Braise, covered, on top of the stove, or in preheated 300 to 325°F oven for suggested time, or until tender. *See also* Stewing (page 170).

Cut	Weight in pounds	Approx. cooking time (in hours)
Shanks	¾ to 1	1½ to 2
Breast	2 to 3	1½ to 2
Rolled breast	1½ to 2	1½ to 2
Shoulder roast	4 to 6	1½ to 2
Arm and blade chops	¾ to 1	¾ to 1
Sirloin steaks	¾ to 1	¾ to 1
Neck slices	¾ to 1	1 to 1½

To stew

Stew covered, on top of the stove, or in a preheated 300 to 325°F oven for suggested time, or until tender. *See also* Stewing (page 170).

Cut	Size of cubes in inches	Approx. cooking time (in hours)
Cuts for stew	1½ to 2	1½ to 2

The national side of lamb

In the United States lamb is not as popular as beef, although the recipes from colonial days calling for mutton and kid would indicate that our forefathers were rather keen on this type of food. John Adams himself, describing a Sunday dinner in his house, lists a "neck of mutton" among the courses served on the occasion.

Nowadays, some self-styled "gourmets" in this country will seek out a French or an Italian restaurant to have *gigot rôti* or *agnello alla romana*. As long as it sounds foreign, they do not seem to mind eating the same American lamb that they reject at the butcher's. And a pity indeed, because American lamb is good all year around. Careful breeding is continuously improving the quality of the meat. It is richer today in proteins and contains less fat and calories than formerly.

Lamb contains iron and B vitamins—niacin, thiamin, and riboflavin—all essential body-building proteins. It is a full-flavored meat and can be prepared in many different ways.

To carve a leg of lamb

Place the roasted leg of lamb on a cutting board with the meatiest side up. Cut a slice off the bottom side so that the leg will rest firmly while you carve it.

Starting from the narrow part of the leg, cut along the bone as far as you can go, without detaching the meat completely.

The roast can then be placed on a platter and garnished. This can be done in the kitchen.

To serve at the table, start again from the narrow end of the leg and slice the meat vertically toward the bone.

Another method of carving is as follows: Place the roast on a serving platter with the narrow part of the leg to the carver's left. Hold this part firmly with a fork in your left hand; with a sharp knife in the other hand, cut thin horizontal slices, parallel to the bone.

For more slices, turn the roast and continue to carve horizontally.

The slices must be thin because when you carve meat with the grain, as you are doing in this instance, meat tends to be tougher. Carving against the grain makes meat more tender.

LAMB CHOPS AND STEAKS

Allow 8 to 12 ounces (227.2–340.8 g) per person for bone-in chops and steaks, and 6 to 8 ounces (170.4–227.2 g) per person for boneless.

Loin chops. These beautifully lean chops contain some of the tenderloin and sometimes some lamb kidney. With the kidney they are called "English chops." They are expensive, so make sure they have been trimmed of "tail meat." Broil or panfry them.

Rib chops. Also expensive, lean, and tender, these chops have little meat on them. They are sometimes cut double. They can be "frenched," that is, have the ends of the ribs trimmed to wear paper frills. Broil or panfry them.

Noisettes are the boned, trimmed meaty hearts of loin and rib chops. Panfry them.

Shoulder chops (arm and blade). These chops are apt to be tough, but some people broil them anyway. Marinating helps tenderize them. Panfry them if they are ¾-inch (1.9 cm) thick or under. They may also be braised.

Sirloin chops or steaks. Cut from the sirloin end of a full leg, these can be broiled or panfried, but they are best cooked that way if they are from Prime or top Choice grades, from a 5- to 7-pound (2.3–3.2 kg) leg. If you are not sure, braise them.

Leg steaks. Center-cut slices from the leg, with the round slice of leg bone in the middle, can be broiled or panfried if they are from Prime or top Choice lamb, from a 5- to 7-pound (2.3–3.2 kg) leg. If you are not sure, braise them.

Cube steaks. Little boneless steaks made from trimmings. They are best panfried.

Shish kebab. Lean 1½-inch (3.8 cm) cubes for skewering are best from the leg.

GROUND LAMB

There is no way to tell what cut supermarket ground lamb comes from. It will most likely be made from shank, neck, and trimmings. There is nothing wrong with this ground lamb except that it may contain more fat than you want. To control the fat content buy shoulder, which has the best flavor, trim away the fat, and grind the lean yourself. Leave a little fat to supply juiciness. One pound (454 g) of ground lamb makes 3 plump patties or 4 thin ones.

Timetable for Broiling, Panbroiling, and Panfrying Lamb

To broil

Cut	Thickness in inches	Distance from heat in inches	Approx. cooking time in minutes per side		
			Rare	Medium	Well done
Loin chops					
English chops	1	2	4 to 5	6	7
Rib chops	1½	2	6	7	8
Sirloin chops or steaks	2	3	8	9	10 to 11
Arm, blade chops					
Leg steaks	¾ to 1	3		5	6 to 7
Shish kebab	1½-in cubes	3 to 4	12 to 15 (total cooking time)		
Patties	plump, 6 ounces each	3		6	7 to 8

(Do not broil cuts of meat less than ¾ inch thick. Instead, panbroil or panfry them.)

To panbroil

Panbroil uncovered, using times given for broiling. Turn frequently.

To panfry

Panfry uncovered, turning often.

Cut	Approx. total cooking time (in minutes)	
	Medium	Well done
Arm, blade chops, leg steaks, ¾ inch thick	8	12
Noisettes	5	8
Cube steaks	3 total	
Patties (4 ounces each)	10 total	

Lamb *alla campagnola* (lamb country style)

3 tablespoons butter
3 tablespoons cooking oil
5 pounds lean lamb cut in cubes
5 anchovies
2 cloves garlic
1½ teaspoons fennel seeds
¼ cup wine vinegar
Salt and freshly ground pepper to taste
1½ tablespoons flour
¾ cup broth or water

Place the butter and oil in a casserole and heat it. Add the lamb and brown the meat, turning it often. While the meat is cooking, prepare the *pesto:* chop together the anchovies, garlic, and fennel seeds; add the vinegar and stir to make a smooth paste. (If you do this in a blender or food processor, add the vinegar to the other ingredients at the beginning.)

Pour off the excess fat from the meat. Keeping the meat over low heat, add salt and pepper and stir. Add the *pesto* and stir again to coat the meat evenly with the sauce. When the vinegar has evaporated, sprinkle the meat with flour. Mix well and add the broth or water.

Cover and simmer until the sauce thickens and the meat is done, about 1 hour. Serves 6 to 8.

Porkopolis

Shortly after the American Revolution the new government taxed the whiskey made from corn, and while this led to the abortive Whiskey Rebellion of 1794, it also led to the fattening of hogs with the surplus grain. This caused a glut of hogs and a great flurry of smoking, pickling, and drying of pork by meat packers. Barrels of the meat were sold to pioneers heading west on riverboats and in covered wagons. Cincinnati, already an important railhead, became the major pork-packing center, known as the "porkopolis" of America.

When the large meat-packing centers moved further west, Cincinnati turned its wealth into industry: first soap, then steam fire engines. Similarly, meat-packing wealth in Springfield, Massachusetts went into the manufacture of the Springfield rifle; in Detroit, to the manufacture of automobiles.

Suckling pig

Suckling pig, or "sucking pig," as it was called, has been a special treat since ancient times. The Romans had only limited amounts of meat, which was usually venison, mutton, or pork. Suckling pig became such a popular dish that the supply could not keep up with the demand, and laws had to be passed forbidding the killing of virgin pigs. Following this edict, suckling pig became a rare and special holiday preparation, as it still is today in various cultures.

However, small suckling pigs are in short supply these days and generally have to be ordered in advance. But, even with advance ordering, the little piglet is more likely to be frozen than fresh.

Roast suckling pig is generally a feature of a luau, a Hawaiian outdoor feast. The pig is roasted in an underground pit that has been fashioned into an oven. Cooked with it are such foods as bananas, sweet potatoes, and breadfruit. Originally the pig had to be wild, but now it is generally a domestic animal.

PORK

Less than a third of the pork produced in the United States is sold as fresh pork; the rest is made into ham, bacon, sausages, lard, and so on. To buy the best fresh pork look for pale, whitish pink flesh and firm white fat. The pinker the flesh, the older the animal. Look for marbling of fat in the flesh, too, as you do in good beef and lamb. Avoid any pork that looks soft and mushy.

An excellent source of high-quality protein, and a good source of iron, niacin, and riboflavin, pork is particularly rich in thiamine, one of the most important of the B vitamins, containing 3 times as much as any other food. New breeding methods, that have increased the protein content in pork, have lowered the calories, too. Calorie content varies greatly. It can range from 237 calories in a 3½-ounce (100 g) serving up to 553, depending on the amount of fat and the method of preparation.

Pork must be cooked to well done—170°F (77°C) internal temperature—to kill the organisms that cause trichinosis. Thick chops are best braised, to be cooked enough to destroy the trichinae without being too dry.

Pork grading. Although there are grades for pork (1, 2, 3, 4, and Utility), the grading is not done as it is with other meat, a whole carcass at a time. Pork is broken up at the slaughterhouse and classified according to the way it will be used. Much of it goes directly to processors for salting and smoking and brand-name pork products; for these purposes, larger animals may be judged the best. Cuts of the smaller animals, suitable for the fresh-pork market, are boxed and sent to the retailer. Fresh pork is judged for maturity—the younger the better. Pork loins are judged for the amount of marbling (flecks of fat) in the flesh—the more the better. The smaller the chop, the younger the pig.

PORK ROASTS, CHOPS, AND STEAKS

Allow 8 to 12 ounces (227.2–340.8 g) per person for bone-in roasts, 6 to 8 ounces (170.4–227.2 g) for boneless. Allow 1 to 2 chops per person, depending on thickness. Steaks are usually enough for 2 to 3 people.

Center-cut loin roast and chops. This cut provides the best and most expensive pork roast and chops, the meatiest and most tender part of the loin, containing the tenderloin. The backbone should be removed or at least cracked in the roast for easy carving.

Thick chops are best braised. Thin ones, ½ inch (1.27 cm) or less, can be panfried.

Center-cut rib roast or chops. With less meat than the center-cut loin, lacking the tenderloin, this is a fine roast and is the cut used for a crown roast (2 or more center-cut rib sections fastened together to form a circle, with a stuffing in the middle). Allow 2 ribs per person. Braise the chops, or panfry if they are ½ inch (1.27 cm) or less.

Loin-end and rib-end roasts and chops. These cuts at each end of the loin, closer to more active muscles, are less tender, and bonier. The rib end is the boniest and fattest, therefore less expensive. The whole loin is sometimes divided in half, making a *full loin half* and a *full rib half*. Chops should be braised.

Fresh ham roasts and slices or steaks. The whole fresh ham, which is the hip and leg, is very large, 10 to 14 pounds (4.5–6.4 kg). It needs to have the hipbone removed, or it can be boneless for easy carving and stuffing. The whole ham is often sold cut in half, making a *butt* and a *shank half*. The butt end is cheaper, but needs to have the hipbone removed. The shank half has the round leg bone in the middle.

Slices or steaks are sometimes cut from the center of the leg. They look like ham steaks. Braise if they are over ½-inch (1.27 cm) thick. Panfry the thinner ones.

Shoulder roasts and steaks. *Picnic* and *Boston butt* roasts come from this section. The roasts are easier to carve if they are boned or semiboned, and they are good for stuffing. They can be braised as well as roasted.

The steaks are *arm* and *blade*. The arm steak looks like the ham steak but is less tender. The blade steak has a lot of bone and fat, but is inexpensive. The steaks are best braised.

Roast suckling pig. It is festive fare, the little roast pig with an apple in its mouth and cranberry eyes. It is 6 to 8 weeks old, and a good size for an oven is 14 to 15 pounds (6.4–6.8 kg). Most of the weight is bone, so *allow about 1¼ pounds (567.5 g) per person*. Order the pig at least a week ahead, and be sure you invite guests who won't be upset by the sight of a pig on a platter.

Stuffed crown roast of pork

This roast will have to be ordered from a butcher, who will fasten the ribs together to make a circle, trim the rib ends, and crack or remove the backbone.

A 12-16- rib pork crown roast (5—6 pounds)
1 clove garlic (optional)
Salt and freshly ground black pepper

Stuffing
2 tablespoons butter
1 medium stalk celery, finely chopped
1 medium onion, finely chopped
4 cups herb-seasoned stuffing crumbs
Pinch of rosemary
Salt and freshly ground black pepper

Wipe the roast with a damp cloth. Rub with the garlic, if used, and salt and pepper inside and out. Set aside while you prepare the stuffing.

Melt the butter in a skillet and slowly cook the celery and onion until soft but not brown. Toss with the crumbs, then add the rosemary and salt and pepper to taste. Fill the crown lightly with the crumb mixture, using more crumbs if needed.

Cover the rib ends with foil to prevent charring and cook, uncovered, in a preheated 350°F oven for 35 to 40 minutes per pound, to an inner temperature of 170°F. The thermometer should be placed between 2 ribs, not touching bones or stuffing.

When the roast is done, remove the foil from the rib ends and decorate with paper frills, pitted olives, or kumquats. Serves 6 to 8.

A word for it

"Bacon" is an old French word that was used to describe pork and cured pork products. During the time of Shakespeare in England, pork was also called "bacon." The present-day French word for bacon is *lard*: fried bacon is *lard frite*; a rasher of bacon is *tranche du lard*. It is not difficult to figure out the origin of the word "lardons," those strips of pork fat that are pushed through roasts before cooking to add flavor and juiciness. The process is called "larding"; the instrument used is called a "larding needle."

Less easily explained is why an actor with limited talent who gives a florid, flamboyant performance is called a "ham actor," or, to move on to another animal, why a complaint is a "beef."

Trichinosis

Trichinosis is a disease peculiar to pigs and humans caused by minute parasitic worms called "trichinae." They are destroyed by freezing and also by heat, which is why fresh pork must be very thoroughly cooked.

Trichinosis is on the wane because pigs are being more carefully fed, but until it is completely wiped out, well-done pork is the answer.

Pork on the spit

This is a loin of pork cooked in the same style of the Roman *porchetta*. It is easier to manage than a suckling pig and every bit as tasty.

2—2½ pounds loin of pork
Salt and freshly ground pepper
Pork skin or caul, enough to wrap the
    entire loin
½ teaspoon fennel seeds

The night before, salt and pepper the meat. Wrap loosely in paper and leave in the refrigerator.

When ready to cook, unwrap the meat and sprinkle it all over with fennel seeds. Spread out the skin or caul, sprinkle lightly with salt and pepper, and place the meat on it. Wrap it securely around the loin and tie with string.

Spit the loin and cook gently for about 2 hours. (It can also be roasted in a 350°F oven. If roasting, place the meat on a rack in a shallow roasting pan.) To make sure that the meat is thoroughly cooked, insert a skewer through an opening of the skin into the meat, as far as it can go. At the removal of the skewer, if the juice runs clear the meat is done; if the juice is pink or bloody, the meat needs more cooking. When ready, carefully remove the meat from the spit (or oven) and take the skin off; slice the meat, place on a serving dish, and surround the slices with strips of crackling skin. The best way to cut the skin is with a poultry shears. Serves 6 to 8.

CUTS OF PORK

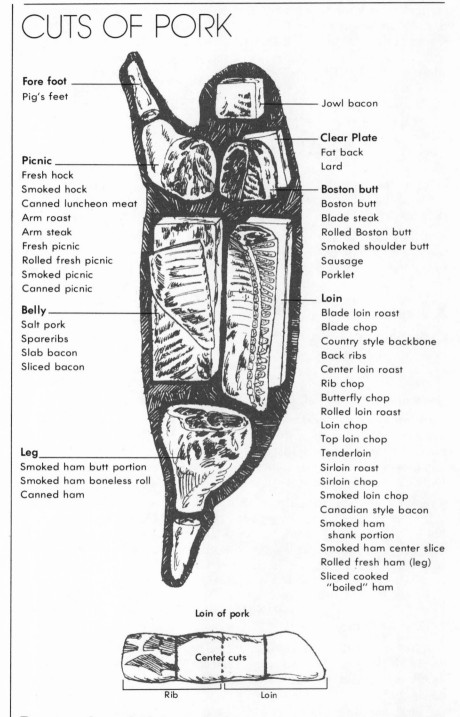

Fore foot
Pig's feet

Picnic
Fresh hock
Smoked hock
Canned luncheon meat
Arm roast
Arm steak
Fresh picnic
Rolled fresh picnic
Smoked picnic
Canned picnic

Belly
Salt pork
Spareribs
Slab bacon
Sliced bacon

Leg
Smoked ham butt portion
Smoked ham boneless roll
Canned ham

Jowl bacon

Clear Plate
Fat back
Lard

Boston butt
Boston butt
Blade steak
Rolled Boston butt
Smoked shoulder butt
Sausage
Porklet

Loin
Blade loin roast
Blade chop
Country style backbone
Back ribs
Center loin roast
Rib chop
Butterfly chop
Rolled loin roast
Loin chop
Top loin chop
Tenderloin
Sirloin roast
Sirloin chop
Smoked loin chop
Canadian style bacon
Smoked ham
    shank portion
Smoked ham center slice
Rolled fresh ham (leg)
Sliced cooked
    "boiled" ham

Loin of pork

Center cuts

Rib   Loin

Roast pork tenderloin. A delicious morsel, not often found whole because it is usually part of loin chops. It only weighs about 1½ pounds (681 g), and can be roasted as is, or opened up and stuffed. It is expensive, but there is no waste.

SPARERIBS. Allow 12 ounces to 1 pound (340.8–454 g) per person. *Country-style ribs* are meatier than regular *spareribs*. Either kind may be cooked in many ways—roasted, baked, barbecued, braised, or boiled (simmered).

Timetable for Roasting Pork

Roast uncovered, in a preheated 350°F oven to 170°F internal temperature.

Cut	Weight in pounds	Approx. minutes per pound	Meat thermometer temperature
Loin roasts			
Center-cut loin or rib	3 to 5	28 to 30	170°F
Loin end or rib end	3 to 4	35 to 40	170°F
Full half, loin or rib	5 to 7	30 to 35	170°F
Rolled loin	3 to 5	35 to 40	170°F
Fresh ham			
Whole ham	10 to 14	25 to 30	170°F
Whole boneless ham	7 to 10	30 to 35	170°F
Butt or shank half	5 to 7	25 to 30	170°F
Shoulder			
Fresh picnic	5 to 8	25 to 30	170°F
Rolled picnic	3 to 5	35 to 40	170°F
Boston butt	4 to 6	35 to 40	170°F
Rolled Boston butt	3 to 4	40 to 45	170°F
Suckling pig	14 to 15	18	170°F
Tenderloin	1½ to 2	about 1 hour total cooking time	170°F
Spareribs		1½ to 2 hours total cooking time, or until tender	

To braise

Braise covered, on top of the stove, or in preheated 300 to 325°F oven until tender and juices run clear, not pink, when meat is pricked. *See also* Braising (page 168).

Cut	Thickness in inches	Approx. cooking time (in hours)
Chops	¾ to 1½	¾ to 1
Steaks	¾ to 1	¾ to 1
Spareribs		1½ to 2

To panfry

Panfry uncovered, over moderate heat, turning often. *See also* Panfrying (page 169).

Cut	Thickness in inches	Approx. cooking time
Chops	under ¾	Cook until brown and juices run clear, not pink, when meat is pricked
Steaks	under ¾	

A Roman favorite

Pork has been a favorite food among the Romans since earliest times. *Fichi e prosciutto,* figs and prosciutto ham, are as popular today as in the time of the Roman emperor Tiberius, who lived in the first century A.D., and *porchetta,* suckling pig, is one of the glories of Roman cuisine. When strolling through the old district of Rome, it is not unusual to see on the tree-shaded porch of a *trattoria,* a modest restaurant, a golden roasted piglet, its skin crisp and oozing droplets of juice, and sporting a collar of red peppers and an orange in its mouth. Its meat is sold to passersby, as well as to the regular diners. The meat is generally cut into chunks and nestled in a crusty *sfilatino,* the savory Roman bread.

During summer festivals, the Romans gorge on *porchetta,* which is sold on every street corner. Carried away by their enthusiasm for the crisp, delicious morsels, many of the people throw discretion to the winds and are left with a *porchetta* hangover the next day.

Streamlined pigs

Some historians claim that pigs were introduced into the New World by the Spanish explorer, Hernando de Soto, when he led his army of one thousand Spanish soldiers to North America in 1538 in search of treasures.

But no matter how the pig reached our shores, the fact is that they adapted very well. In Virginia during the eighteenth century pigs had multiplied so successfully that almost every household was well supplied with ham and pork. As one can see, Virginia ham goes back a long way.

Not much thought was given to improving new swine breeds over the years, and lard pigs were the leading species. Then lard fell out of fashion. The public grew concerned with replacing animal fats with vegetable and seed oils, and pork breeders focused their efforts on increasing the yield in ham, bacon, and pork chops. To produce carcasses that are high in lean cuts and low in fatty cuts, pigs are fed largely on alfalfa, barley, skim milk, and protein supplements, along with corn, the basic fodder of hogs.

The pigsty is a thing of the past. Pigs, which formerly cost nothing to keep, are now raised on the range in clean, modern pig barns.

Tracing the family tree

Pigs were first domesticated by the Chinese over five thousand years ago, and even today they are China's dominant livestock animal. Mongol armies took pigs along on their military expeditions in order to assure themselves of a supply of meat and cooking fat. The pigs performed their functions and were little trouble, for, being scavengers, they could be depended upon to scrounge for their own food.

During the Middle Ages, some Chinese pigs were crossed with European pigs to produce lard pigs.

In medieval Europe, most of the city dwellers were peasants who had abandoned the land for economic reasons. They continued to conduct their lives as if they were still in the country. They used the patches of land near the houses to cultivate vegetables and raise their animals. Pigs were kept around the house in the same way as chickens and cows. But, while the cows stayed in the stable and chickens scratched around close to home, the pigs strayed. In the Paris of the twelfth century pigs created traffic jams that endangered the safety of the citizens.

Of course, pigs also performed a useful operation in removing most of the food refuse that was thrown carelessly in the street to rot. And that was not a task to be ignored, considering that there were few street cleaners. And, apart from providing food, sometimes pigs provided entertainment. Pigs were greased and set loose in enclosures, and serfs amused the nobility by trying to chase and capture the slippery creatures. This was not the end of their careers as performers; in the eighteenth century Louis XIV of France had his court tailors design special clothes for the pigs for the entertainment of his court.

PORK FOR STEW. Allow 8 ounces (227.2 g) per person.

Pork makes a wonderful stew. One-and-one-half-inch (3.8 cm) cubes from the shoulder are the best.

PORK HOCKS AND PIGS' FEET. Allow 1 pound (454 g) per person.

Hocks are usually found smoked, and pigs' feet pickled, but they are available fresh. Fresh, they are simmered in water to cover completely, with plenty of seasonings.

GROUND PORK. Some local laws forbid the grinding of pork in the same machine in which other meat is ground because of the danger of trichinosis. Butchers either have a separate machine, or do all their pork for the day at one time and then thoroughly clean the machine, in which case they cannot grind it to order without some advance notice. To grind pork yourself, buy shoulder, picnic, or lean trimmings from other parts. After grinding, wash every part of the machine is soapy water, and rinse well in boiling water. Dry with a clean cloth.

Ground pork is good in meat loaves, alone or with beef and veal.

Timetable for Stewing Pork

Simmer covered, on top of the stove or in a 300 to 325°F oven until tender. *See also* Stewing (page 170).

Cut	Method	Approx. cooking time (in hours)
Cubes for stew	Stew	1 to 1½ or until tender
Spareribs	Boil	2 to 2½ or until tender
Hocks	Boil	2 to 2½ or until tender
Pigs' feet	Boil	4 to 5 or until tender

VEAL

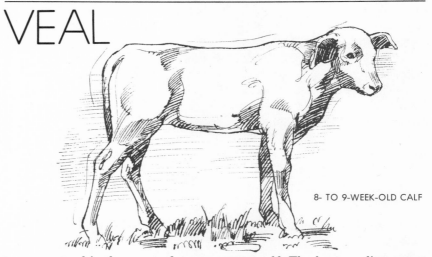

8- TO 9-WEEK-OLD CALF

Veal is the meat of a very young calf. The best quality comes from an animal between five and twelve weeks old, which has been milk-fed. The flesh is smooth, firm and velvety, pale grayish pink in color, with no marbling. The bones are soft and reddish. Meat of this quality is sold to hotels and restaurants and is available generally from specialty butchers only. After twelve weeks, or whatever age at which the veal calf leaves its milk diet and begins to eat grain or grass, the flesh becomes increasingly rosy, and while it can make acceptable eating, it does not have the delicacy, flavor or tenderness of the milk-fed veal. These olders vealers can be from fourteen weeks to one year and weigh about 250 pounds (114 kg). From them comes most of the veal found in American markets. It ranges from dark pink to light red in color and is, as you might expect, lower in both quality and price than the milk-fed veal. There is something on the market called "Plume de Veau," a brand-name veal (not USDA graded) which, in spite of its fancy name, you will have to evaluate as you do any veal—by its appearance.

Because of the lack of fat within the fiber of the meat, veal steaks and chops cannot be broiled. They need to be panfried slowly in fat, or braised. Veal roasts need some fat around or on them to supply juiciness, and they should be roasted to an inner temperature of 160°F (71°C). If a veal roast is only slightly too dark a shade of pink when you buy it, it can still be good, but it should be cooked in some liquid. Veal roasts, unlike those of beef, pork, and lamb, are sometimes cooked on a bed of vegetables and basted throughout the cooking.

Grades of veal. The grades of veal we see are Prime, Choice, and Good. Lower grades do not appear on the retail market. Since there is no marbling in the flesh of veal, this is not the criterion for grading, as it is for beef, lamb, and pork. Veal is graded, as you will judge it, for the color of the flesh and signs of youth in the bones.

VEAL ROASTS

Allow 12 ounces to 1 pound (340.8–454 g) per person for loin and rib roasts with the bone in. For other bone-in roasts, allow 8 to 12 ounces (227.2–340.8 g) per person. For boneless roasts, allow 6 to 8 ounces (170.4–227.2 g) per person.

LOIN AND RIB. These are very good but expensive roasts, and since they are more often cut into chops, they are not readily available and will need special ordering.

The glamorous *saddle of veal* is the double loin, right and left sides intact. It can also be boned and rolled.

A *crown roast*, like lamb and pork crown roasts, is made of 2 or more rib sections fastened together in a circle with the ribs upright. The rib ends are trimmed of meat and can be decorated after cooking with pitted olives, kumquats, or paper frills. Fill the center with a stuffing to cook with the meat, or fill with a green vegetable, crisp watercress or parsley, after cooking. Allow 2 ribs per person.

LEG ROASTS. These can be *standing rump, rolled rump, center leg*, or *shank half*, all good, and nearly as expensive as loin and rib roasts.

SIRLOIN. A tender roast from the hip section, it can also be a *double sirloin*, with both right and left sides intact.

SHOULDER ROASTS. Less expensive roasts, these are *arm, blade* and *shoulder*, usually boned. They are good for stuffing and are particularly good braised. For oven roasting, they should have some fat on or around them.

Scaloppine alla Marsala
(Veal Scallops with Marsala)

1½ pounds veal round, cut for scaloppine and pounded very thin into 4-by-4-inch squares
2 tablespoons butter
1 tablespoon olive oil
Salt and freshly ground black pepper
⅓ cup dry Marsala

Pat the veal scallops dry with paper towels. In a heavy skillet, melt the butter with the oil over moderate heat. When the foam subsides, add the scallops, a few at a time, and cook for 2 to 3 minutes per side until nicely browned. Sprinkle with salt and pepper as they brown. Remove them as they are done to a heated platter and keep warm.

Pour the excess fat from the pan, leaving just a film. Add the Marsala, stirring to incorporate any browned bits in the pan. Boil briskly for 1 to 2 minutes, then pour over the scallops and serve immediately. Serves 4.

Veal on a budget

A few generations ago, it was not unheard of for thrifty housewives to stretch their chicken salad or creamed chicken dishes with as much veal as could be disguised by the other ingredients to pass for chicken. Wouldn't these women be surprised if they knew that today chicken breasts and lean loin of pork are known as "poor man's veal"?

Although choice veal roasts and chops will scarcely fit into a tight meat budget, there are some less costly cuts that can be used for some elegant dishes. The boned breast, for instance, can be stuffed and rolled for a preparation such as *cima alla Genovese,* a superb dish from Italy that includes fresh peas in the stuffing and looks like a colorful mosaic when cut.

Using shoulder or, again, the breast, the French make their exquisite *blanquette de veau,* its rich cream sauce studded with mushrooms. Veal Marengo, claimed by both France and Italy and dubiously connected with Napoleon's getting angry either before or after the battle of Marengo, is another fine dish that can be made with any stewing cut.

Ossobuco literally means "bone with the hole" or hollow bone. Made with the shanks of veal, this regional specialty from Milan, Italy has become popular all over the world. The cut costs comparatively little, unless it is bought from an Italian butcher who regards it as a great delicacy, which indeed it is. On the other hand, the Italian butcher will probably give you the best quality *ossobuco* available, but often supermarkets will have fine, meaty veal shanks, which, properly prepared, will give a good account of themselves. The preparation of this dish is simple, and recipes for it are to be found in many cookbooks.

CUTS OF VEAL

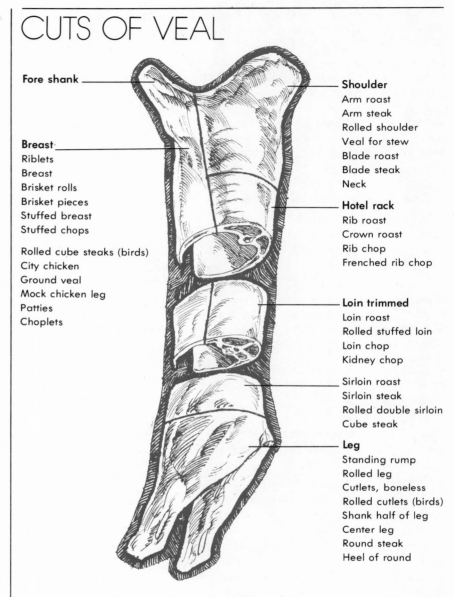

Fore shank

Breast
Riblets
Breast
Brisket rolls
Brisket pieces
Stuffed breast
Stuffed chops

Rolled cube steaks (birds)
City chicken
Ground veal
Mock chicken leg
Patties
Choplets

Shoulder
Arm roast
Arm steak
Rolled shoulder
Veal for stew
Blade roast
Blade steak
Neck

Hotel rack
Rib roast
Crown roast
Rib chop
Frenched rib chop

Loin trimmed
Loin roast
Rolled stuffed loin
Loin chop
Kidney chop

Sirloin roast
Sirloin steak
Rolled double sirloin
Cube steak

Leg
Standing rump
Rolled leg
Cutlets, boneless
Rolled cutlets (birds)
Shank half of leg
Center leg
Round steak
Heel of round

CHOPS AND STEAKS

Allow 1 to 2 rib or loin chops per person; 1 shoulder steak or chop per person; 8 to 12 ounces (227.2–340.8 g) of sirloin steak per person: and 4 to 6 ounces (113.6–170.4 g) lean veal round or scallops per person.

Rib and loin chops. Rib chops have less meat on them than loin, but they can look pretty with the end of the rib trimmed (frenched) and decorated with a paper frill for serving. Loin chops include the tenderloin and may also include a piece of kidney. Braise if they are over ¾-inch (1.9 cm) thick, panfry if they are ½ to ¾ inch (1.27–1.9 cm) thick. They can be breaded or plain.

Shoulder steaks and chops. *Arm* and *blade* chops and *shoulder* steaks have a lot of bone. They should be braised.

Sirloin steaks. Coming from the hip section, these have portions of backbone and hipbone. They should be braised if they are about 1-inch (2.54 cm) thick, panfried if they are under 1-inch (2.54 cm) thick.

Round steaks or cutlets. Cut from the center of the leg, this steak has the round slice of the leg bone in it. It can be cooked whole or cut into smaller pieces, sometimes called "cutlets." Cut thin, they make veal scallops. Braise or panfry if they are ½-inch (1.27 cm) thick or less. Weiner schnitzel is breaded veal cutlet.

Scallops. These lean, thin, boneless pieces of veal are most often cut from the leg, but can also be from the rib or loin. They are usually pounded to a thickness of between ⅛ and ¼ inch (0.3–0.6 cm) and all kinds of wonderful things can be made from them—veal birds, *saltimbocca*, and veal *parmigiana*, to name a few. They are called *escalopes* in French and *scaloppine* in Italian, and they are also fine just panfried, breaded, or plain, served with a slice of lemon.

Timetable for Roasting Veal

Roast uncovered, in oven preheated to 300 to 325°F.

Veal should be cooked until it is well done. Meat thermometers give 170°F as the degree for well-done veal, but to avoid the chance of dryness, cook to 160°F, then prick the roast, and if the juices run clear, it is done. If the juices are still pink, cook a little longer.

Cut	Weight in pounds	Approx. minutes per pound	Meat thermometer temperature
Loin	4 to 6	30 to 35	160°F
Saddle	8 to 12	30 to 35	160°F
Rib	3 to 5	35 to 40	160°F
Crown	12 to 15	35 to 40	160°F
Leg roast	4 to 8	25 to 35	160°F
Sirloin	3 to 4	35 to 40	160°F
Shoulder	4 to 6	40 to 45	160°F

Cube steaks. These little steaks can come from any cut. They have been tenderized by being passed through a machine that breaks down the fibers. They are of questionable quality. Panfry them.

BONY CUTS. Allow 12 ounces to 1 pound (340.8–454 g) per person.

Breast of veal. A very bony cut, this often has a pocket cut in it for stuffing. It can also be boned and rolled. It should be braised, a method of cooking to which it lends itself in an interesting variety of liquids and seasonings.

Shank. This is good for braising or stewing. The famous Italian dish called *osso buco* is made from the shank, cut in 3-inch (7.6 cm) pieces.

GROUND VEAL. Neck, flank, shank, or breast meat is used for grinding, rather than the more expensive cuts. Since veal is so lean, it needs to have some fat ground with it, or to be mixed with ground pork for patties (called *fricadelles* in French). Add 2 ounces (56.8 g) of ground pork fat to 1 pound (454 g) of ground veal, or mix half-and-half, or 2 to 1 with ground pork. A mixture of pork and veal is used in pâtés, and a mixture of beef, pork, and veal is sold for meat loaves.

Veal Marengo

5 tablespoons cooking oil
3 pounds boned, cubed veal (shoulder or breast)
1 onion, chopped
Salt and freshly ground pepper
2 tablespoons flour
1 cup dry wine
1 cup broth or stock
6 to 7 firm, ripe tomatoes, peeled and coarsely chopped
1 clove garlic, mashed
1 bay leaf
2 tablespoons butter plus 1 teaspoon oil
16 small white onions
16 small mushrooms
1 tablespoon chopped fresh parsley
6 slices white bread, cut in triangles and fried

Heat 5 tablespoons of oil in a skillet and brown the meat. Add the chopped onion, salt, and pepper. Stir and sprinkle with the flour. Stir again until all the ingredients are well blended. Add the wine, then stir and scrape the brown particles at the bottom and sides of the pan. Cook until the wine evaporates.

Add the broth, bring to a boil, and add the tomatoes, garlic, and bay leaf. Cover the pan and simmer for 45 minutes, or until the meat is tender.

In another pan, melt the butter, add the teaspoon of oil, and saute the small white onions briefly in this fat. Reserve.

Wipe the mushrooms clean and add, along with the sauteed onions, to the meat. Cook for 15 minutes, then remove from the heat and let the meat rest.

Skim the fat from the surface of the meat and, if necessary, reheat the meat. Transfer to a heated platter, sprinkle with parsley, and arrange the bread triangles around the meat. Serves 6 to 8.

One pound (454 g) of ground meat makes 3 to 4 patties. Allow 1 to 2 per person.

One pound (454 g) of ground meat in a meat loaf yields 3 to 4 servings.

Timetable for Braising and Panfrying Veal

To braise

Braise covered, on top of the stove, or in a preheated 300 to 325°F oven. Cook until tender and juices run clear, not pink, when meat is pricked. *See also* Braising (page 168).

Cut	Weight in pounds	Thickness in inches	Approx. cooking time (in hours)
Chops		½ to ¾	½ to 1
Steaks		1 to 1¼	¾ to 1
Cutlet		½ to ¾	¾ to 1
Rolled roast	4 to 6		3½ to 4
Breast	3 to 5		1½ to 2½
Shanks	3 to 4		1½ to 2½
Patties	⅓ pound		15 to 20 min.

To panfry

Panfry uncovered, until meat is brown and juices run clear, not pink, when meat is pricked. *See also* Panfrying (page 169).

Cut	Thickness in inches (cm)	Approx. cooking time (in minutes)
Chops	½ to ¾	20 to 30
Steaks	¾ to 1	25 to 35
Cube steaks	¼ to ½	3 to 5
Scallops	⅛ to ¼	6 to 8

CUTS FOR STEW

For a boneless stew, allow 8 ounces (227.2 g) per person. For a bony stew, allow 12 ounces (340.8 g) per person.

Two famous French stews, *blanquette de veau* and veal Marengo, are made here with *shoulder*, but in France the blanquette is made with *breast* cut into small pieces. Stew meat can also be *shank*, *rump*, *neck*, or *riblets*. Bones, particularly veal bones, give flavor and texture to stews; a few bones or bony pieces can be added to a boneless stew.

Timetable for Stewing Veal

Stew covered, on top of the stove, or in a preheated 300 to 325°F oven until tender. *See also* Stewing (page 170).

Cut	Weight in pounds	Approx. cooking time (in hours)
Riblets	2 to 4	¾ to 1¼
Other cuts for stew	2 to 4	1½ to 2½

VARIETY MEATS

Variety meats offer an interesting change of pace for menu planning. In texture alone there is the creamy softness of brains and sweetbreads, the fork-tender delicacy of calves' liver, and the slight chewiness of tripe. For flavor, the palate can be delighted with something as exotic as sweetbreads sauced *à la Perigordine* (truffles and Madeira), or as down-to-earth hearty as beef-and-kidney stew.

Variety meats are relatively inexpensive, and they are a definite bargain in nutrients. They are high in protein, B vitamins, vitamin A, phosphorus, and iron. Liver is particularly high in iron. Although they are not too high in calories, variety meats do contain a large amount of cholesterol.

BRAINS AND SWEETBREADS. Allow 4 to 6 ounces (113.6–170.4 g) per serving.

Brains. Although they all taste about the same, whether beef, lamb, pork, or veal (calf), veal brains are the most prized. They are very perishable and should be eaten within 24 hours of purchasing. Look for soft, plump, pinkish gray brains, avoiding any that look dry and shriveled. Brains may be panfried, broiled, braised, or cooked in liquid.

Sweetbreads. These are the thymus glands of young animals (when the animal matures, the glands disappear). Veal sweetbreads are considered the best, and they are the most readily available. Sweetbreads have a slightly nuttier taste than brains, but otherwise the two are much alike; they are equally perishable and also interchangeable in recipes. Look for sweetbreads that are soft, plump, and creamy white.

Beef breads, the pancreas glands of beef, are a coarser version of sweetbreads that are treated in the same way. The most expensive of the variety meats, and the most prestigious, sweetbreads may be panfried, broiled, braised, or cooked in liquid.

HEART. Allow about 8 ounces (227.2 g) per serving.

Beef hearts are the largest, feed the most people, and take the longest to cook. Beef and pork hearts are too tough to panfry or broil. Lamb and veal hearts may be panfried if they are young, but all hearts are best braised or stewed. Look for firm, bright red ones without any grayish tinge. Before cooking, cut in half, trim out large vessels and tubes, and wash well. Big beef hearts may be stuffed, making a fine meal for several people. If the heart is to be stuffed, leave the halves joined after trimming.

KIDNEYS. Allow 6 to 8 ounces (170.4–227.2 g) per person.

Veal and lamb kidneys are the most tender and can be panfried or broiled, sliced or whole. They can also be cooked on skewers. Beef and pork kidneys are tougher and need to braise or stew longer than the others. All should be trimmed of membranes, tubes, and knobs of fat. Some cooks say lamb and veal kidneys should not be washed before cooking because of their delicacy.

Kidneys alla fiorentina

1 pair veal kidneys
1 tablespoon olive oil
1 tablespoon butter
Salt and freshly ground pepper
Juice of ½ lemon
1 tablespoon chopped fresh parsley

Trim away the fat on the kidneys, then wash and pat dry. Cut into small pieces.

Heat the oil and butter in a small skillet and sauté the kidneys over medium heat so that they do not cook too quickly. It should take about 10 minutes. Add salt and pepper, stir, then add the lemon juice. Cook for 2 or 3 minutes, add the parsley, stir, and serve at once.

This recipe will serve four as an appetizer and two as a main course.

Chitterlings

Chitterlings (or chitlins) are the thoroughly cleaned and fried small intestines of the pig. The name is a corruption of the Middle English word "chiterling," which means "rag and tatter," describing their appearance on the plate. Although other innards from lamb and veal are sometimes called "chitlins," this extension of meaning is not recognized in the American South, where the dish is a popular one—and tastier than you might think.

Offal

Variety meats must have been named by some clever merchandiser to get around a genteel prejudice against the words "innards" or "offal," and what they represent—liver, tongue, kidneys, and so forth.

Offal, although it is an unpleasant word, has a logical origin. It came from "off-fall," the name given to all parts of the animal that fell off the cutting block when the carcass was being dressed. This meant everything from the inside of the animal, including the blood, as well as head, feet, and tail.

Approximate Cooking Time for Variety Meats

Kind	Panfried uncovered (in minutes)	Broiled (in minutes)	Braised covered (in hours)	Cooked in liquid, covered (in hours)
Brains	8 to 10	10 to 15 4 to 5 inches from heat	20 to 25 min.	15 to 20 min.
Sweetbreads				
Heart				
Beef				
Whole			3 to 4	3 to 4
Sliced			1½ to 2	
Lamb	2 to 3		2½ to 3	2½ to 3
Pork			2½ to 3	2½ to 3
Veal (calf)	2 to 3			
Whole			2½ to 3	2½ to 3
Kidney				
Beef		10 to 12 3 inches from heat	1½ to 2	1 to 1½
Lamb	3 to 5	10 to 12	¾ to 1	¾ to 1
Pork			1 to 1½	¾ to 1
Veal	8 to 10	10 to 12 4 inches from heat	¾ to 1	¾ to 1
Liver				
Beef				
piece 3 to 4 lbs.			2 to 2½	
sliced			20 to 40 min.	
Lamb, sliced	4 to 5	8 to 10		
Pork, whole 3 to 3½ lbs.			1½ to 2	
Veal (calf) sliced	4 to 5	8 to 10		
Tongue (fresh)				
Beef				3 to 4
Veal				2 to 3
Tripe				1 to 2
Oxtails			2 to 3	2 to 3

LIVER. Allow 4 to 6 ounces (113.6–170.4 g) per serving.

Veal and young calves' liver is the most tender. Beef liver is darker and a little tougher. Lamb liver looks very much like calves' in color, but it is smaller and should be cheaper. Pork liver is inexpensive if you can find it, and it is preferred for pâtés. Remove all membranes before cooking or they will make the liver curl up. Liver may be panfried, broiled, braised, or cooked in liquid.

TONGUE. Allow 4 to 6 ounces (113.6–170.4 g) per person.

Beef and veal tongues are the ones you are likely to find fresh. Lamb and pork tongues are usually processed before reaching the retail market. Fresh tongues should be cooked in seasoned water to cover.

TRIPE. Allow 4 to 6 ounces (113.6–170.4 g) per person.

Honeycomb tripe, considered the best, is the lining of the second stomach of beef. There is also *plain* or *smooth tripe*, not quite as delicate. It is thoroughly cleaned and partially cooked before being sold, but still needs long cooking in liquid before being used in most recipes. Tripe has a subtle flavor and a pleasant chewiness, and many interesting dishes are made with it—including the famous *tripe à la mode de Caen*.

OXTAILS. Allow 12 ounces to 1 pound (340.8–454 g) per person.

There is quite a lot of meat on oxtails, fatty though they are, and they have a flavor all their own. They may be braised, stewed, or boiled.

FURRED GAME

In large cities there are specialty stores that carry game in season. If the game comes from reputable game farms, the carcasses will have been federally inspected and will very likely be of high quality.

Game brought home by hunter friends or family can pose a problem. There are butchers across the country who will do the butchering and aging for you, if you can find them. Anyone planning a hunting trip might well line up a butcher beforehand. Aging, for hygienic reasons, should always be done under controlled conditions—proper sustained temperature and adequate airiness. Furred game is hung for 1 to 2 weeks.

The meat of game should be moist and velvety, not wet and flabby. Small-game flesh should be springy to the touch.

Gloves should be worn whenever game is handled in the field in order to avoid the danger of tularemia. This bacterial infection is transmitted by ticks or other insects in the hair of the game.

VENISON

Venison has come to mean the flesh of deer and other antlered animals like moose and elk, although the original definition meant the meat of any wild animal taken by hunting.

The best meat comes from young buck (male) less than 2 years old, identified by small, smooth hoofs, and bones that are spongy and red inside. The anatomy is much like that of domestic animals and, like them, tenderest cuts come from the less used muscles of the ribs and of the loin.

The fat of venison is inedible and should be trimmed away. This necessitates barding (covering with strips of bacon or other fat) the roast as well as larding, if possible. Marinating is usually recommended, both for flavor and tenderizing. Marinate for 24 to 36 hours. A young, tender cut can be roasted or broiled. If the animal is older, or if there is doubt as to age, venison is pot roasted or braised.

The sporting life

Hunting, a necessity for human survival during prehistoric times, became a leading sport in later centuries. It was performed with great panoply and ceremony and in special settings.

Some of the most famous châteaus and palaces were built with this purpose in mind. Fontainebleau started life as a hunting lodge, as did Chambord. Francis I rebuilt it in its Renaissance splendor at the beginning of the sixteenth century and used it for hunting and entertaining. During his reign, the aviary of the chateau housed more than three hundred falcons. They were trained to hunt the game in which the surrounding marshy regions abounded. The park of Chambord today is a game-breeding and wildlife preserve.

It is not surprising to find that some of the most famous dishes from this region, the Orléanais, are game inspired. *lapereau* à la solognote, made with wild rabbit, and the very rich *lièvre en terrine*, a savory preparation made with hare meat, are favorites.

Wild game in pioneer days

One has only to glance through a collection of recipes used by the pioneer housewives to appreciate the importance of wild game in the early days of our country. The pages are studded with directions for cooking a haunch of venison, wild turkey, wild duck, wild goose, partridge, opossum, groundhog, turtle, frog, quail, and rabbit, among other creatures of the forests and ponds. The recipes were not designed for cooks who didn't know their way around the kitchen. "Cook until done," directed the recipes.

Fresh butter, lard, and bacon fat were the fats called for; the meats were dusted with flour or "pounded cracker"; seasoned with such ingredients as salt and pepper, vinegar, onions, and walnut catsup. The meats were barbecued, grilled, braised, boiled, or baked. Directions were simple and basic. To cook a raccoon, for example, the cook is told to clean and gut it, then "leave it soak all night in salt water. Parboil the coon for a while and then take out and fill the chest cavity with sweet potatoes. Then bake until brown and tender."*

A vivid picture of the rigors of providing meat for a family in those days before refrigeration may be seen in the directions for dry-curing or brine-curing beef, buffalo, venison, elk, and deer. The recipes begin with the proportion of ingredients needed to treat each hundred pounds (45.4 kg) of meat.

The pioneers and Indians always carried strips of dried meat, called "jerky," in their shirt pockets or jackets. Any meat from beef to caribou was used, but never pork. Preparing jerky was a process that took from fifteen to twenty-five hours, during which time a smoky fire had to be kept going continuously. When the strips of meat became black and brittle, they were considered done. It was said that excellent stew could be made from the dried jerky. Jerky was also used to make pemmican, another meat preparation that could keep indefinitely. It consisted of ground jerky mixed with ground marrow fat or suet and ground raisins.

Certainly the pioneer women had no problem with what to do with their leisure time!

Venison roasts. Allow 6 to 8 ounces (170.4–227.2 g) per serving for boneless roasts and 12 ounces (340.8 g) for bone-in ones.

Leg, *rib*, and *loin* are good for roasting if they are from a young animal. Loin is best, or a 5- to 6-pound (2.3–2.7 kg) *saddle* (both loins). The leg to be roasted should also weigh about 5 to 6 pounds (2.3–2.7 kg), no more; larger roasts should be braised or pot roasted. Rib-roast weights depend on how many ribs you buy; just be sure you have meat from a young animal. Cooking beyond medium rare may make the meat tough.

Timetable for Roasting Venison Roast uncovered, in a preheated 350°F oven to desired inner temperature.		
Cut	Approx. minutes per pound	Meat thermometer temperature
Leg, rib, loin and saddle		
Rare	15 to 20	125 to 130°F
Medium rare	22 to 25	140 to 145°F
Medium	25 to 27	155 to 160°F
Well done	27 to 30	165 to 170°F

Chops and steaks. Allow 4 to 6 ounces (113.6–170.4 g) per person for boneless chops and steaks, 8 to 12 ounces (227.2–340.8 g) for bone-in.

As with all chops and steaks, the best are from the *rib* and *loin*. Others are better braised. Since the meat is so lean, rib steaks and rib and loin chops are good panfried in plenty of butter. If they are broiled, they should be brushed with butter as they cook.

Timetable for Cooking Venison Steaks and Chops

To broil

Cut	Thickness in inches	Distance from heat in inches	Approx. minutes per side
Rib or loin chops or steaks	1	2 to 3	3 to 5
	1½	3 to 4	5 to 6

To panfry

Cook uncovered, 3 to 4 minutes per side for rare, a minute or two more for medium, and another minute or two for well done.

About braising venison. The words are "until tender" with venison. How long the cooking will take depends on so many variables—the age of the animal, how long it was hung, and so on. The time can be from 1½ hours for a braised steak to 4 hours or more for a haunch or some other large cut.

SMALL FURRED GAME

Lepre in salmi (Hare in salmi)

The hare in Italy has always been considered a delicacy. The Romans were exceedingly fond of its meat, and it appeared frequently in their banquets. The meat was made into pâtés and shaped to resemble other animals or art objects. Trimalchio, the extravagant Roman merchant famous for his feasts, once served a hare fashioned to look like a winged Pegasus.

This is a classic Italian recipe fit for a Roman banquet, a modest one.

1 large hare (about 3 pounds)

Marinade:
2 carrots, sliced
1 onion, sliced
2 stalks celery, diced
1 pinch each sage, marjoram, and rosemary
2 bay leaves
1 teaspoon juniper berries
Salt and freshly ground pepper
3 cups dry red wine
1 tablespoon flour
¼ cup cooking oil
 or
4 tablespoons butter

Wash the hare quickly, pat dry, and cut into serving pieces. Include the heart, lungs, and liver. Mix the marinade ingredients together. Add the hare meat and refrigerate for 2 days, turning a number of times.

When ready to cook, remove the hare from the marinade and wipe dry with a paper towel. Reserve the marinade.

Heat the butter and oil in a heavy casserole. Ideally one should use an earthenware casserole. Coat the pieces of hare with flour and brown them well in the hot fat.

Strain the marinade. Add to the casserole the vegetables of the marinade, discarding the juniper berries. Stir the meat and vegetables together, cook briefly, and add the liquid of the marinade.

low heat, stirring occasionally. When tender, remove the pieces of hare from the casserole and keep warm. Scrape the bottom of the casserole and mash the sauce through a strainer. Return the pieces of meat to the casserole, cover with sauce, reheat, and serve.

In the north of Italy, this is always served with polenta, a corn mush. Serves 6 to 8.

Brunswick stew

Brunswick County, North Carolina and Brunswick County, Virginia both claim to be the place of origin for Brunswick stew. Wherever it came from this rich, thick stew is a kind of succotash with added vegatables and meat. The meat was originally squirrel and a ham hock, but now the squirrel is usually replaced by chicken or, in some areas, rabbit.

Brunswick stew is one of those stews that could be described as "more vittles than drink," having very little liquid when it is finished. Thickened with potatoes, it can barely be stirred—a kind of glorious mush, but with all the ingredients retaining their identity.

Rabbit stew

1 rabbit 3– 4 pounds, cut up
2 tablespoons butter
1 tablespoon oil
1 medium onion, finely chopped
1 stalk celery, finely chopped
1 clove garlic, minced
3 tablespoons all-purpose flour
½ teaspoon thyme
1 bay leaf, crumbled
¼ cup finely chopped parsley
1 teaspoon salt
½ teaspoon freshly ground black pepper
1 bottle dry red wine

Dry the rabbit pieces for browning.

Heat the butter and oil in a heavy, lidded casserole. Brown the rabbit pieces on all sides. Add the onion, celery, and garlic and cook, stirring over low heat for 2 to 3 minutes. Sprinkle in the flour, thyme, bay leaf, parsley, salt, and pepper. Stir gently to mix the flour and seasonings with the rabbit pieces. Add enough wine to barely cover the pieces, stirring to incorporate any bits stuck on the bottom of the pot, and bring to a boil. Turn down to a simmer, cover, and cook on top of the stove, or in a preheated 300– 325°F oven for 1 to 1½ hours or until tender. Skim off the fat before serving. Serves 4.

Rabbit, when young, weighs about 3 pounds (1.4 kg), has a delicate taste not unlike chicken and, like it, can be fried, stewed, or roasted. Rabbit is usually marinated and should be barded—that is, covered with strips of bacon or other fat for roasting.

Hare or **jack rabbit** is gamier than rabbit, tougher, and larger. *Leveret*, or young hare, weighs about 6 pounds (2.7 kg) and can be barded and roasted like rabbit, but older hares need to be marinated, then braised or stewed. Hare or jack rabbit that is "jugged" is pot roasted or stewed in a traditional pot, like a bean pot, called a "jug."

Raccoon, opossum, woodchuck, and muskrat. These can all be roasted like rabbit if they are very young, but to be sure of tenderness they are usually braised or pot roasted. The fat is not palatable and should be removed before cooking.

Squirrel. Gray squirrels are less gamy than red and can be roasted, but they need to be covered with bacon or some other fat; they are often braised. Gray squirrel is a traditional ingredient in Brunswick stew.

Cooking time for small game. The words for small game are "until tender." The length of time for cooking varies with the size and age of the animal, how long it has been hung, and how long it has marinated.

Roast rabbit, uncovered, in a preheated 350°F (177°C) oven for about 1½ hours, or until tender. Leveret, or young hare, will take twice as long as rabbit, squirrels a little less.

Braise, pot roast, or stew, covered, on top of the stove or in a preheated 300–325°F (149–163°C) oven. Squirrel and small rabbit will take 1 to 1½ hours; larger, older animals 2 to 3 hours. Cook until tender.

FISH AND SHELLFISH

For kings and peasants

Fish has gone through various stages of gastronomic popularity since the days of prehistory, when primitive people either found sustenance on coastal shores or went hungry. In the Greece of seven or eight centuries before the beginning of the Christian era, eating fish was a sign of poverty. However, in later ages as the population increased, fresh fish became a luxury. Aristotle is said to have been a connoisseur of fresh fish.

The people in Elizabethan England ate whale, seal, and porpoise, along with their beef, pork, and mutton. "Fish days" were strictly enforced by law. Inns were not allowed to serve meat on Fridays and sometimes Wednesdays, or during Lent. This had less to do with religion than the Crown's interest in supporting the fisheries. But, for the poor, almost every day was fish day. "Poor-John," the cheap food of England's underprivileged, was dried salted hake or cod. Turbot, trout, salmon, whiting, and sole, among others, were eaten in that period, but seafood was mostly for fast days and for the poor.

The French at the time of Louis XIV ate sardines, oysters, and salmon, but they generally avoided fish whenever they could and found fast days a trial. English royalty felt otherwise. They loved herring pies and stewed lamprey. The lamprey is a fat, eel-like creature that sucks the blood of other fish. Queen Elizabeth I doted on lamprey. One of her passions, she said.

For the English who crossed the ocean and founded homes in the New World, seafood was an almost daily food staple. The colonists would have been badly off without the bounties of the sea. They depended on fish as much as the poor back home in England. Scrod, a young filleted cod, was one of the first distinctly New England dishes. Many American fortunes were based on the production and shipping of New England codfish.

Unless perfectly fresh, fish is unfit to use." This unequivocal advice, offered at the end of the Civil War by the *Picayune*, New Orleans' leading newspaper, attempted to educate suddenly cookless and servantless southern housewives. The advice still stands today, although it is much easier to come by a fresh fish in this age of fast transportation and modern refrigeration. It is after you get a fresh fish in the kitchen that the other half of the battle begins. It must be handled and cooked properly, for unless cooked right, fresh fish is unfit to eat. Well, perhaps fit to eat, but certainly not as palatable as it should and can be.

In seeking out a good-quality fresh fish, your geographical location is important. Generally speaking, if you live in or near a major metropolitan area within one day's travel of a sea or lake fishing port, you should be able to buy fresh fish. For instance, Florida's fish arrive in excellent condition at New York's Fulton Fish Market after a hard-driving 24-hour trip. If you live in the right place, you should have a wide choice of fresh fish and seafood at your disposal.

FRESH, FRESHER, FRESHEST

It is almost axiomatic that the fresher the fish, the better the fish dish will be. Freshness depends not only on when the fish left the water, but also on how it fared during storage and transportation. A freshly caught cod, eviscerated (gutted) immediately and kept at 32°F (0°C) in moist cold will stay fresh for 8 days. Elevate the temperature to 41°F (5°C) and the same cod will stay fresh only 4 days. Spoilage starts in the entrails first, and then in the mucous-covered skin. The slime or mucous on a fresh fish is a protective coating that keeps the fish from developing a "dishwater hands" skin condition in its natural element.

The flesh under the skin is sterile when a fish comes out of the water, but bacterial growth will start early without proper handling (gutting and icing). When fish skin undergoes temperature rise, the surface bacteria increase astronomically, producing a substance called "trimethylamine," that is responsible for the "fishy" odor that gave rise to all the age-old gags about fish smells.

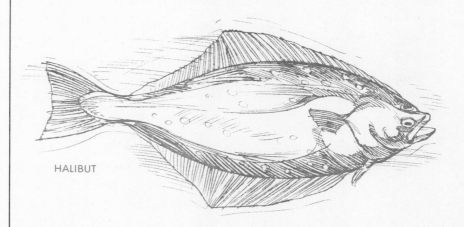

HALIBUT

Professional fishermen gut their larger catches as they come from the net (small fish catches, too, if the vessel will not make port in a short time) and bed them down in flake ice. If they did not, we would not have very fresh fish available. Unfortunately, sport fishermen are sometimes unaware of the high perishability of fish, and often let their catch lie ungutted and un-iced until ready to depart, and then may heave it into an airless car trunk for the trip home.

Where to buy fish. With professional handling and modern transportation, then, people today enjoy much fresher fish than in the post-Civil War days of slow boats, slower horse-drawn cartage, and no refrigeration. One can now anticipate that the fish will be fresh in any competent retail operation. The average retail fish store will offer the finest-quality fish available, but the prices will be higher than those charged at supermarket chain-store counters. The independent dealer buys his needs from day to day, while most chain operations buy huge quantities at remote points and receive shipment only once a week. It is a dismal experience to see the woebegone specimens offered in some chains, where even the most inexperienced shopper knows something is amiss. Some of the smaller supermarket chains receive twice-weekly deliveries from local distribution points, enabling them to offer much fresher fish to their customers. The best retail fish operations seem to be located in the smaller coastal towns where the clean, sea-fresh smell of a sparkling display of ice-bedded fish and shellfish delights the eye and nose, and titillates the appetite.

How much fish to buy. It takes about 6 ounces (170.4 g) of fish to satisfy a small appetite and 8 ounces (227.2 g) for the average good appetite. Fish fillets are 100 percent edible and fish steaks are about 90 percent edible. The following table shows how much edible flesh is available in other market forms of fish:

Market form	% Edible flesh
Whole or round	43–47
Eviscerated (gutted) only	46–50
Dressed (eviscerated, head and fins off)	65–69

Nutritional information. Fishery products are excellent sources of high-quality, complete protein, many valuable minerals, and essential B-complex vitamins. Fish are, with few exceptions, low in fats, and what fat is present is of the polyunsaturated type. Calorie counts are very low: 80 or less per 3½ ounces (100 g) for the leaner-meated fish such as cod, haddock, sole, and flounder. As the fat content of fish goes up, calories and protein values increase. A salmon with a fat content of 14 percent has about 220 calories per 3½ ounces (100 g) and protein content is about 22 percent. Cod has less than 1 percent fat, 78 calories per 3½ ounces (100 g) and 17.6 percent protein by contrast. Shellfish are lean, but they contain more cholesterol than regular fish. Carbohydrates are totally absent from fish and occur in very low concentrations in shellfish. Sodium (salt) content is quite low in *both* fresh-water and salt-water fish; it is medium high in shellfish.

Fish eating around the world

Considering that at least seventy percent of the earth's surface is water, of which four-fifths is a mile or more deep, there is less universal interest in the sea life that abounds there than might be expected.

In 1976, Americans ate an average of 12.9 pounds of fish per person. This in a country with one of the world's greatest natural fishery resources. Icelandic people ate 86.2 pounds. (It is not surprising they waged their "cod war" with Great Britain.) The Japanese ate 80.2 pounds, the Danes 78.3 and the Swedes 45.9 pounds per person. Britain and France managed 18.1 and 17.4 pounds respectively.

Argentina, a large beef producer like the United States, was low on the fish-eating totem pole with an annual fish consumption of 5.5 pounds.

Flying fish

Don't look askance at a fish dealer who offers you a handsome Pacific salmon or a lively Maine lobster even though you may be 3,000 miles from where it was caught. Major metropolitan areas throughout the United States receive fish and seafood delicacies by air once or twice each week. The fish is packed in special chilled containers and arrives in prime condition.

Low-fat frying

Modern Teflon- and porcelain-coated skillets make frying with minimum fat much easier. Because of diet restrictions, many fish eaters avoid panfrying because of the added calories caused by the oil. In any event, these coated skillets are a boon to seafood lovers. They permit less fat and breading to be used, thus enhancing the natural flavor of fresh fish and shellfish.

Fishy stories about fish

Kennebec salmon on restaurant menus doesn't come out of the Kennebec, of course. Best bet is Washington or Alaska. . . . Sole is what anybody cares to call some type of flounder. American enterprise uses the name for snob value, but the real sole—Dover sole—comes only from the English Channel area. The U.S. permits two flatfish, the gray sole and the lemon sole, to be called "sole," but they are not related to the Dover sole. The gray sole is the premier flatfish of the East Coast. The important West Coast soles (read "flounder") are rex sole and California sole. . . . The ever popular "turbot" does not exist in American waters. It is a highly regarded western Atlantic and English Channel fish that does not find its way to this country. The most common "turbot" sold in America is a frozen import that used to be sold here as "Greenland halibut" until the government stopped the importers from degrading the good name of American halibut. It is at best a very poor substitute for the highly regarded true turbot. . . . Steelhead salmon can be a great disappointment. The name seems to suggest a superior kind of salmon, which indeed would be trying to gild the lily. Actually, a steelhead is a sea-running rainbow trout that somehow escaped its stream and went to sea. It attains a huge size compared to the average rainbow trout. Its flesh is beautiful orange red and looks like true salmon flesh, but is coarse and dry by comparison. . . . Don't ever turn your nose up if you are offered shark. At least not at the mako, blue, or blacktip, that rank in texture and flavor with choice swordfish. English fish-and-chips eaters might be surprised to find out that grayfish is largely used. In America we call grayfish "sand shark" or "dog shark" or "dogfish." . . . Red snapper is one of America's most prized fish, which has led importers to market a red snapper look-alike. It is offered mainly as frozen red snapper fillets. They come from Japan but bear no resemblance in texture or flavor to the American red snapper. . . . "Sandy," "granular," "tough," "dry," and "tasteless" are some of the comments heard from people who eagerly try their first highly vaunted turtle steaks. It might turn out to be your dish, but these comments are passed along to be recalled after you disregard them and try

How to recognize a fresh fish. Recognizing a fresh fish is easy, provided the head is still on. Look at the eyes. If they are dull, glazed, and sunken, pass on! If they are bright and bulge a bit, right on! If you come upon a shining, bright blue eye surrounded by a golden cornea, you have hit the jackpot. The color of the iris fades to darker blue to black and the golden cornea becomes grayish white as time passes.

Other indicators of freshness are a moist, shining appearance, firm and resilient flesh, tight scales, and red gills under the gill flaps. If there is doubt about any of these signs, pick up the fish, push back the gill covers and hold the fish to your nose. This is the ultimate test used by experienced fish handlers. The slightest sour smell is instant warning of the onset of staleness. *Fresh fish do not smell!*

If the head is off, look for the cut end to be neat, fresh looking, and to have a shining, translucent quality. There should be no discoloration.

Handling fish in the home. Fish should go into the coldest part of the refrigerator immediately upon arrival home. If fish is to be held overnight, repackage it in fresh wrapping and slip it into an airtight plastic bag. The store wrapping will often have been applied by someone with fish moisture on the hands. This causes the wrapping to smell after a few hours, so it is best to discard it before odors develop and make you think the fish has spoiled. Purists will even place cracked ice cubes around the package to further cut down moisture loss overnight. Protection against moisture loss cannot be overemphasized. It is this loss that steals flavor and causes dryness. Although fresh fish can be stored for a day or two, it is always best to use it as soon as possible.

If you feel you must wash a steak or a fillet before cooking, do it quickly in cold water, preferably salted, and paper-towel it dry before escaping juices are neutralized by the water. Dressed fish can be handled much more roughly because the skin is still there to protect the tender flesh.

Freezing fish at home. If you have more fresh fish than your immediate needs, wrap the fish (first cleaning it if it is whole) tightly in freezer wrap, slip it into an airproof container, and place it in the freezing compartment of your refrigerator. Don't try to hold it more than a week or two because the average home refrigerator freezer does not achieve a sufficiently low temperature for long storage. Unless held at −10°F (−23°C) or more, enzymatic changes will take place that reduce flavor and change flesh texture. Fish with high fat content, such as mackerel, salmon, or shad, do not hold as well as leaner fish in freezer storage.

When you get around to using the fish you have frozen, it should be removed from freezer to refrigerator the night before use, still wrapped in its airtight container. When the package is opened the next day you will find it dry inside, not full of leaked-out juices that result from too-quick thawing. The fish will look almost as good as when you froze it, and the texture and flavor will be close to fresh. Don't thaw fish at room temperature or, worse, try to thaw it out quickly in water.

GETTING YOUR MONEY'S WORTH

First find out what is in season and most plentiful at the moment. When fish are abundant they are usually at their cheapest and in their best condition of the year, having eaten well and waxed fat and healthy. Of course, in today's economy there is rarely a chance at a bargain buy of the elite species such as red snapper, salmon, halibut, swordfish, sea bass, or pompano, but the more humble species can often be had at bargain prices in season. Try a "new" species for yourself and you may be richly rewarded.

If you are interested in economy, consider buying large whole fish rather than fillets or steaks. The most convenient sizes for individual portions are usually snapped up by restaurant buyers who pay premium prices for them. The larger fish are better buys because they will yield a high percentage of edible flesh. Don't be afraid to buy enough for several meals or for splitting with someone else. Fillets and steaks are easier to handle, but then you have to foot the bill for high-priced labor. Also, you lose the makings for fish stocks and fish soups and chowders that a good cook depends on. Any really good fish sauce calls for a fish-stock base.

People who are within traveling distance of a wholesale fish market or a port where sport or commercial fishing boats dock can take advantage of the chance to pick up fish bargains at wholesale prices. There's always someone eager for a cash sale. If you are required to buy wholesale amounts, usually about 10 pounds (4.5 kg) or more, make the trip a community party. The savings will be substantial and the freshness should be superior.

your first turtle steak anyway. . . . Fish as brain food? While seafood is high in phosphorus and the human brain contains the body's highest concentration of phosphorus, it has never been proved that eating fish will make a dullard any smarter. On the other hand, fish is rich in protein, vitamins, and minerals that promote good health and mental alertness, and fish meals do not produce extended waistlines and a state of torpor. . . . Oysters as an aphrodisiac? Never, says the scientific community. But whoever first uttered the phrase implanted an idea that public fancy has kept alive for centuries. The power of suggestion can move mountains, and it is an accepted fact that mental attitudes influence human sexuality.

Quantity storage

Special arrangements are generally needed for overnight storing of packages too big for the refrigerator, such as a bushel of clams, a crate of lobsters, a basket of hard crabs, or a shallow flat of soft crabs. If possible, they should be placed on the floor in a cool cellar. The crabs and lobsters should have a porous covering on top (several sheets of newspaper or a piece of burlap) that is kept wet and chilled with sprinklings of crushed ice. Make sure there is normal air flow. Chunks of ice can be thrown directly on top of clams and oysters.

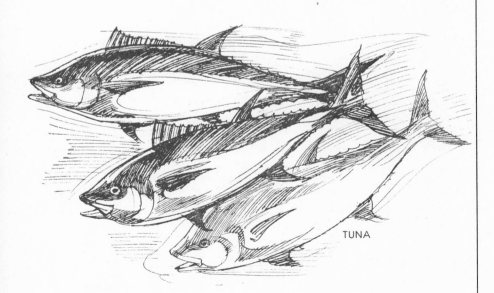

TUNA

Is fresh always better?

No rule is without an exception. "Just out of the water" big specimens of fish negate the "fresher is better" rule, particularly those fish with low-fat content. Cod, haddock, and fluke, lean meated, with gleaming, bulging eyes and just hours out of the sea, are bland and disappointing dishes. Even striped bass, with higher fat content, tastes better the third day than the first. Enzymotic changes take place in fish flesh that release flavor and have a tenderizing effect. If you catch a big one or are able to buy one right off the boat, wait a day or two to enjoy it fully.

Snappy travelers

Consider that red snapper are taken far at sea in the deepest waters of the Gulf of Mexico, landed several days later and then driven in fast refrigerated trucks to northern markets. They have been out of the water a week or more, but command top prices because they are in fine, fresh condition. They stay fresh because they are gutted when caught, iced inside and outside the body cavity, and kept under constant refrigeration until they arrive at northern markets. Every seafood restaurant in major northern cities offers fresh red snapper as one of its choicest menu items.

Is it fresh or frozen?

Human nature being what it is, a shopper at times will be confronted by an offering of thawed-out frozen fish for fresh. The eye should pick up such telltale hints as dull-looking flesh, generally limp aspect, and a lack of translucency in the visible flesh. There is often a mushy look. Thawed fish flesh releases its moisture, which causes the dead white color that goes with translucency loss. This is very easy to spot in fish fillets and steaks that were once frozen.

HANDLING A WHOLE FISH

To scale a fish. If you have been lucky enough to get a good fish outside normal retail channels, you can make fillets or steaks for yourself. First comes the scaling. To prevent flying scales, fill your sink with cold water and hold the fish under it as you scale. With a fish scaler or the back of a short-bladed kitchen knife use short, pushing strokes and gently but firmly work from tail to head. Be careful when moving your hands around the back fins; they can be very sharp. Use gloves until you get the hang of it. Don't let the mass of fish scales run down the drain or you will be risking a plumbing job.

To gut a fish. Slit the belly from anal vent to chin and remove everything inside the stomach cavity. Beneath the exposed backbone under a thin membrane lies the blood pocket. If the fish is really fresh the blood will still be liquid; it congeals as the fish ages. Scrape this blood pocket out with the knife tip. Do not remove the head if you want to bake or broil the fish whole. With the head left on, flavorful juices are retained during the cooking period and the fish will cook more quickly than without the head.

To cut fish steaks. To steak a fish, scale and gut as above. Then slice it crossways in steaks about an inch thick. Make the slices uniform so that all the steaks will be done at the same time in cooking. A heavy hammer and a cleaver may be necessary if the fish is of any size. If you obtain your fish from a market, the fishman will steak any fish you order. Fish regularly cut into steaks are cod, pollock, striped bass, halibut, salmon, swordfish, tilefish, tuna, king mackerel, large bluefish, large drums, groupers, large ling cod, and sablefish, among others.

PIKE

To fillet a fish. Filleting is the graduate course in fish butchering. It is much easier than it sounds, so don't be discouraged by the awkward verbiage necessary for written instructions. Use a very sharp knife of good steel (not stainless, which will not keep a sharp edge). A 6- or 7-inch blade (15.2–17.8 cm) is recommended. The fish does not have to be scaled or gutted before being filleted, but it is recommended that this be done initially until you acquire skill with the knife and a greater knowledge of fish anatomy.

Cut off the head with a diagonal slash from each side that includes the gills and pectoral fins (the two slender fins on the belly just behind the gills). If the knife fails to sever the backbone, use pressure on the head against the table edge to snap the bone.

Start the fillet cut at the head end and slice gently in toward the backbone. You should feel and keep pressure on the spines projecting from the backbone; they will guide the knife as you slice down toward the tail. Feel that you are cutting with the end of the knife rather than the full blade. Don't let the knife go in past the midline of the backbone as you cut the length of the fish.

Now lift the half-loosened fillet and, cutting gently with very small, knife-tip strokes, slice the flesh away from the ribs. Keep the knife pressed against the guiding rib bones. Cut to, but not through, the belly skin. As you reach the end of the rib cage, elevate your hand slightly to keep pressure on the spines on the other side of the backbone; this will save precious flesh. When the whole fillet is loosened, run the knife through the belly skin. Turn the fish over and repeat the operation to free the second fillet.

To skin the fillet, get a fingertip grip at the tail end. Cut down to the skin and flatten the knife against it. Slide the knife forward firmly toward the head end, keeping it at an angle to lower resistance to the blade; bias cuts require much less pressure than straight cuts.

SALMON

Amateurs vs. professionals

Sportfishermen, believe it or not, have been catching about 1.6 billion pounds of fish per year according to U.S. government statistics, almost the same amount produced by our commercial fishermen. And this figure does not include amateur catches of clams, oysters, lobsters and other shellfish.

A digestible comestible

For many centuries fish and shellfish have been considered to be easily digestible. Recent research has shown that 90 to 100 percent of fish protein is digestible. This percentage is higher than that of beef or chicken.

About fish oil

The oil in fish can play a significant role in human health. Because fat in fish has a unique chemical nature, fish is often recommended in diets designed to lower cholesterol in the hope of reducing the risk of heart disease. The reason for this is that fish oil (fat) is high in polyunsaturated fatty acids that are effective in reducing cholesterol in many people.

A fish vanishes

People who live along the East Coast may recall the popularity of the blowfish during and immediately after World War II. In case this fish sounds unfamiliar, it was also known as "swellfish," "globefish," "puffer," and "swell toad." Shunned for years by both sport and commercial fishermen as trash fish, the blowfish (an unappetizing name that an enterprising industry transformed into the more fashionable "sea squab" and "chicken of the sea") became such a delicacy that it reached a peak of $1.85 per pound at the wholesale level before it was literally fished out.

Soaring fish prices

Rising costs of fish and seafood have caused many fish eaters to pass up or cut down on consumption of their favorites. Prices in general are 250 to 350 percent higher than they were just 10 years ago. More and more consumers are going outside the normal commercial channels to procure fish and seafood. How to get the most out of your fish dollar is a pressing issue for many.

Make your own fish scaler

If you don't have a fish scaler handy, you can make a most efficient one simply by nailing several serrated-edge bottle caps to the end of a piece of wood 2 bottle-caps wide and 8 inches long. The serrated edges will provide fine scraping surfaces.

Sauce for the fish

One approach to fish cookery is that of the French, who have an old saying, *C'est la sauce qui fait manger le poisson*, meaning it is the sauce that makes the fish dish acceptable. By the addition of indisputably superb sauces, the French chef can make any fish a delicacy. But here in America, unless we have gourmet inclinations and the time to indulge them, we look for the fish itself to provide a good fish dish. Of course, for those who cannot get good fresh fish, *la sauce* for *le poisson* becomes more important. Butter or margarine, salt, and lemon provide the only "sauce" needed when a good fresh fish is at hand.

Water broiling

"Water broiling" is a technique that can be used successfully at any time, but particularly when your fillet or steak seems to be a bit on the dry side. Proceed as in the broiling instructions, but add salted water (a little dry white wine can be an added fillip) to the pan up to one-third the thickness of the fish. It provides moisture during broiling and will result in a juicier dish.

Spencer method for fish cooking

Broiling is the preferred cooking method for fillets and steaks, but there is another satisfactory way called the "Spencer method" that is highly recommended. Cut fillets or steaks into individual portions. Preheat the oven to 500°F. Soak the fish for 3 minutes in salted milk—1 teaspoon of salt to ½ cup of milk. Drain, then roll in bread crumbs. (You may add some chopped parsley and grated Parmesan cheese to the bread crumbs for additional interest.) Place the fish on a foil sheet in the pan and dot with butter or margarine. Place the pan on the top rack of the preheated oven and bake for 10 to 12 minutes. (Thin pieces may cook in a shorter time.) The fish should be juicy inside and crisply brown outside.

COOKING METHODS

The purpose of this chapter is to help you choose a good fish, handle it properly, and then cook it perfectly. In coastal cities people flock to fine fish restaurants because the fish is cooked just right. The flavor of good fish is completely lost when overcooking dries out the natural juices. All the flavor in a lean-meated fish is in its juices; it does not have the fat content or muscle tissue (both of which add to flavor) found in meat. The purpose of exposing fish to heat is to coagulate the protein, not to tenderize and cook the flesh. Indeed, fish flesh is edible in its raw state. The Japanese cut fish into slender strips, dip it in a sauce of horseradish, ginger root, and mustard, and eat their *sashimi* heartily. Good fish cookery is based on "How quickly can I cook this fish?" rather than "How long do I have to cook it?"

When is fish done? The flesh of raw fresh fish and shellfish has a translucent, "live" look. When cooked a short period of time the flesh becomes opaque, or solid, in appearance. Fish is "done" when the last bit of translucency disappears. "Test for doneness with a fork," and "When the fish flakes readily it is done," are the usual fish cooking directions—and they have led to more overdone fish dishes than there are fish in the sea. Unless the fork is thrust in at the precise moment, the action means nothing. And who is so sensitive at fork thrusting that he or she can tell the difference between cooked fish flesh and uncooked soft fish flesh? The only way to learn when fish is done is to slice the fish open for a peek to see how much "live" or translucent flesh is left—or to put it another way, to see if any raw flesh is still visible.

After one gets the feel of fish cookery, one will know just by looking at the thickness of a piece of fish, and whether it has a soft- or hard-textured flesh, exactly how long to cook it. A safe precaution is *always* to slice a peephole in the cooking fish about one minute before you think it will be done. If you see just a thin line of raw flesh, take it out and the heat in it will finish the cooking job on the serving platter. If the thickness of the piece of fish is uneven, by all means rescue the thinner parts as they become ready to take out. An experienced fish chef will always allow the fish to finish cooking en route to the table. If it is cooked until completely "done" in the oven, it will be slightly overdone by the time it is eaten.

PANFRYING. Panfrying is the easiest way to cook small fish, thin fillets, and steaks. In a heavy skillet place enough oil or butter (or margarine), or a combination of both, to accommodate the fish you plan to fry. Use as little oil as possible and bring it to just below the smoking point before the fish is added. The fish may be coated with flour, fine bread crumbs, or cracker meal. Fry fish to a light brown on each side. If you have to check for doneness, make a tiny slit with a knife tip, part the flesh, and check for translucency (raw flesh).

DEEP FRYING. If your diet allows, fry half-portion or one-portion size pieces of fish—no more than ½ inch (1.27 cm) thick—in deep fat. It is preferable to use a frying basket; otherwise frying can be a bit messy, even dangerous. Dip pieces in batter of egg and milk or egg and water, then in a preferred crumb mixture. Fry a few pieces at a time; the pieces should not touch each other. Lower the basket into hot oil that has been preheated to 375°F (190°C). You may need a thermometer to know when the fat is hot enough, although you can also test with a 1-inch (2.54 cm) cube of bread (it should brown in one minute). Fry until a light golden brown. Drain and serve immediately.

SWORDFISH

Varieties of fish

Bass. Fish nomenclature can be most confusing, for the same fish can be known by different names, depending on locality, and in some cases the same name can be used for fish of varying species. This is well illustrated in the bass family. Sea bass is a saltwater fish, but the name "bass" is also applied to a large variety of popular freshwater game fish that includes the *sunfish* and the *crappie*. The word "bass" is generally accompanied by a word that describes the category, such as "largemouth," "smallmouth," "striped," "white," or "black," among other names used locally. These fish are abundantly distributed throughout streams, lakes, and rivers in various parts of the United States. They vary in weight from 1 to 4 pounds (.45—1.8 kg).

Bluefish. This fine-tasting, blue green fish is fairly common along the Atlantic and Gulf coasts. The usual weight is 3 to 6 pounds (1.4—2.7 kg), although it can be more. The fish is sold whole, or as steaks or fillets. It can be broiled or baked and requires only the simplest seasonings. Available all year.

Butterfish. These small, delicately meated silvery fish are caught in great quantities off the Atlantic coast and are available in eastern markets all year. They average about 8 ounces (227.5 g). They may be broiled or fried.

Carp. Carp is a scaly fish and needs careful preparation. It sometimes has a muddy flavor, particularly in the summer, but this can be overcome by skinning the fish and soaking it in lightly salted water for 3 or 4 hours. Generally sold whole, it may also be available in fillets or steaks. It can be poached, baked, deep fried, steamed, stewed, or braised. Available all year.

Catfish. These fish are caught in the Great Lakes, the Mississippi Valley, and central United States and are rarely sold in coast markets. Among the common varieties are the *bullhead* or *horned pout*, *channel*, *yellow* or *goujon*, and *spotted* or *fiddler*. The fiddler cat is considered to have the best flavor. Catfish must be skinned before cooking. It is sold whole or skinned and dressed, or as fillets, steaks, or chunks. Available all year.

Cod. A fish of great importance, cod comes mainly from the banks of New-
(continued)

(Varieties of fish, continued)

foundland, from New England waters, and from the coasts of Norway. Average weight is 10 pounds (4.5 kg). Available whole or in steaks, fillets, or sticks. *Scrod* is a young cod weighing from 1½ to 2½ pounds (0.7–1.1 kg). Young haddock, pollock, and other similar fish are often called "scrod." May be broiled, fried, baked, or poached. Available all year.

Flounder. The flounder family provides what is usually sold under the name of "sole." Included are *blackback, dab, fluke, gray sole, lemon sole, southern,* and *yellowtail.* May be fried, baked, broiled, poached, or deep fried. Available whole or as fillets. Available all year.

Haddock. Haddock and cod are closely related, but the haddock is generally smaller. It is sold whole but more commonly as fillets. Smoked fillets are known as *finnan haddie.* Haddock is one of the leanest of all fish. Available all year.

Hake. Hake is probably more often eaten than recognized. It is frequently sold along with haddock and cod as "deep sea fillets." The flesh is delicate, soft, and white. It is sold whole and in fillets. Available all year.

Halibut. Native to the North Atlantic and North Pacific oceans, a halibut can weigh over 100 pounds (45.4 kg). Small members of the species, weighing up to 9 pounds (4.1 kg) are known as *chicken halibut* and are considered the finest. The flesh is white and meaty. It is usually bought in steaks, sometimes in fillets. A slice about 1½ inches (3.8 cm) thick is ideal for broiling. Available all year.

Mackerel. This is a strongly flavored fish that averages about 2 pounds (508 g). It is available whole, in cuts, or filleted. It can be poached, broiled, fried, or stuffed and baked. Available from April through November.

Mullet. There are about one hundred varieties that live in the Atlantic and Gulf regions. Mullet, marketed chiefly in the South, is usually sold whole but also as fillets. Available all year.

Ocean perch. This name is applied to *rosefish, redfish,* and *red perch,* and has become the official trade name for frozen fillets made from these fish. The flesh is firm and bland and appeals to people who do not like a strong fish flavor but are fond of the texture of fish.

BROILING: The broiling compartment must be preheated at "broil" heat, 550°F (288°C) for at least 10 minutes. The preheating is essential for even cooking and proper gauging of cooking time.

Broiled *fish fillets* cook very quickly. A fillet from a small fish will cook in 3 or 4 minutes, particularly in an electric stove broiler (not a portable broiler, which is unpredictable). Place the fillets on a sheet of aluminum foil in the broiling pan. The foil serves to keep the pan clean, but more important, it can be used to lift the broiled fillets from the baking pan when they are done. If the fillets are left in the pan, they will continue cooking past the point of doneness. Dust the fillets with bread crumbs, dot quite generously with small dabs of butter or margarine, and then place the pan in the broiler. The top of the fillets should be 2 inches (5.1 cm) from the source of heat. Broil the fillets the length of time indicated on the chart. Do not turn. (All timing charts are courtesy of the Fishery Council of New York and Middle Atlantic Area, Inc.)

Broiling Fish Fillets			
Name of fish	Thickness of fillets vary from (in inches)	Baste during broiling	Broiling time (in minutes)
Bluefish	¼–¾	once	6
Carp	¼–1¼	once	8–10
Cisco (lake herring)	¼–½	once	5–7
Cod	½–1	twice	8–10
Flounder	¼–½	once	5–7
Fluke	¼–⅔	twice	5–8
Haddock	⅓–⅔	twice	5–8
Hake	¼–½	twice	6–8
Mackerel	¼–1¼	once	6–8
Mullet	¼–¾	twice	6–8
Pike	¼–⅔	once	6–8
Pollock	½–1	twice	6–8
Porgy	¼–⅝	twice	6
Rockfish	¼–½	twice	5
Sea bass	¼–½	twice	5
Sole (lemon)	¼–¾	twice	5–8
Sole (gray)	¼	once	5
Weakfish (sea trout)	¼–¾	twice	6
Whitefish	¼–¾	once	6–8
Whiting	¼–¾	twice	5

The thickness of *fish steaks* will vary from about ½ to 1 inch (1.27–2.54 cm). Follow the same directions as for preparing fish fillets for the broiler. Broil steaks 2 inches (5.1 cm) from the source of heat. A choice presents itself in broiling fish steaks as to whether or not to turn them during the broiling period. The chart calls for turning them, but they are just as well if not turned. If you elect to broil without turning, place them 1 inch (2.54 cm) farther away from the flame.

Broiling Fish Steaks

Types of steaks	Thickness (in inches)	Time on 1st side (in minutes)	Time on 2nd side (in minutes)	Extra bastings
Cod	½	3	5	1
	1	5	5	1
Salmon	½	3	3	
	1	3	5	
Swordfish	½	3	3	
	1	3	5	
Tuna (fresh)	½	3	3	
	1	4	5	
Halibut	½	3	3	1
	1	4	5	1
Striped bass	½	3	3	1
	1	4	4	1

Any fish that will fit in your oven can be *split* for broiling. A split fish that is cooked with the skin on and the bone left in will yield more edible flesh and retain more juices and flavor than a fillet. To split the fish, proceed as in the instructions for filleting. Prepare split fish for broiling as you would fillets or steaks; follow the chart for cooking time.

Broiling Split Fish

Name of fish	Distance from source of heat (in inches)	Thickness of fish (in inches)	Broiling time (in minutes)
Bluefish	3	¾	8
Bonito mackerel	3	½–1½	10
Croaker	2	¾	8
*Carp	6	½–1½	12–14
Cisco (lake herring)	3	¼–1	9–11
Hake	3	1	6–8
Mackerel	2	¾–1	8–10
Mullet	3	¼–1	10–12
Porgy	3	½–1	6–8
*Pike	3	¼–1¼	8–10
Rockfish	3	½–1	6–8
Sea bass	3	½–1	6–8
Weakfish (sea trout)	2	½–¾	6–8
Whitefish	3	½–1½	10–12
Whiting	3	¼–½	6–8

*Carp and pike should be basted twice during the broiling period instead of the single basting recommended for the other varieties.

Pike and pickerel. Popular among anglers as sportfish, pike and pickerel have special local names such as *jack pike, grass pike,* and *Northern pike.* Eastern pickerel is known as *chain pickerel* in the North and *jack pickerel* in the South. They come to market whole if small, and filleted if large. They are lean fish and fat should be added when broiling. They may also be poached, braised, or stuffed and baked. Pike is finely ground for the delicate poached fish cakes called *quenelles de brochet* ("forcemeat of pike"). Available all year.

Pike perch. Also known as *yellow pike* and *walleye,* pike perch is not related to pike but is in the same family as the yellow perch, as is *sauger* or *sand pike.* They average 1 to 1½ pounds (454–681 g) but may weigh up to 4 pounds (1.8 kg). They are excellent food fishes with firm white flesh. They may be fried, baked, or broiled. Available all year, whole or filleted.

Pompano. Considered by some the finest fish caught in American waters, pompano is a thin fish with a beautiful silvery skin and delicate white meat. It is caught mainly off Florida and in the Gulf, and only a small amount is shipped north. It may be baked, broiled, or sautéed.

Porgy. Porgy, or *scup,* is found in nearly all American coastal waters. It is sold whole, rarely filleted. It is best fried. Available from January to November.

Red snapper. This magnificently colored Gulf Coast fish is regarded as one of the choicest offerings of the sea. It ranges from 1½ to 10 pounds (0.7–4.5 kg) or more. The smaller ones are often sold whole; the larger are cut into steaks and fillets. Excellent prepared in any manner. Available all year.

Salmon. This peerless fish is native to both the Atlantic and Pacific coasts of North America. The *Pacific king salmon,* or *chinook* is a deep, bright coral pink color. It is considered by some connoisseurs the finest, while others prefer the *Atlantic* or *Eastern salmon,* which is taken from Canadian waters. The latter is a pale blush pink and is firmer, meatier, and has a more pronounced fish flavor. The *silver* or *Coho,* also from the Pacific, is paler pink and mild in flavor. Available whole, or as steaks, fillets, or chunks. May be broiled, baked, steamed, fried, or

(continued)

(Varieties of fish, continued)

braised. King salmon is available April through October; Atlantic, July to December.

Sea bass. The *common* or *black sea bass* ranges from 1 to 5 pounds. The *white sea bass* caught along the California coast is not a true bass. Sea bass is sold whole or sometimes cut into steaks or fillets. Black bass is available all year.

Sea trout. In the sea trout family are the *gray sea trout* or *weakfish,* the *spotted weakfish* or *speckled trout,* and the *white weakfish* or *sand trout.* Weakfish does not imply fragility, but tenderness of flesh. The smaller fish are sold whole and the larger ones are cut into steaks or filleted. Available all year.

Shad. Native to Europe and the Atlantic coast, shad was transplanted in 1870 to the Pacific, where it has flourished. Shad has such an intricate bone structure that boned fillets are the most desirable for general use. It is also sold whole, but great care must be taken in removing the bones. The roe of the shad is greatly prized. In season from January to May.

Smelt. Related to the salmon, this small fish is a migrating saltwater fish found in the oceans and rivers. Some species can be oily or may absorb unpleasant flavors from rivers. They may be fried very crisp with the bones left in, or bones removed. Available September through April.

Sole. There is no genuine sole in North American waters. It must be imported from England, Belgium, and Denmark. The *English* or *Dover sole* is considered the finest.

Striped bass. Also known as *rockfish,* this delicious fish grows to a huge size, but the usual market size is 2 to 25 pounds (0.9–12.7 kg). It comes to market whole or in steaks or fillets. Available all year.

Swordfish. This fine game fish is caught in most coastal waters around the world. The meat, firm and well flavored, is generally sold in steaks that can be broiled, baked, or sautéed. The flesh tends to be dry if not basted during cooking. Available April through August from the Atlantic; September through November from the Pacific.

Trout. There are many varieties of trout in this highly prized food and sportfish family. Among them are *brook trout, rainbow*

The chart for broiling *whole dressed fish* calls for broiling on both sides except for flatfish (flounder, fluke, sole). Follow the chart until you know your way around the risks of overcooking, and then you may choose to broil whole dressed fish without turning them. It is not a must. Preheat the broiler to 550°F (288°C). Place the fish on a foil sheet in the pan. Brush with oil. Add a cup (240 ml) of water to the pan to provide moisture during cooking.

Broiling Whole Dressed Fish

Name of fish	Distance from source of heat (in inches)	Time on 1st side (in minutes)	Time on 2nd side (in minutes)
Bluefish	3	4	5
Butterfish	3	4	5
Carp, up to 3 lbs. (1.4 kg)	6	12	14
Cisco (lake herring)	6	4	5
Croaker	6	5	8
Flounder	3	10	
Fluke	3	8	
Mackerel	6	3	5
Mullet	6	5	9
Pike	6	5	8
Porgy	3	3	6
Rockfish	6	5	6
Sea bass	6	5	6
Weakfish (sea trout)	6	3	5
Whitefish	6	5	8
Whiting	6	4	5

STRIPED BASS

BAKING: Fish should be baked with the head on. If it is removed before cooking, the flesh at the cut end will dry and toughen. More importantly, the head seals in the juices to maintain flavor and hastens cooking time. You must know the *exact* weight of the fish, because this determines cooking time. If you don't have a kitchen scale, get one or find out the exact weight from your fish dealer. The oven should be preheated to 400°F (204°C), moderately hot. If you doubt your oven, use a cooking thermometer, because it is important that the temperature be constant. Do not slash the fish; this causes loss of juices and flavor. Add a cup or two (240–480 ml) of water to the baking pan to maintain moisture during baking. Some people like to brush the fish with oil before baking, but it is not necessary and adds calories. If the fish will be in the oven for a prolonged period, baste once or twice with pan juices. Follow directions in the baking chart. If you find you must bake a headless fish, you will see that it takes longer than with the head on. Here is where it will be necessary to rely on the translucency test.

Baking Fish

Name of fish	Thickness (in inches)	Baking time, head on (in minutes)
Small fish		
Bluefish	1½	1½ per oz.
Butterfish	½	3 per oz.
Croaker	1½	1½ per oz.
Flounder	1	2 per oz.
Herring	1	1½ per oz.
Mackerel	2½	2 per oz.
Pike	2¼	1¼ per oz.
Porgy	2	1 per oz.
Rockfish	1½	1⅔ per oz.
Sea bass	1½	1⅔ per oz.
Mullet	2	1½ per oz.
Weakfish (sea trout)	1½	1⅔ per oz.
Whiting	2	1¼ per oz.
Large fish or pieces		
Carp	2½	12 per lb.
Cod	2¾	9 per lb.
Florida mackerel	2½	17 per lb.
Haddock	3¼	10 per lb.
Halibut	2¾	
Salmon	2¼	
Sea trout	3½	14 per lb.
Striped bass	2½	12 per lb.
Whitefish	1½	15 per lb.

trout, *steelhead trout,* and *Dolly Varden,* all delicious and well meated. Brook trout is considered one of the best. The smaller ones can be fried whole. They may also be baked, broiled, or poached. Available all year.

Tuna. Caught on both coasts, some varieties of tuna can weigh 4 pounds (1.8 kg) and others up to 1,000 pounds (454 kg). The *albacore,* or *bonito,* has white meat. The others are not so white, varying from an amber to a purply red. Available occasionally fresh, although most is canned. The fish is sold whole, in steaks, and in fillets. It can be grilled, baked, sautéed, or poached.

Whitebait. These minnowlike fish from the Atlantic provide good eating. They should be soaked in ice water for a couple of hours, drained on a towel, rolled in cornmeal, and fried quickly in oil.

Whiting. Also known as *silver hake,* whiting is a member of the cod family. The flesh is white and delicately flavored. Whiting is available whole or as fillets and is on the market all year. May be prepared in any manner.

Yellow perch. Some consider this the best of all freshwater fish. The fish averages under a pound (454 g). Avoid those longer than 14 inches (35.6 cm); they tend to be bony, with inferior-quality flesh. They may be broiled, deep fried, or sautéed. They come to market whole or filleted. Available all year.

Watch the fish in the oven!

Firmly fleshed fish like red snapper and striped bass take a little longer to cook than soft-fleshed fish like white hake, flounder, and whiting. It is imperative, if you are looking for perfectly cooked fish, to become familiar with the translucency-opacity test for "doneness."

Another consideration is that fish are fatter or leaner depending on the season of the year. Lean-meated and soft-fleshed fish as a rule will come to "doneness" faster than fish of higher fat content. Always be ready to ignore the clock and check a minute or so ahead of time to prevent overcooking.

Sauté Meunière

Sauté meunière is a popular method of cooking fish. It must be avoided, sadly, by those who have to watch their calorie and fat intakes. But for those whose health permits them to fly before the wind gastronomically, it is a lip-smacking treat.

Season the fish or shellfish, dust lightly with flour, and place in a skillet in which you have heated a generous amount of butter to a point below burning. Sauté until lightly browned on one side, then turn and do the other side. Remove the fish or shellfish to a heated plate. Squeeze a few drops of lemon juice over it and sprinkle with parsley. Melt some extra butter in the pan and pour it over the fish. Serve at once.

POACHING: Poaching and simmering mean the same thing. The idea is to keep the water temperature just below the boiling level. Tiny bubbles are what we are looking for. Simply place the fish, in whatever form, in hot liquid deep enough to slightly cover the fish. When the water returns to a simmer, cook for 8 to 10 minutes. Rely on the translucency test for exact poaching time. Another method is to place the fish with a little salt, onion, and celery in a watertight foil package and simmer it for 10 minutes if the fish is about an inch (2.54 cm) thick or for about 8 minutes if the fish is about ¾ inch (1.9 cm) thick. Smoked cod fillet is delicious poached in milk rather than in water.

STEAMING: If you don't have a steamer, improvise one by using anything handy to keep the fish above the water during the steaming process. A platter propped up by two glasses in a large roasting pan with a cover does nicely. Wrap the fish in cheesecloth to facilitate handling. Put about an inch (2.54 cm) or less of water in the bottom of the pot and bring it to a boil. Place the fish in the upper part of the steamer or suspended above the water. It must not touch the water. Cover tightly, and when you hear the steam again, count cooking time as for poaching.

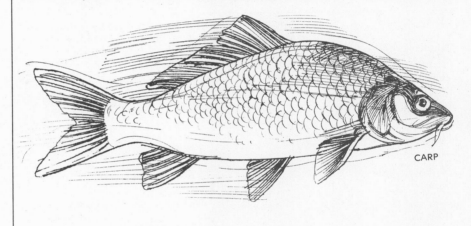

CARP

Most Common American Fish				
Most common name	**Other names**	**Main producing areas**	**Weight (lbs.)**	**Fat or lean**
Barracuda, California		Pacific	3 to 6	Lean
Bass (*See* Sea Bass, etc.)				
Bluefish		Atlantic, Gulf	1 to 7	Lean
Buffalofish	Winter Carp	Lakes, rivers	3 to 25	Lean
Butterfish	Harvestfish, California Pompano	Atlantic, Pacific	¼ to 1	Fat
Carp	Summer or German Carp	Lakes, rivers	2 to 8	Lean
Catfish and Bullheads		Lakes, rivers	1 to 40	Lean
Chub	Longjaw, Blackfin, Bluefin	Great Lakes	3 to 8 per lb.	Fat
Cod		Atlantic, Pacific	1½ to 10	Lean
Croaker	Hardhead, Tomcod	Atlantic, Pacific	½ to 2	Lean
Drum				
Black	Oystercracker, Oyster or Sea Drum	Atlantic, Gulf	1 to 40	Lean
Red	Redfish, Channel Bass	Atlantic, Gulf	2 to 25	Lean

Most Common American Fish

Most common name	Other names	Main producing areas	Weight (lbs.)	Fat or lean
Eels		Atlantic	1 to 5	Fat
Flounders				
Blackback	Winter Flounder	Atlantic	¾ to 2	Lean
Dab	Sand Dab, Sea Dab	Atlantic, Pacific	¾ to 2½	Lean
Fluke	Summer Flounder	Atlantic	2 to 12	Lean
Gray Sole		Atlantic	¾ to 4	Lean
Lemon Sole		Atlantic	¾ to 4	Lean
Southern		Atlantic, Gulf	2 to 12	Lean
Yellowtail	Rusty Dab	Atlantic	¾ to 2	Lean
Sole (Not a true Sole)				
California	Common Sole, Pointed Nose Sole	Pacific	1 to 4	Lean
Fringe	Spotted Flounder, Sand Sole	Pacific	1 to 5	Lean
Petrale	Round Nosed Sole over 5 lbs.	Pacific	5+	Lean
Rex		Pacific	1 to 2	Lean
Round Nosed	English Sole, Jordan's Flounder	Pacific	1 to 5	Lean
Gaspergeau	Sheepshead	Gulf	¾ to 10	Lean
Grouper	Red, Nassau, Yellowfish, Black and Gag Grouper	Gulf, Atlantic	5 to 12	Lean
Haddock		Atlantic	1½ to 7	Lean
Hake				
Red		Atlantic	2 to 5	Lean
White	Common, Squirrel	Atlantic	2 to 5	Lean
Halibut		Atlantic, Pacific	5 to 75+	Lean
King Mackerel	Kingfish, Cero	Atlantic, Gulf	5 to 20	Fat
Kingfish	King Whiting, Whiting	Atlantic, Gulf	¾ to 3	Lean
Lake Herring	Cisco, Bluefin	Great Lakes	⅓ to 1	Lean
Lake Trout		Great Lakes	1½ to 10+	Fat
Lingcod	Cultus Cod, Greenling, Blue Cod	Pacific	3 to 20	Lean
Mackerel	Common, Boston	Atlantic	½ to 2½	Fat
Mullet	Striped, Silver, Jumping	Atlantic, Gulf	½ to 3	Lean
Ocean Perch	Rosefish, Redfish, Red Perch	Atlantic, Pacific	½ to 2	Lean
Pickerel	Jack, Grass Pike, Northern Pike	Great Lakes, rivers	2 to 10	Lean
Pollock	Boston Bluefish	Atlantic	1½ to 12	Lean
Pompano	(California Pompano is actually a Butterfish)	Gulf	½ to 3½	Fat
Porgy	Scup	Atlantic	½ to 1½	Lean
Rockfish (*See* Striped Bass)				
Chilipepper	Red Rock Cod	Pacific	2 to 5	Lean
Bocaccio	Rock Cod, Grouper	Pacific	2 to 5	Lean
Black	Bluefish, Priestfish	Pacific	2 to 5	Lean
Rockfish	(Several other species are called simply "Rockfish")	Pacific	2 to 5	Lean
Sablefish	Black Cod, Coal Fish	Pacific	3 to 15	Fat

(continued)

Most Common American Fish

Most common name	Other names	Main producing areas	Weight (lbs.)	Fat or lean
Salmon				
Atlantic		Atlantic	5 to 10	Fat
Chinook	King Salmon	Pacific	5 to 30	Fat
Silver	Coho	Pacific	5 to 18	Fat
Steelhead	(Not a true salmon, but a sea-run Rainbow Trout)	Pacific	5 to 30	Fat
Sauger	Sand Pike	Great Lakes	1 to 1½	Lean
Scup (*See* Porgy)				
Sea Bass				
Black	Giant Bass	Pacific	60 to 600+	Lean
Common	Black Sea Bass, Blackfish	Atlantic	½ to 4	Lean
Kelp	Rock Bass, Sand Bass, Cabrilla	Pacific	1 to 5	Lean
White	(Related to Atlantic Weakfish or Sea Trout. Not a true Bass)	Pacific	15 to 20+	Lean
Sea Trout (Weakfish)				
Gray		Atlantic	1 to 6	Lean
Spotted	Speckled Trout	Atlantic, Gulf	1 to 4	Lean
White	Sand Trout	Gulf	½ to 1½	Lean
Shad		Atlantic, Pacific	1½ to 5	Fat
Sheepshead	Freshwater Drum, Gaspergeau	Lakes, rivers	1½ to 5	Lean
Smelt				
Atlantic Smelt	Capelin	Atlantic, Great Lakes	1 to 2 ozs.	Lean
Eulachon	Candlefish, Hooligan, Smelt	Pacific	1¼ to 2 ozs.	Fat
Jack Smelt	Silver or California Smelt	Pacific	2 to 4 ozs.	Lean
Bay Smelt	Least or Little Smelt	Pacific	1 to 2 ozs.	Lean
Snapper, Red	Redfish	Gulf	1½ to 10	Lean
Spanish Mackerel	Florida Mackerel	Atlantic, Gulf	1 to 4	Fat
Spot	Goody, Lafayette, Roach, Chub	Atlantic	¼ to 1¼	Lean
Striped Bass	Rockfish	Atlantic, Pacific	2 to 25+	Lean
Suckers	Mullet, Redfin	Lakes, rivers	1½ to 6	Lean
Swordfish	Broadbill	Atlantic, Pacific	50 to 400+	Lean
Tilefish		Atlantic	5 to 30	Lean
Trout, Rainbow	(Common commercial variety)	Hatchery raised	⅓ to 2	Fat
Trout	(Numerous sportfishing species)	Streams, rivers	⅓ to 15+	Fat
Tuna				
Albacore	Longfin Tuna	Pacific	15 to 25	Fat
Bluefish	Horsemackerel	Atlantic	75 to 1000	Fat
Little	Bonito, Albacore	Atlantic	4 to 10	Fat
Turbot	(European fish. Not sold in U.S. Pseudo specimens offered here.)			
Weakfish (*See* Sea Trout)				
Whitefish		Great Lakes	1½ to 6	Fat
Whiting	Silver Hake	Atlantic	¾ to 3	Lean
Yellow Perch	Lake Perch	Lakes, rivers	½ to ¾	Lean
Yellow Pike	Pike Perch, Walleye	Lakes	1½ to 4	Lean

SHELLFISH

Fish eaters are, as a matter of course, shellfish enthusiasts, but many people who do not eat fish will avidly seek out shellfish. The mere thought of the tender and tasty morsel offered by the clam, crab, lobster, scallop, or oyster will make fish eaters salivate. Hardship cases will often drive hundreds of miles for a good fresh clam or oyster fix. Once you obtain your shellfish, keep in mind that you have an extremely perishable product, particularly when the weather is hot. You have to exercise more than ordinary precaution to keep it alive and/or fresh until eating time. Keep it cold; a temperature of 32°F (0°C) and a moist atmosphere are most desirable.

Don't try to keep shellfish alive in a tub of water, thinking they will stay fresher. It will kill them. If the weather is very warm and humid, circulating air is a necessity; a fan must be used or the mortality rate will climb. Don't try to keep lobsters and crabs more than 24 hours (unless you capture them yourself, of course), and soft crabs should be eaten as soon as possible. The strength of soft crabs is at its lowest ebb after the laborious molting process, and they do not have the vitality they possess when they wear their hard shells.

People who enjoy gathering their own shellfish should exercise great caution about where they do their gathering. In this day of polluted waters, shellfish should be taken only from areas that have been certified as safe for swimming. It is always advisable to check with town authorities before embarking on a shellfishing expedition, not only for health reasons, but also because many towns jealously guard all their shellfish assets and forbid unlicensed interlopers. Commercial shellfish harvesting is permitted, of course, only in areas where the waters are unpolluted.

How much shellfish to buy. An average appetite could be satisfied with about ½ pound of shellfish meat; smaller appetites take less. But since so much of the weight of shellfish is in the part that is discarded, it is something of a challenge to figure correct amounts. The following table shows the percentage of edible flesh present in shellfish.

Oysters yesterday and today

Oysters have been prized and enjoyed since the beginning of time. The ancient Greeks and Romans doted on them, and as early as 100 B.C. the Romans established oyster beds to guarantee a dependable source of supply.

The American Indians were eating oysters before the colonists arrived, and the mollusks were enthusiastically made an important part of the early settlers' diet. They found the coast lines laden with oysters.

By the mid-nineteenth century in the United States, oysters had become a national passion as well as a status symbol, like champagne and terrapin. Even before railroads, oyster expresses from Baltimore rushed great Chesapeake Bay oysters across the Alleghenies deep into inland settlements. Every eastern city had oyster houses, and oyster peddlers hawked their wares in the streets. Earlier, in the 1840s, there were eating places that served all the oysters you could eat for six cents, a mind-boggling thought today, with the cost of oysters spiraling up in the direction of Beluga caviar. However, it was rumored that owners of the oyster emporiums would slip a bad oyster into a plate to keep the customer from eating too many. In any event, oysters in every form—raw, pickled, fried, scalloped—were eaten by the millions.

A now-famous concoction of oysters baked with spinach and bacon was created at Antoine's, the famous New Orleans restaurant, at the turn of the century. The story goes (and it may be apocryphal) that a patron on tasting it approvingly said, "It's as rich as Rockefeller." And so the dish "oysters Rockefeller" was born.

Changing biological and ecological conditions have greatly thinned out the nation's oyster beds, but new efforts and research are being directed toward restoring the industry.

Bill Johnston's Manhattan clam chowder

36 large chowder clams (quahogs) or 2 cans (7 to 8 ounces each) minced clams
4 tablespoons (½ stick) sweet butter
1 large onion, diced (1 cup)
1½ cups diced potatoes (2 medium)
1 cup diced celery
¾ cup diced carrots (2 medium)
¼ cup diced green pepper
1 can (2 pounds, 3 ounces) Italian-style plum tomatoes, drained
1½ teaspoons leaf thyme, crumbled
¼ teaspoon white pepper
⅛ teaspoon curry powder

Shuck the clams; reserve the broth. Chop the clams coarsely (if using canned clams, drain and reserve the broth). Broth from the clams should measure 2 cups; if not, add water or bottled clam broth.

Melt the butter in a large saucepan. Sauté the onions until lightly browned.

Add the remaining ingredients and extra water, if needed, to cover vegetables. Bring to a boil; lower the heat, cover, and simmer 30 minutes, or just until the vegetables are tender.

Add the fresh or canned clams; turn off the heat; cover and let stand 2 minutes, or just until the clams are thoroughly hot. Serve with warm buttered pilot crackers, if you wish.

Serves 6. This recipe was adapted with permission from *Family Circle* magazine.

Percentage of Edible Flesh in Shellfish

Market form	Where found	% Edible flesh
Uncooked		
Clams		
Hard	New England	14.5
	Chesapeake	10.0
	Middle Atlantic	14.0
	South Atlantic	9.5
	Pacific	25.0
Soft	New England	22.7
	Chesapeake	18.5
Surf	Middle Atlantic	20.0
Oysters		
Eastern	New England, Middle Atlantic	11.0
	South Atlantic	6.3
	Gulf	6.5
Pacific		11.3
Mussels	Atlantic and Pacific	17.0
Cooked in shell		
Crabs		
Hard	Atlantic and Gulf	10 to 18
Soft	Atlantic and Gulf	90
Dungeness	Pacific	22 to 26
Lobsters	New England	35 to 37
Shucked		
Clams, oysters, bay and sea scallops		100
Shrimp, in shell	South Atlantic, Gulf	50 to 60
Cooked meat		
Crabs, lobsters, shrimp		100

CLAMS

Many species of clams are found in the tidal flats of America's vast coastline, with every region having its own particular varieties. They can be purchased alive in the shell or as freshly shucked meats in their own juices. They may be served raw on the half shell with lemon juice and spicy sauce or cooked in countless ways, one of the most popular being as the main ingredient in steaming chowder.

Peak season. Available all year.

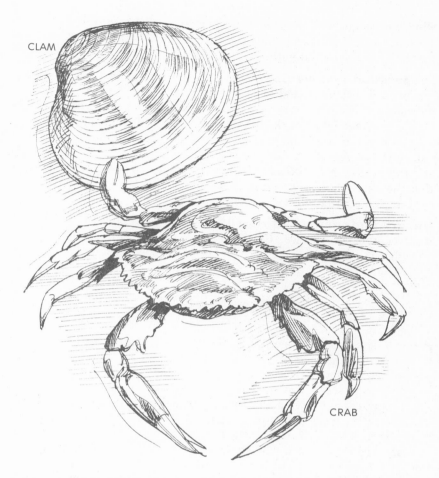

CLAM

CRAB

Amount to buy. You can buy clams in the shell by the pound, or shucked clams by the quart (960 ml). For steamed clams, figure on about 20 per person. Two dozen small hard-shelled clams will serve 4 to 6 as an appetizer. Large hard-shelled clams are used in chowder and other recipes. For 6 main-dish portions you will need about a quart (960 ml) of shucked clams. It takes approximately 8 quarts (7.7 l) of clams in the shell to yield about 1 quart (960 ml) of shucked clams.

Varieties. There are two basic types: hard shelled and soft shelled. Large hard-shelled clams are sometimes called "quahogs" and are used for chowders. The small ones are littlenecks; the medium size, cherrystones. These are served raw on the half shell, or broiled or baked. Soft-shelled clams are used for steaming.

Selection. Look for clam meats that are plump, moist, and glistening. Color will vary from grayish green to beige to a light or dark orange, according to locality. There should be little or no free liquid in a container of freshly shucked clams. They should have a fresh odor and be free of shell particles. When purchased in the shell, shells should be tightly closed or tighten immediately when tapped. Unless the shells have been scrubbed, there may be a slight off odor, but it will be a "good" one of the bottom mud, and not unpleasant.

Opening clams

Use a regular clam or oyster knife; don't try it with a kitchen knife unless you are an expert. Very cold clams will open more easily. The cold relaxes the muscle that clamps the shells together. Clams and oysters that won't yield readily should be "billed." ("Billing" is simply breaking off an edge with pliers or a hammer to permit easier entry for the knife.)

To open a clam, take it in your left palm (if right-handed) with the thickest part of the clam hinge nestled against the flesh pad at the base of the thumb. Place the knife in a likely looking spot between the shells and grasp it firmly with the fingers of the left hand. Close the left hand, pressing the blade into the opening as if your hand were a vise. If the knife slips, your fingers will contact the clam with no harm done. With the blade between the shells as deep as you can press it, twist it with your other hand to force the shells apart. Run the knife around to the back hinge, riding it against the top shell to cut through the muscle attachment. Cut the muscle at the other side of the top shell. Repeat the process with the bottom shell. To save the juice, open the clams over a large pot.

White clam sauce

To make a great white clam sauce for spaghetti, use small tender clams if you can (otherwise chop up large clam meats) and retain all the juice when they are opened. Fifteen to 20 "littlenecks" (smallest of the East Coast hard-shelled clams) make an ideal portion for one serving, and they don't have to be chopped. Cover the bottom of a heavy skillet with good olive oil and heat slowly. When hot, add 4 garlic cloves and sauté until golden brown. Discard the garlic. Add the clam juice and (for two) about 1 teaspoon of crushed garlic and some chopped parsley. Simmer the juice, garlic, and parsley for 10 to 15 minutes. (Don't reduce the liquid too much or it will be too salty.) As you set the spaghetti on the table, pop the clam meats into the pan. Stir them around for about 2 minutes, no more. Don't heat the meats until they start to contract. Pour over the spaghetti and serve. (If the heat is turned off under the skillet when the clam meats are added, there will be less danger of overcooking the clam meats.) Serve with freshly grated Parmesan cheese.

A big family

Various regions of the United States have their own particular type of crab. The dungeness (pronounce the G as in George), with its fine, meaty claws and lump crab meat in the back, is taken from Pacific waters. It is much larger than the blue crab, weighing up to 3½ pounds. Rock crab and Jonah crab are caught off New England and California shores, and the blue crab flourishes in the Atlantic and Gulf regions. Stone crabs are found mostly in Florida. The Alaskan king crab from the North Pacific is named for its great size; it can weigh up to 20 pounds. And then there is the tanner crab, red crab, green crab, lady crab (also known as "sand" or "calico crab"), and more. Most of these are available fresh only in their local areas.

A special talent

Stone crabs are unique. Only the large claws are used. They are broken off the live crabs which are then returned to the sea, where they obligingly grow a brand new set. An enviable ability, to be sure.

Can this crab be saved?

If you are about to clean a soft-shelled crab that shows no sign of life, you can make a simple test to determine whether or not it is safe to use. Lift the back shell and sniff the gill area. If it smells the same as a live crab, it can be used. If it smells sour or "off," discard it.

When preparing soft-shelled crabs and you find one with a back shell that has stiffened and seems inedible, don't discard the crab. Tear off the back shell and go ahead with the cooking. After dipping in batter or breading, the absence will not be noticed and you will have gotten your money's worth.

Hard shells into soft shells

When a crabber sees a blue crab about to shed its shell, he puts the so-called peeler in a special float until the molting process has taken place. The crab is then kept in the water for another hour to give the new shell time to harden a bit so the crab can be shipped. The whole process takes about 6 or 8 hours, during which time the crabber keeps a fairly close watch over his charges.

Storage. Good-quality clams will keep well in the refrigerator for a week or more if necessary, but there will be a gradual loss of flavor. It is better if they are used within a day or two.

Preparation and serving. Clams can be sandy, so they should be scrubbed well and soaked in salt water—⅓ cup (79.5 ml) of salt to a gallon (3.8 l) of cold water—for 20 minutes to draw out the sand. Clams should be steamed or cooked in a covered pot with a small amount of water only until they open—5 to 10 minutes—and no longer, or they will toughen. Add them as the last ingredient in chowders and stews, shutting off the heat the instant they are added to the pot. Remember that they are edible raw and they need warming and not cooking. Discard any clams that do not open in cooking.

Dietary information. Three-and-one-half ounces (100 g) of raw clam meat contain 82 calories. Clams are high in protein, potassium, and phosphorus.

CRABS

Fresh cooked crabs or live crabs are not easily come by unless you live in a major metropolitan marketing area or fairly close to the natural habitat of the crab. Only those who live near crabbing waters seem to know and relish hard-shell crabs in their natural state. They have a short shelf life and must be frozen to travel. Consequently, most people take their crab in the form of fresh crab meat, or they use frozen or canned.

Crabs are either hard shelled or soft shelled. The soft-shelled crab that is eaten shell and all is not a separate species; it is the blue, or common crab that has molted and not yet grown its new shell.

FRESH CRAB MEAT

Cooked fresh crab meat, picked from the shell, is available in specialty fish stores and is sold by the pound (454 g). It comes packed in tins.

Amount to buy. One pound (454 g)—or about 3 cups (720 ml)—will provide 3 to 4 main-course portions or 6 to 8 appetizer portions.

Varieties. Fresh-cooked crab meat comes in several grades: lump meat (whole lumps from the large body muscles), flake meat (small pieces of white meat), combination of lump meat and flake meat, and claw meat of a brownish color. The lump meat is distinguished for its spendid, firm lumps of crab without stiff tendons or bits of shell. It is the best and, as you might expect, the most expensive.

Selection. How you plan to use it (and the state of your budget) will determine which grade you will want to buy. The lump meat is superb for seafood cocktails and salads where appearance and texture will be apparent. For crab cakes or similar preparations, lesser grades can be used.

Storage. Fresh crab meat must always be kept under refrigeration and eaten the day of purchase. It discolors and becomes yellowish as it ages.

Preparation and serving. Crab meat must be picked over carefully to remove stiff tendons and bits of shell. It is ready to be served as it comes from the can, cold with mayonnaise, or in a soufflé or casserole, deviled, or made into crab cakes. Fresh crab meat is easily ruined by overcooking and must be handled gently if sautéed.

Dietary information. Fresh crab meat contains 93 calories in 3½ ounces (100 g) and is high in protein, calcium, phosphorus, vitamin A, and one of the B vitamins.

HARD-SHELLED CRABS

Live, hard-shelled crabs are unknown in many parts of the country since they are sold only in areas where they are caught. East, West, and Gulf Coast crabs are marketed as hard-shelled crabs.

Peak season. Available all year but most plentiful in the summer.

Amount to buy. The number you need will depend upon the weight of the crabs. The only edible parts are the meat in the claws and in the body shell. Allow at least 10 ounces (284 g) of prepared crab per serving.

Selection. Crabs are sometimes available in the fish market already cooked and prepared. If buying a fresh crab, make sure it has both claws and is heavy for its size. Hard-shelled crabs should be alive and active before they are cooked.

Storage. Crabs should be used the day of purchase.

Preparation and serving. Grasp the crab with tongs and rinse it under cold water. Plunge it headfirst into boiling, salted water to which you have added the juice of ½ lemon, a bay leaf, a few sprigs of parsley, and 5 or 6 peppercorns. Boiling time will depend on the size of the crab, but they cook quickly. A 2½- to 3-pound (1.1–1.4 kg) crab will cook in 15 to 20 minutes. As soon as they turn bright red they are done. To eat immediately, cool the crab with cold water for comfortable handling. Snap off the claws and crack them open, reserving them for later eating. Unless you have a sizable crab, break off and discard the legs. With a sturdy thumbnail or knife tip, dig under the edge of the back shell and lift it off. Scrape away the spongy gill tissue at the sides and remove the soft entrails. This is done most easily under running water, but some flavor will be lost. Remove all visible crab meat, scraping it from the shell with a spoon. The backfin lumps are the choicest.

Dietary information. *See* Fresh Crab Meat.

SOFT-SHELLED CRABS

Most soft-shelled crabs are blue crabs that have bright blue claws before they are cooked and are found all along the Atlantic coast. Fishermen take them from the water just after they have molted their hard shells in the annual growth process, and before the new shell has begun to harden. They are completely edible after they have been cleaned and cooked.

Peak season. May through September.

Crab Cakes with mustard sauce

1 pound fresh lump crab meat
1 egg
½ cup mayonnaise
¼ cup minced scallions
2 tablespoons finely minced celery
1 teaspoon Worcestershire sauce
1 tablespoon lemon juice
2 slices white bread, crust removed
1 egg white
2 tablespoons water
½ cup all-purpose flour
½ cup bread crumbs
½ cup cooking oil

Beat the egg lightly and combine with the crab meat. Add the mayonnaise, scallions, celery, Worcestershire sauce, and lemon juice and mix carefully so you don't break up the crab lumps completely. Crumble the bread fine and add to the crab mixture. Form into 16 small balls about the size of a large walnut (as an appetizer) or 8 larger ones (as a main course).

Beat the egg white to a froth and add the water. Place a mound of flour on one square of waxed paper and a mound of bread crumbs on another. Dip the crab cakes lightly into the flour, then egg white, then crumbs. Refrigerate until time to cook. Then heat the oil in a heavy skillet and brown the cakes quickly on all sides. Add more oil if needed. Serve with mustard sauce (below). Serves 8 as appetizer, 4 as main course.

Mustard sauce

2 tablespoons butter or margarine
2 tablespoons all-purpose flour
1 cup milk
½ cup chicken broth
2 tablespoons prepared mustard
1½ tablespoons Worcestershire sauce
1 teaspoon grated onion
Freshly ground pepper

In a small saucepan melt the butter, blend in the flour, and slowly stir in the milk, beating with a wire whisk. Reduce the heat and mix in the chicken broth. Add the remaining ingredients and cook for 2 or 3 minutes over low heat, beating with a wire whisk until the sauce is smooth and thickened. (Use a mild mustard—not a strong Dijon type—so the sauce will not overpower the taste of the crab meat.) Keep the sauce warm until ready to serve, but do not let it boil. If it gets too thick (it should be the consistency of heavy cream), thin it out with a tablespoon or so of consommé. Yields 1½ cups.

Where have the frogs gone?

People who dote on frog's legs probably wonder. There are a number of reasons for the decline in numbers of these pop-eyed little creatures, the biggest of which might weigh as much as 5 pounds, although the average is about 1 pound. First, frogs are hard to raise domestically. Like some people, frogs are finicky eaters. And there has been a sizable decrease in swamplands. Thousands of acres have been drained by irrigation projects that dried up both the land and the wildlife in it. As an example, in 1936 Louisiana sold more than 2½ million pounds of frogs for frog's legs, and about 30 years later it sold less than 42,000 pounds. This decrease was because of lack of supply, not demand.

The French, who have a particular fondness for *cuisses de grenouilles* (frog's legs), get theirs from a number of sources, including the Danube delta. The United States has acquired frogs mostly from Japan.

Prices have more than doubled over the last few years. In 1938 Louisiana bullfrogs sold for 2½ cents a pound, but science and research laboratories need them and they have bid the price up to about 80 cents.

Amount to buy. Two or three soft-shelled crabs will generally do for a serving, although a hearty eater could eat double or more that number.

Selection. Soft-shelled crabs are usually available in the market cleaned and ready for cooking. If they have not been cleaned and prepared, they should be alive when you buy them and alive when you place them in your refrigerator. The smaller they are, the more tender.

Preparation and serving. To prepare soft-shelled crabs, wash them in several waters. Place the live crab on a board, face down. Make an incision just behind the eyes and cut out the face. Place your thumb and index finger in the spot where the eyes were and squeeze them together. This will pop out the bubble of bitter fluid that the crab spurts at enemies when attacked. Lift the tapering points on each side of the back shell and remove the sandbag and spongy gills. Turn the crab on its back and remove the small pointed apron at the lower part of the shell. The crab is now completely edible.

The best cooking method for soft-shelled crabs is sautéing or broiling, although they can be deep fried. Brush them with melted butter or margarine, dust them lightly with good, unseasoned bread crumbs, and fry them or broil them. In either case, just a light browning is required—2 to 3 minutes on each side for smaller crabs and 3 or 4 minutes for larger ones. Serve with lemon wedges and tartar sauce.

FROG'S LEGS

Fresh frog's legs are in short supply commercially, but are available if you happen to live near a frog farm or catch your own. The edible species include the common bullfrog, largest of the species, and the green frog, the southern bullfrog, the leopard frog, and the pickerel frog. Frogs are more numerous in the southern states, particularly Florida and Louisiana, than in the north. They are a delicious morsel, resembling tender chicken in texture and flavor. The smaller legs are the most tender.

Amount to buy. You will need from 3 to 6 or more frog's legs per serving, depending on size.

Storage. Refrigerate and use within a day.

Preparation and serving. Frog's legs are usually bought skinned and ready to use. If the frogs are not prepared, cut off the hind legs close to the body. These are the only parts of the frog that are used. Wash them in very cold water and chill; then strip off the skin, beginning at the top. Dry them thoroughly, dust lightly with flour, and sauté them in hot fat as you would shellfish meats. Turn them carefully and frequently as they cook to prevent sticking. They cook quickly, 6 to 8 minutes. Lemon, salt, pepper, chopped parsley, and a generous amount of garlic to zip up the flavor (frog's legs can be bland) are usual additives when preparing sautéed frog's legs.

Dietary information. There are 73 calories in 3½ ounces (100 g) of uncooked frog's legs. They are high in protein, minerals, and one of the B vitamins.

LOBSTERS

Lobster is one of the most popular of all shellfish delicacies, with a world-wide demand that exceeds supply. They are often sold ready cooked, which must take second place to being alive when bought and prepared in your own kitchen. Taken fresh from a trap at sea, a lobster can be plunged into boiling sea water and be ready to eat in 3 to 4 minutes after the water has returned to a boil. This bit of information is offered by way of warning not to cook lobsters too long. This applies also to spiny lobsters, crayfish, crawfish, or any other members of the family.

Peak season. May, June, and September through December are prime season for lobsters, although they are available all year. They shed their shells for growth purposes in July and August. The "new shells," as they are called by lobstermen, are not as fully packed with meat, and consequently hard-shelled, full-meated lobsters are even more expensive during July and August.

Amount to buy. A lobster weighing from 1 to 1½ pounds (454 to 681g) is generally adequate for one serving. It is difficult to be precise about how much to buy, since a hungry trencherman would have no trouble with a 3- or 4-pounder (1.4–1.8 kg). In most cases, the weight and number of lobsters needed are dictated by purse and appetite, in that order.

Varieties. The northern or Maine lobster is dark greenish blue, mottled with reddish orange or brown. It turns bright red when cooked. Lobsters range in size from the 1-pound (454 g) chicken lobster to the 2½- to 4-pound (1.1 to 1.8 kg) "jumbos."

Selection. Be sure you are buying a live lobster. It will move its legs and its tail will curl under its body when it is picked up. If the tail hangs flaccid and loose, the lobster is undoubtedly dead.

Storage. Cook soon after purchase. Do not store.

What size lobster?

Large lobsters are scarce now, but when they were plentiful people believed that any lobster over 5 pounds was tough. The big ones ended up in Chinese restaurants. A few hundred years earlier even the Plymouth colonists could hardly gather up the courage to eat the great, formidable-looking clawed lobsters that washed up on their beaches. However, nothing daunted, the Chinese cooks found that by steaming them they became tender and most palatable for use in sauces and various lobster dishes. Some notable chefs use this cooking method and prefer larger lobsters.

Commercial lobsters come in four sizes, from the 1-pound chicken lobster through medium and large to jumbo, about 4 pounds. The general preference, however, is for lobsters weighing between 1 and 2 pounds.

Never too late

If the lobster shows no movement when cooking time comes, but was alive when placed under refrigeration, go right ahead with the cooking. Texture and flavor may be slightly diminished but will still be acceptable. As with all other fish and shellfish, the loss of body moisture, which is usually the cause of the lobster's demise, is responsible for loss of flavor.

How to eat a lobster

Begin with the premise that it is hard to be neat when eating a lobster, which is why seafood restaurants supply a bib for the procedure and follow it up with a finger bowl.

Equipment and accompaniments should include individual bowls of melted butter or sauce, lemon wedges, a bowl for shell scraps, a nutcracker and nutpick or oyster fork, and lots of paper napkins.

Start by twisting off the claws and tail. Many people eat the meat in the tail first to satisfy the most urgent cravings. Be sure to remove the intestinal tract from the tail. If the tail is split lengthwise down the middle, the tract is easily seen. To remove the meat from the tail, break off the flippers, and with an oyster fork or pick push the meat from the end of the tail where you have broken off the flippers toward the large end. The tail meat should emerge in one piece from the large end. Dip each piece of the lobster meat in the butter or sauce. The tail and two large claws and knuckle meat are the major areas of tender, solid meat, but there is some sweet meat in the small claws and in the general body area that is worth getting at. The small claws may be twisted off the body and the meat sucked out of them.

For the chest meat, pull the body out of the chest shell and discard the feathery gills on the outside of the chest. Be sure to eat the greenish tomalley and the coral roe, if present, or scoop it out and save it to spread on your crusty roll. Break the chest in half, lengthwise, and dig out the tender meat between the cartilage with a nutpick or oyster fork.

Cleaning mussels

Virginia Lee, the widely known cooking expert, suggests the following procedure to facilitate cleaning mussels if time permits: place the mussels in a bucket of cold, salted water as soon as you get them home. Throw in ½ cup or so of cornstarch and a filming of vegetable oil. Allow the mussels to soak for an hour or longer. The mussels will feed on the cornstarch and oil and excrete their dirt and grit. Discard any mussels that float to the top. Rinse the mussels well and scrub them to remove all dirt and proceed with the preparation.

Preparation and serving. Lobsters should be alive when plunged into boiling water. For the squeamish cook, a blow between the lobster's head and tail shells with a heavy cleaver or knife will sever its equivalent of a spinal cord and make it insensitive to the proceedings. Rinse the lobster in cold, running water, grasp it firmly, and plunge it head first into a large pot of boiling, salted water—¼ cup (60 ml) salt to 1 gallon (3.8 l) of water. The lobster should be well covered with water. Don't put more lobsters in the pot than can comfortably fit on the bottom. Cover the pot, return the water to the boil, then reduce the heat and simmer 5 minutes for the first pound (454 g) and 3 minutes more for each additional pound. Remove the lobster from the water and place it on its back. With a heavy knife, helped along with a mallet, if necessary, split from end to end starting at the head. Crack the large claws and split the tail so that the meat can be removed easily at the table. The green material in the body cavity is the liver (tomalley) and the coral substance is roe, if you happen to have a female lobster. Both are edible and delicious, and should not be removed unless you want to put them aside to be used in a sauce or mixed with bread crumbs and seasoning for a stuffing for broiled or baked lobster.

The only inedible part of the lobster is the stomach sac, about 2 inches (5.1 cm) below the head, and the dark intestinal vein that runs down the center and ends at the opening in the tail. These must be removed.

Serve the lobster hot with melted butter and lemon wedges or cold with mayonnaise.

Lobsters may also be broiled, stuffed and baked, or steamed. For steaming, proceed as in directions for steaming fish; allow 18 to 20 minutes for a 1-pounder (454 g) and 5 minutes more for each additional pound. Some experts feel that boiling or steaming a lobster produces the finest result with the least risk of drying out the delicate meat, which can occur when the lobster is baked or broiled.

Dietary information. There are 95 calories in 3½ ounces (100 g) of cooked lobster meat. It is high in protein, minerals, and one of the B vitamins.

MUSSELS

Mussels are one of America's most abundant and unappreciated seafoods and rate more attention on our menus than they get. The ubiquitous blue mussel found on American shores is exactly the same species as *moule*, beloved by the French, and the *cozze* of the Italians, many of whom regard it more highly than any other mollusk. Mussels are sold alive in the shell and, unlike clams and oysters, they are never eaten raw. The meats range in color from a pale tea-with-milk to a deep orange.

Peak season. Available all year.

Amount to buy. Allow about 1 quart (960 ml) of undrained, shucked mussels, or about 3 quarts (2.9 l) of unshucked, for 4 servings.

Selection. Be sure the shells are tightly closed or close immediately when tapped.

Storage. Mussels should be stored in the coldest part of the refrigerator and used within a day of purchase.

Preparation and serving. Mussels are distinguished by the presence of a beard. They may be served either with or without it. Removing the beard is a refinement dictated solely by aesthetics. Prepare the mussels by first scrubbing the shells clean with a stiff brush. Discard any with open or broken shells. You may cut away the beard with a scissors or a sharp knife. Mussels have rough shells to which seaweed and other marine growths cling tightly at times. Some fish experts feel that the shells do not have to be scrubbed too vigorously because this nonforeign matter that clings to them merely adds to the fortitude of the broth. Steam the mussels in a deep, heavy pot containing ½ inch (1.27 cm) of water or white wine that you may wish to season with thyme, bay leaf, and chopped scallions or shallots. Cook, closely covered, over medium heat until the shells open, approximately 6 to 8 minutes. Remove from the heat and strain the broth through cheesecloth. Discard any mussels that have not opened. After steaming, mussels may be removed from the shell, bearded, and served like oysters or clams; or they may be served with a sauce or melted butter, shell and all. Some people use the beard as a handle when they pluck the mussel from the shell and pop it into their mouths. You *must* use your fingers when you separate the shells in eating mussels—there's no other way.

Dietary information. Mussels are high in protein, phosphorus, calcium, iron, and sodium. There are 95 calories in 3½ ounces (100 g) of mussel meat.

OYSTERS

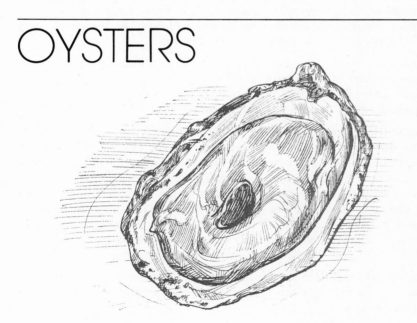

Contrary to folklore that deals with oysters and the necessity of avoiding them during the months that lack the letter *R*, oysters are edible and available all year. Sophisticated methods of cultivation and harvesting have extended their production throughout the 12 months. However, they are at their best from September until the first of May.

Moules Marinière

Probably the most popular mussel dish in American restaurants is *moules marinière* ("mariner's mussels"), a classic French recipe.

1 cup dry white wine
8 tablespoons (1 stick) butter
1 large onion, chopped
1 large garlic clove, crushed
4 parsley sprigs
¼ teaspoon thyme
½ bay leaf
Pinch freshly ground black pepper
2 to 3 quarts mussels, scrubbed and cleaned
½ cup coarsely chopped parsley

Place the white wine, half the butter, onion, garlic, parsley, thyme, bay leaf, and pepper in a large kettle and bring to a boil. Add the mussels to the kettle, cover tightly, and steam over medium heat. Try to shake the kettle a few times (with your hands properly protected, of course) so the mussels change their levels and cook evenly. Cook until the shells open—5 minutes or so. Add the remaining butter and chopped parsley. Taste and correct the seasonings, then serve in large bowls with some of the broth—and be sure you have plenty of warm, crisp French bread or rolls to sop up the broth. Serves 3 to 4.

Mussel upswing

Mussels have always been more popular in Europe than in the United States. In some European countries mussels are raised in huge undersea farms to meet the enormous demand that runs to hundreds of millions of pounds each year. But reports from American fish dealers indicate that the demand for mussels has recently quadrupled, which would put American consumption at about 4 million pounds per year. The increased demand is no doubt due to the astronomical prices of other shellfish. Mussels have more protein than any other shellfish. Both the Atlantic and Pacific coasts could produce much larger quantities of mussels if public demand increased.

To open oysters

"Bill" the oysters by twisting off part of the fragile shell edge with pliers. A hammer can be used, but you may end up breaking off more than just an edge. Hold the oyster in the palm of the left hand (if you are right-handed), deep shell down, and insert the edge of an oyster knife into a likely spot between the shells. Twist it to force the shells apart and run it around to the hinge of the shell. Work over a bowl and strainer to catch the juice. Turn the knife to pry and lift the upper shell sufficiently to insert the knife and cut the hinge muscle. For half-shell eating, serve the oyster in the deep half that will hold the juice more efficiently than the shallow half.

Freezing clams and oysters

If you have more clams and oysters than you need, don't try freezing them for future use. A frozen clam or oyster has about as much character as a banana put through a thresher. The delicate flesh tissue simply breaks down and releases its flavorful moisture, and the texture changes to that of limp mush.

Fried oysters

A product as delicate as an oyster does better in a simple sauté than a thick batter coating and deep frying.

Heat a ¼-inch layer of oil in a large skillet. While it is heating, place ½ cup of unseasoned bread crumbs in a sturdy paper bag and add a cup of oyster meats. Shake well by upending the bag briskly a few times. The crumbs will not adhere as much as a batter coating, but enough will stick for an adequate coat. Add the breaded oysters to the pan when the oil is very hot but before it reaches the smoking stage. The oysters should not touch each other in the pan. A minute or two of frying on each side will be enough to lightly brown the oysters and heat the meats. Serve immediately with lemon wedges and tartar sauce. This may also be done with clam meats. Serves 2.

Almost every state that borders on the sea has an abundance of oysters, and some of the larger inland cities are fortunate enough to have many fine varieties flown in. Oysters vary greatly in size, flavor, texture, and degree of saltiness. Even oysters from the same bay but from different beds can be entirely different. They come in various shades of gray green, off white, and coppery tan, depending on the waters they come from. They can be served raw or cooked, and many people feel there is no finer appetizer in all of gastronomy than a half-dozen succulent oysters on the half shell nestled on a bed of crushed ice.

Amount to buy. Oysters are sold raw by the dozen, in the shell or on the half shell; or shucked, by the pint (480 ml) or quart (960 ml). For 6 main-dish portions you will need from 36 to 48 oysters in the shell, or 1 to 1½ quarts (1.4 l) of shucked oysters. If you are planning to cook them, it is easier to buy them already shucked.

Varieties. Varieties found on the Pacific coast include the tiny Olympia oyster, the size of a thumbnail, and the large Pacific (or Japanese) oyster numbering from 10 to 40 in a quart (960 ml). The Eastern oyster from the Atlantic ranges in size from extra large to very small and represents the greatest percentage of the oyster catch in this country.

Selection. The oyster should be shiny, plump, and sweet smelling. Shucked oysters should not have more than 10 percent liquid by weight. An excess amount of liquid indicates watering for weight, poor handling, and poor quality. Added liquid bloats the meats and causes loss of flavor. If you buy them in the shell, they should be alive with shell tightly closed. If they gape and do not close quickly in handling, discard them. Also discard any with broken shells. If the shells have not been scrubbed there could be an odor, but it will be of bottom mud, very different from that given off by a dead oyster.

Storage. Oysters store very well under refrigeration. They will hold for a week or more but gradually lose flavor, so it is better to use them as soon as possible. Shucked oysters packed in their natural juices will keep for about a week in a tightly closed container.

Preparation and serving. Scrub shells well and open them according to the directions on this page. Oysters may be eaten raw or baked, steamed or deep fried. They can be served in a cream sauce (scalloped) or be dazzling in stew. But, like clams, they need only be warmed and not cooked. They should be added as a last ingredient in a soup or stew, with the heat turned off when they are added to the other ingredients. Oysters will not toughen as much as clams in cooking, but you may have trouble recognizing what you are eating. Oysters have also played a traditional role on Thanksgiving Day in turkey stuffing.

Dietary information. One pound (454 g) of oyster meat contains 299 calories and is high in vitamin A, calcium, phosphorus, iron, potassium, and other minerals.

SCALLOPS

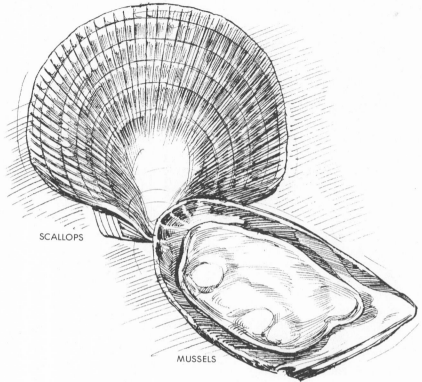

SCALLOPS

MUSSELS

Cooking scallops

Both bay and sea scallops lend themselves to a large variety of preparations. Raw bay scallops are delicious when marinated in lemon or lime juice for a few hours, then drained and tossed with oil seasoned with chopped green onions, garlic, and parsley; then a dash of salt and Tabasco, and served cold.

They are also the basis for the famous *coquilles Saint-Jacques*, a preparation invented by the French in the eleventh century. Bay scallops are simmered in white wine and mixed with a rich cream sauce studded with chopped mushrooms. This is served in scallop or clam shells and topped with grated Parmesan cheese and bread crumbs and run under the broiler for a minute to brown.

Sea scallops make a fine cold salad with green mayonnaise. Cut scallops in half and simmer them in a combination of water and dry white wine seasoned with onion, parsley, and bay leaf. Blend mayonnaise with chopped raw spinach, parsley, chives and dill, and toss.

Sea scallops may also be served on skewers and broiled. Paint scallops with melted butter or margarine and roll them in bread crumbs. Broil 2 to 3 minutes on each side.

Scallops in shells

The scallop morsel we eat is the big muscle that the scallop uses to open and close its shell. In the process of closing its shell, the scallop ejects water that propels it around the bay or sea bottom. In Europe scallops are sold in their shells alive; the red tongue, or coral, is highly prized. In America the muscle is the only part marketed. The rest of the scallop, representing 90 percent of its total weight, is discarded at sea as waste.

But there is good reason for taking only the muscle. Whole scallops are extremely perishable because they cannot retain sea water for moisture as do clams and oysters, and the muscle by itself is much hardier.

Scallops are a smaller industry than clams, shrimp, crabs, or lobsters, but all shellfish fanciers are familiar with these sweet, tender morsels and find them very good indeed. There are two types: the small bay scallops and the larger sea scallops built like lopsided marshmallows. Sea scallops are more plentiful and less expensive than bay scallops, but both are delicious.

Peak season. Sea scallops and southern bay scallops are available all year. Peak season for Long Island bay scallops is from September until December.

Varieties. Fresh bay scallops are cream colored with a pinkish tinge, sometimes approaching a light amber color. They are about ½ inch (1.27 cm) in diameter. Sea scallops are cream to beige in color with a pinkish cast and may be as big as 2 inches (5.1 cm) in diameter. The smaller bay scallops lack the bold flavor of the sea scallops, but they are especially tender and sweet.

Selection. Fresh scallops should have a translucent and glistening appearance. Shun the dead white scallop! That opaque look is never present in a fresh scallop. The opaque scallop may have been frozen and thawed out with running water (soaking in fresh water causes scallops to whiten), or they may have been immersed in water to be rejuvenated with added moisture (and weight). Or they may simply have been frozen and thawed. The flavor of such scallops bears no resemblance to that of fresh.

Shrimp scampi

"Shrimp scampi," or "scampi," has become a popular dish in restaurants all over the country. "Scampi" in the United States refers to a method of preparation, not to the name of the shellfish being offered. The true Italian *scampi* are small lobsters of the variety *Nephrops norvegicus* and run about 7 to the pound. They are known in Ireland as "Dublin Bay prawns" and were considered the best of all prawns by André Simon of London Wine and Food Society fame.

To make the American restaurant dish at home, shell and de-vein shrimp and pat dry with a paper towel. Butterfly the shrimp. (To do this, split them lengthwise almost through, as you would cut a frankfurter roll, being careful to leave the two halves attached. Leave the little tail shell on for a handle.) Sauté or broil them in any mixture of butter, oil, garlic, parsley, paprika, and any other herbs that may suit you—oregano or basil, perhaps. Turn them while cooking. They are done when they turn pink. Most restaurants broil them, and too often they are overcooked to the point where they are hard and dry. A sauté is a safer preparation.

To the rescue

Virginia Lee, the well-known cooking authority, suggests a first-aid procedure for shrimp that have spent a few hours too many in your refrigerator and, while still edible, have developed a slight "off" odor. She recommends that you rub the shrimp with baking soda and let them stand for a short time. Then rinse the shrimp thoroughly in cold water to remove every trace of soda. They will smell and taste totally clean.

A shrimp by any other name

Large shrimp are often called "prawns," although the true prawn is really a species of lobster and not a shrimp at all. As stated elsewhere, prawns are *scampi* in Italian, and in Spanish *camerones*. Shrimp in Europe are usually much smaller than our shrimp from the Gulf of Mexico, although we, too, have some baby-sized shrimp. The French call the little shrimp *crevettes*; the Spanish call them *gambaros*, or *gambis*.

Preparation and serving. Scallops are ready for use just as you buy them. Rinse in cold water and dry thoroughly. Since sea scallops are not uniform in size, it is advisable to cut the big ones to match the smaller so that all will cook in the same length of time. The same admonition applies in cooking scallops as in all shellfish cookery. Do it quickly! Overcooking toughens the tender texture of the flesh. Scallops may be fried or broiled, but the small bay scallops should not be prepared in any way other than frying. Do not disguise the delicate flavor with a batter coating. Dip the scallops in milk, drain, and shake them lightly in a bag with bread crumbs. Heat a thin film of oil in a heavy skillet and fry them quickly, shaking the pan a few times so they do not stick and will brown evenly. Cook only until the scallops lose their translucent quality and become opaque. Serve at once with lemon wedges and, if desired, tartar sauce.

Dietary information. Scallops contain phosphorus, iron, potassium, and some vitamin A. There are 367 calories in 1 pound (454 g).

SHRIMP

Fresh shrimp is available mainly near production points the year-round, but some large cities receive daily shipments of it. Our southern waters produce the larger varieties, and our northern waters produce the tinier kind (several hundred to a pound). For fried shrimp, stuffed shrimp, shrimp cocktail, and the ambivalent "shrimp scampi," only the larger shrimp will do. For salads, sandwiches, soups, and bisques, the tiny shrimp are fine. The tiny shrimp may be available near you in a peeled-and-fresh, or peeled-and-cooked form, but most are offered on the frozen market. They have sweetness and tenderness, but lack the full shrimp flavor of South Atlantic or Gulf shrimp. People in the fishing industry on the East Coast say the finest shrimp available anywhere come to port in North Carolina in the fall months. This shrimp is particularly firm meated and resilient and has a more piquant flavor than species from warmer waters. With rare exceptions, colder waters produce more flavorful fish and shellfish.

Selection. Shrimp is marketed headless and shell on in the fresh state. It is also sold shelled and deveined and, in some stores, already cooked. Fresh shrimp have an almost total absence of odor, as does fresh fish. The meat is firm and of a "live" (here's that word again), translucent quality. Color of the shell may vary from a light grayish green to a light pink or tan, depending on the point of origin. You may be offered "green shrimp," but in the industry "green" is a term meaning "fresh." A frozen shrimp that has been defrosted will give itself away by its appearance. It may be limp and lack the translucency of the fresh, and appear moist from the leaking juices.

Amount to buy. One pound (454 g) of shell-on shrimp will serve two or three. It takes about 1½ pounds (681 g) of shell-on shrimp to yield 1 pound (454 g) of shelled shrimp.

Storage. As with all seafood, shrimp should be used as soon as possible after purchase, but it may be stored overnight in the refrigerator, cooked or uncooked, in a tightly covered container.

Preparation and serving. Shrimp may be cooked shelled or unshelled, but the shells add a degree of flavor. Drop the shrimp into a pot of boiling, salted water, cover the pot, and as soon as the water has returned to the boil, reduce the heat and simmer for 3 to 5 minutes depending on the size. As soon as the shrimp turn pink they are done. They should have a firm texture when cooked and shelled. Never boil shrimp; they will repay your efforts by toughening. Drain. Remove the shells as soon as they are cool enough to handle. Slip a blunt knife between the flesh and the shell, then peel away the body shell and the small crawler claws with your fingers. Remove the vein with a small pointed knife or the end of a toothpick. Large or jumbo-sized shrimp may also be sautéed, deep fried, or broiled. They may be served hot or cold as an hors d'oeuvre, an appetizer, in a salad or seafood cocktail, or in a curry, soup, or sauce.

Dietary information. There are 285 calories in 1 pound (454 g) of raw, unshelled shrimp. It is high in minerals, protein, and one of the B vitamins.

SQUID

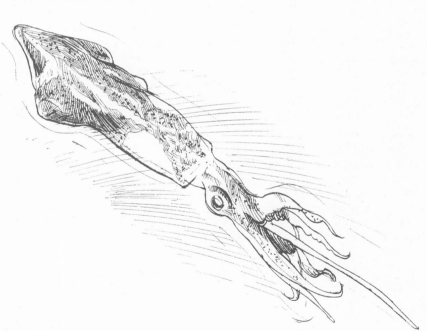

The squid is a small member of the octopus family and is classified as a shellfish. The squid we have in the United States corresponds to the larger Italian squid, *calamari* and *calamaroni*. The body below the eyes, also called the "mantle" or "sac," and the tentacles are edible. Fresh squid is an off-white color speckled with purple. The body, exclusive of tentacles, measures from 3½ inches (8.9 cm) to 6 or 7 inches (15.2–17.8 cm) in length. Fish markets sell cleaned, dressed squid.

Squid is a favorite seafood in many fish-loving countries from Italy to Japan, but it has never been very popular with Americans. However, as

Bigger is not better

All shrimp are costly, but the larger shrimp—under 10 to a pound—go for ridiculously high prices, considering the fact that smaller shrimp are far more tender and flavorful. The huge ones tend to be woody, with texture instead of taste. When they get larger than 16 to 20 to a pound, they are better forgotten.

To clean a squid

Hold the sac (or body) in one hand and pull off the tentacles with the other. If you grasp them gently but firmly, all of the contents of the sac should come away attached to the tentacles. Cut the tentacles above the eyes, put the tentacles aside, and discard everything else from the eyes down. Inside the sac is a quill-like bone that ends in a beak at the end of the body. Remove it and wash out the inside of the sac, removing all its contents. Peel off the sac's outer skin. (If you do this under running water, it will come off as easily as a banana peel.) Also under running water peel off as much of the skin of the tentacles as you can. Rinse the sac and tentacles in several waters until the water runs clear. Dry thoroughly. The squid is now ready to be cooked.

Stewed squid

3 tablespoons cooking oil
1 small onion, finely chopped
1 teaspoon garlic, finely chopped
1 tablespoon parsley, finely chopped
¾ cup canned Italian tomatoes, coarsely
    chopped, with their juice
2 pounds small squid, cleaned
Salt and freshly ground pepper

Heat the oil in a large, heavy skillet with a tight-fitting cover. Add the onion and cook until it becomes limp and golden. Add the garlic and cook 3 minutes longer, then add the parsley and tomatoes and simmer gently for 10 minutes.

Cut the tentacle clusters into two and slice squid sacs into rings about 1-inch wide. Add to the skillet with salt and pepper, stir, cover, and simmer gently for 35 to 45 minutes. Taste and correct seasonings. The cooking time will vary according to the size and toughness of the squid. You'll have to test with a fork from time to time. When you can pierce the squid easily it is done. Serves 4 to 6.

About abalone

Abalone is a large sea snail found only in the Pacific Ocean. It has an oval-shaped pink or red shell and usually measures 7 or 8 inches across at maturity. Abalone flesh is tough and rubbery and must be filleted and tenderized before it can be eaten. Once abundant, it is now becoming rare because of the insatiable appetite of both humans and sea otters for abalone meat. More than 95 percent of the fresh and frozen abalone sold in the United States is consumed in California. It was intiially regarded as a coarse, common shellfish, perhaps because it needed so much tenderizing, but it is now considered a great delicacy and is very expensive. However, price is no deterrent to abalone fanciers.

other seafoods become scarcer, more squid is being sold. When properly cooked it can be delicious, and an adventuresome eater can find it a rewarding experience, one worth repeating often.

Peak season. Available fresh all year, but the sweetest, tastiest squid come to the market in early spring.

Amount to buy. Depends on size and method of preparation, but generally figure 8 ounces (227.2 g) per serving.

Selection. The smaller squid, 5 to 6 inches (12.7–15.2 cm) are preferable to the larger ones because they are more tender. Select squid that are a pure, milky white color.

Storage. Squid will hold refrigerated for a day or two, although it is better to use them at once. Once cooked, squid can be refrigerated for a few days.

Preparation and serving. Squid can be stewed, braised, fried, or used in a fish soup. Cooking time varies with the size and toughness of the squid and can range from 25 to 50 minutes. It must be watched and tested. It is done when it feels tender when you prick it with a fork. Frying is the quickest and easiest method. Prepare and wash the squid and dry very thoroughly with paper towels. Cut the squid body sac into rings about ½-inch (1.27 cm) wide and cut the tentacles into bite-sized pieces. Dust them lightly with flour and fry them quickly in about 1 inch (2.54 cm) of hot fat; don't crowd the pan. When golden, turn and fry the other side. Drain on paper towels, sprinkle with salt, and serve with lemon wedges.

Dietary information. There are 84 calories in 3½ ounces (100 g) of raw squid. It contains appreciable amounts of protein, calcium, phosphorus, and one of the B vitamins.

Most Common American Shellfish

Most common name	Other names	Main producing areas
Clams		
Butter		Pacific
Hard	Quahog, Hard-shell	Atlantic
Sizes	Chowder (lge)	
	Cherrystone (med)	
	Littleneck (sml)	
Littleneck		Pacific
Razor		Pacific
Soft	Steamer, Soft-shell	Atlantic
Surf	Skimmer	Atlantic
Crabs		
Blue		
Hard	Hard-shell Crab	Atlantic, Gulf
Soft	Soft-shell Crab	Atlantic, Gulf
Dungeness		Pacific
Rock		Atlantic
Lobsters		Atlantic
Lobsters, Spiny	Crawfish, Crayfish	Atlantic, Pacific, Gulf
Mussels		Atlantic, Pacific
Oysters		
Eastern		Atlantic, Gulf
Pacific	Japanese	Pacific
Olympia	Western	Pacific
Scallops		
Bay		Atlantic, Gulf
Sea		Atlantic, Pacific
Shrimp	Prawns	Atlantic, Pacific, Gulf
Squid	Calamari	Atlantic, Pacific

POULTRY AND GAME BIRDS

ere's a variation on an old theme: Which came first to the New World, the chicken or the explorer? We know that wild game, turkeys and such, had been scratching about North and South America for as long as anyone can determine. But whether the chicken, or a close approximation thereof, actually greeted fifteenth-century Spanish and Portuguese pathfinders when they landed, or was simply on board the ships as part of the cargo, is anyone's guess. Check the manifests of Marco Polo, the Mayflower settlers, or Captain Cook, and one will always find poultry inventoried—and for good reason: these fine-feathered friends were inexpensive to stock, nutritious and delicious to eat, and such good travelers that they became a ship's only self-perpetuating food supply!

Poultry is still one of the most reasonably priced items in anyone's larder. Chicken today, for instance, is the most inexpensive source of high-quality protein available, costing barely more than it did twenty years ago. This rather startling counterinflationary situation is due to the industrialization of the poultry business. Through feed experimentation and equipment improvements, a full-weight, fleshy bird is ready for the market in ever shorter periods of time. Today's broiler is marketed at seven to seven and a half weeks and weighs, feathers and all, about 4½ pounds (2 kg). Ten years ago, it took nine weeks to produce a bird that weighed less. Shorter growing time means less feed and fewer man-hours, which add up to an inexpensive bird.

HOW TO BUY FRESH POULTRY

oultry, like meat, is inspected for wholesomeness by the U.S Department of Agriculture. The USDA's circular mark of inspection can be found on a paper wing tag, giblet wrap, or insert, or on an overwrap. All poultry, whether chicken, turkey, goose, duck, or guinea fowl, will be inspected if it is to be shipped across state lines. Most poultry is. Usually the inspection takes place in the processing plant itself. An inspector checks whether the bird comes from a healthy flock, has been processed under rigid sanitary conditions, contains no chemicals or additives considered harmful by the Food and Drug Administration, and is properly packaged and truthfully and informatively labeled.

U.S. Grading. Although USDA inspection is usually mandatory, grading (which also comes under the aegis of the USDA) is provided only if it is requested, and paid for, by the poultry processor. The highest quality bird is given a Grade A shield, found near the inspection tag. Grades B and C are allocated to lower quality birds, and if a bird ranks in one of these classes, often no grading shield is attached to the bird. Graders, much like dog-show judges, look for conformation (is the bird well shaped?), meatiness, amount of fat (it should have a layer of fat), freedom from feathers (was it well plucked?), discoloration, and cuts or blemishes of the skin and flesh. One interesting note: a whole chicken with a blemish on a wing would have the wing cut off and be graded C. However, if the rest of the bird is in top condition, it can be cut up, and the separate parts sold with a Grade A shield.

Poultry stock
If you are the kind of cook whom everyone admires, you have your stockpot always full, so you can make delicious sauces and soups. A little concentrated poultry stock, always at the ready, in either refrigerator or freezer, will give your gourmet sauces a lot of character. Both a brown and a white poultry stock are useful to have on hand.

Brown poultry stock. Take whatever poultry parts (backs, necks, gizzards, hearts, bones, scraps, but not livers) you have squirreled away in the freezer for just this purpose and chop them into small pieces. Dry them thoroughly, then brown them in hot cooking fat with some sliced onion and carrot. When they are really brown, pour off the browning fat and add 2 or more cups of canned beef bouillon or chicken broth (preferably your own). Throw in a couple of parsley sprigs, a pinch of thyme and a bay leaf. Add enough water to this pot to cover by half an inch. Cover partially and simmer for 2 hours or so, skimming off scum as it rises. Strain, chill, and remove congealed grease from the surface.

White poultry stock. Use the same method, but do not brown the ingredients, and use chicken stock (your own or canned) instead of bouillon.

When is poultry kosher?
Poultry is considered kosher when it has been slaughtered according to Jewish law by a schochet, who is often, but not necessarily, a rabbi. The most important element of the kosher process is that the bird be slaughtered in a swift, humane manner. The live chicken must be a healthy specimen up to the moment the schochet makes his swift, clean incision in the throat. Most blood is drained out immediately. The bird is eviscerated, soaked in clear water, salted, and placed on a tilted drain board for an hour, so that any remaining blood will be drawn out. Then it goes back into cool water to be rinsed once again. A kosher bird will taste slightly saltier than its brethren, and will be more expensive, due to the extra labor and the cost of machine maintenance (all that salting does terrible things to equipment). A kosher bird, or parts thereof, can cost double the price of an ordinary supermarket bird.

Government grading

Grading of food is not required by federal law. It is voluntary, requested and paid for by the packer or processor and there are many good foods that do not carry the USDA grade. However, some food manufacturers use the official grade on their products, feeling that it gives the consumer assurance that the poultry is wholesome, unadulterated, truthfully labeled and has been processed hygienically. The official inspection mark looks like this:

It may appear on a paper wing tag, on the giblet wrap, on an insert, or be printed on the overwrap or transparent wrapper. It does not denote quality; it is purely an assurance of wholesomeness.

The mark that tells the grade or quality of a bird looks like this:

The grades are U.S. Grade A, B, or C. The lower grades, however, are rarely used on poultry labels. A trained government grader determines the quality of each bird only after the bird has first been inspected for wholesomeness.

There are no federal rules that govern the period of time within which a slaughtered bird must be sold. Unlike milk, which usually has a last day of sale stamped on it, there is no expiration date for the sale of poultry. However, birds are usually transported quickly and can often be found in stores within twenty-four hours of being slaughtered.

A poultry inspector talks about buying poultry: "The best guide to the condition, that is the wholesomeness of a bird, is your own nose. Therefore, number one, pick out the bird you want and then open the wrapping so you can put your nose to it. Don't worry about what other shoppers are thinking. You have every intention of taking that particular bird home with you, if it's good. If it *should* prove to be off, take it to the manager. He will be grateful that it has been found, and will then scrutinize the others on the shelf very carefully. If there is a package of giblets inside or alongside, open that too, because these are the first parts to produce a bad odor. You ask, how will you know by the smell? You will! Once decomposition sets into poultry, it goes bad very rapidly. There is a definite and absolute off-condition odor that you couldn't possibly miss.

"Be aware, too, of how the bird feels to the touch. A sound bird should be pretty firm. It shouldn't be sticky or slimy (as opposed to just moist). These are the first signs of decomposition, and usually the beginnings of a bad smell will be there too. Look for good, fairly solid color, either white or yellow. However, there will always be a slightly darker color along the feather track of the breast, about midway up. This is the center of concentration of the feather follicles and is perfectly normal.

"In areas far removed from poultry processors, you may occasionally encounter a bird that has been frozen, then defrosted and is being retailed as "fresh" poultry. Unfortunately, there is no reliable guide for detecting this masquerade, outside of a possible bluish or brownish tint to the skin caused by freezer burn. Luckily, it's a rare occurrence."

Where to buy the best, the freshest. Grade A poultry is Grade A poultry, and there is no reason why a Grade A bird in a supermarket should be any less good than its Grade A brother or sister in a fancy meat market. Supermarket poultry may, in fact, reach store shelves somewhat sooner than those birds destined for higher-class retailers. The reason for this seeming social inequity is that the supermarkets deal directly with the processor, eliminating the middleman. This makes it possible for truckloads of birds to be shipped straight to the stores, whereas fancy butchers, who deal in smaller numbers, buy from middlemen, all of which takes time.

The advantage of having a first-class butcher is that he tends to your needs and whims—for a price. And it may be worth every penny to you! Not only that, he is guaranteed, by his wholesaler, the absolute tops in all birds. In fact, some processors will privately grade their best birds with an AA mark, meaning that these are to be set aside for their carriage-trade butchers. All these birds are fed the same food, raised in the same manner, go to the same schools, so there is no real reason for one to taste better than the other. It's all a matter of cosmetics: AA birds may be prettier. It's up to you to decide.

Hormones and additives. Commercially raised birds are normally fed low-level antibiotics and chemicals to aid in growth, feed efficiency, and pigmentation—in this case meaning skin color. In the Northeast, for instance, consumers prefer yellow-skinned chickens, whereas white skins seem to be favored in the West. Color makes no difference in taste or nutritional value; it's just that consumers *think* it does. So marigold petals and/or a yellowing chemical are given to birds destined for the Northeastern marketplace. The FDA carefully supervises what a bird ingests, and nothing is allowed to be fed to it that would be harmful to the consumer. That's the law. The only trouble with the law is that what was acceptable yesterday may suddenly be harmful today. As an example, for decades poultry was routinely fed penicillin and tetracycline. Now the FDA is proposing a ban on both antibiotics except to combat an actual disease or infection. The reason is apprehension that, with constant use, a superbacteria might develop that would be immune to these antibiotics—a bacteria that might be transmitted to the consumer. Female hormones are sometimes fed to larger male broilers in order to fatten them up to a roasting size of 6 to 7 pounds (2.7 to 3.2 kg). These hormones, which in effect chemically, rather than surgically, desex the broiler so that it becomes known as a capon, are completely harmless to the consumer, according to the FDA. The only way for a consumer to know what has gone into today's poultry in the way of food, chemicals, and hormones is to inquire of the FDA and the USDA.

Seasonal shopping for value. The price of poultry goes up and down with about as much regularity as the stock market. It's the old principle of supply and demand. If there are too many birds this week the prices go down, and next week's short supply will drive it up again. During holiday seasons, turkey and goose are often good buys.

How to keep poultry until cooking time. There's nothing less appetizing than the odor of poultry left in your refrigerator more than two days, still covered in its original store wrapping. And if you try to cook it, masking its odor in curries and spices, it will still taste strange. To avoid this, unwrap the bird as soon as you bring it home from the store, place it on a platter, rewrap it loosely in waxed paper, and put it in the refrigerator. Remove the giblets (neck, liver, heart, etc.) and refrigerate separately. The bird will now stay fresh for one or two days, but no longer. If you are planning to stuff the poultry, don't place the mixture inside the bird until you are ready to put it into the oven. And once in the oven, or on the fire, don't partially cook the bird with the idea of returning it to the refrigerator and finishing cooking it later. With poultry, cook all at once. Doing otherwise gives unfriendly bacteria additional opportunity to grow.

Is poultry nutritious? Brimful of high-quality protein, poultry is a fine source of iron and B vitamins also. In view of its generally good value, the wise thing is to serve poultry frequently.

"A chicken in every pot"
For centuries a cooked chicken has been a symbol of abundance and plenty. Those people who were around during the depression of the 1930s will remember the political slogan that circulated during Herbert Hoover's administration: "A chicken in every pot and two cars in the garage." Actually, the chicken segment of this slogan originated with Henri IV, the sixteenth-century French king who is reputed to have said that he wished there would be no peasant in all his kingdom who was too poor to have a chicken in his pot every Sunday.

To disjoint a bird

Supermarkets generally charge more for poultry that has been halved or quartered than for whole birds. Doing the cutting or disjointing yourself is simple, money saving, and in many cases tidier.

To split a small bird in two, place it breast side up on a board and with a sharp knife or poultry shears cut lengthwise down and through the breastbone and then through the backbone. If you wish, you can divide each half in two by slicing the leg portion away from the wing portion.

Disjointing a bird will give you eight individual pieces. The neck, giblets, and back of the carcass that are left can be stewed along with the chicken or frozen for chicken stock at a later date.

Start by slitting the skin around the drumstick with a sharp knife. Pull the leg out at right angles to the body to break open the thigh joint at the small of the back. Cut the whole leg away, then cut through the joint at the knee to separate the drumstick from the second joint, or thigh, portion.

Cut through the wing joint, taking a little piece of the breast meat attached, to provide a good serving. Repeat on the other side of the bird. You now have the breast remaining on the carcass. With poultry shears—or knife, if you prefer—cut through the rib cage and end of shoulder at each side to separate the breast from the lower carcass. Chop the breast in two, crosswise.

CHICKEN

In order to gain a proper perspective on the chicken, it is fitting for the reader to know that there are more chickens in the world today than there are people. On any given day in the United States you could count about 2.3 billion chickens eating and growing fat just for the sake of the American palate. The average American consumes 40 pounds (18 kg) of this gallinaceous delight annually.

A little chicken for whatever ails you. Chicken is a fine choice for weight watchers, as it ranks lowest in calorie count of all popular meats. Three and one-half ounces (100 g) of a combination of white and dark roasted chicken meat contain 171 calories. No meat is lower in fat content. And the fat it does contain has 64 percent unsaturated fatty acids, which makes it highly desirable for those on low-cholesterol or low-fat regimes. Just as chicken soup is often considered the panacea for anyone feeling sickly, chicken meat is a fine prescription for anyone desiring an easily digestible meal. Mother Nature gave chickens short muscle fibers, which our digestive systems break down easily.

Besides high-quality protein, and a large percentage of essential amino acids, chicken is also a good source of calcium, phosphorus, and iron. Add to that the fact that chicken loses few vitamins and probably none of its protein during cooking, and you can appreciate how its reputation was acquired.

Amount to buy. Count on buying ¾ pound (336 g) of a whole chicken for each serving, and slightly less if you're buying chicken in parts. The bird you see in the store today has an established cooked edible yield of 51.1 percent—slightly better than veal cutlets, and not quite as generous as pork chops, rib roasts, or hamburger. In all cases, however, it is considerably less costly.

Selection. In addition to the USDA inspection and grading marks, and the "nose test" spoken about previously, you can tell a bird's age, and presumably its tenderness, by pressing against the tip of its breastbone. If it's bendable, it's a young bird. If not, it's seen better days as a tender young thing but is just coming into its own as a flavorful bird for stewing, fricasseeing, or braising.

ROCK CORNISH HEN. The smallest member of the chicken family, at six weeks it weighs only 1½ pounds (681 g) or less, just enough for one person. The 2-pounders (908 g) will serve two. A tender, plump-breasted bird, Rock Cornish hen is good roasted, broiled or sautéed. The bird itself was originally from Cornwall, in England, and some enterprising American crossed it with a White Plymouth Rock chicken back in the 1880s.

BROILER-FRYER. A young meaty bird about seven and one-half weeks old, weighing 1½ to 3½ pounds (681 g to 1.6 kg). Don't be misled by its name: a broiler-fryer may be roasted, simmered, or sautéed successfully and will come up with moist, succulent meat. The broiler-fryer has the mildest of chicken flavors.

ROASTER. A little older and larger than the broiler-fryer, the roaster weighs 3½ to 5 pounds (1.6 to 2.3 kg). It is about twelve weeks old and has tender meat. It may also be jointed and braised or potted.

CAPON. A desexed rooster weighing 4 to 7 pounds (1.8 to 3.2 kg). The capon has fine flavor and a generous proportion of white meat. It is usually roasted.

HEN, STEWING CHICKEN, FOWL, OR BROILER HEN. A plump, meaty laying hen about 1½ years old that weighs 4½ to 6 pounds (2 to 2.7 kg), it makes excellent soup and is good for leisurely stewing. October is often the month when egg farmers sell off their older hens that can no longer compete in the egg-laying race with their younger sisters. They need a couple of hours in the stewpot, but their meat is rich in flavor.

CHICKEN PARTS. Chicken is also available in prepackaged parts. Whole chickens are generally a more economical buy, except for those families with such decided preferences for either white or dark meat that the remaining parts would be wasted. Boned, skinned chicken breasts (called "chicken cutlets") can be sautéed, braised, or poached for a quick and satisfying meal.

Roasting timetable. Meat should be allowed to come to room temperature before cooking. If it is chilled, add 15 to 30 minutes to the cooking time. Use the lower figure for large birds and the higher one for small birds.

Roaster	300°F	30 to 45 minutes per pound
Capon	325°F	22 to 30 minutes per pound

Followers of the faster-roasting school of thought use the following timetable:

¾ pound	350°F	30 to 40 minutes
1½ pounds	350°F	40 to 50 minutes
3 pounds	350°F	70 to 80 minutes
5¼ pounds	350°F	1½ to 1¾ hours

To cook chicken breasts

There are many times when you can use some white-meat chicken—for sandwiches, salads, aspics, stuffings for crêpes, among many others—and the boned and skinned fresh chicken breasts, already prepackaged in supermarkets can fill the need. The simplest cooking method is to poach them in the oven in broth.

Preheat the oven to 400°F. Wipe the breasts with a damp cloth, pat dry, and cut them in two. Peel off the membranes and trim away all strips of fat. Season lightly with salt and pepper and place in a baking dish that holds them snugly. Add just enough chicken broth to almost cover; ½ cup is usually enough for two whole breasts. Cover the baking dish tightly with aluminum foil and bake for 30 minutes, at which time the breasts will be completely cooked, soft, juicy, and ready to use hot or when chilled.

Carving a turkey

There are two methods of carving a bird. One is the traditional method, and the other is an easier "side carving" style.

Traditional method

1. Remove the drumstick and thigh by pressing them away from the body. The joint connecting the leg to the backbone will often snap free, or you may cut it with a knife.

2. Separate the drumstick and thigh by slicing through the connecting joint, and slice off the dark meat from each bone, if desired.

3. Place the knife parallel to, and as close to, the wing as possible on the breast. Make a deep cut into the breast, cutting right to the bone.

4. Slice the breast perpendicular to the previous cut. Start each new slice slightly higher up on the breast.

Side carving method

1. Place the bird on its side, breast away from the carver. Remove the last two joints of the wing by lifting the tip up firmly and severing at the joint.

2. Slice the dark meat off the drumstick and thigh if desired, until the bone is exposed. Lift the drumstick and cut off at the thigh joint. Slice the meat from the drumstick.

3. Run the knife point completely around the thigh bone, loosening it. Pry one end up, grasp, and pull free. Slice the dark meat from the body of the bird. Make a deep vertical cut in the breast just in front of the wing joint to serve as a base for all breast meat slices.

4. Start from the center of the breast, cut toward you, making large, even slices. Turn the bird and repeat the process on the other side.

Turkey vs. eagle

If Ben Franklin had had his way, you would not only stare with awe at the Thanksgiving turkey gracing your festive table, you'd have to stand up, salute, and sing the national anthem. Ben wanted the turkey for the Great Seal of the United States instead of the eagle. Of the avian controversy he said: ". . . the Turkey is a much more respectable Bird, and withal a true native of America."

TURKEY

There are really only two things you can say about a turkey: it's as delicious as it is dumb and hard to raise. Turkeys will stand out in the rain until they drown; the young ones catch cold if they get wet feet; and the older ones sometimes panic and suffocate from pressing together in their terror. The American tom turkey has been bred to such a huge size that it can no longer reproduce naturally, and all breeding is now done by artificial insemination. One pound (454 g) of bird is produced for every 2 pounds (908 g) of feed. Two billion pounds of turkey come through the processing plants every year. It takes eighteen weeks to produce a hen of marketable size, and twenty-two weeks for a tom to get to the store.

Amount to buy. Three-quarters of a pound (340.5 grams) will serve a person nicely. If you have a large turkey—over 12 pounds (5.4 kg)—allow ½ to ¾ pound (227 to 340.5 g) per serving because bigger birds have a higher proportion of meat to bone weight. Turkeys range in size from 6 to 25 pounds (2.7 to 11.4 kg).

Selection. Many food experts prefer a tom over a hen for tasty eating. You can tell a turkey's age by its feet, if you happen to buy one that still has them. A young turkey has black feet, a three-year-old pink feet, and an old turkey gray feet. As with chickens, look for a plump, moist bird with a smooth complexion free of feathers and bruises.

Storage. As with chicken, when you get your bird home, unwrap, rewrap in loose waxed paper, and refrigerate. Use within two days.

Dietary information. Turkey meat ranges from 121 to 263 calories per 3½ ounces (100 g), depending on the age of the bird. White meat from a young bird (twenty-four weeks and under) is the lowest. It is rich in protein and B vitamins.

Roasting timetable. At 325°F (163°C)

8 to 10 pounds	20 to 25 minutes per pound
10 to 16 pounds	18 to 20 minutes per pound
18 to 25 pounds	13 to 15 minutes per pound

DUCK

A duck farmer shares his recipe

"Take a 4- to 5-pound duckling and salt and pepper it inside and out. Use freshly ground pepper. Preheat the oven to 375°F. Truss the duck with string. Place in a roasting pan on its back and bake for 30 minutes. Pour or spoon out accumulated fat and return the pan to the oven for another 30 minutes, having placed the bird on its right side. Remove and pour out the fat (not the nonfat juices). Increase the oven temperature to 400°F. Turn the duck breast side down and return to the oven for another 30 minutes. Turn the bird onto its left side, and roast for 30 minutes longer. Remove the bird and discard trussing string. Place the bird back in the oven, back side down, for 10 more minutes. You can rub it all over with garlic before putting it back in the oven for the final baking."

Mrs. Orville Freeman's wild duck recipe

Skin and wash ducks thoroughly. Soak them for at least 10 hours in a pan of water, laced with 2 tablespoons of salt and 1 tablespoon of baking soda for each gallon of water; this will draw out the gamy taste. Rinse well. Stuff the birds lightly with chunks of apple, onion, celery, and carrot. (You don't have to close the bird, as the stuffing will be discarded. Its purpose is to absorb the strong flavor and add its own flavors to the meat.) Roast, covered, in a 325°F oven for 2 to 2½ hours, but test for doneness after 1½ hours. Salt the birds when half done.

In deference to those who are not enamored of wild game, and to make sure that no one goes hungry, the wife of the former Secretary of Agriculture also serves turkey or roast chicken at the same time.

Pity the poor goose

The astronomical cost of a tin of imported French pâté de foie gras, that delicious, creamy mixture of ground goose liver and other ingredients, is not to be wondered at when you consider what the poor goose and the hard-working farmer were put through to produce it.

Foie gras means, literally, "fat liver," and goose liver is considered the finest for a pâté, although it can be made with the livers of other birds or animals. The goose has its liver enlarged by force-feeding, an unpleasant practice that originated in ancient Egypt. Three times a day a funnel is placed in the bird's throat and a mash poured down it. It must be worked with a milking motion so that the bird cannot cough it up. This is done for three to five weeks; nearly 70 pounds of cooked, salted mash will be pushed down its unwilling gullet. When the goose is slaughtered, the liver will weigh from 1 to 1½ pounds, and in some cases up to 4 pounds.

Young farm wives faced with a flock of ten or twenty reluctant geese are understandably unwilling to be burdened with the task of fattening them, even apart from the inhumanity of the procedure, and pâté de foie gras grows ever more expensive and in short supply.

Most of our domestic ducks, the so-called Long Island ducklings, are descended from the white Peking duck, a Chinese mallard type that immigrated here in 1890. Now it is our most important domestic duck. Long Island roaster duckling is marketed at eight or nine weeks and weighs 4 to 5½ pounds (1.8 to 2.5 kg). Restaurants generally serve half a 5-pound (2.3-kg) bird per person. At home, however, you may wish to serve smaller portions.

Selection. There is not much choice when you buy a duck, since close to 90 percent of them are frozen. Your best chance to find a fresh bird is at a fancy meat market, and then probably only on special order. If you should be lucky enough to find a bird with its head still on, you can check on its freshness by wiggling its underbill. This will be pliable if the bird is fresh.

Amount to buy. Two people can dine off a 4-pound (1.8-kg) bird, and you could, in a pinch, serve four not too voracious people with a 5½-pounder (2.5 kg). Duck is a rich bird, and if you serve it with wild rice, which is a favorite accompaniment, and a sweet sauce, such as orange or cherry, the smaller portions may be welcome.

Storage. As with other poultry, don't buy it until you are ready to cook it, or the day before. Keep it loosely wrapped in waxed paper in the refrigerator.

Dietary information. There are 325 calories in 3½ ounces (100 g) of uncooked duck with the skin, 165 calories in the same amount of meat only.

GOOSE

A commercially grown goose is ready to eat at age ten weeks, but in any case no goose older than six months should be purchased since the older ones tend to be tough. Oven-ready fresh geese weigh in at anywhere from 4 to 14 pounds (1.8 to 6.4 kg), the most popular size being in the 7- to 11-pound (3.2 to 5 kg) range. Figure 1 to 1½ pounds (454 to 721 g) of ready-to-cook goose per serving.

Storage. Place immediately in the coldest part of the refrigerator, loosely wrapped, with some air circulation. Do not store longer than three days. Giblets should be removed from the bird immediately, cooked promptly, and refrigerated until ready to use.

Roasting time. Twenty to twenty-five minutes per pound (454 g) in a 300°F (149°C) oven.

A hint to the tidy. In order to save your oven from goose-grease spatterings, place the bird, breast side down, in a brown paper bag on a rack in the roasting pan. When two-thirds done, poke pencil-sized holes in the top of the bag and turn over the bag and bird. All the fat will drain out into the roasting pan.

Dietary information. In 3½ ounces (100 g) of cooked, roasted goose with the skin there are 441 calories; the flesh only contains 233.

GUINEA HEN

The guinea hen, with its bulbous, big-breasted body, is thought of as the sweater girl of the fowl world. Not as profitable a poultry product as chickens, guinea hens are produced by poultry men only for the gourmet market. Similar to pheasant in flavor and in cooking preparation, their meat is dry, requiring thick strips of salt pork to be inserted under the breast skin and additional fat to be added during cooking. Guinea hen is so noisy a bird that some farmers use it as a watchdog; it makes a terrific racket when strangers approach. A guinea hen weighs about 2 pounds or a bit more (1 kg) and serves two. Some connoisseurs prefer splitting and grilling guinea hen to any other method of preparation, but it may also be roasted. Roasting takes from 30 to 45 minutes in a 350°F (177°C) oven. However you cook the bird, the usual accompaniment to a guinea hen is Cumberland sauce.

Dietary information. There are 156 calories in 3½ ounces (100 g) of uncooked guinea hen.

SQUAB

GUINEA HEN

SQUAB

Cumberland sauce for guinea hen

1 8-ounce (227-g) glass currant jelly
1 egg yolk
2 tablespoons (30 ml) vinegar
¾ teaspoon (3.75 ml) dry mustard
2 tablespoons (30 ml) granulated sugar
Salt and freshly ground pepper to taste
Raisins (optional)

Over hot water, stir the currant jelly until soft. Beat in the egg yolk, vinegar, dry mustard, sugar, salt, and pepper. Stir the sauce for about 15 minutes, until it is thickened. You may want to add raisins.

Nonlethal fare

It is interesting to note that there are both fish in the sea and plants in the field that are distinctly poisonous, but there does not appear to be any poisonous bird. A complete list of edible birds would have to include every known species from the giant albatross to the tiniest little figpecker and lark. However, some birds are so tough that it is unlikely that anyone except a sailor marooned on a barren island would think of eating them.

Potted pigeons or squabs

6 squabs
1 cup flour
1 teaspoon salt
½ teaspoon freshly ground pepper
¼ teaspoon thyme
¼ cup chopped onion
1 carrot, diced
¼ cup chopped celery
4 tablespoons butter
1 cup boiling chicken stock
1 cup sliced mushrooms
½ cup sour or sweet cream

Preheat oven to 350°F. The squabs may be cut into pieces or left whole. Dredge them with the flour that has been mixed with the salt, pepper, and thyme and sauté them slowly in the melted butter in a large, heavy skillet. When they are just seared, place them in a casserole. Add the onion, carrot, and celery to the fat remaining in the skillet and cook for 3 or 4 minutes. Add the boiling chicken stock, mix well, and pour over the birds. Cover the casserole and cook until tender, 45 to 60 minutes. Add the sliced mushrooms the last 15 minutes. If the liquid is drying out, add more chicken stock. Just before serving, stir in the sweet or sour cream and mix well. Serve with hot, fluffy rice or wild rice. Serves 6.

Squab is a plump young pigeon, which is sold at about four weeks of age, when it weighs from 12 to 14 ounces (340.5 to 398 g). There is enough meat—all of it dark—for one person per bird. Squab can often be purchased fresh from quality meat markets. Occasionally you may find a few feathers still attached to the bird. Simply use a blunt knife and your fingers and pluck them out.

Roasting. A thick piece of bacon or salt pork may be placed across the breast. Or you can brush the entire bird with melted butter and dredge it with flour. Rub the inside with salt, then roast, uncovered, in a 325°F (163°C) oven for 45 minutes or more, until tender. Baste while cooking, then remove the bacon.

Dietary information. Four ounces (113.6 g) of squab meat and skin contain 333 calories; the same amount of meat only, 161.

THE PHEASANT FAMILY

The pheasant family is large, so large that it includes chickens and turkeys and peacocks. Three other relatives, the quail, partridge, and the ring-necked pheasant, are the most common domesticated game birds available in the United States. These birds are raised just like the commercial chicken. They do not get to fly around like their wild cousins. The domestic bird is purchased and prepared like chicken. The wild varieties must be hung first.

PHEASANT Benjamin Franklin was unsuccessful in promoting the turkey as our national emblem. His son-in-law, however, succeeded in promoting the importation of the ring-necked pheasant as a symbol of gourmet delight. These birds grow to a length of about 36 inches (91 cm), half of which is tail feathers. Their plumage is marked by an iridescent emerald neck, and copper body accentuated by azure, ruby gold, and black.

QUAIL

PARTRIDGE

Vanishing wildlife

Time was when America abounded with wild pigeons, also known as "wood pigeons," "turtle doves," or "passenger pigeons." They were so numerous that on occasion huge flocks of them darkened the skies. According to food historian James Trager, some estimates place the total number of passenger pigeons as high as 9 billion, which is about twice the number of all land birds in America today. The Pilgrims considered the birds a threat to their crops, although they were grateful for them when a crop failure in 1648 reduced their food supply and threatened to leave them hungry.

Passenger pigeons made good eating and were easy to kill. The birds were so cheap that farmers fed them to their hogs. You could still buy six pigeons for a penny in Boston as late as 1736, although the huge flocks that had winged their way from the Gulf of Mexico north to Canada were beginning to thin out in the East. In the latter half of the nineteenth century, millions of birds were shipped by railroad at a wholesale price of fifteen to twenty-five cents a dozen in the Midwest.

But this state of affairs was not to last, and in the end the passenger pigeon, like so much other wildlife, was exterminated. Authorities are not certain of why this happened with such stunning finality. Some experts do not believe that it was caused only by wholesale slaughter. They suspect that it was brought about by a combination of other factors: shrinking areas of forest lands that provided breeding ground and the peculiar mating habits of the birds. As they decreased in numbers and became more widely scattered across the continent, it became more difficult for them to find mates. When they did find a mate, something was lacking in their mating process—perhaps the stimulus of seeing hundreds of other birds on the same tree, all engaged in a similar pursuit. Individual pairs of wild pigeons were never bred successfully in captivity.

Other game birds that are now extinct are the Labrador duck, the Eskimo curlew, and the heath hen. Birds that were once plentiful—some species of quail, prairie chickens, rail, woodcock, and snipe—are considered endangered species. And canvasback duck is rarely enjoyed by anyone except the actual hunters.

Some people believe that it is the fabled phoenix, which cremated itself only to be reborn in a glorious likeness of itself. Beautiful to look upon, it is even better to eat.

Pheasants weigh 2 to 3 pounds (908 g to 1.4 kg) each. Allow one bird to two people. (Baby pheasants, usually found frozen, weigh about 1 pound (454 g) and are a great delicacy.) A hen is thought to be more tender and better tasting than a cock.

QUAIL. The most widely sold game birds are the quail and the pheasant. The bobwhite is one of thirty-three species of quail and is considered a great delicacy in the southern states. Many quail are raised on game farms for the commercial market. They have a less gamy taste than other wild birds. They should not be hung or they will lose their delicate flavor. Birds weigh approximately 5 ounces (142 g), so be prepared to serve two birds per person. Sautéing is usually considered the best method of cooking. If roasting, be sure to lard the bird well, as it is almost totally lacking in body fat. In Japan quail are raised mostly for their small eggs, which the Japanese consider a great treat.

PARTRIDGE. These birds have darker meat than pheasant, and a more pungent taste. Naked on a platter, however, a partridge and a baby pheasant are almost identical. The pheasant has a high, pointed breastbone, although in the baby it is not very well developed; the partridge breastbone is more rounded. Partridge sells for twice the price of its baby cousin. The wild birds must be hung three or four days before being cooked. Serve one bird per person.

Partridge can be cooked by any method that is used for chicken. Since it is somewhat drier than chicken, however, it is frequently larded before roasting. Truss the bird and roast like a chicken in a 300°F (149°C) oven for 30 to 45 minutes. Baste frequently. It is customary to serve partridge with the unthickened pan juices, to which lemon juice, sherry, or port may be added.

A note on domesticated wild game birds

In many states the only wild duck, geese, and pheasants you can buy must be raised on a licensed game preserve. These birds, unlike their truly wild relatives, don't fly around and scratch about for their food. They eat a better, more balanced diet, and as a result they are more tender, have meatier breasts, and are also fatter than their wild relatives.

Snaring the wild bird

Small wild game birds have never been as popular in the American cuisine as in the European. Each autumn all over southern Europe, small birds juicy with berries are eagerly hunted. In some places, whole flocks of birds are trapped in nets as they migrate through mountain passes. Millions of birds are shot during the Italian hunting season that begins in the early fall, and in England the opening of the grouse season stirs up a good bit of excitement.

A hunting practice that was once common in England and is still in use in some parts of Europe involves stripping the leaves off small trees and spreading lime on the branches. Like flies on flypaper, the birds' little feet become stuck in the gummy lime and the birds are easily captured.

Robin pie was a popular dish in America in the early part of the nineteenth century. While this dish has disappeared from the scene along with the passenger pigeons, Americans do eat squab, which are commercially raised pigeons, descendants of the Rock pigeons.

WILD GAME BIRDS

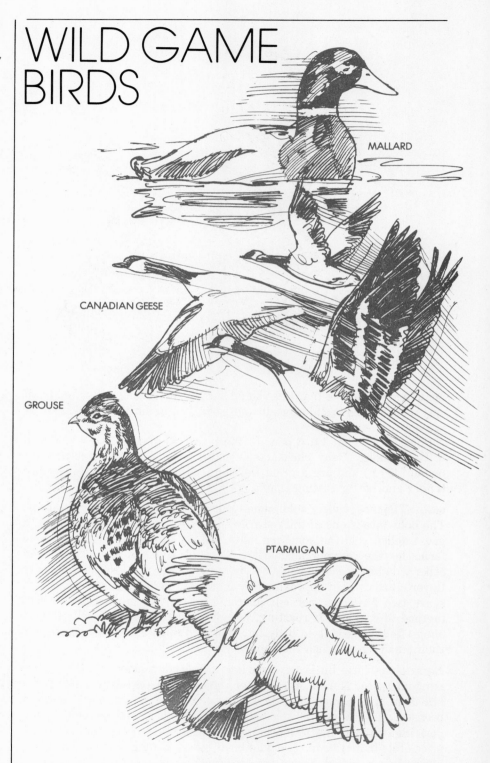

MALLARD

CANADIAN GEESE

GROUSE

PTARMIGAN

Wild game birds (pheasant, quail, partridge, duck, and goose) can be hunted only during special seasons in the United States and Canada, and the rules change from state to state, province to province. In season some specialized meat markets, depending upon state laws, sell these birds. These wild game should not be confused with their commercially raised and domesticated cousins, which can be purchased at any time of the year, often frozen.

Scotch grouse, traditionally considered the ultimate in game birds, is ironically the least acceptable to the American palate because it has a very strong taste and is served very rare. Importation of frozen Scotch grouse has ceased during the last several years because of an outbreak of a poultry disease in Great Britain.

Another game bird to know about, just in case you're lucky enough to come across one, is the ptarmigan, a red-meated bird from Scandinavia. The ptarmigan lives in northern near-Arctic regions and is common as a gourmet dish in its various homelands. This wild bird, or a similar variety called "winter snow grouse" or "snow ryper," is imported from Sweden, weighs about 12 ounces (340.5 g), and is as expensive as it is delicious.

If a hunter friend happens to give you a freshly killed game bird, the easiest way to handle it is to ask your "friendly" butcher to hang, dress, and eviscerate it. Hanging tenderizes the flesh and develops the gamy taste. Game birds are hung, unplucked and undrawn, by their beaks or by their feet in a cool spot. After one or two days they are usually ready. You can tell if the bird is "ripe" when the tail feathers can be pulled out easily. For really good eating, a game bird should be young. Unfortunately, this is a determination that cannot be made until it is too late— from the bird's point of view. In young birds, the beak and feet will be pliable; their plumage is soft and the breast plump. Younger birds can be roasted; older ones require long, slow cooking over low heat in a covered pot with liquid added (braising).

Preparation of wild game birds. Dry-pluck fowl after hanging. It is easier to pluck and draw a bird that is thoroughly chilled.

Wild birds are hunted with a shotgun, which is apt to leave BB-sized shot in the bird. After plucking, look for darkish spots on the bird, which indicate the place of entry, and remove pellets with tweezers or a pointed utensil. Cut out the meat that has discolored near the shot.

After plucking, wipe the bird with a damp cloth. Wild fowl should not be washed before cooking. Salt the interior of the bird or rinse it with a bit of brandy or sherry. The gamy taste can be reduced by placing an apple, an onion, a carrot, or a few celery stalks inside the cavity of the bird when cooking. The fillers are discarded before serving.

Wild birds are leaner than the domestic varieties and generally need additional fat. Wrap the breast with a piece of salt pork or bacon, which is discarded after cooking.

Cooking procedures. The cooking procedures for *pheasant, quail,* and *partridge* have been described earlier.

For wild duck, place a cut-up onion and some orange rind inside each duck. Tie a piece of salt pork over the breast. Roast on a rack in a 350°F (177°C) oven for 45 to 60 minutes, basting with melted butter a few times while cooking. Figure half a duck per person.

As for wild goose, an old goose will need long, slow cooking in a covered pot; a young one, between 5 and 6 pounds (2.3 to 2.7 kg), may be roasted. Place apple quarters in the cavity of the goose, truss, and sprinkle with salt and pepper. Roast on a rack in a 500°F (260°C) oven for 30 minutes. Reduce the heat to 300°F (149°C), cover with aluminum foil, and continue to cook for 2 to 3 hours, or until tender. Remove the foil covering during the last 30 minutes. Baste often with chicken stock and pour off fat as it accumulates. Figure 1 pound (454 g) per person.

Marinated wild birds

Pheasant, partridge, or grouse may be used. Classic accompaniments for wild fowl are a dressing of chestnuts or wild rice, a tossed salad of crisp greens, and a side dish of a tangy conserve such as quince or gooseberry. Sour cream or wine sauces do well with wild game, but they should not be too highly seasoned.

Clean and disjoint the bird. Place in a casserole and cover with the following marinade (the marinade should cover the pieces completely):

Marinade
1 small onion, cut into quarters
1 bay leaf
1 clove garlic, minced
2 cups port wine
1 teaspoon salt
½ teaspoon freshly ground pepper

Refrigerate for three days. Remove the pieces from the marinade and pat dry with paper towels. Reserve the marinade.

Preheat the oven to 375°F. Melt 2 tablespoons of butter in the casserole. Brown and roast the pieces for about 45 minutes, turning them a number of times. Strain the marinade and pour it over the pieces. Return to the oven and cook uncovered for another 30 minutes, or until tender. Remove the pieces from the casserole and reduce the sauce over high heat. Taste and correct seasoning. Transfer the pieces to a warmed platter and cover with sauce. Serve with noodles or wild rice. Serves 2.

APPENDIX

THE METRIC SYSTEM

The United States is the only major country that has not yet converted to the metric system, but from signs and portents on the horizon, it would appear that we are on our way. In the metric system, weight is expressed in grams and kilograms; liquid volume in liters and milliliters; and length in meters, centimeters, or millimeters. Temperature will be measured in Celsius instead of Fahrenheit. It is also expected that the calorie will be expressed in terms of kilojoules (KEE-lo-jowles). One calorie equals approximately 4.2 kilojoules.

The cook will not encounter too many difficulties in following metric recipes. Metric "cup and spoon" measures can, in most cases, be used interchange-ably with the customary "cup and spoon" measures commonly used in American households. Measurements in pounds and ounces will be expressed in grams. To convert a recipe to metric, just remember that a pound is about 450 grams and an ounce is about 30 grams. To convert a Celsius temperature to Fahrenheit, multiply the Celsius temperature by 2 to obtain, quite closely, the corresponding Fahrenheit temperature. This method of conversion is accurate within 9 degrees for Fahrenheit temperatures within the 240–400 degree range.

We have included metric equivalents throughout the text of *Fresh Food* to familiarize the reader with the metric system.

Conversion Tables for Metric Measurements
(approximate measurements)

Length

American Inches (in)	Metric Equivalent Centimeters (cm)
¼ inch	.63 cm
½ inch	1.25 cm
1 inch	2.5 cm
3 inches	7.5 cm
6 inches	15.2 cm
8 inches	20.3 cm
12 inches	30.5 cm
39½ inches	1 meter

Temperatures

Fahrenheit (F)	Celsius (C)	Fahrenheit (F)	Celsius (C)
*32°	0°	**212°	100°
60°	16°	250°	121°
75°	24°	300°	149°
80°	26.7°	350°	177°
95°	35°	400°	205°
150°	65°	450°	232°
175°	79.4°	500°	260°

*water freezes   **water boils

To convert Fahrenheit into Celsius; subtract 32, multiply by 5, divide by 9.
To convert Celsius into Fahrenheit; multiply by 9, divide by 5, add 32.

Liquid Measures

American Measures	Metric Equivalent Milliliters (ml)
1 teaspoon	5 ml
1 tablespoon	15 ml
1 fluid ounce	29.56 ml
¼ cup (2 ounces)	59.125 ml
½ cup (4 ounces)	118.25 ml
1 cup (8 ounces)	236 ml
1 fluid pint	473 ml
1 fluid quart	946 ml
1 gallon	3,785.4 ml
1 liter	1,000 ml

1 liter = 10 deciliters (dl) = 100 centiliters (cl)
To convert ounces into milliliters, multiply the ounces by 29.573.

Weight

American Ounces	Metric Equivalent Grams (g)
⅓ ounce	10 g
½ ounce	15 g
1 ounce	30 g
3½ ounces	100 g
4 ounces (¼ pound)	114 g
9 ounces	250 g
16 ounces (1 pound)	454 g
2.2 pounds	1 kilogram (kg)

To convert ounces into grams, multiply the ounces by 28.3495.

TABLE OF FOOD EQUIVALENTS

Food	Amount	Yield
Dairy products		
Butter	1 pound (4 sticks)	2 cups
	½ pound (2 sticks)	1 cup
	1 ounce	2 tablespoons
Cheese		
Cottage cheese	8 ounces (½ pound)	1 cup
Cheeses, grated	1 pound	4 to 5 cups
	2 ounces	½ cup (about)
Eggs		
Whole	5 large	1 cup (about)
Egg white	1 egg white	1½ tablespoons
	8 large	1 cup (about)
Egg yolk	1 egg yolk	1 tablespoon
	12 large	1 cup (about)
Fresh fruits		
Apples	1 pound (3 medium)	3 cups (about), pared, diced, or sliced
Apricots	1 pound	3 cups, cooked, drained
Bananas	1 pound (3 or 4)	2 cups sliced; 1½ cups, mashed
Blueberries	1 quart	3½ cups
Cherries	1 pound	2⅓ cups (about), pitted
Cranberries	1 pound	3 to 3½ cups, sauce
Dates	1 pound	2½ cups whole, or pitted, and cut up
Figs	1 pound	2⅔ cups, chopped
Grapefruit	1 medium	1⅓ cups pulp; ⅔ cup juice
Lemons	1 medium	3 tablespoons juice (about) 2 teaspoons grated rind
Limes	1 medium	1½ to 2 tablespoons juice
Oranges	1 medium	⅓ to ½ cup juice; 2 to 3 tablespoons grated rind
	1 pound	2 cups, orange sections
Peaches	1 pound	2 cups, sliced
Pears	1 pound	2 cups, sliced
Pineapple	1 medium	2½ to 3 cups, cubed
Plums	1 pound	2¼ cups, halved and pitted
Rhubarb	1 pound	2 cups, cut and cooked
Strawberries	1 quart	4 cups, whole; 2 cups, pureed
Nuts and herbs		
Almonds	5⅓ ounces, blanched	1 cup
	4 ounces ground, lightly packed	¾ cup
	1 pound in shell	2⅔ cups ground
Chestnuts	1½ pounds in shell	1 pound, shelled
	1 pound in shell	2½ cups, peeled
Peanuts, shelled	1 pound	2¼ cups

Food	Amount	Yield
Pecans, shelled	1 pound	4½ cups (about)
	3½ ounces	1 cup
Walnuts, shelled	1 pound	4 cups (about)
	4½ ounces	1 cup, chopped
Herbs		
Fresh leaves	¼ cup pressed down	½ ounce or 2 tablespoons, chopped
	1 tablespoon fresh herbs	⅓ to ½ teaspoon, dried
Fresh vegetables		
Beets	1 pound (4 medium)	2 cups, diced and cooked
Cabbage	1 pound	4 cups, shredded
Carrots	1 pound (7 or 8 medium)	2½ cups, diced
Cauliflower	1 large head	4 to 6 servings
Celery	1 long branch	¾ cup, diced (about)
Corn	2 ears	1 cup kernels (about)
Eggplant	1½ pounds	2½ cups (about), diced and cooked
Greens for salad	2 cups loosely packed	1 serving
Mushrooms	1 pound (36 medium)	4 cups, sliced, uncooked
Onions	1 pound (4 or 5 medium yellow)	2–2½ cups, chopped
	1 medium	½ cup chopped
Peas, green	1 pound, small	1 cup, shelled
	1 pound, large	1½ cups, shelled
Peppers (Bell)	1 pound (3 to 6)	4 cups, chopped
Potatoes	1 pound (4 medium)	1½ to 2 cups, mashed
Potatoes, sweet	1 pound (3 medium)	2 cups, mashed
Pumpkin	1 pound	1 cup and a little more
Rutabaga	1 pound	2 cups, cooked
Shallots	1 shallot (½ ounce)	1 tablespoon
Spinach		
Raw	1 pound	4 cups
Cooked	1 pound	1½ cups
Tomatoes	1 pound (3 medium)	1½ cups, peeled, seeded, and juiced
Zucchini	1 pound	3½ cups, sliced
Meat and poultry		
Chicken		
Whole	3½ pounds (raw, cleaned)	3 cups (about), cooked
Chicken breast	1 large (raw)	2 cups, cooked and diced
Miscellaneous		
Breadcrumbs		
Dry	1 slice dry bread	⅓ cup crumbs
Soft	1 slice fresh bread	¾ cup soft crumbs
Sugar		
Granulated	1 pound	2¼ to 2½ cups
Brown	1 pound	2⅛ to 2¼ cups
Confectioners'	1 pound	4 cups unsifted

BIBLIOGRAPHY

Ackart, Robert. *Fruits in Cooking*. Macmillan, 1974.

Allen, Jana, and Margaret Gin. *Innards and Other Variety Meats*. 101 Productions, 1974.

Anderson, Jean, and Elaine Hanna. *The Doubleday Cookbook*. Doubleday, 1975.

Aresty, Esther B. *The Delectable Past*. Simon & Schuster, 1964.

Beard, James. *American Cookery*. Little, Brown, 1972.

Bloch, Barbara. *The Meat-Board Meat Book*. Benjamin, 1977.

Blue Goose, Inc. *The Buying Guide for Fresh Fruits, Vegetables, Herbs and Nuts*. 6th Edition, 1976.

Child Julia. *Mastering the Art of French Cooking*. Knopf, 1966. *The French Chef*. Knopf, 1967. *From Julia Child's Kitchen*. Knopf, 1975.

Chu, Grace Zia. *The Pleasures of Chinese Cooking*. Simon & Schuster, 1962.

Claiborne, Craig. *The New York Times Cook Book*. Harper & Row, 1961. *An Herb and Spice Cookbook*. Harper & Row, 1963.

Culpepper's Complete Herbal. W. Foulsham & Co. (undated).

de Groot, Roy Andries. *Feasts for All Seasons*. McGraw-Hill, 1976.

Doole, Louise Evans. *Herbs, How to Grow and Use Them*. Oak Tree Press, 1962.

Doyle, Rodger P., and James L. Redding. *The Complete Food Handbook*. Grove Press, 1976.

Drury, John. *Rare and Well Done*. Quadrangle, 1966.

Encyclopedia Britannica. Encyclopedia Britannica, Inc., 1971.

Encyclopedia of Cookery. William H. Wise, 1954.

Evans, Travers Moncure, and David Greene. *The Meat Book*. Charles Scribner's Sons, 1973.

Fabricante, Thomas, and William J. Sultan. *Practical Meat Cutting and Merchandising*. Vols. 1 and 2. Avi, 1974.

Friedlander, Barbara, and Ira Friedlander. *The Vegetable, Fruit, and Nut Book*. Grosset & Dunlap, 1974.

Genders, Roy. *The Perfect Vegetable and Herb Garden*. Drake, 1972.

Goldbeck, Nikki, and David Goldbeck. *The Supermarket Handbook*. New American Library, 1976.

Hazan, Marcella. *The Classic Italian Cook Book*. Knopf, 1976.

Jones, Evan. *The World of Cheese*. Knopf, 1976.

Kaufman, William I. *The Nut Cookbook*. Doubleday, 1964.

Kraus, Barbara. *Calories and Carbohydrates*. Grosset & Dunlap, 1971.

Lampert, Lincoln. *Modern Dairy Products*. Chemical Publishing Co., 1975.

Langer, William L., editor. *An Encyclopedia of World History*. Houghton Mifflin, 1972.

Langseth-Christensen, Lillian, and Carol Sturm Smith. *The Complete Kitchen Guide*. Grosset & Dunlap, 1968.

Levie, Albert. *The Meat Handbook*. Avi, 1970.

Limburg, Peter. *Chickens, Chickens, Chickens*. Thomas Nelson, 1975.

McClane, A.J. *McClane's Standard Fishing Encyclopedia and International Angling Guide*. Holt, Rinehart & Winston, 1965.

The Encyclopedia of Fish Cookery. Holt, Rinehart & Winston, 1977.

McCully, Helen. *Nobody Ever Tells You These Things*. Holt, Rinehart & Winston, 1967.
Things You've Always Wanted to Know about Food and Drink. Holt, Rinehart & Winston, 1972.

Medlin, Faith. *A Gourmet's Book of Beasts*. Paul S. Eriksson, 1975.

Meyers, Perla. *The Seasonal Kitchen*. Random House, 1975.

Miloradovich, Milo. *The Home Garden Book of Herbs and Spices*. Doubleday, 1952.

Montagné, Prosper. *Larousse Gastronomique*. Crown, 1965.

Moyer, Anne, editor. *The Green Thumb Cookbook*. Rodale Press, 1977.

National Live Stock and Meat Board. *Lessons on Meat*. Chicago, Illinois (undated).

National Turkey Federation publications.

New Book of Knowledge. Grolier, Incorporated, 1975.

New Columbia Encyclopedia. Columbia University Press, 1975.

Ogilvy, Susan. *Making Cheese at Home*. Crown, 1976.

Pappas, Lou Seibert. *Egg Cookery*. Scribner (undated).

Pomeroy, Ruth Fairchild, editor. *The Redbook Cookbook*. McCall, 1971.

Rombauer, Irma, and Marion Rombauer Becker. *The Joy of Cooking*. Bobbs-Merrill, 1972.

Rosenthal, Sylvia. *Live High on Low Fat*. Lippincott, 1975.

Simon, André L. *A Concise Encyclopaedia of Gastronomy*. Bramhall House, 1952.

Smith, Page, and Charles Daniel. *The Chicken Book*. Little, Brown, 1975.

Trager, James. *The Foodbook*. Grossman, 1970.

United States Department of Agriculture. Food publications. Consumer and Food Economics Institute, Agricultural Research Service, Washington, D.C., 1975.

Waldo, Myra. *The Complete Round the World Cookbook*. Doubleday, 1962.

Wason, Betty. *Cooks, Gluttons, and Gourmets*. Doubleday, 1962.

Watt, Bernice K., Annabel L. Merrill, and others. *Composition of Foods*. U.S. Department of Agriculture, 1963.

Witty, Helen, and Burton Wolf, editors. *The Garden-to-Table Cookbook*. McGraw Hill, 1976.

Wright, Richardson. *The Story of Gardening*. Dover, 1934.

INDEX

Numbers in italics refer to text in outer columns.